GEGE AKUTAMI

Being caught in a pinch should be seen
as an opportunity! But an opportunity
can also turn into a pinch!

GEGE AKUTAMI published a few short
works before starting *Jujutsu Kaisen*, which began
serialization in *Weekly Shonen Jump* in 2018.

JUJUTSU KAISEN

VOLUME 7
SHONEN JUMP MANGA EDITION

BY GEGE AKUTAMI

TRANSLATION **Stefan Koza**
TOUCH-UP ART & LETTERING **Snir Aharon**
DESIGN **Joy Zhang**
EDITOR **John Bae**
CONSULTING EDITOR **Erika Onabe**

JUJUTSU KAISEN © 2018 by Gege Akutami
All rights reserved.
First published in Japan in 2018 by SHUEISHA Inc., Tokyo.
English translation rights arranged by SHUEISHA Inc.

The stories, characters and incidents mentioned
in this publication are entirely fictional.

Printed in the U.S.A.

Published by VIZ Media, LLC
P.O. Box 77010
San Francisco, CA 94107

10 9 8 7 6 5 4
First printing, December 2020
Fourth printing, May 2021

viz.com

JUJUTSU KAISEN

7

THE ORIGIN OF OBEDIENCE

STORY AND ART BY GEGE AKUTAMI

JUJUTSU KAISEN CAST OF CHARACTERS

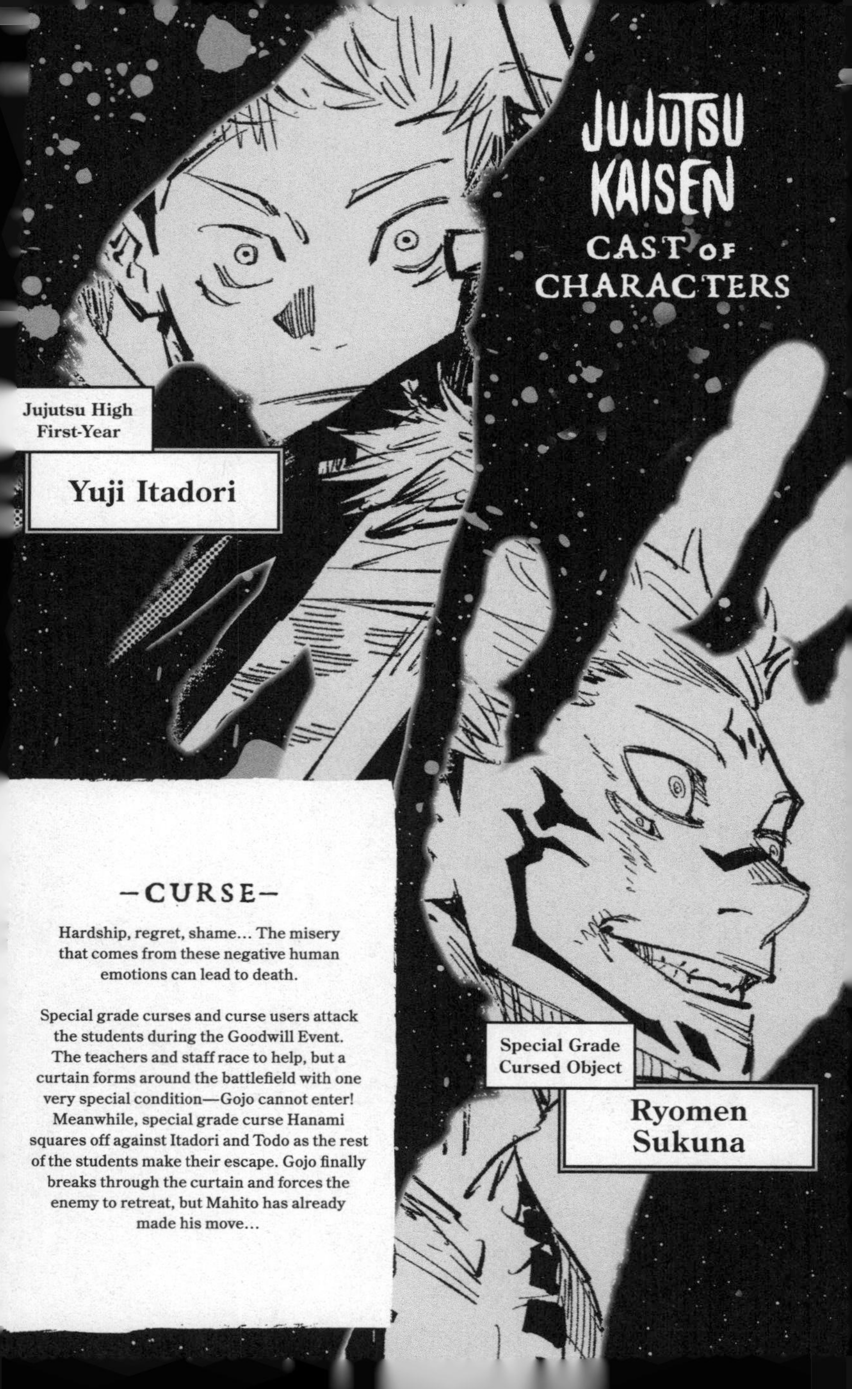

Jujutsu High First-Year
Yuji Itadori
Special Grade Cursed Object
Ryomen Sukuna

—CURSE—

Hardship, regret, shame... The misery that comes from these negative human emotions can lead to death.

Special grade curses and curse users attack the students during the Goodwill Event. The teachers and staff race to help, but a curtain forms around the battlefield with one very special condition—Gojo cannot enter! Meanwhile, special grade curse Hanami squares off against Itadori and Todo as the rest of the students make their escape. Gojo finally breaks through the curtain and forces the enemy to retreat, but Mahito has already made his move...

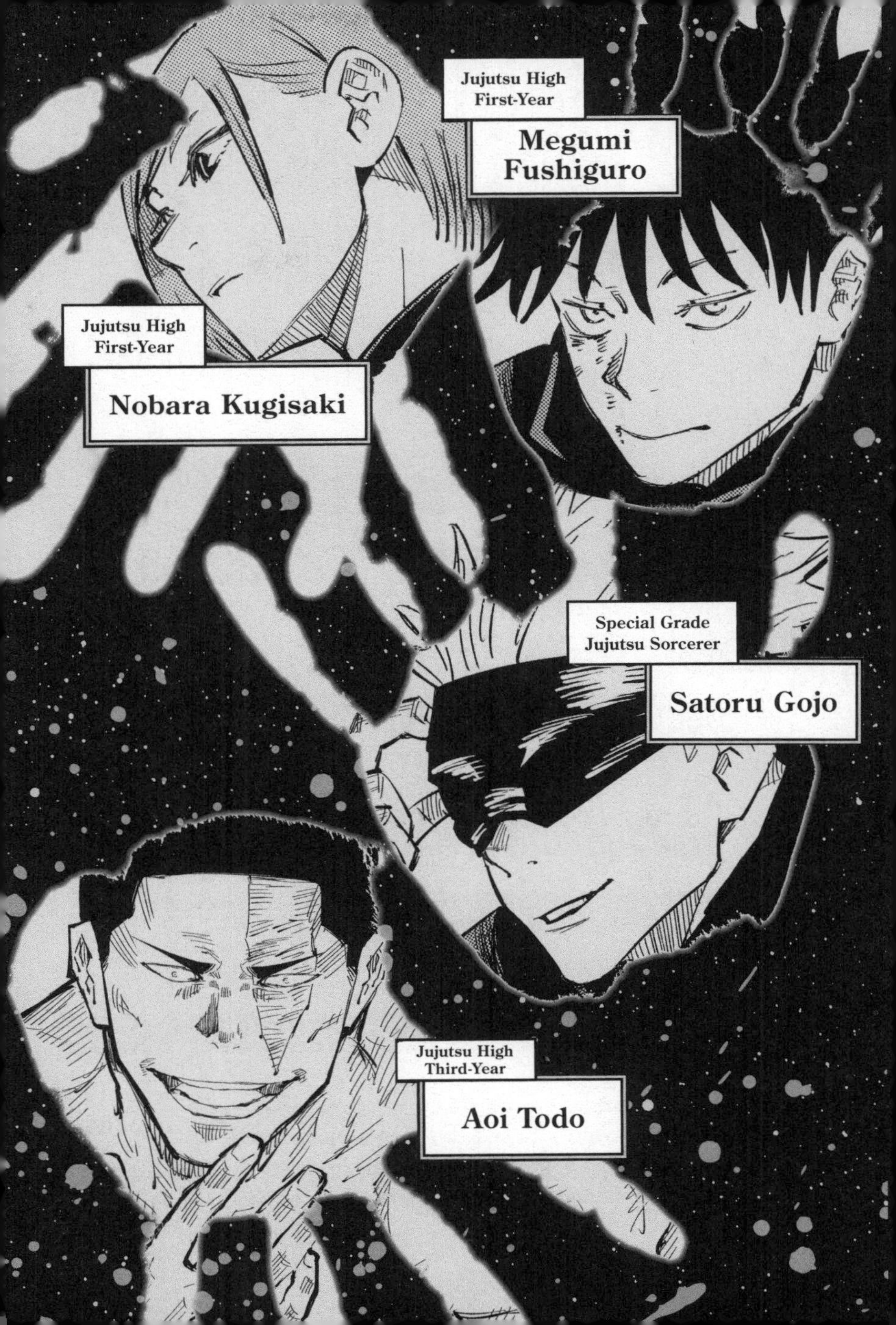
Jujutsu High
First-Year
Megumi Fushiguro
Jujutsu High
First-Year
Nobara Kugisaki
Special Grade
Jujutsu Sorcerer
Satoru Gojo
Jujutsu High
Third-Year
Aoi Todo

JUJUTSU KAISEN

7

THE ORIGIN OF OBEDIENCE

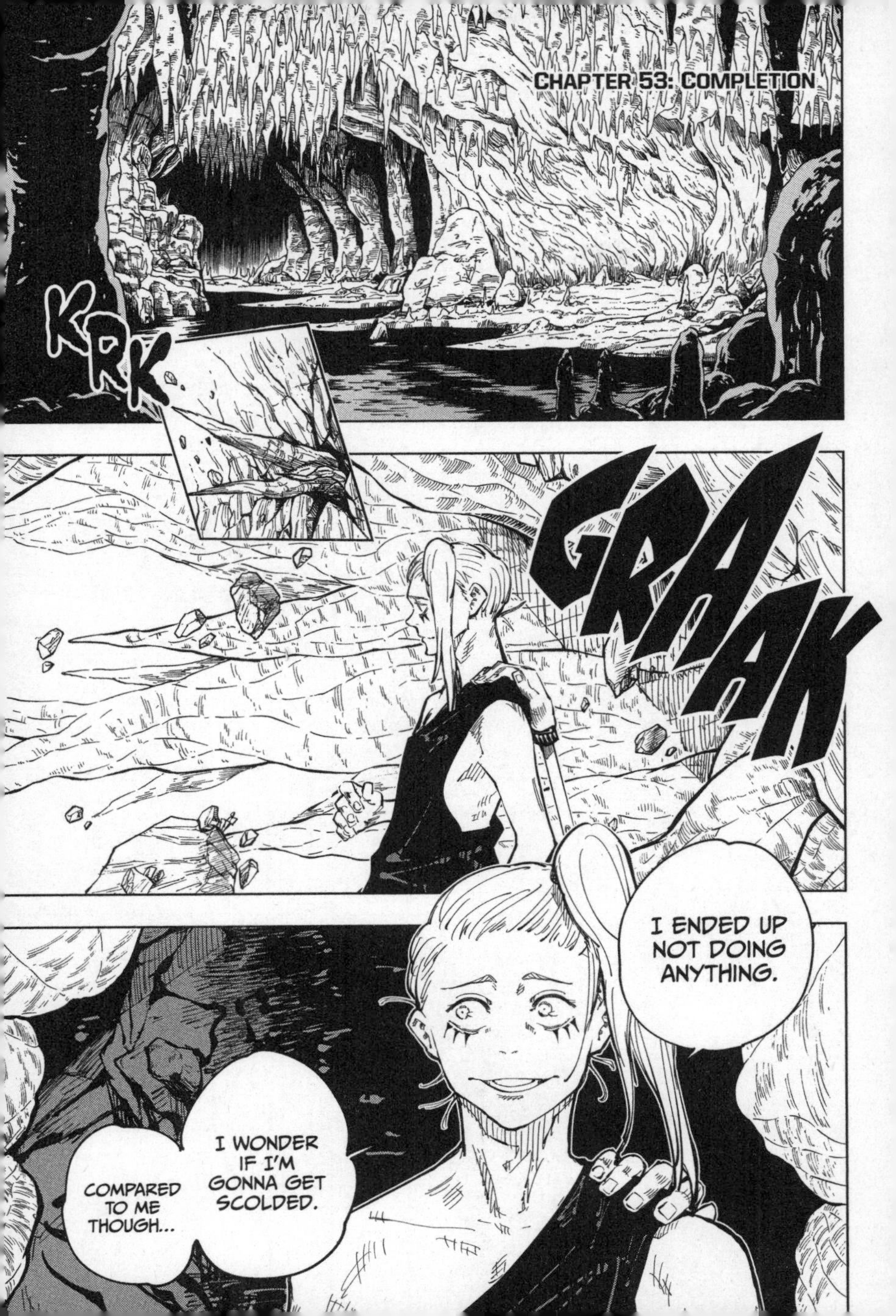
CHAPTER 53: COMPLETION
KRK
GRAAK
I ENDED UP NOT DOING ANYTHING.
I WONDER IF I'M GONNA GET SCOLDED.
COMPARED TO ME THOUGH...

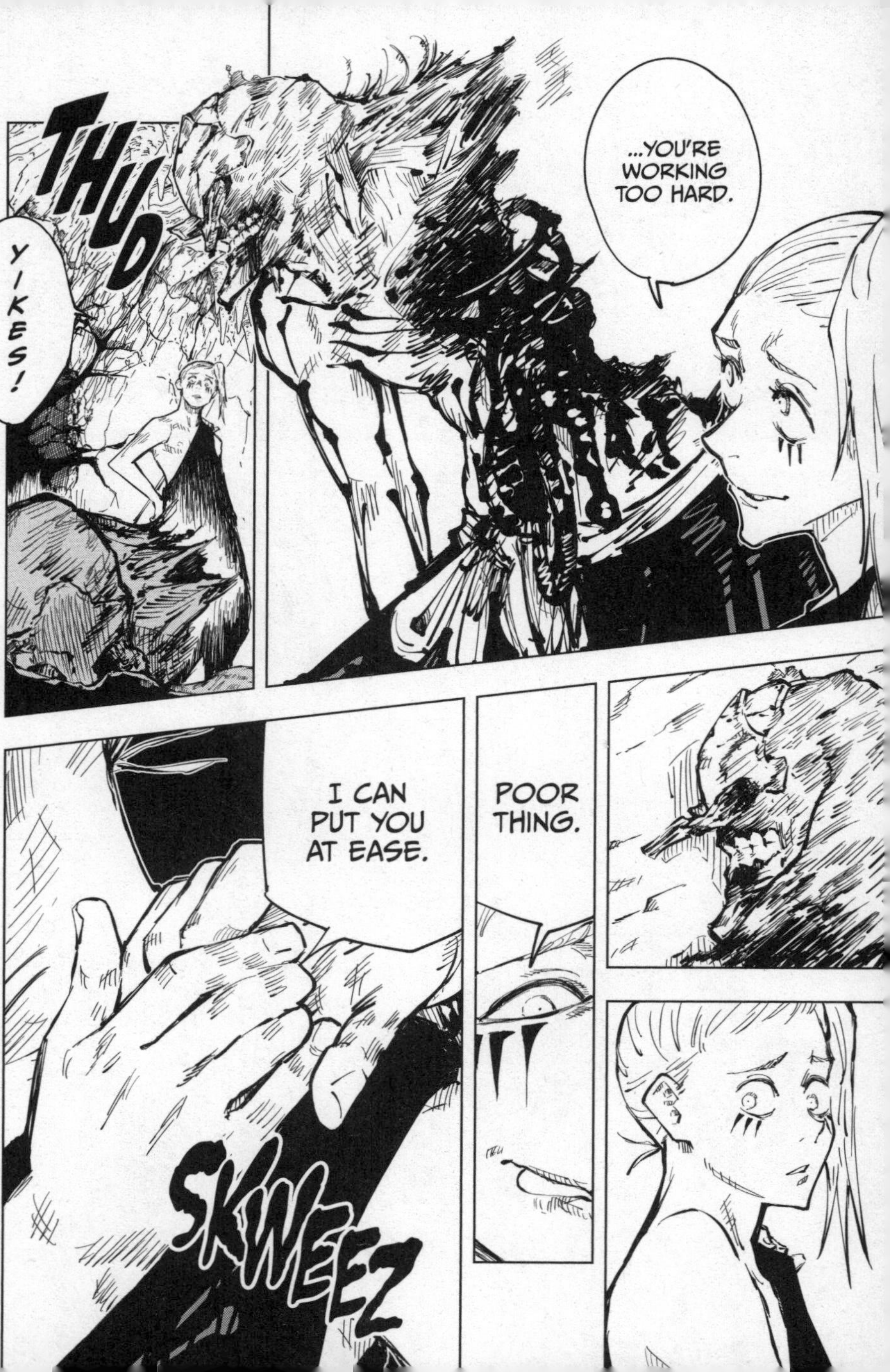
...YOU'RE WORKING TOO HARD.
THUD
YIKES!
POOR THING.
I CAN PUT YOU AT EASE.
SKWEEZ

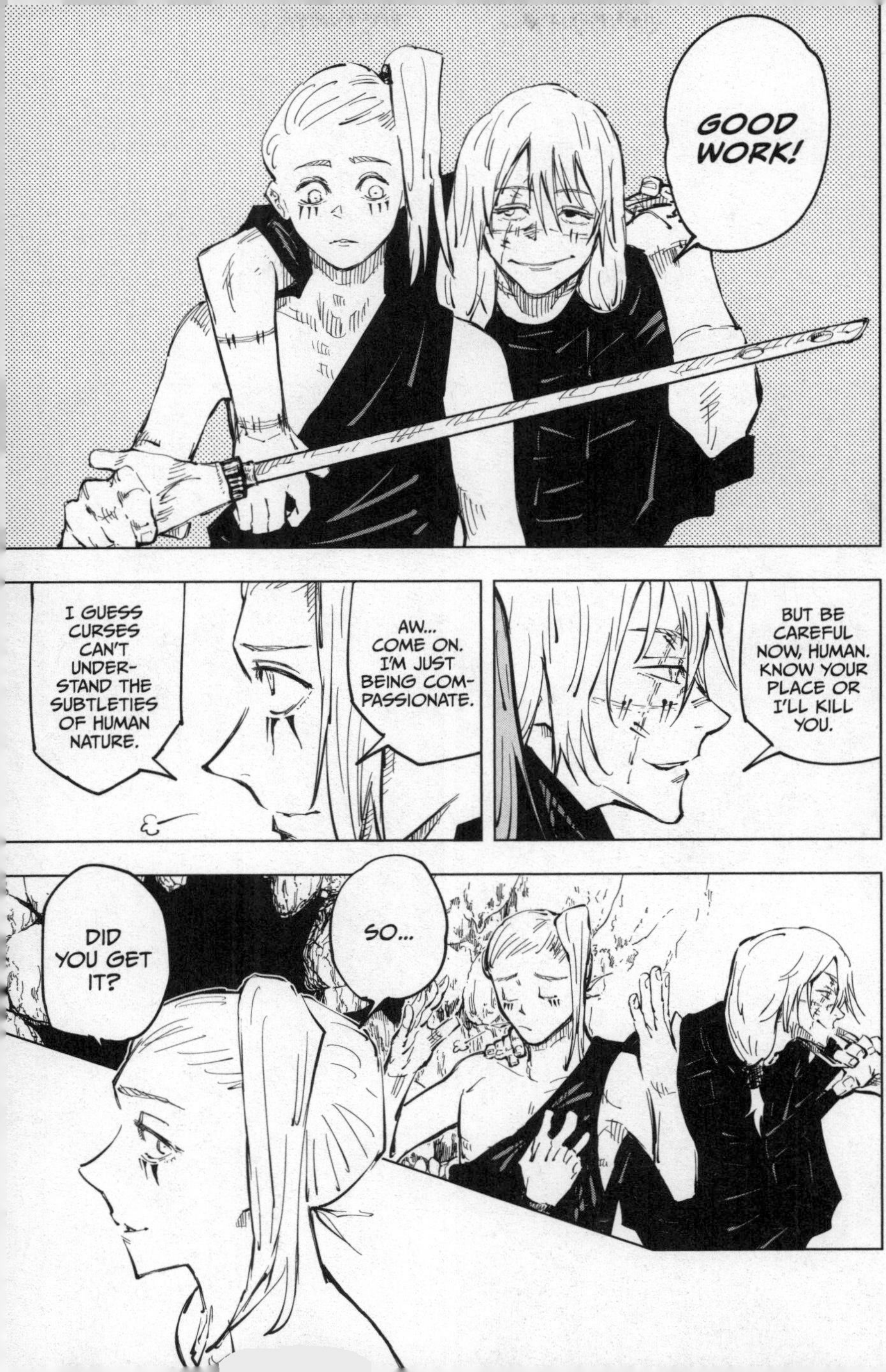
GOOD WORK!
BUT BE CAREFUL NOW, HUMAN. KNOW YOUR PLACE OR I'LL KILL YOU.
AW... COME ON. I'M JUST BEING COMPASSIONATE.
I GUESS CURSES CAN'T UNDERSTAND THE SUBTLETIES OF HUMAN NATURE.
SO...
DID YOU GET IT?

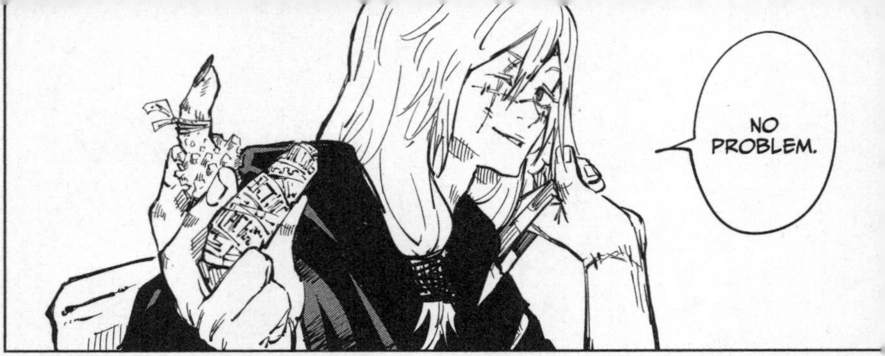
NO PROBLEM.

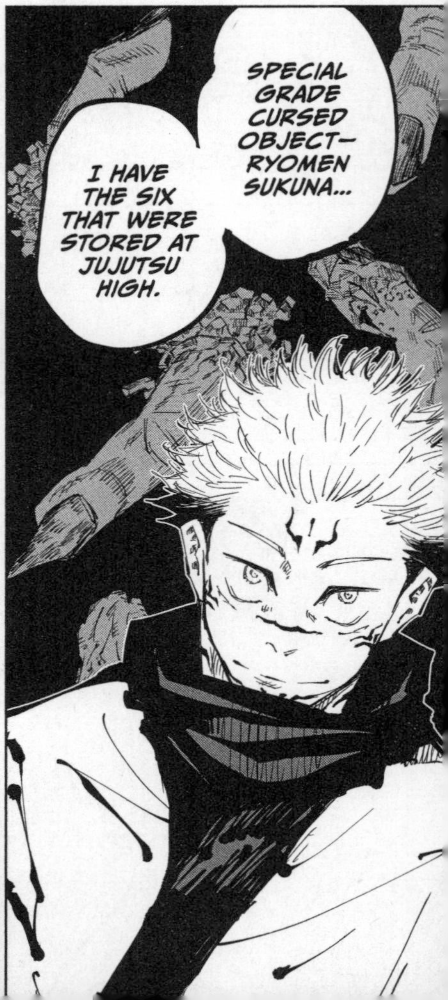
SPECIAL GRADE CURSED OBJECT—RYOMEN SUKUNA...
I HAVE THE SIX THAT WERE STORED AT JUJUTSU HIGH.

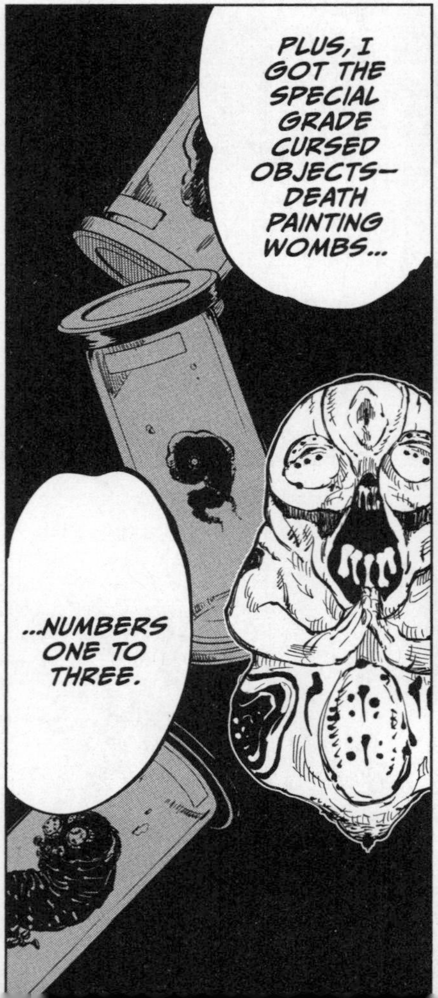
PLUS, I GOT THE SPECIAL GRADE CURSED OBJECTS—DEATH PAINTING WOMBS...
...NUMBERS ONE TO THREE.

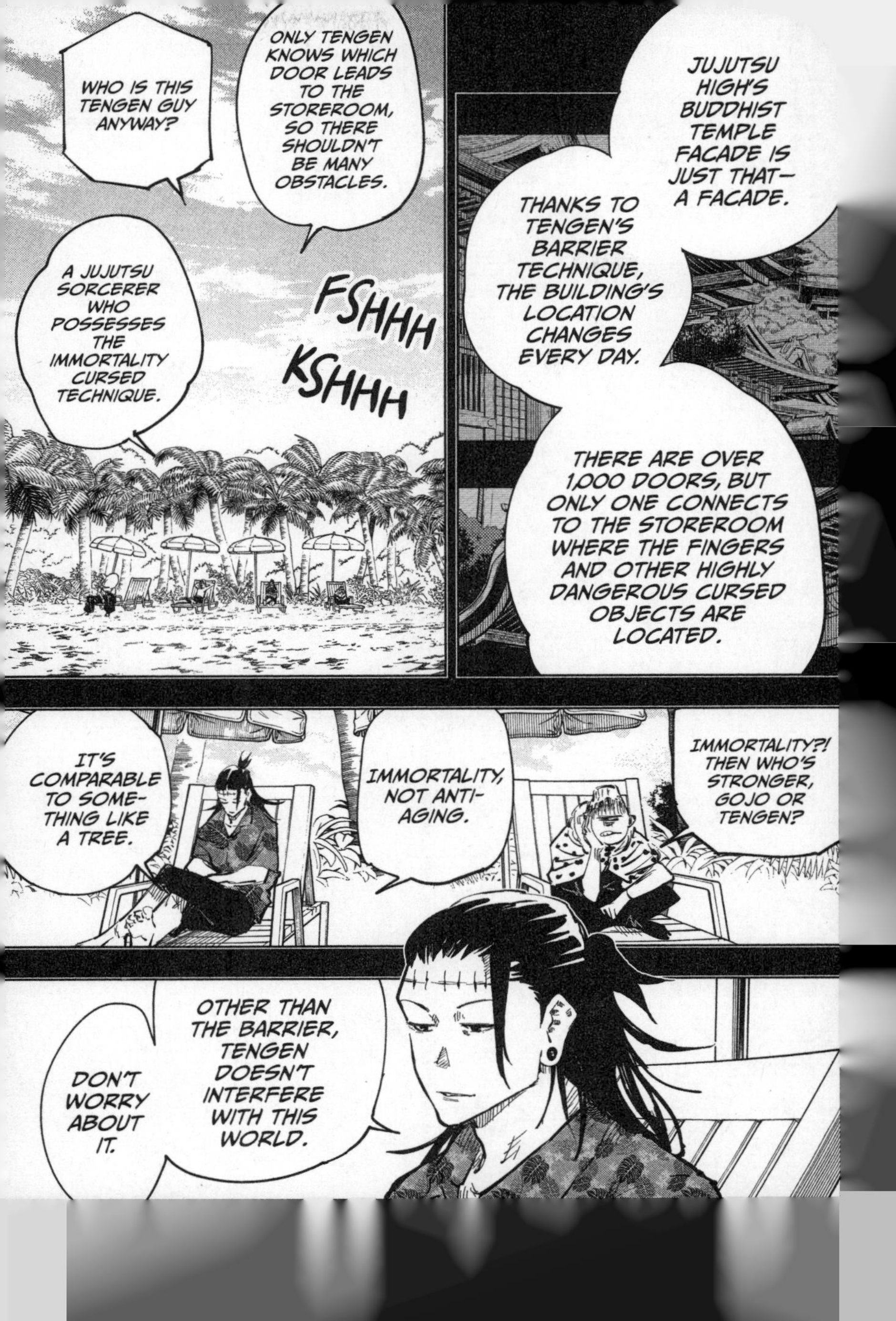
JUJUTSU HIGH'S BUDDHIST TEMPLE FACADE IS JUST THAT—A FACADE.
THANKS TO TENGEN'S BARRIER TECHNIQUE, THE BUILDING'S LOCATION CHANGES EVERY DAY.
THERE ARE OVER 1,000 DOORS, BUT ONLY ONE CONNECTS TO THE STOREROOM WHERE THE FINGERS AND OTHER HIGHLY DANGEROUS CURSED OBJECTS ARE LOCATED.
ONLY TENGEN KNOWS WHICH DOOR LEADS TO THE STOREROOM, SO THERE SHOULDN'T BE MANY OBSTACLES.
WHO IS THIS TENGEN GUY ANYWAY?
FSHHH
KSHHH
A JUJUTSU SORCERER WHO POSSESSES THE IMMORTALITY CURSED TECHNIQUE.
IMMORTALITY?! THEN WHO'S STRONGER, GOJO OR TENGEN?
IMMORTALITY, NOT ANTI-AGING.
IT'S COMPARABLE TO SOMETHING LIKE A TREE.
OTHER THAN THE BARRIER, TENGEN DOESN'T INTERFERE WITH THIS WORLD.
DON'T WORRY ABOUT IT.

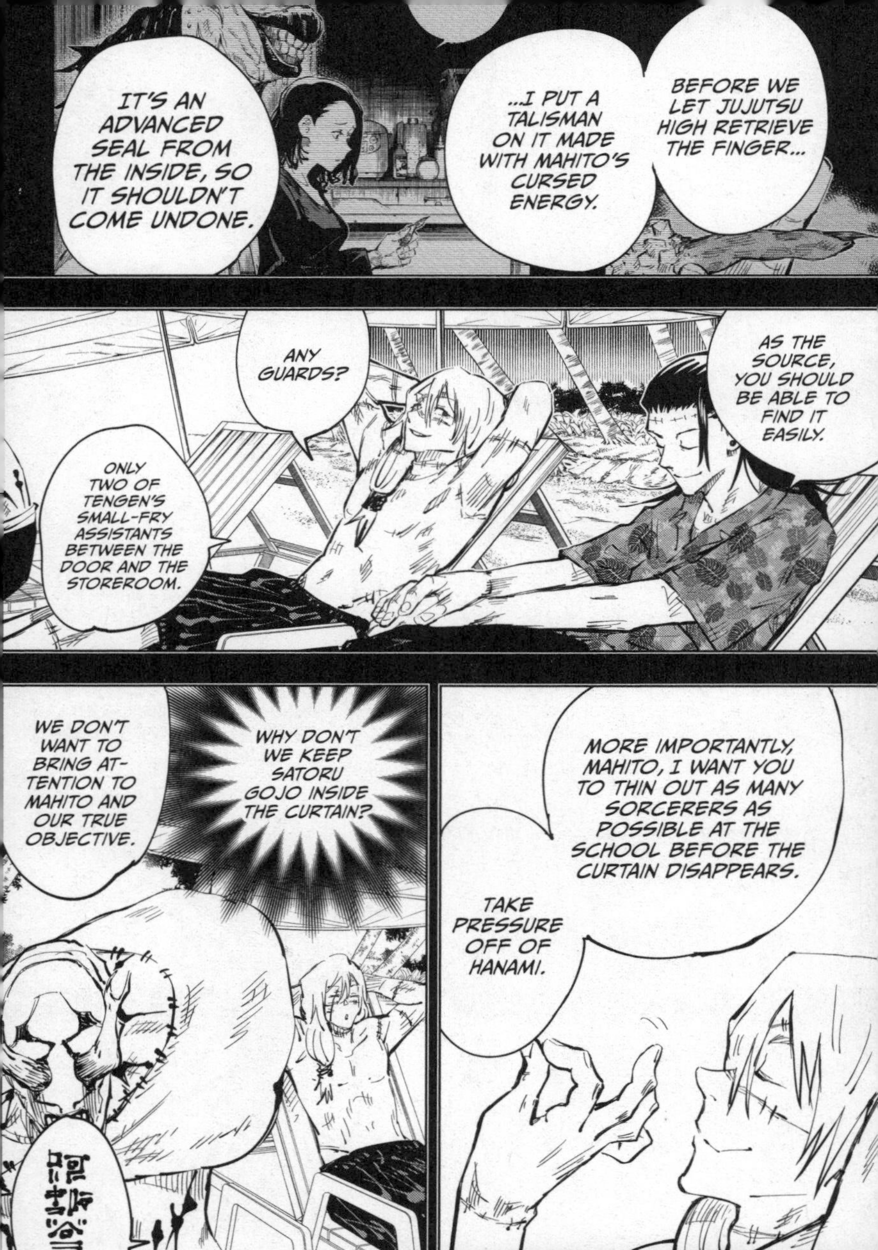
BEFORE WE LET JUJUTSU HIGH RETRIEVE THE FINGER...
...I PUT A TALISMAN ON IT MADE WITH MAHITO'S CURSED ENERGY.
IT'S AN ADVANCED SEAL FROM THE INSIDE, SO IT SHOULDN'T COME UNDONE.
AS THE SOURCE, YOU SHOULD BE ABLE TO FIND IT EASILY.
ANY GUARDS?
ONLY TWO OF TENGEN'S SMALL-FRY ASSISTANTS BETWEEN THE DOOR AND THE STOREROOM.
MORE IMPORTANTLY, MAHITO, I WANT YOU TO THIN OUT AS MANY SORCERERS AS POSSIBLE AT THE SCHOOL BEFORE THE CURTAIN DISAPPEARS.
TAKE PRESSURE OFF OF HANAMI.
WHY DON'T WE KEEP SATORU GOJO INSIDE THE CURTAIN?
WE DON'T WANT TO BRING ATTENTION TO MAHITO AND OUR TRUE OBJECTIVE.

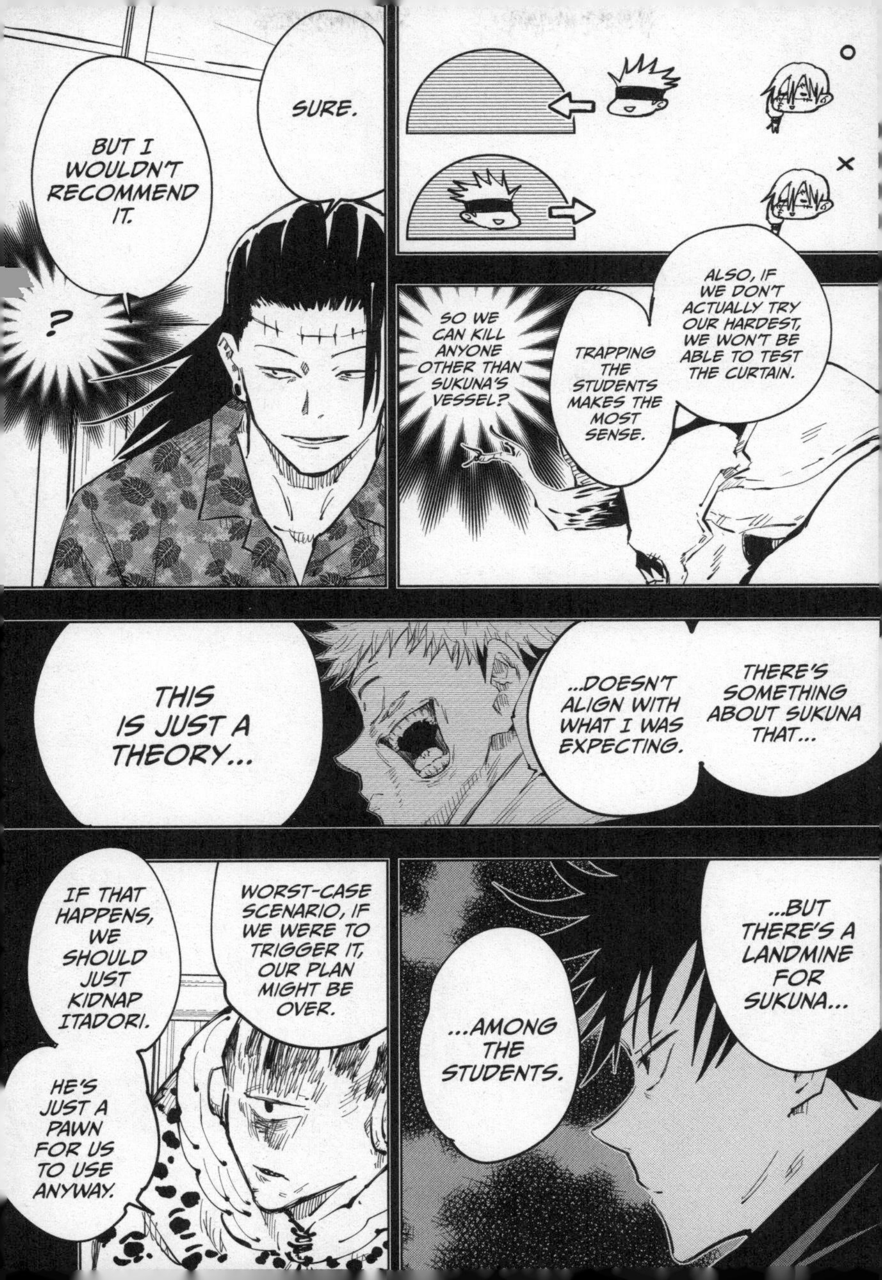
○
×
ALSO, IF WE DON'T ACTUALLY TRY OUR HARDEST, WE WON'T BE ABLE TO TEST THE CURTAIN.
TRAPPING THE STUDENTS MAKES THE MOST SENSE.
SO WE CAN KILL ANYONE OTHER THAN SUKUNA'S VESSEL?
SURE.
BUT I WOULDN'T RECOMMEND IT.
?
THERE'S SOMETHING ABOUT SUKUNA THAT...
...DOESN'T ALIGN WITH WHAT I WAS EXPECTING.
THIS IS JUST A THEORY...
...BUT THERE'S A LANDMINE FOR SUKUNA...
...AMONG THE STUDENTS.
WORST-CASE SCENARIO, IF WE WERE TO TRIGGER IT, OUR PLAN MIGHT BE OVER.
IF THAT HAPPENS, WE SHOULD JUST KIDNAP ITADORI.
HE'S JUST A PAWN FOR US TO USE ANYWAY.

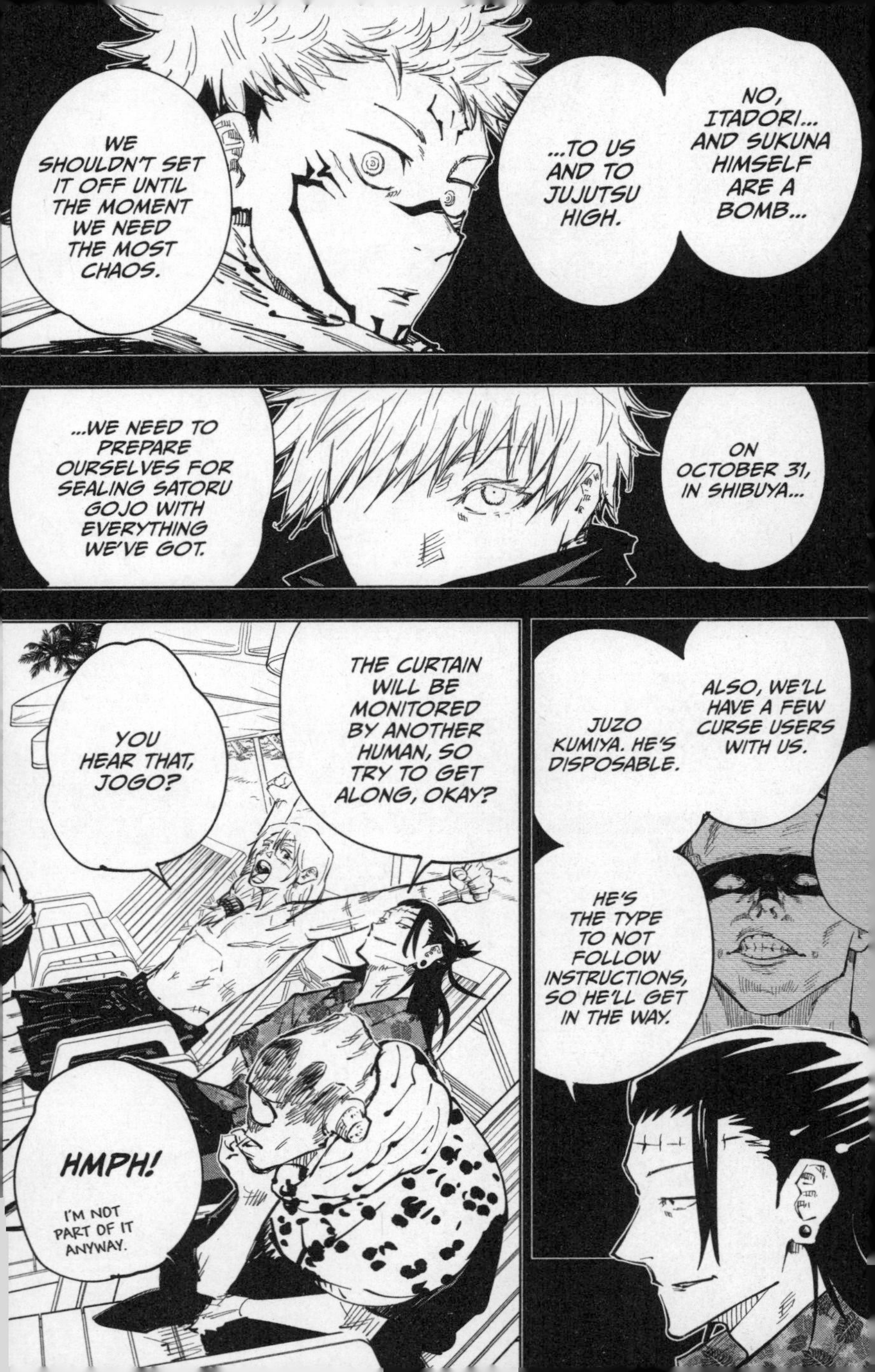
NO, ITADORI... AND SUKUNA HIMSELF ARE A BOMB...
...TO US AND TO JUJUTSU HIGH.
WE SHOULDN'T SET IT OFF UNTIL THE MOMENT WE NEED THE MOST CHAOS.
ON OCTOBER 31, IN SHIBUYA...
...WE NEED TO PREPARE OURSELVES FOR SEALING SATORU GOJO WITH EVERYTHING WE'VE GOT.
ALSO, WE'LL HAVE A FEW CURSE USERS WITH US.
JUZO KUMIYA. HE'S DISPOSABLE.
HE'S THE TYPE TO NOT FOLLOW INSTRUCTIONS, SO HE'LL GET IN THE WAY.
THE CURTAIN WILL BE MONITORED BY ANOTHER HUMAN, SO TRY TO GET ALONG, OKAY?
YOU HEAR THAT, JOGO?
HMPH!
I'M NOT PART OF IT ANYWAY.

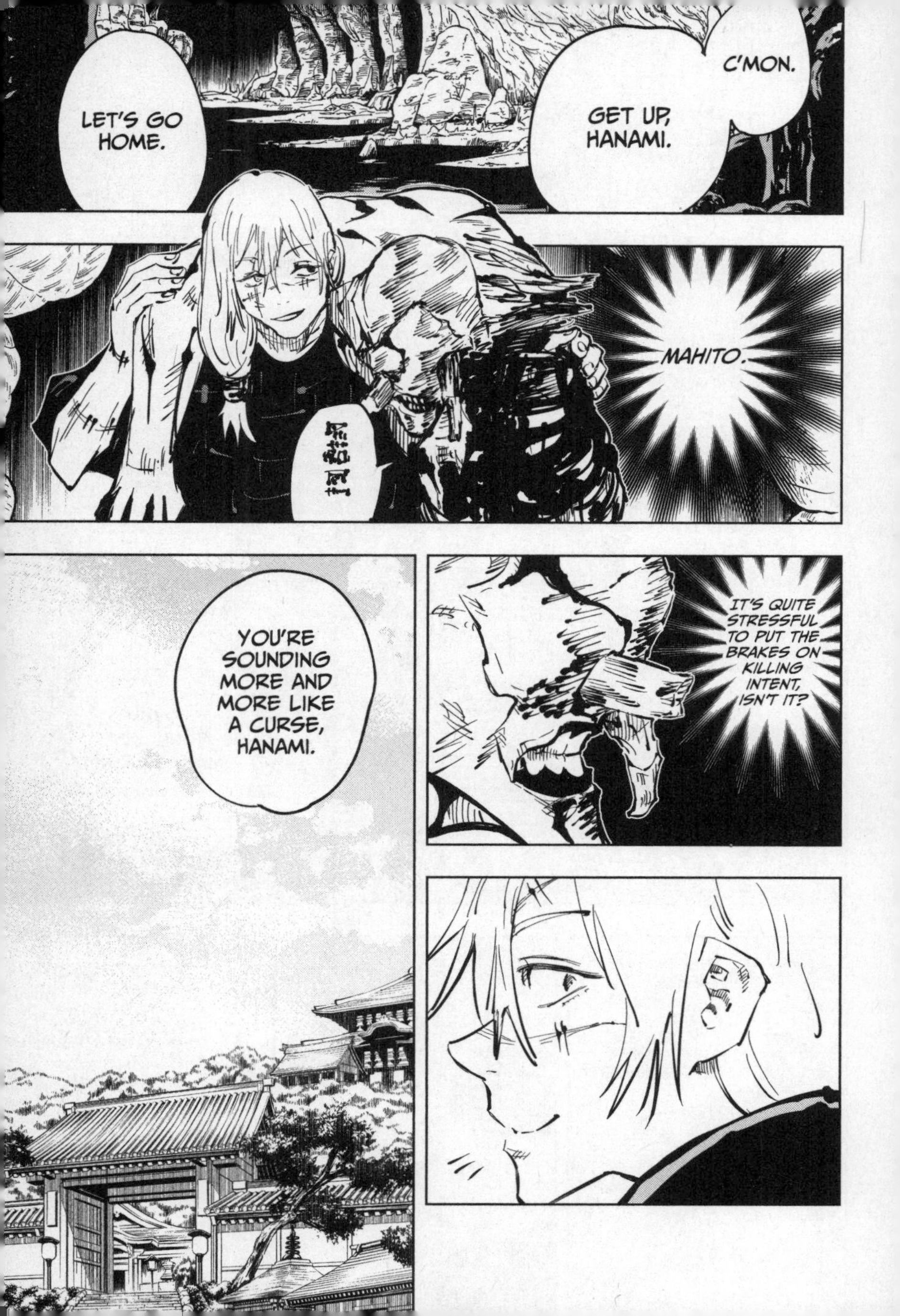
C'MON.
GET UP, HANAMI.
LET'S GO HOME.
MAHITO.
IT'S QUITE STRESSFUL TO PUT THE BRAKES ON KILLING INTENT, ISN'T IT?
YOU'RE SOUNDING MORE AND MORE LIKE A CURSE, HANAMI.

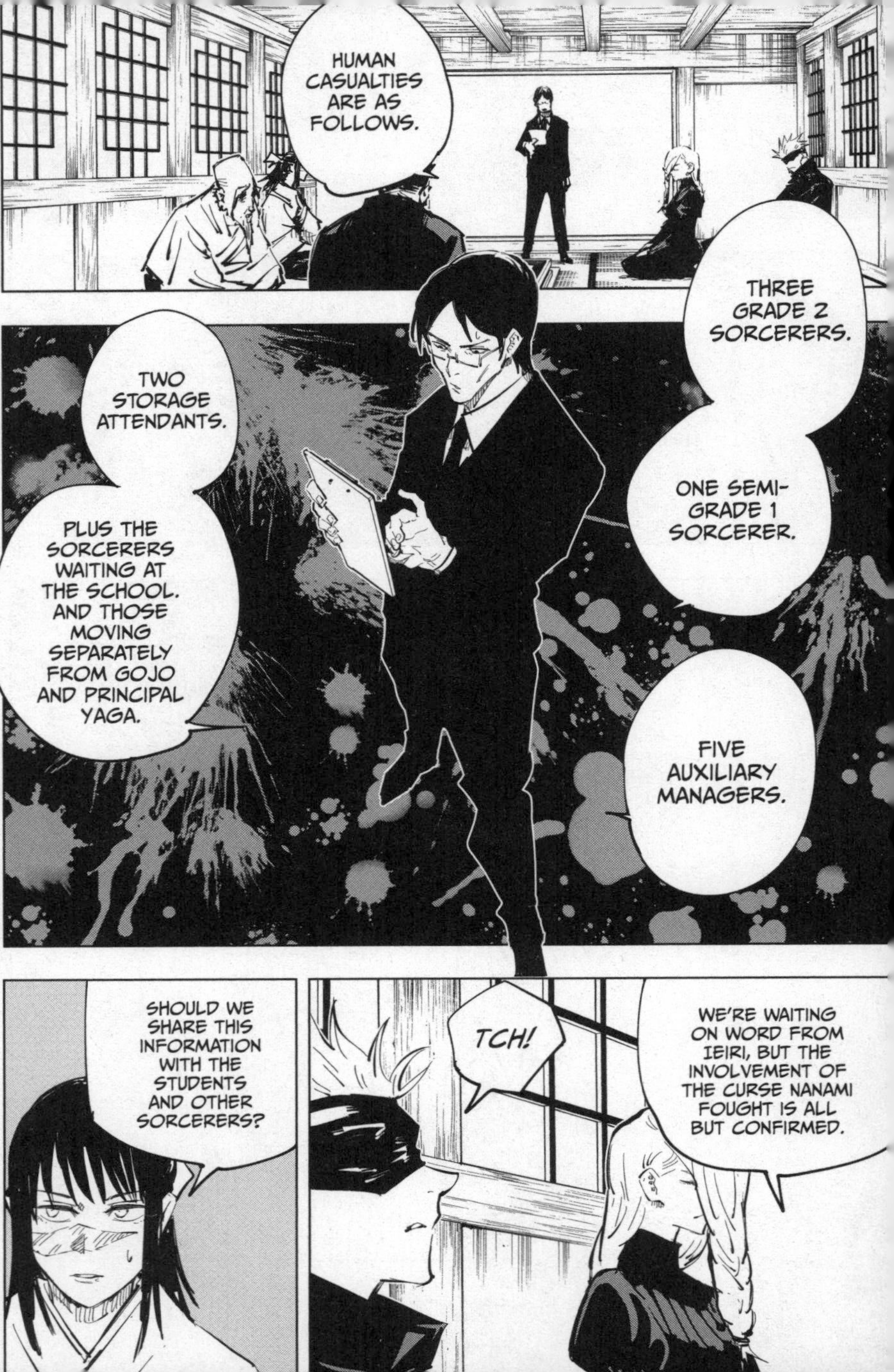
HUMAN CASUALTIES ARE AS FOLLOWS.
THREE GRADE 2 SORCERERS.
ONE SEMI-GRADE 1 SORCERER.
FIVE AUXILIARY MANAGERS.
TWO STORAGE ATTENDANTS.
PLUS THE SORCERERS WAITING AT THE SCHOOL. AND THOSE MOVING SEPARATELY FROM GOJO AND PRINCIPAL YAGA.
WE'RE WAITING ON WORD FROM IEIRI, BUT THE INVOLVEMENT OF THE CURSE NANAMI FOUGHT IS ALL BUT CONFIRMED.
TCH!
SHOULD WE SHARE THIS INFORMATION WITH THE STUDENTS AND OTHER SORCERERS?

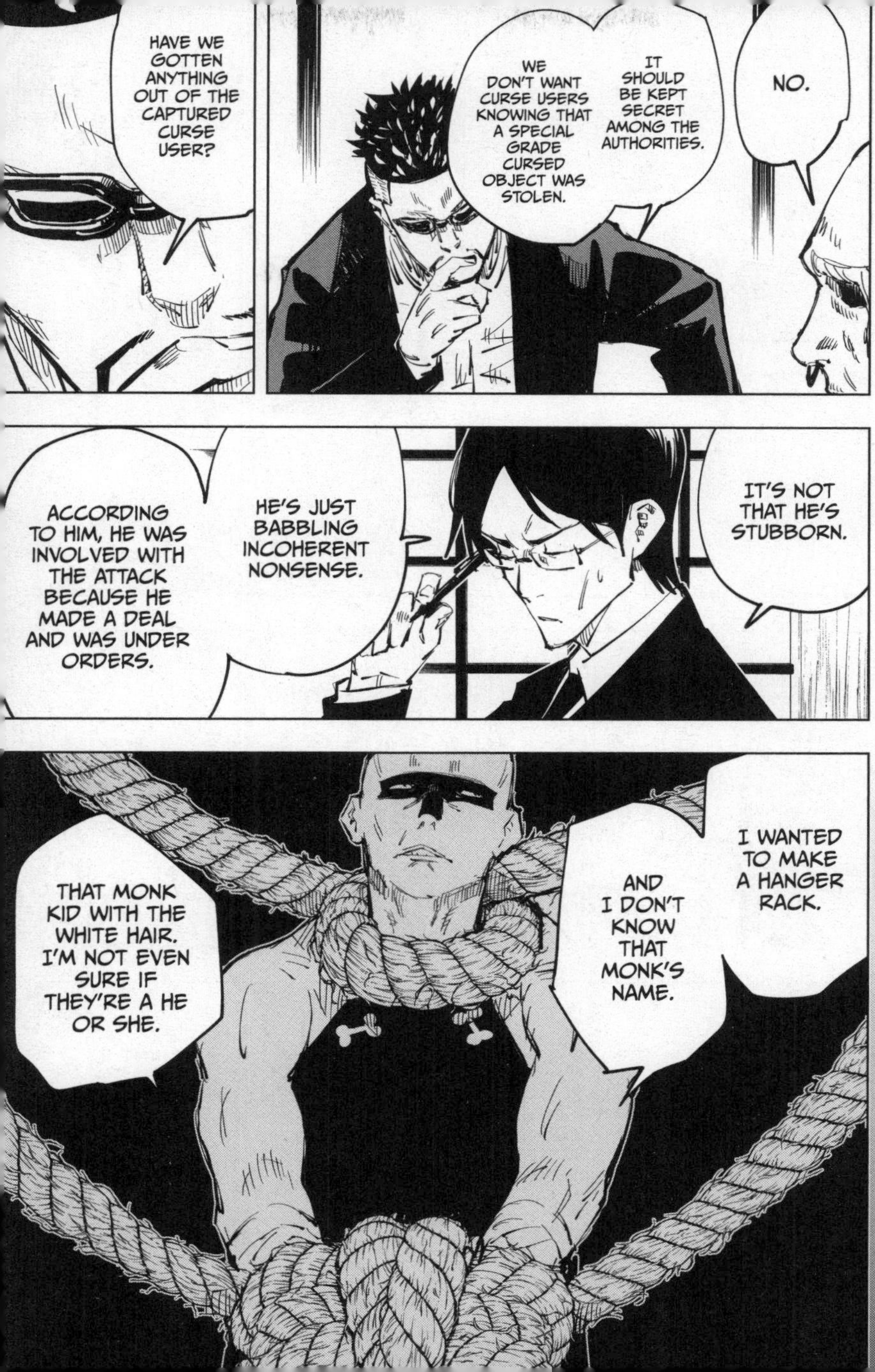
NO.
IT SHOULD BE KEPT SECRET AMONG THE AUTHORITIES.
WE DON'T WANT CURSE USERS KNOWING THAT A SPECIAL GRADE CURSED OBJECT WAS STOLEN.
HAVE WE GOTTEN ANYTHING OUT OF THE CAPTURED CURSE USER?
IT'S NOT THAT HE'S STUBBORN.
HE'S JUST BABBLING INCOHERENT NONSENSE.
ACCORDING TO HIM, HE WAS INVOLVED WITH THE ATTACK BECAUSE HE MADE A DEAL AND WAS UNDER ORDERS.
I WANTED TO MAKE A HANGER RACK.
AND I DON'T KNOW THAT MONK'S NAME.
THAT MONK KID WITH THE WHITE HAIR. I'M NOT EVEN SURE IF THEY'RE A HE OR SHE.

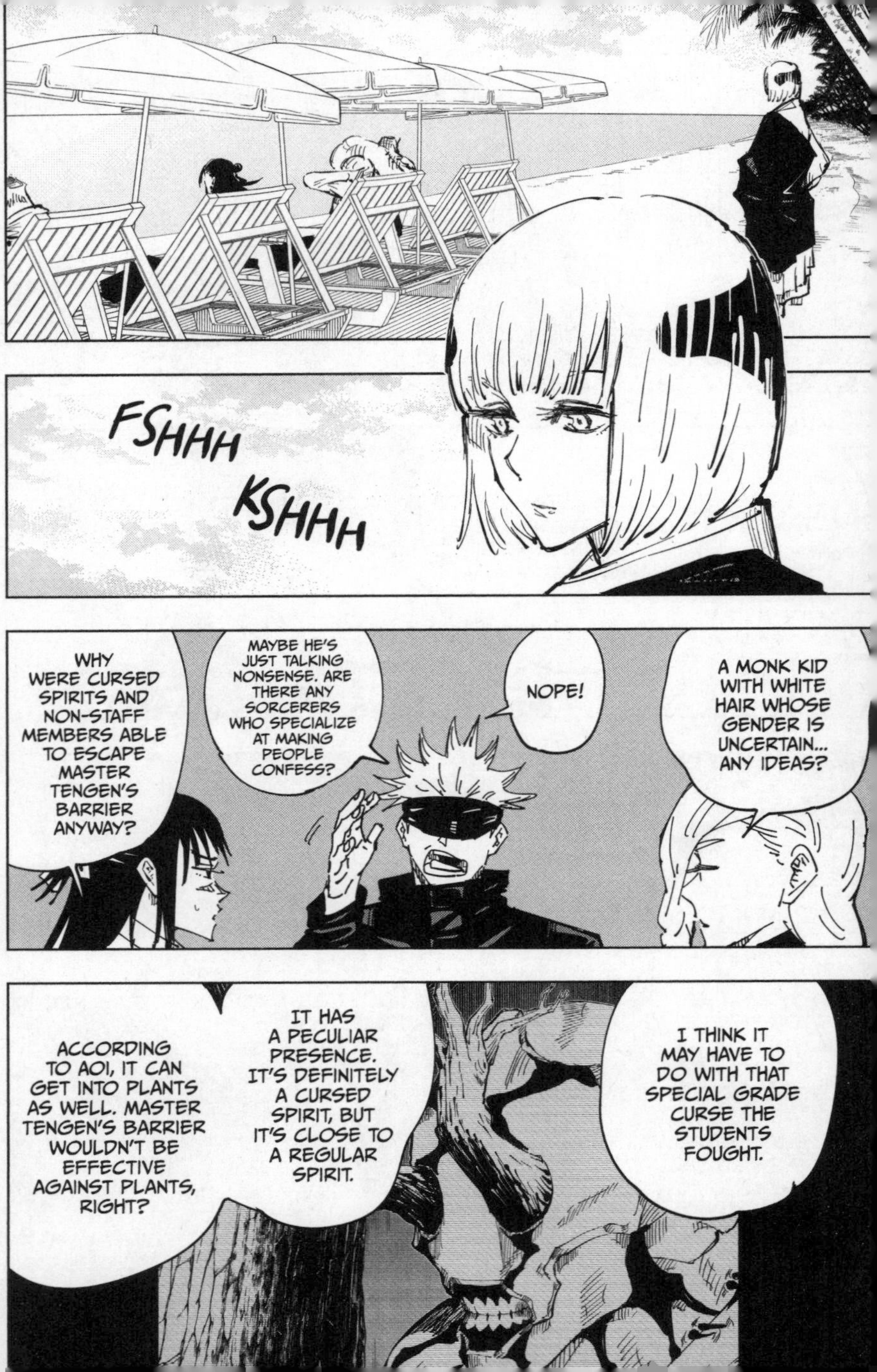
FSHHH
KSHHH
A MONK KID WITH WHITE HAIR WHOSE GENDER IS UNCERTAIN... ANY IDEAS?
NOPE!
MAYBE HE'S JUST TALKING NONSENSE. ARE THERE ANY SORCERERS WHO SPECIALIZE AT MAKING PEOPLE CONFESS?
WHY WERE CURSED SPIRITS AND NON-STAFF MEMBERS ABLE TO ESCAPE MASTER TENGEN'S BARRIER ANYWAY?
I THINK IT MAY HAVE TO DO WITH THAT SPECIAL GRADE CURSE THE STUDENTS FOUGHT.
IT HAS A PECULIAR PRESENCE. IT'S DEFINITELY A CURSED SPIRIT, BUT IT'S CLOSE TO A REGULAR SPIRIT.
ACCORDING TO AOI, IT CAN GET INTO PLANTS AS WELL. MASTER TENGEN'S BARRIER WOULDN'T BE EFFECTIVE AGAINST PLANTS, RIGHT?

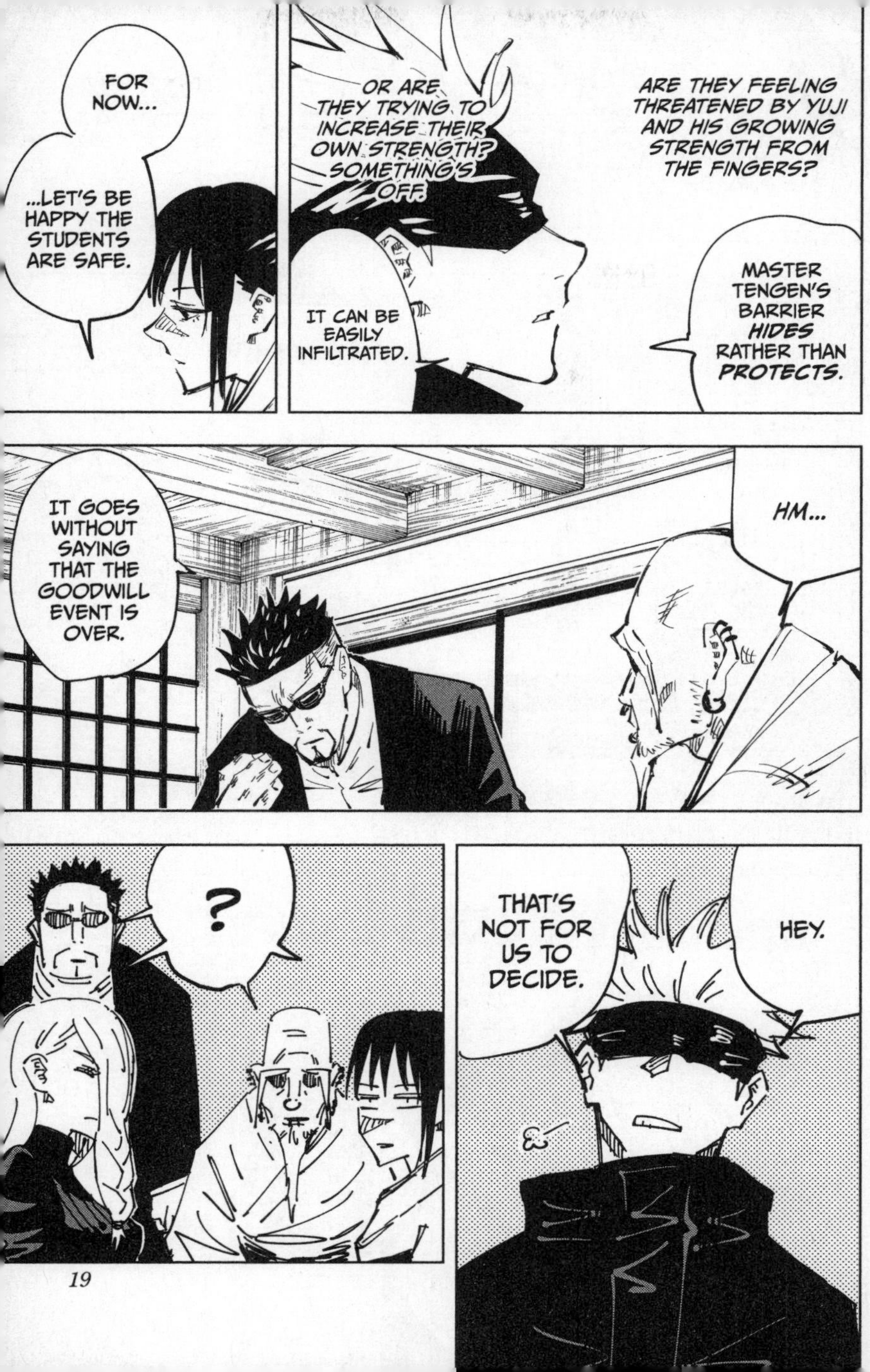
ARE THEY FEELING THREATENED BY YUJI AND HIS GROWING STRENGTH FROM THE FINGERS?
OR ARE THEY TRYING TO INCREASE THEIR OWN STRENGTH? SOMETHING'S OFF.
MASTER TENGEN'S BARRIER *HIDES* RATHER THAN *PROTECTS.*
IT CAN BE EASILY INFILTRATED.
FOR NOW...
...LET'S BE HAPPY THE STUDENTS ARE SAFE.
HM...
IT GOES WITHOUT SAYING THAT THE GOODWILL EVENT IS OVER.
HEY.
THAT'S NOT FOR US TO DECIDE.
?

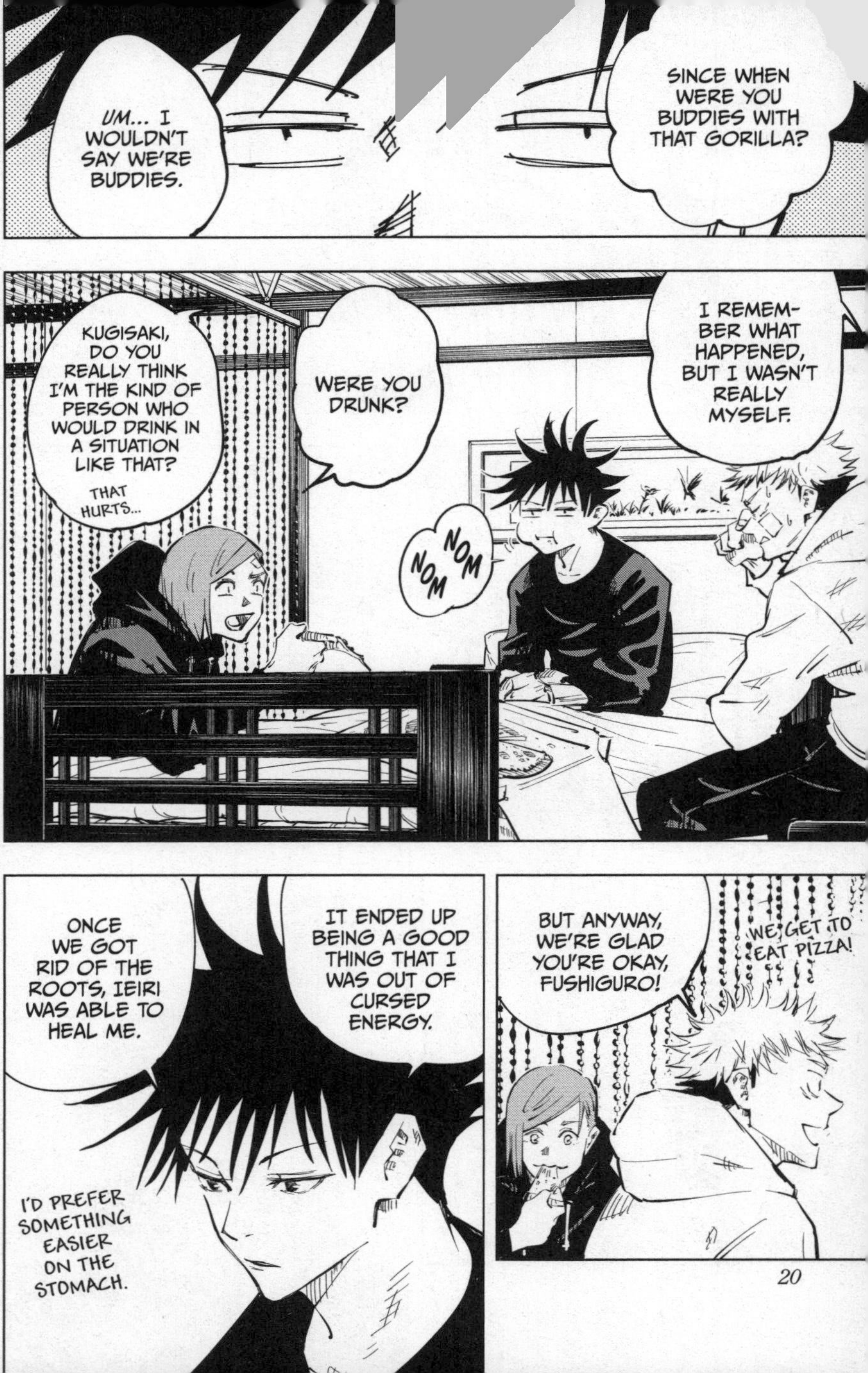
SINCE WHEN WERE YOU BUDDIES WITH THAT GORILLA?
UM... I WOULDN'T SAY WE'RE BUDDIES.
I REMEMBER WHAT HAPPENED, BUT I WASN'T REALLY MYSELF.
WERE YOU DRUNK?
KUGISAKI, DO YOU REALLY THINK I'M THE KIND OF PERSON WHO WOULD DRINK IN A SITUATION LIKE THAT?
THAT HURTS...
NOM NOM
BUT ANYWAY, WE'RE GLAD YOU'RE OKAY, FUSHIGURO!
WE GET TO EAT PIZZA!
IT ENDED UP BEING A GOOD THING THAT I WAS OUT OF CURSED ENERGY.
ONCE WE GOT RID OF THE ROOTS, IEIRI WAS ABLE TO HEAL ME.
I'D PREFER SOMETHING EASIER ON THE STOMACH.

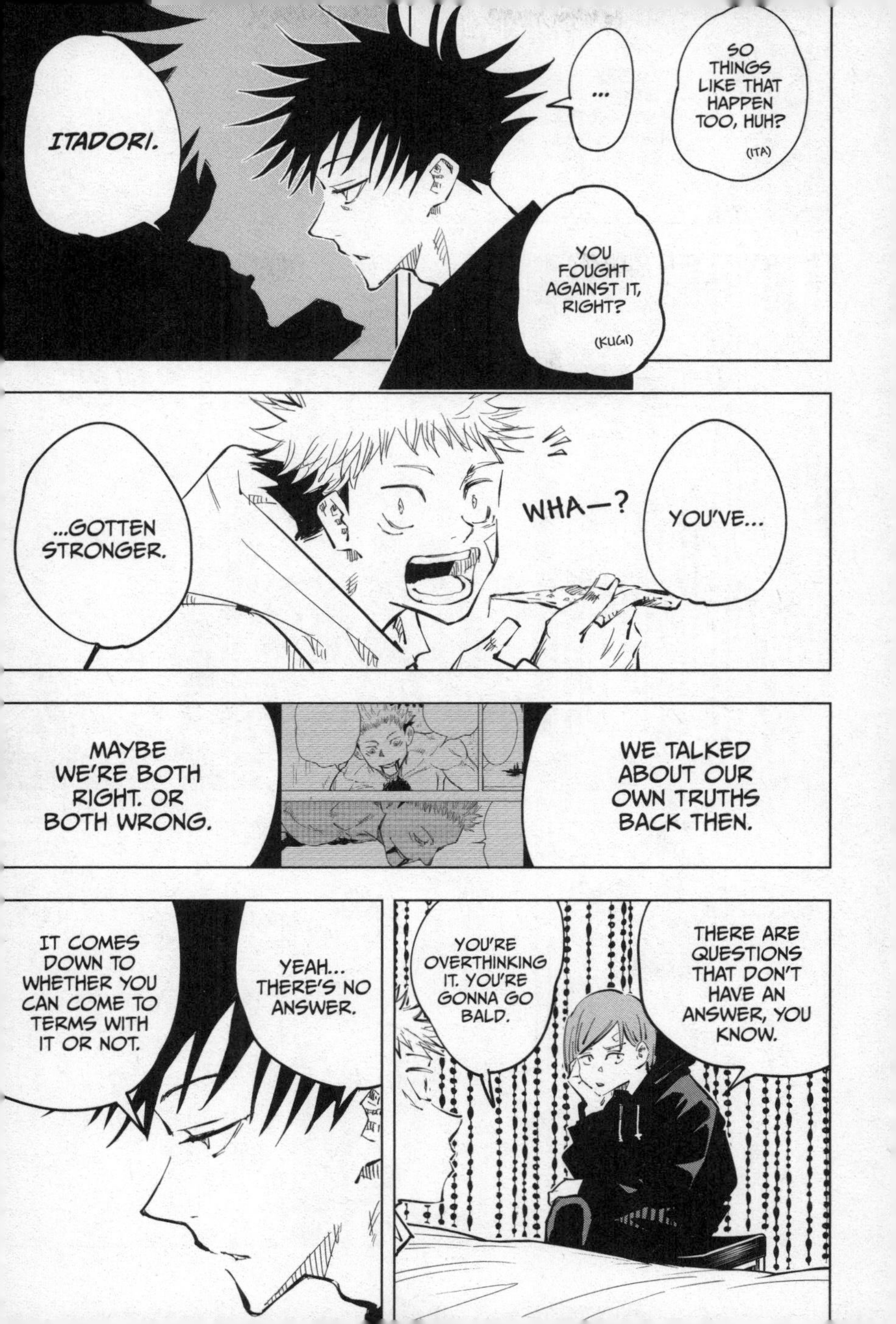
SO THINGS LIKE THAT HAPPEN TOO, HUH? (ITA)
...
YOU FOUGHT AGAINST IT, RIGHT? (KUGI)
ITADORI.
YOU'VE...
WHA—?
...GOTTEN STRONGER.
WE TALKED ABOUT OUR OWN TRUTHS BACK THEN.
MAYBE WE'RE BOTH RIGHT. OR BOTH WRONG.
THERE ARE QUESTIONS THAT DON'T HAVE AN ANSWER, YOU KNOW.
YOU'RE OVERTHINKING IT. YOU'RE GONNA GO BALD.
YEAH... THERE'S NO ANSWER.
IT COMES DOWN TO WHETHER YOU CAN COME TO TERMS WITH IT OR NOT.

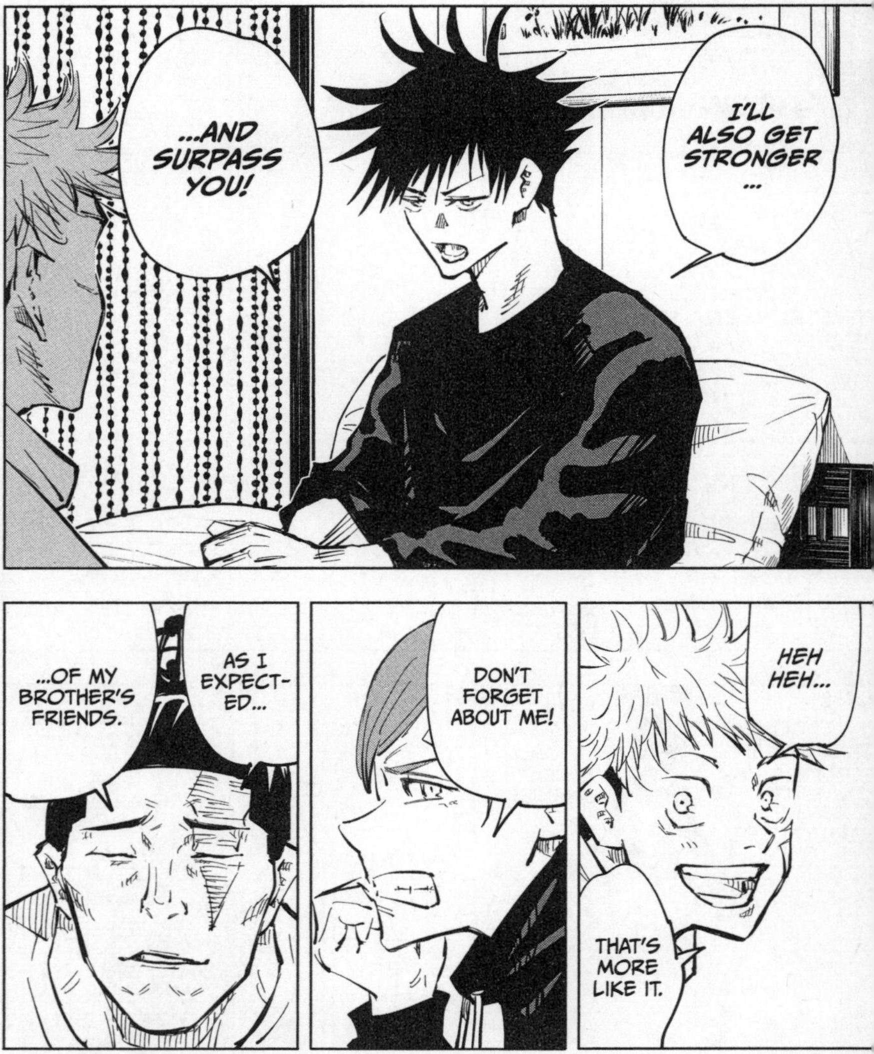
I'LL ALSO GET STRONGER ...
...AND SURPASS YOU!
HEH HEH...
THAT'S MORE LIKE IT.
DON'T FORGET ABOUT ME!
AS I EXPECT-ED...
...OF MY BROTHER'S FRIENDS.

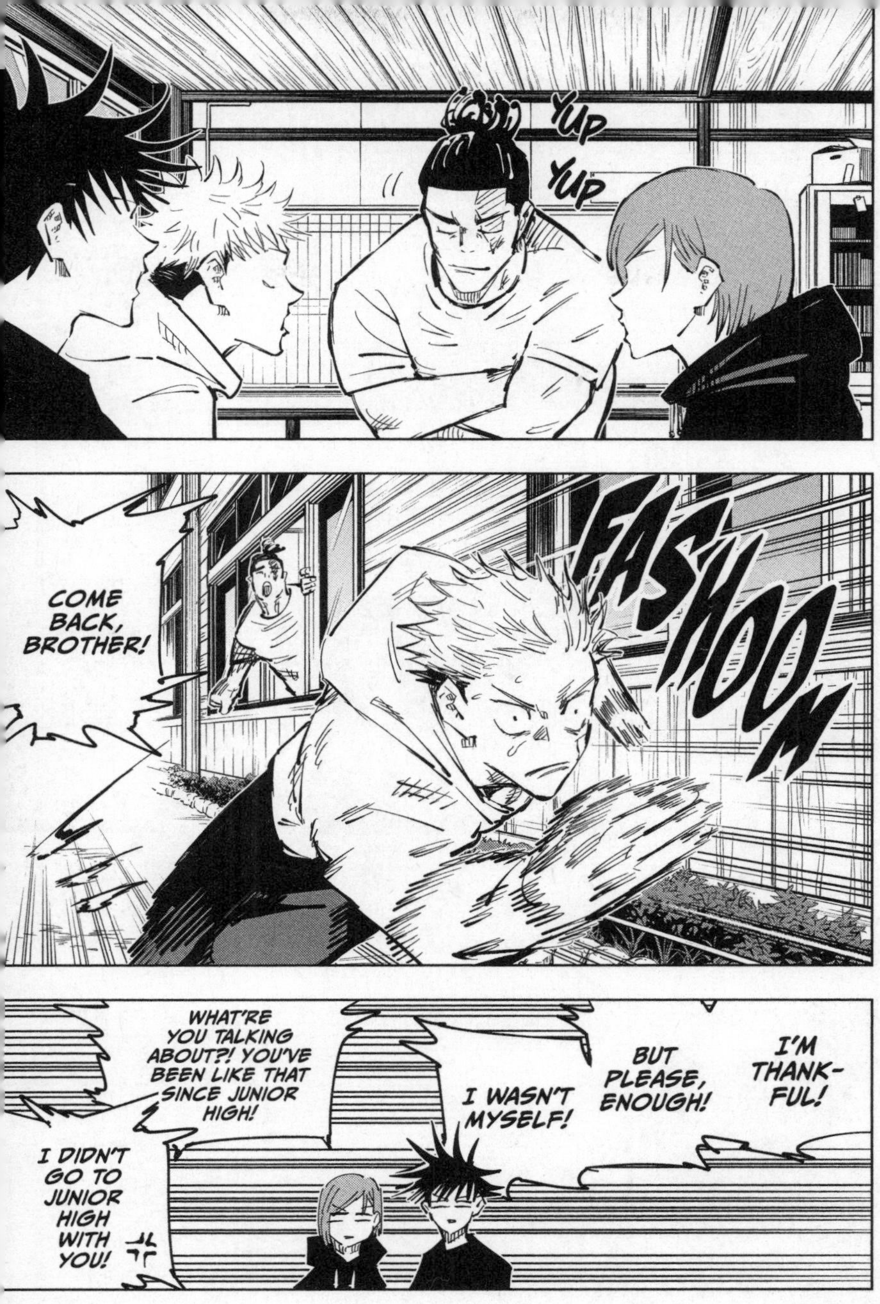
YUP
YUP
FASHOOM
COME BACK, BROTHER!
I'M THANKFUL!
BUT PLEASE, ENOUGH!
I WASN'T MYSELF!
WHAT'RE YOU TALKING ABOUT?! YOU'VE BEEN LIKE THAT SINCE JUNIOR HIGH!
I DIDN'T GO TO JUNIOR HIGH WITH YOU!

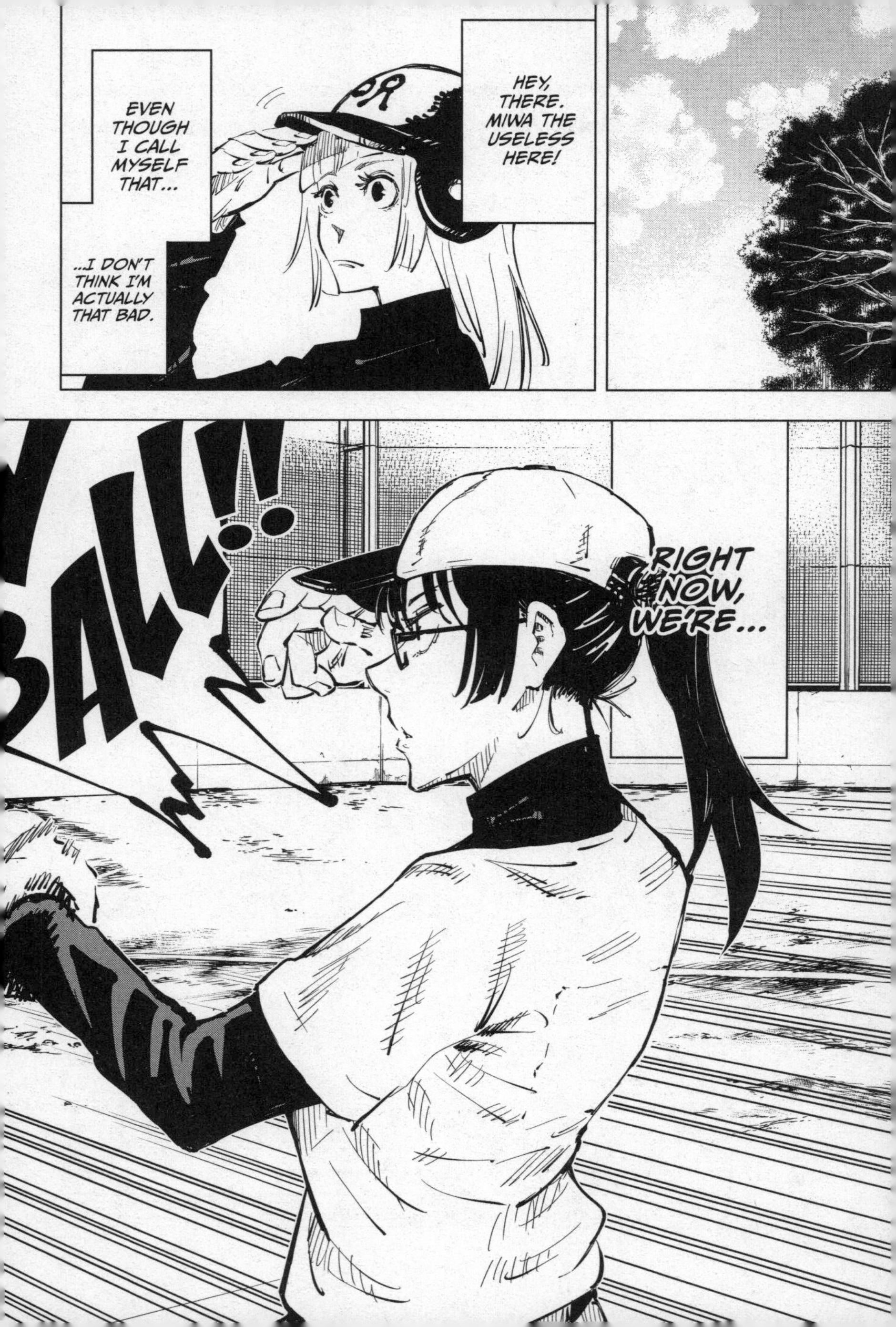
HEY, THERE. MIWA THE USELESS HERE!
EVEN THOUGH I CALL MYSELF THAT...
...I DON'T THINK I'M ACTUALLY THAT BAD.
RIGHT NOW, WE'RE...
BALL!!

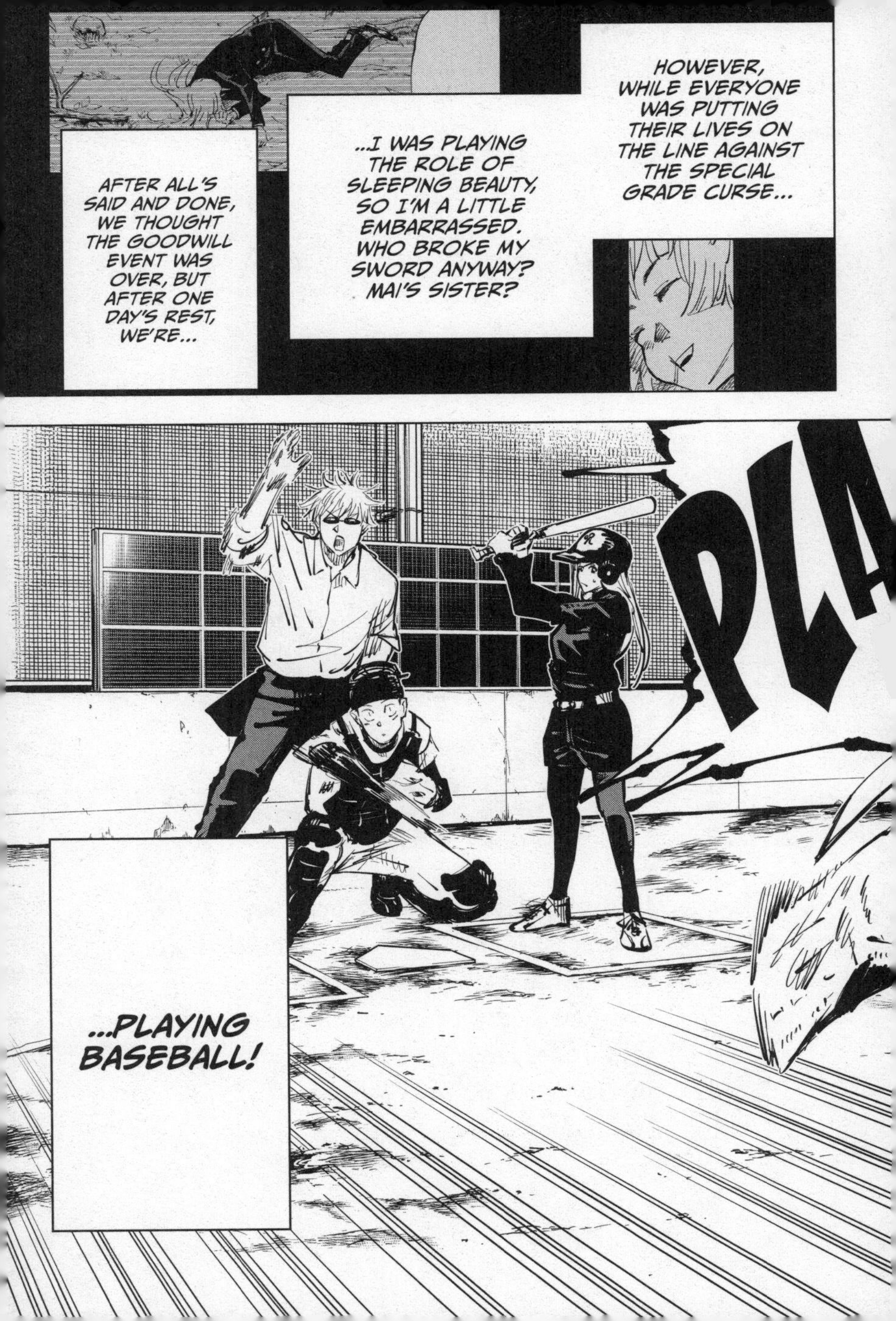
HOWEVER, WHILE EVERYONE WAS PUTTING THEIR LIVES ON THE LINE AGAINST THE SPECIAL GRADE CURSE...
...I WAS PLAYING THE ROLE OF SLEEPING BEAUTY, SO I'M A LITTLE EMBARRASSED. WHO BROKE MY SWORD ANYWAY? MAI'S SISTER?
AFTER ALL'S SAID AND DONE, WE THOUGHT THE GOODWILL EVENT WAS OVER, BUT AFTER ONE DAY'S REST, WE'RE...
PLA
...PLAYING BASEBALL!

SUPPLEMENTARY INFO

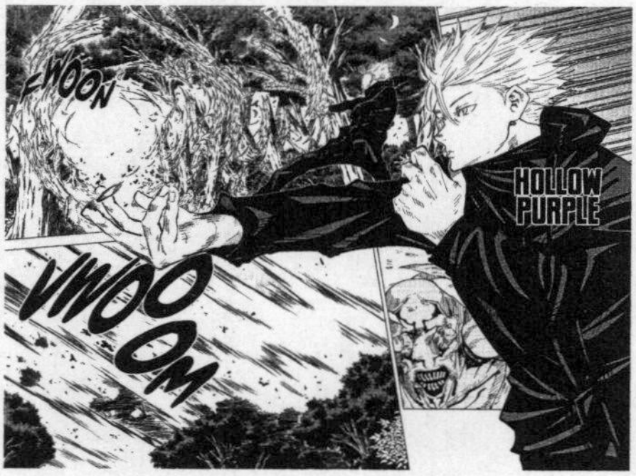
HOLLOW PURPLE
FWOON
VWOOOM

In the final pages of the previous volume, it looks like Gojo swooped in to steal the kill. However, this was just a lack of communication with Todo. Gojo isn't familiar with the specifics of Todo's cursed technique.

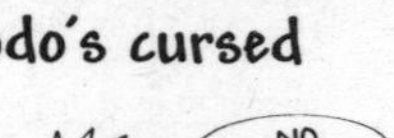
NO WORRIES!

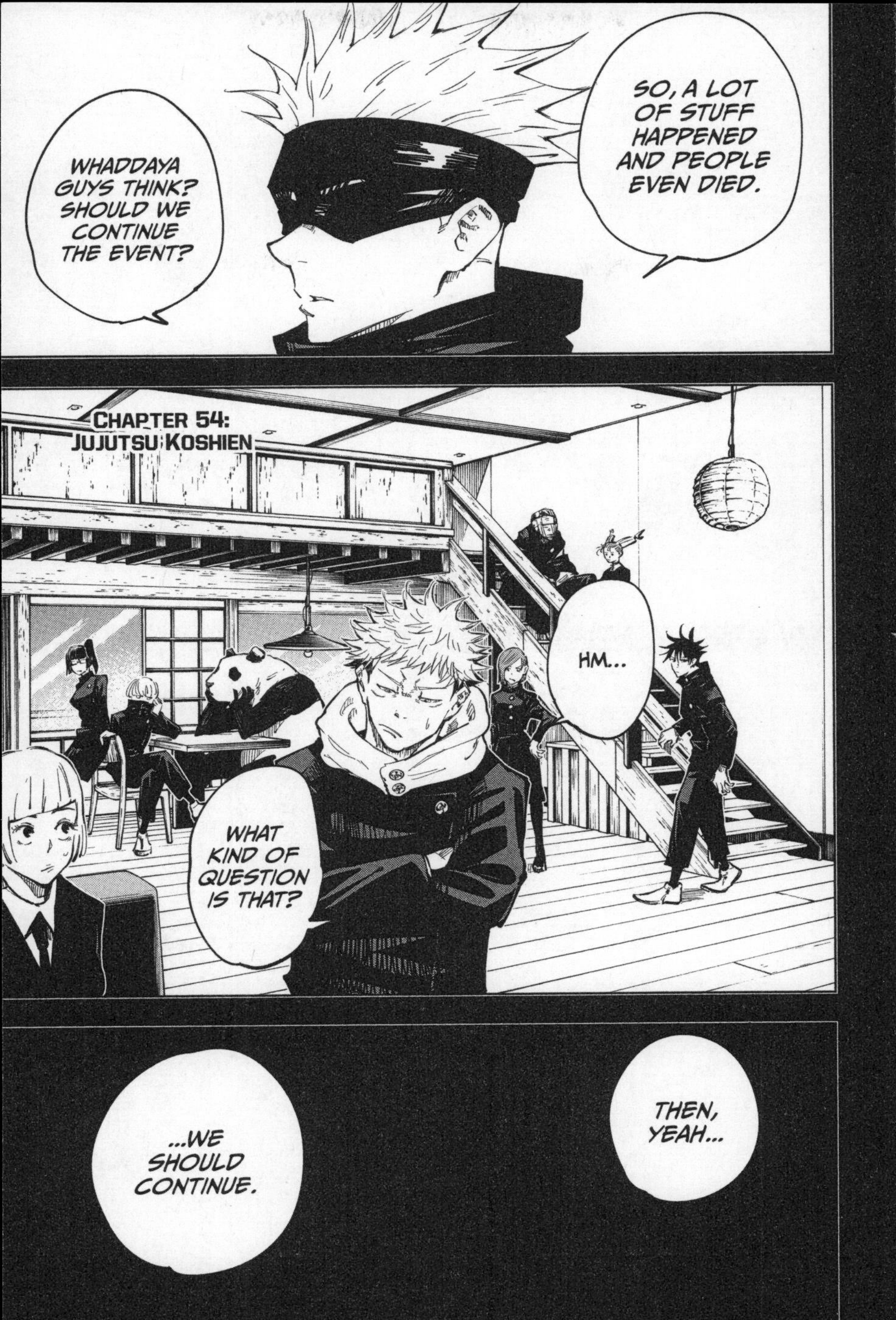
SO, A LOT OF STUFF HAPPENED AND PEOPLE EVEN DIED.
WHADDAYA GUYS THINK? SHOULD WE CONTINUE THE EVENT?
CHAPTER 54: JUJUTSU KOSHIEN
HM...
WHAT KIND OF QUESTION IS THAT?
THEN, YEAH...
...WE SHOULD CONTINUE.

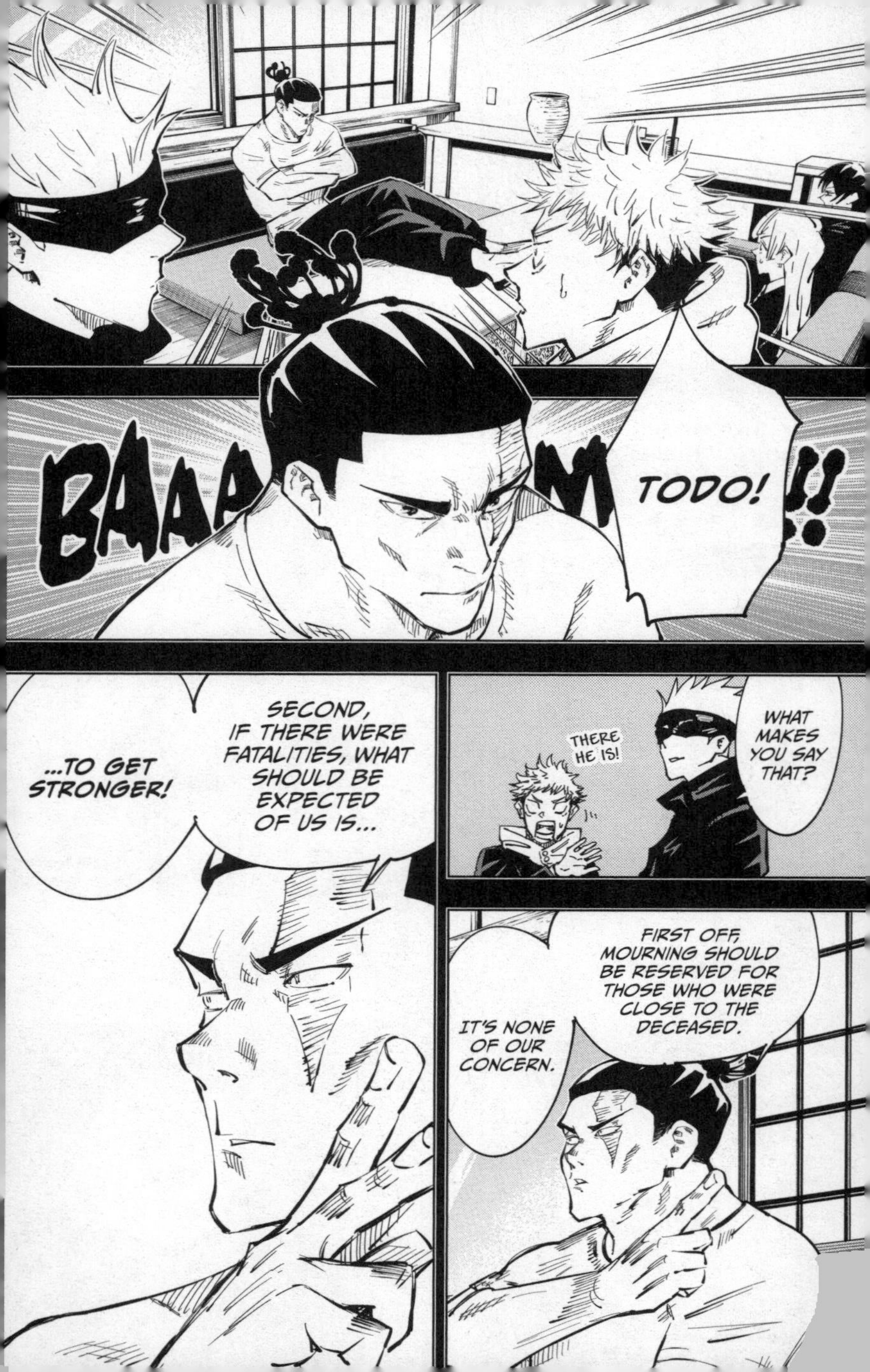
TODO!
WHAT MAKES YOU SAY THAT?
THERE HE IS!
FIRST OFF, MOURNING SHOULD BE RESERVED FOR THOSE WHO WERE CLOSE TO THE DECEASED.
IT'S NONE OF OUR CONCERN.
SECOND, IF THERE WERE FATALITIES, WHAT SHOULD BE EXPECTED OF US IS...
...TO GET STRONGER!

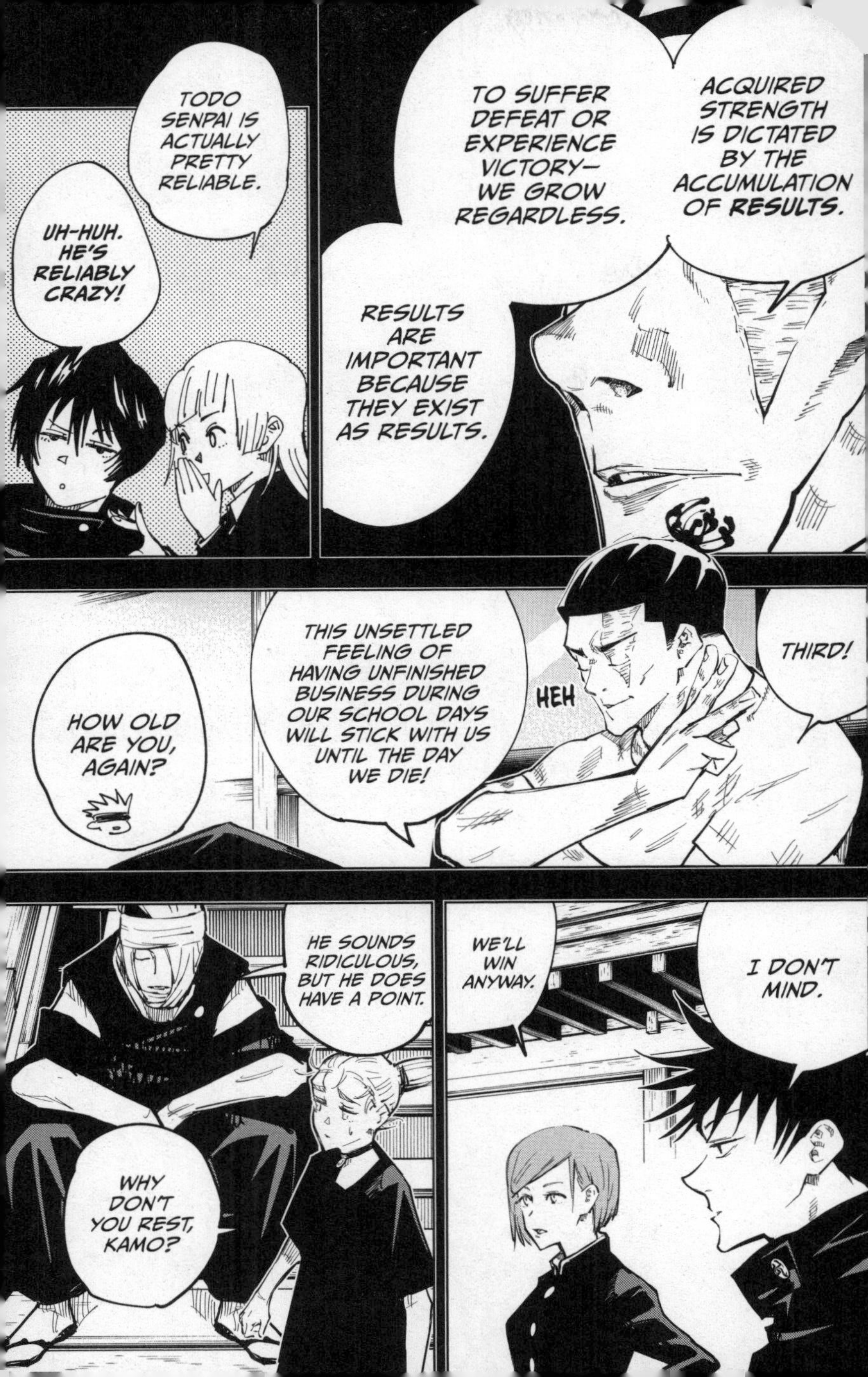
ACQUIRED STRENGTH IS DICTATED BY THE ACCUMULATION OF RESULTS.
TO SUFFER DEFEAT OR EXPERIENCE VICTORY— WE GROW REGARDLESS.
RESULTS ARE IMPORTANT BECAUSE THEY EXIST AS RESULTS.
TODO SENPAI IS ACTUALLY PRETTY RELIABLE.
UH-HUH. HE'S RELIABLY CRAZY!
THIRD!
HEH
THIS UNSETTLED FEELING OF HAVING UNFINISHED BUSINESS DURING OUR SCHOOL DAYS WILL STICK WITH US UNTIL THE DAY WE DIE!
HOW OLD ARE YOU, AGAIN?
I DON'T MIND.
WE'LL WIN ANYWAY.
HE SOUNDS RIDICULOUS, BUT HE DOES HAVE A POINT.
WHY DON'T YOU REST, KAMO?

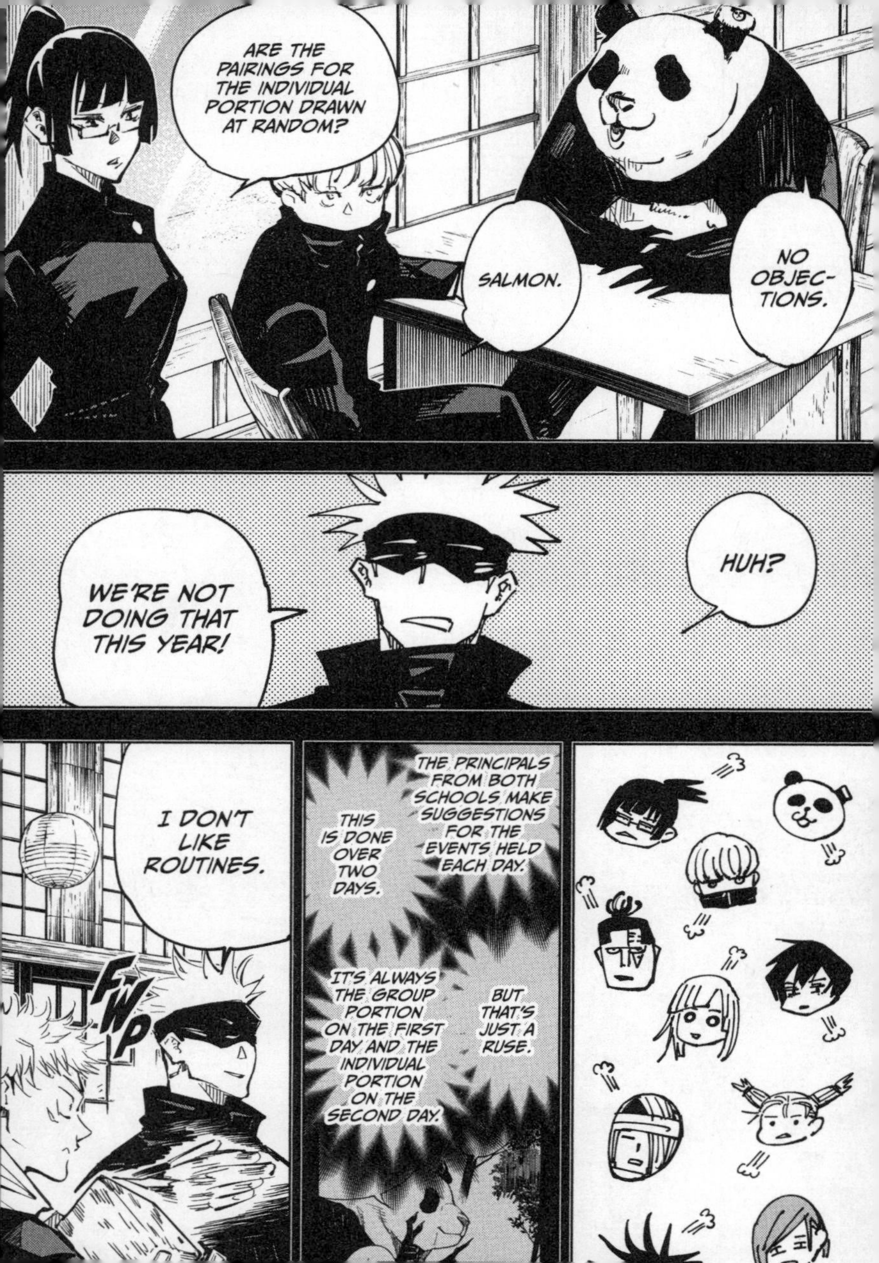
ARE THE PAIRINGS FOR THE INDIVIDUAL PORTION DRAWN AT RANDOM?
NO OBJECTIONS.
SALMON.
HUH?
WE'RE NOT DOING THAT THIS YEAR!
THIS IS DONE OVER TWO DAYS.
THE PRINCIPALS FROM BOTH SCHOOLS MAKE SUGGESTIONS FOR THE EVENTS HELD EACH DAY.
IT'S ALWAYS THE GROUP PORTION ON THE FIRST DAY AND THE INDIVIDUAL PORTION ON THE SECOND DAY.
BUT THAT'S JUST A RUSE.
I DON'T LIKE ROUTINES.
FWP

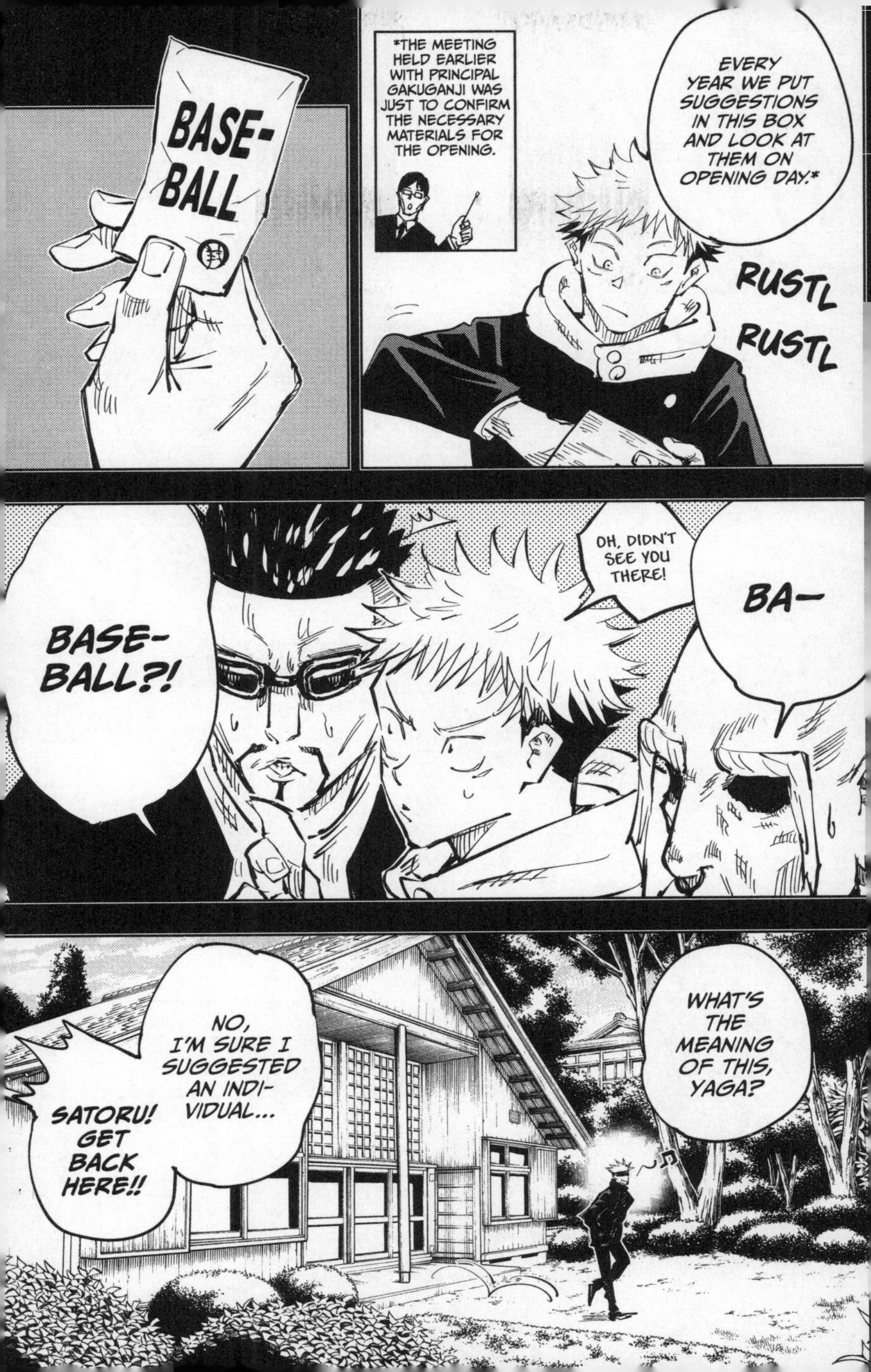
EVERY YEAR WE PUT SUGGESTIONS IN THIS BOX AND LOOK AT THEM ON OPENING DAY.*
RUSTL RUSTL
*THE MEETING HELD EARLIER WITH PRINCIPAL GAKUGANJI WAS JUST TO CONFIRM THE NECESSARY MATERIALS FOR THE OPENING.
BASE-BALL
BA—
OH, DIDN'T SEE YOU THERE!
BASE-BALL?!
WHAT'S THE MEANING OF THIS, YAGA?
NO, I'M SURE I SUGGESTED AN INDIVIDUAL...
SATORU! GET BACK HERE!!

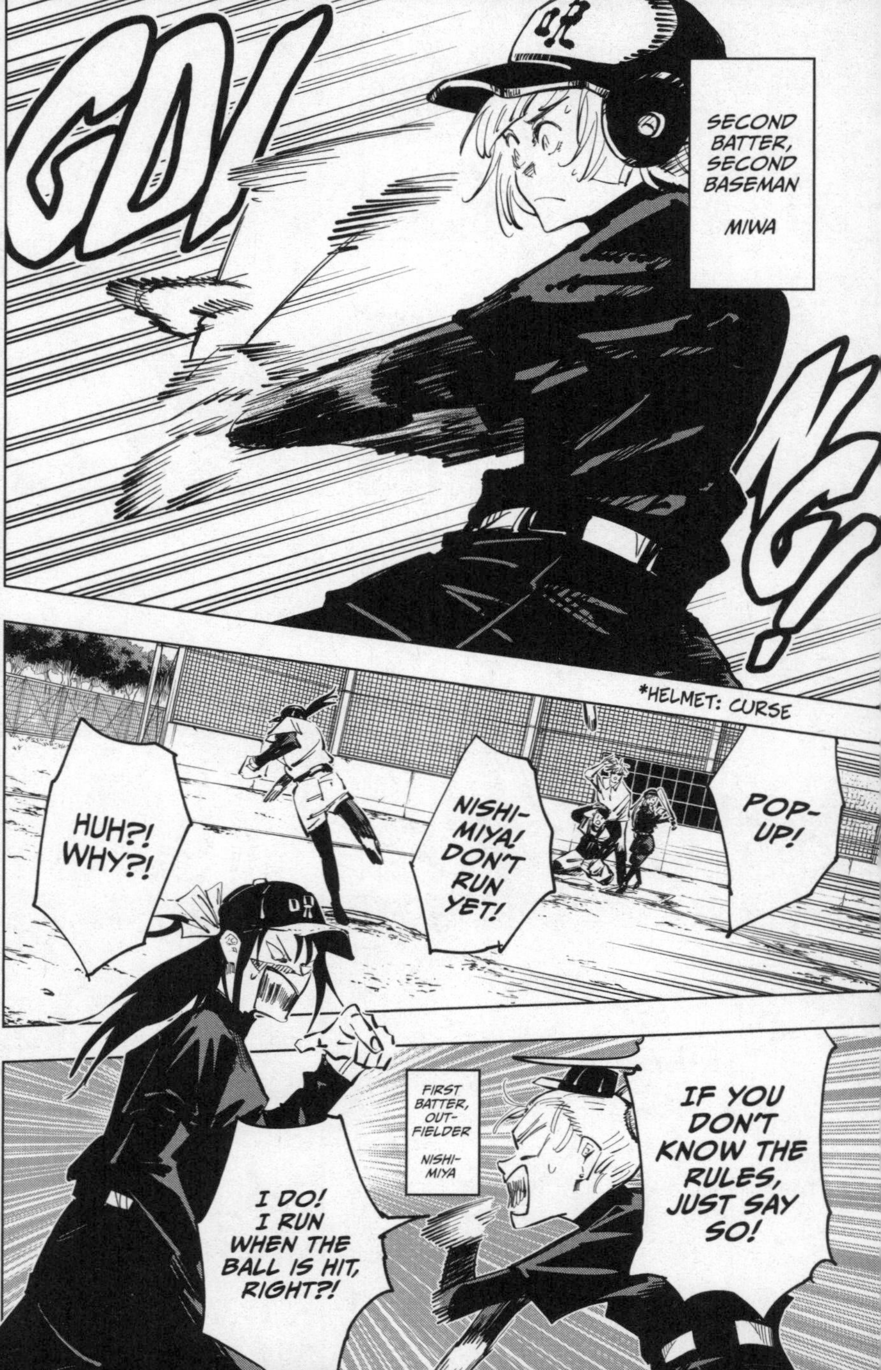
SECOND BATTER, SECOND BASEMAN
MIWA
GON
NNG!
*HELMET: CURSE
POP-UP!
NISHIMIYA! DON'T RUN YET!
HUH?! WHY?!
IF YOU DON'T KNOW THE RULES, JUST SAY SO!
FIRST BATTER, OUTFIELDER
NISHIMIYA
I DO! I RUN WHEN THE BALL IS HIT, RIGHT?!

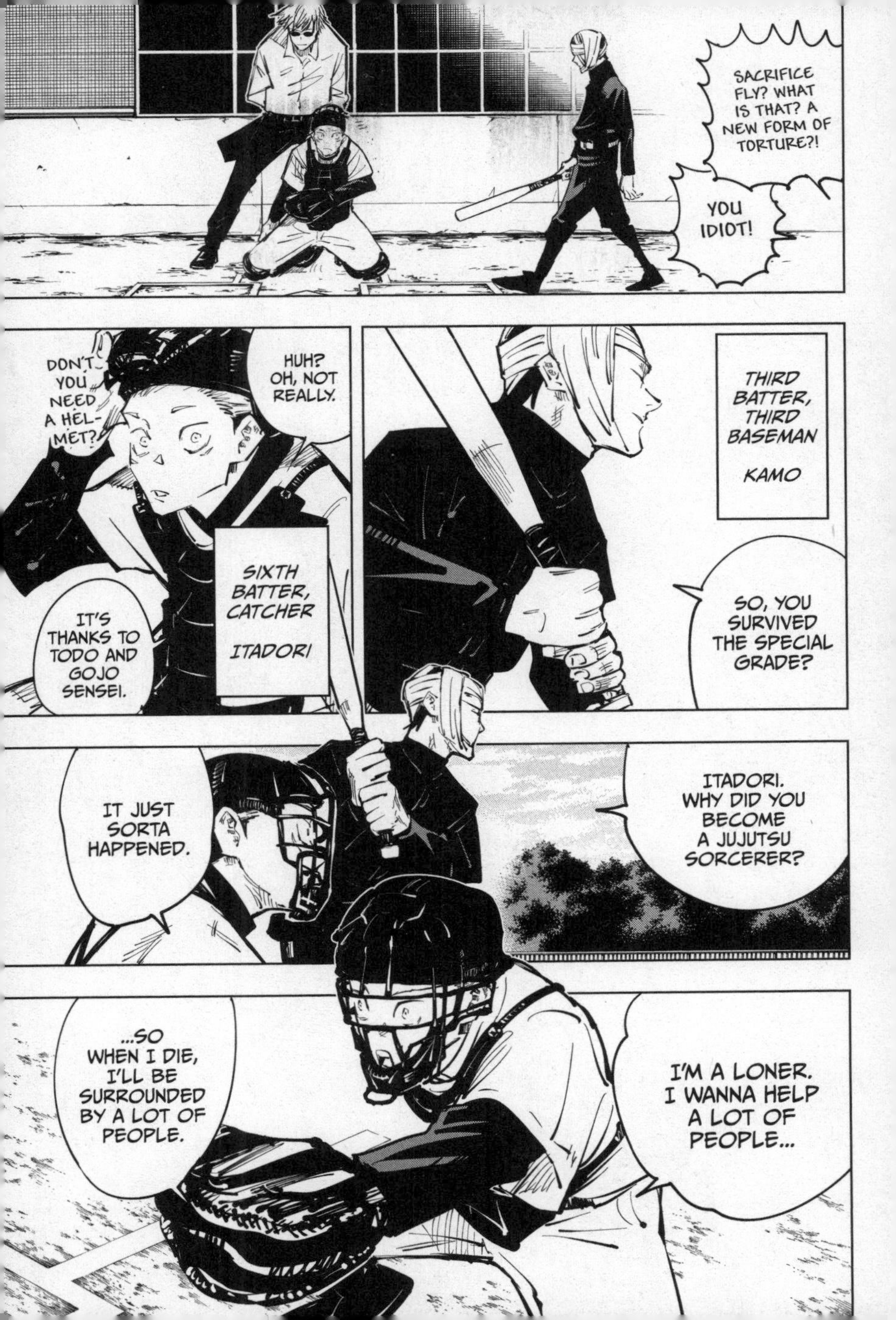
SACRIFICE FLY? WHAT IS THAT? A NEW FORM OF TORTURE?!
YOU IDIOT!
THIRD BATTER, THIRD BASEMAN
KAMO
SO, YOU SURVIVED THE SPECIAL GRADE?
HUH? OH, NOT REALLY.
DON'T YOU NEED A HEL-MET?
SIXTH BATTER, CATCHER
ITADORI
IT'S THANKS TO TODO AND GOJO SENSEI.
ITADORI. WHY DID YOU BECOME A JUJUTSU SORCERER?
IT JUST SORTA HAPPENED.
I'M A LONER. I WANNA HELP A LOT OF PEOPLE...
...SO WHEN I DIE, I'LL BE SURROUNDED BY A LOT OF PEOPLE.

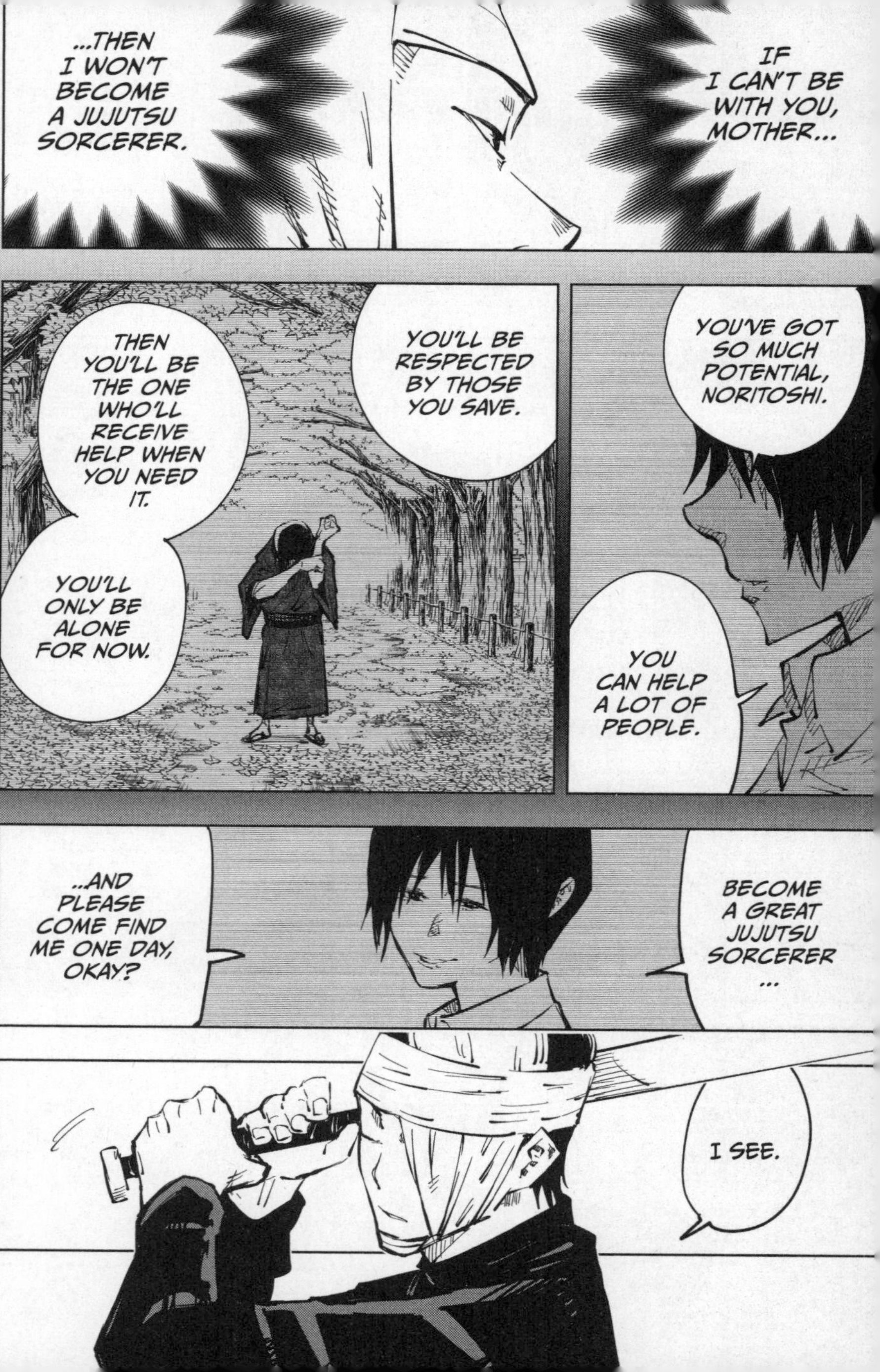
IF I CAN'T BE WITH YOU, MOTHER...
...THEN I WON'T BECOME A JUJUTSU SORCERER.
YOU'VE GOT SO MUCH POTENTIAL, NORITOSHI.
YOU CAN HELP A LOT OF PEOPLE.
YOU'LL BE RESPECTED BY THOSE YOU SAVE.
THEN YOU'LL BE THE ONE WHO'LL RECEIVE HELP WHEN YOU NEED IT.
YOU'LL ONLY BE ALONE FOR NOW.
BECOME A GREAT JUJUTSU SORCERER ...
...AND PLEASE COME FIND ME ONE DAY, OKAY?
I SEE.

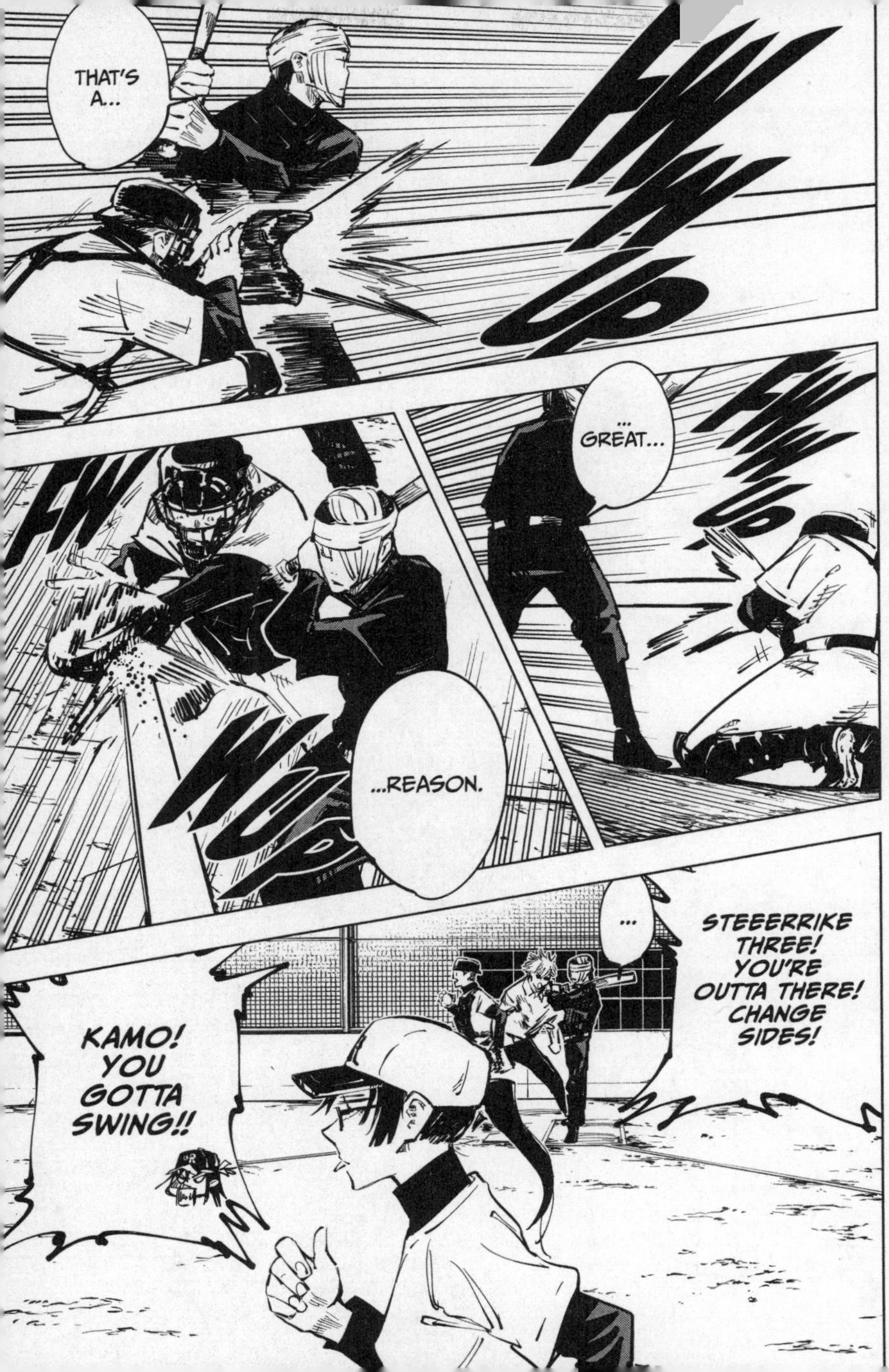
THAT'S A...
... GREAT...
...REASON.
STEEERRIKE THREE! YOU'RE OUTTA THERE! CHANGE SIDES!
...
KAMO! YOU GOTTA SWING!!

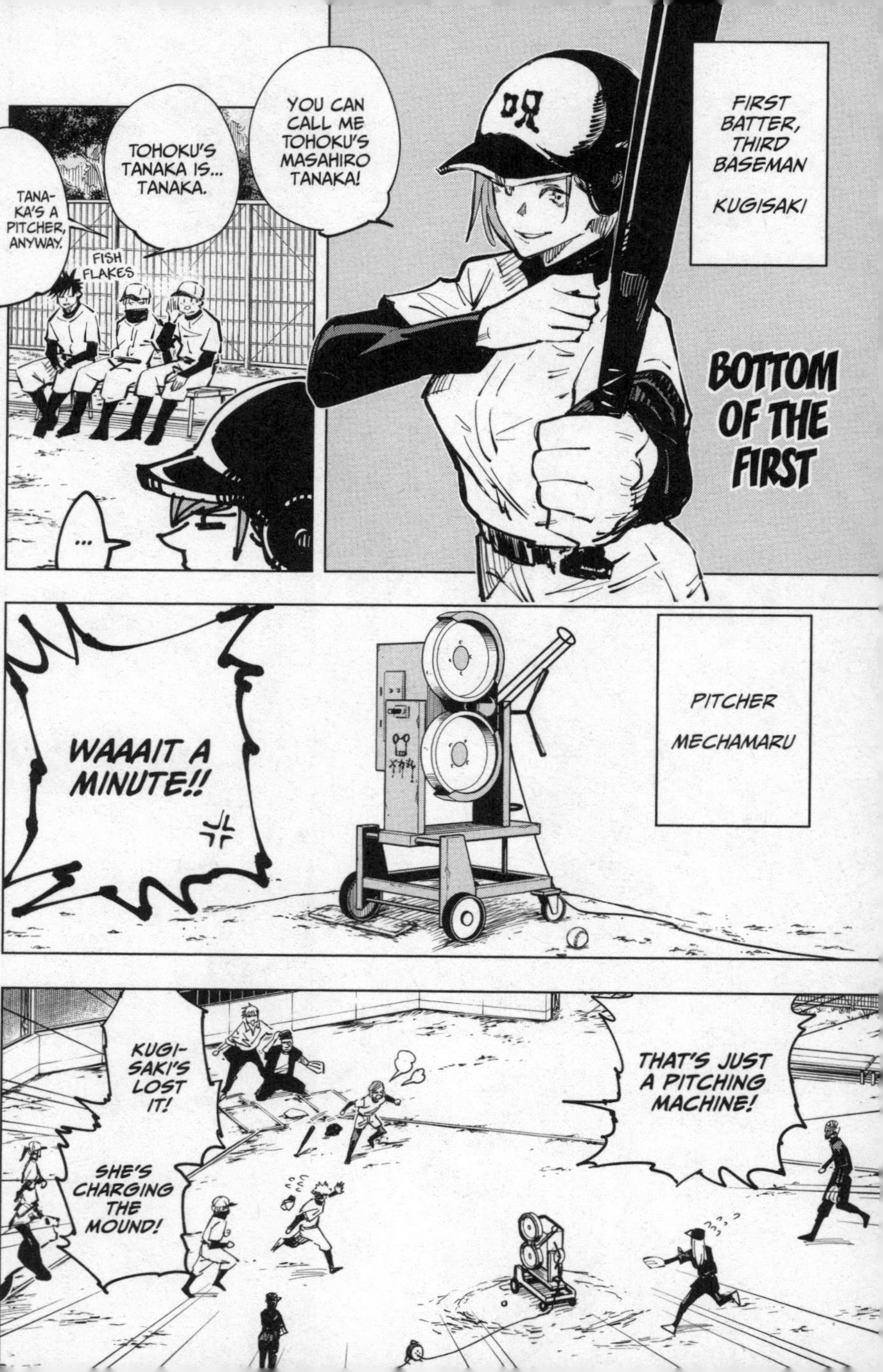
FIRST BATTER, THIRD BASEMAN
KUGISAKI
BOTTOM OF THE FIRST
YOU CAN CALL ME TOHOKU'S MASAHIRO TANAKA!
TOHOKU'S TANAKA IS... TANAKA.
FISH FLAKES
TANA-KA'S A PITCHER, ANYWAY.
...
PITCHER
MECHAMARU
WAAAIT A MINUTE!!
THAT'S JUST A PITCHING MACHINE!
KUGI-SAKI'S LOST IT!
SHE'S CHARGING THE MOUND!

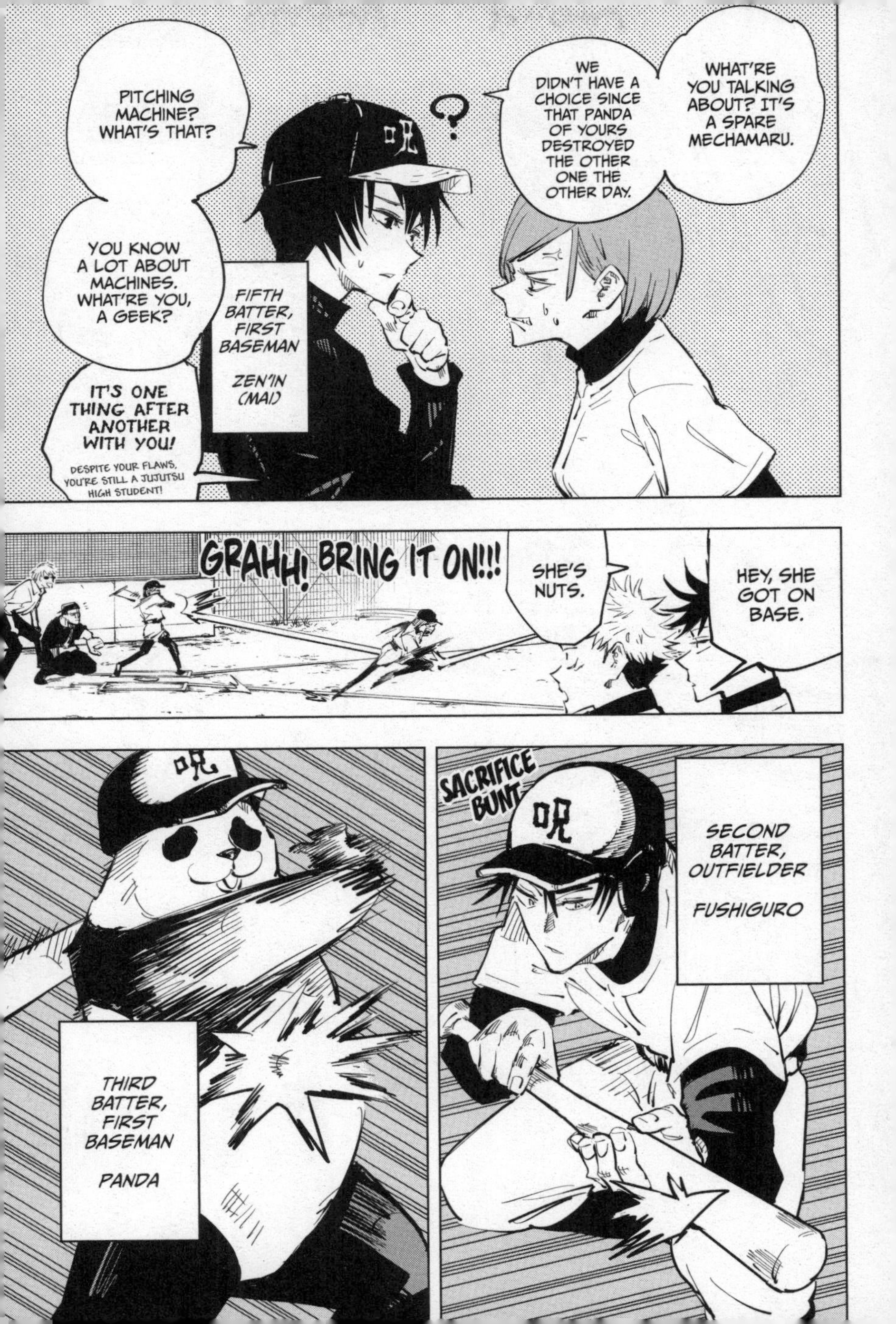
WHAT'RE YOU TALKING ABOUT? IT'S A SPARE MECHAMARU.
WE DIDN'T HAVE A CHOICE SINCE THAT PANDA OF YOURS DESTROYED THE OTHER ONE THE OTHER DAY.
?
PITCHING MACHINE? WHAT'S THAT?
FIFTH BATTER, FIRST BASEMAN
ZEN'IN (MAI)
YOU KNOW A LOT ABOUT MACHINES. WHAT'RE YOU, A GEEK?
IT'S ONE THING AFTER ANOTHER WITH YOU!
DESPITE YOUR FLAWS, YOU'RE STILL A JUJUTSU HIGH STUDENT!
HEY, SHE GOT ON BASE.
SHE'S NUTS.
GRAHH! BRING IT ON!!!
SACRIFICE BUNT
SECOND BATTER, OUTFIELDER
FUSHIGURO
THIRD BATTER, FIRST BASEMAN
PANDA

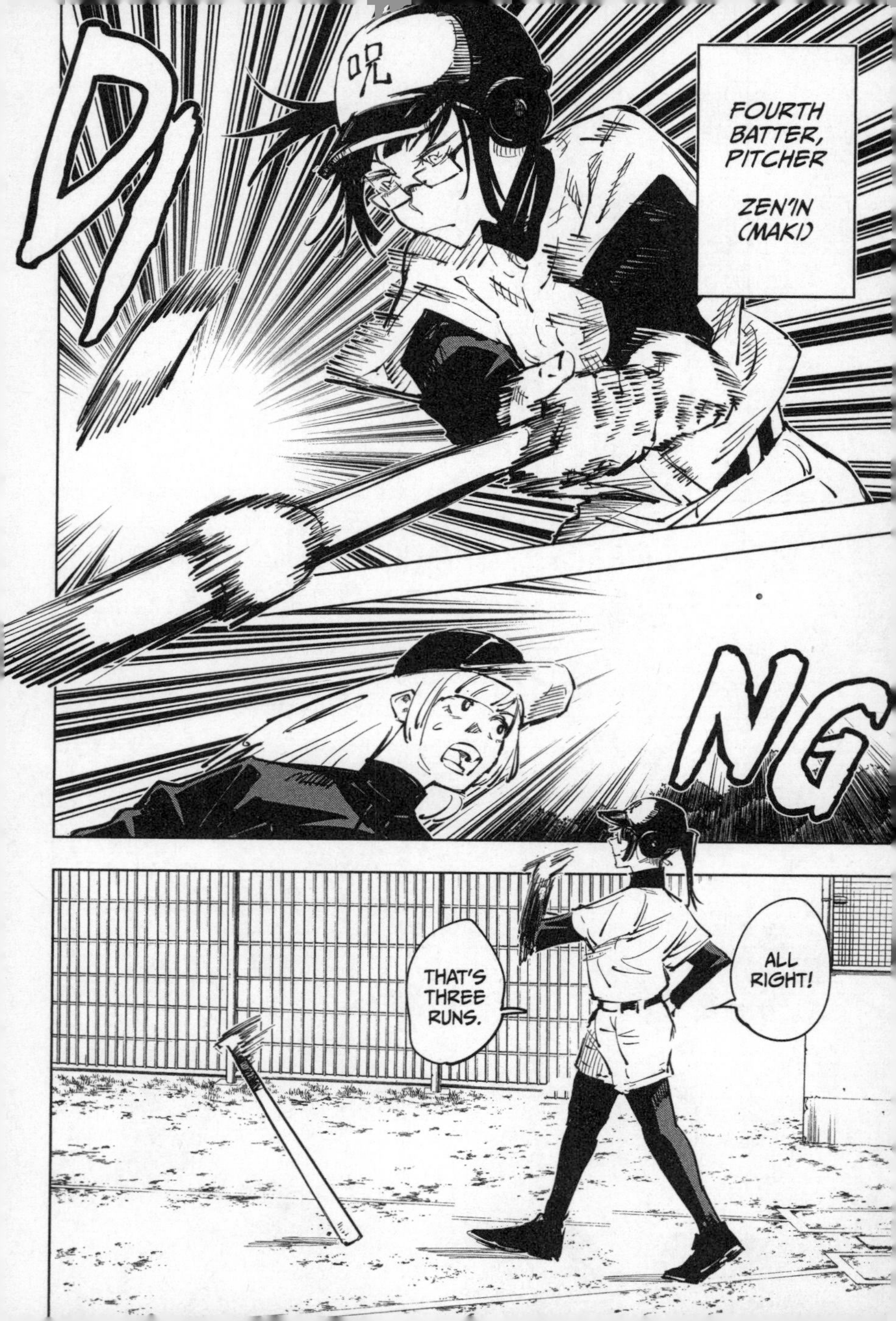
FOURTH BATTER, PITCHER
ZEN'IN (MAKI)
DING
ALL RIGHT!
THAT'S THREE RUNS.

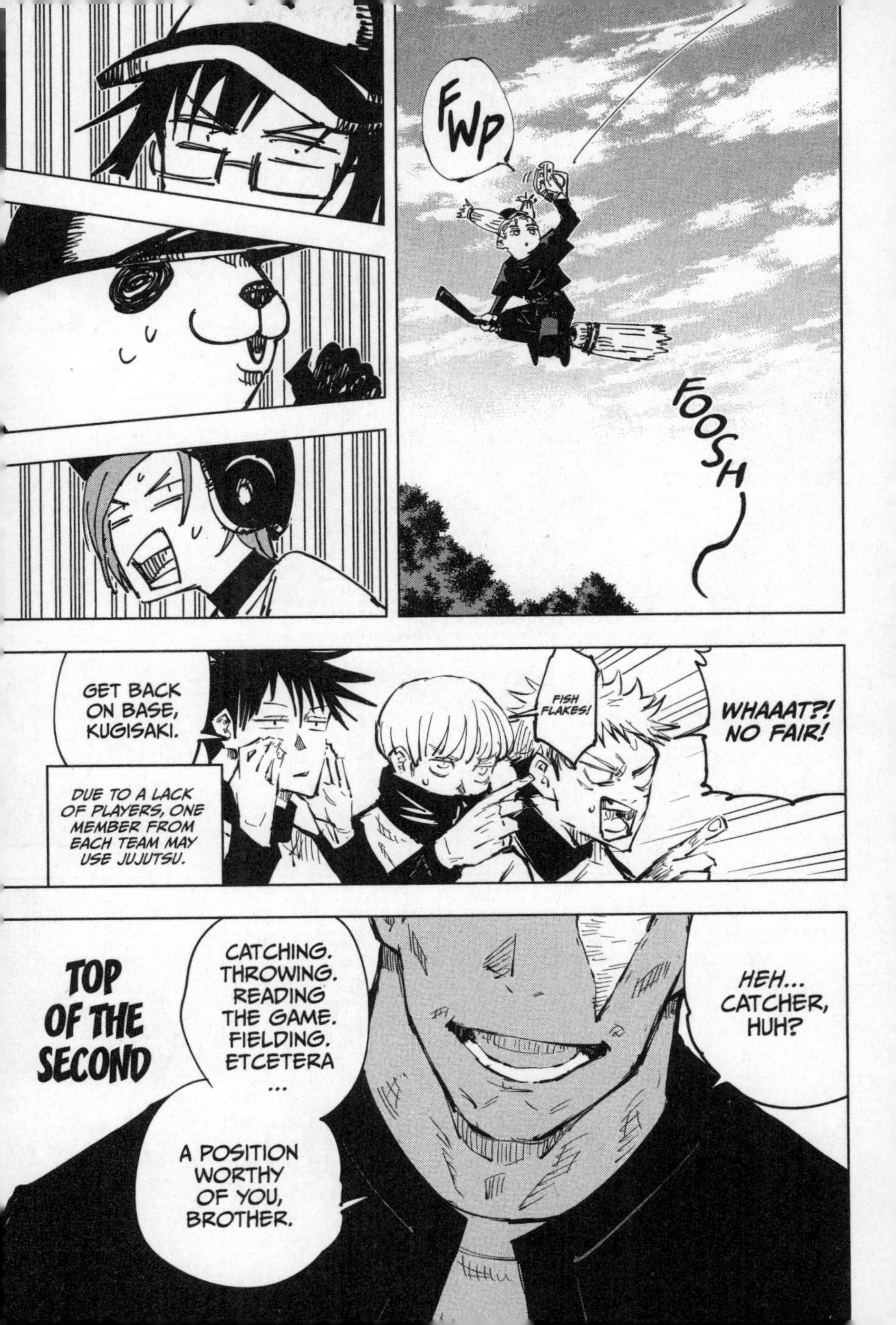
FWP
FOOSH
WHAAAT?! NO FAIR!
FISH FLAKES!
GET BACK ON BASE, KUGISAKI.
DUE TO A LACK OF PLAYERS, ONE MEMBER FROM EACH TEAM MAY USE JUJUTSU.
HEH... CATCHER, HUH?
CATCHING. THROWING. READING THE GAME. FIELDING. ETCETERA ...
TOP OF THE SECOND
A POSITION WORTHY OF YOU, BROTHER.

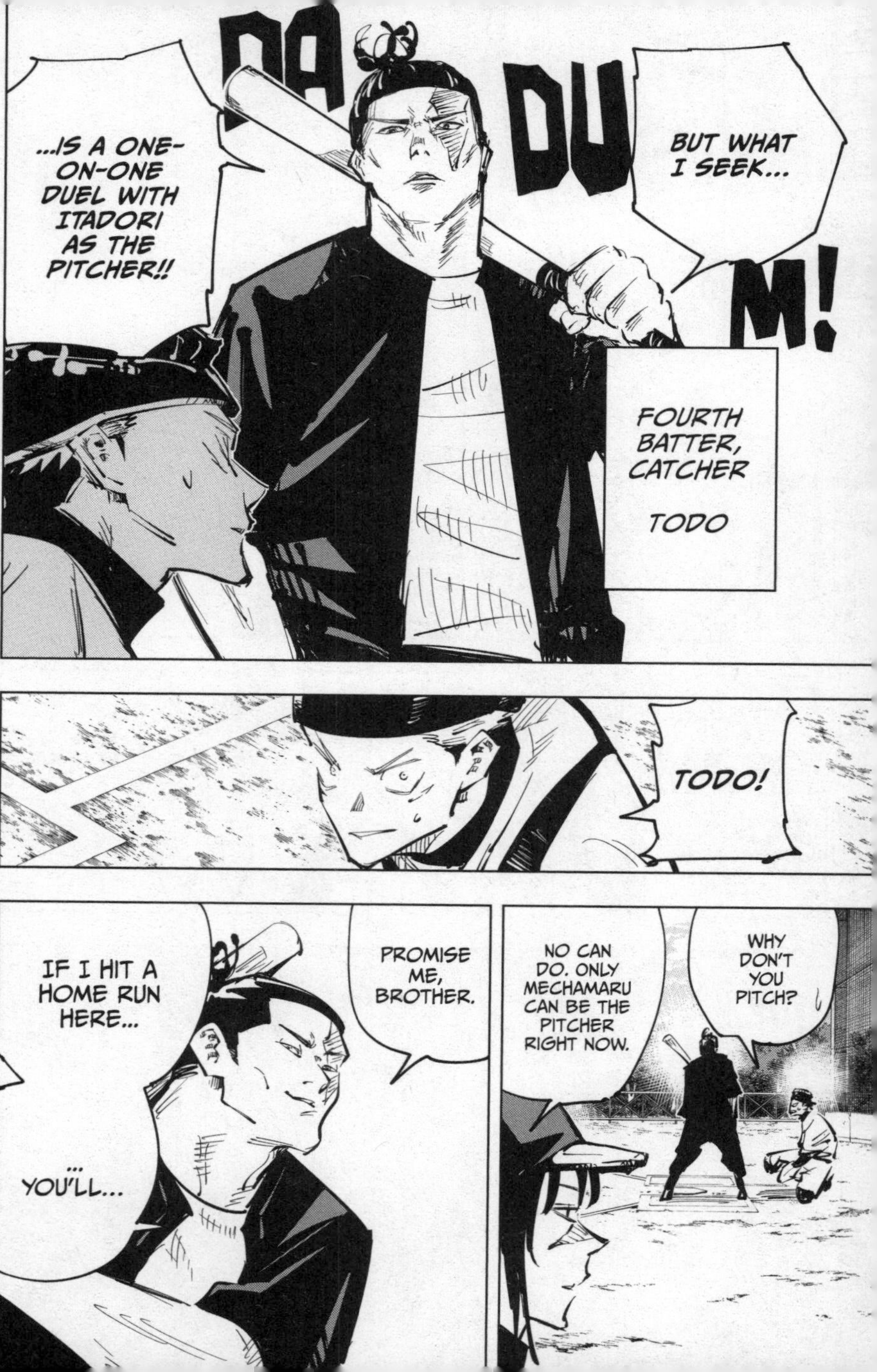

BUT WHAT I SEEK...
...IS A ONE-ON-ONE DUEL WITH ITADORI AS THE PITCHER!!
DADUM!
FOURTH BATTER, CATCHER TODO
TODO!
WHY DON'T YOU PITCH?
NO CAN DO. ONLY MECHAMARU CAN BE THE PITCHER RIGHT NOW.
PROMISE ME, BROTHER.
IF I HIT A HOME RUN HERE...
...YOU'LL...

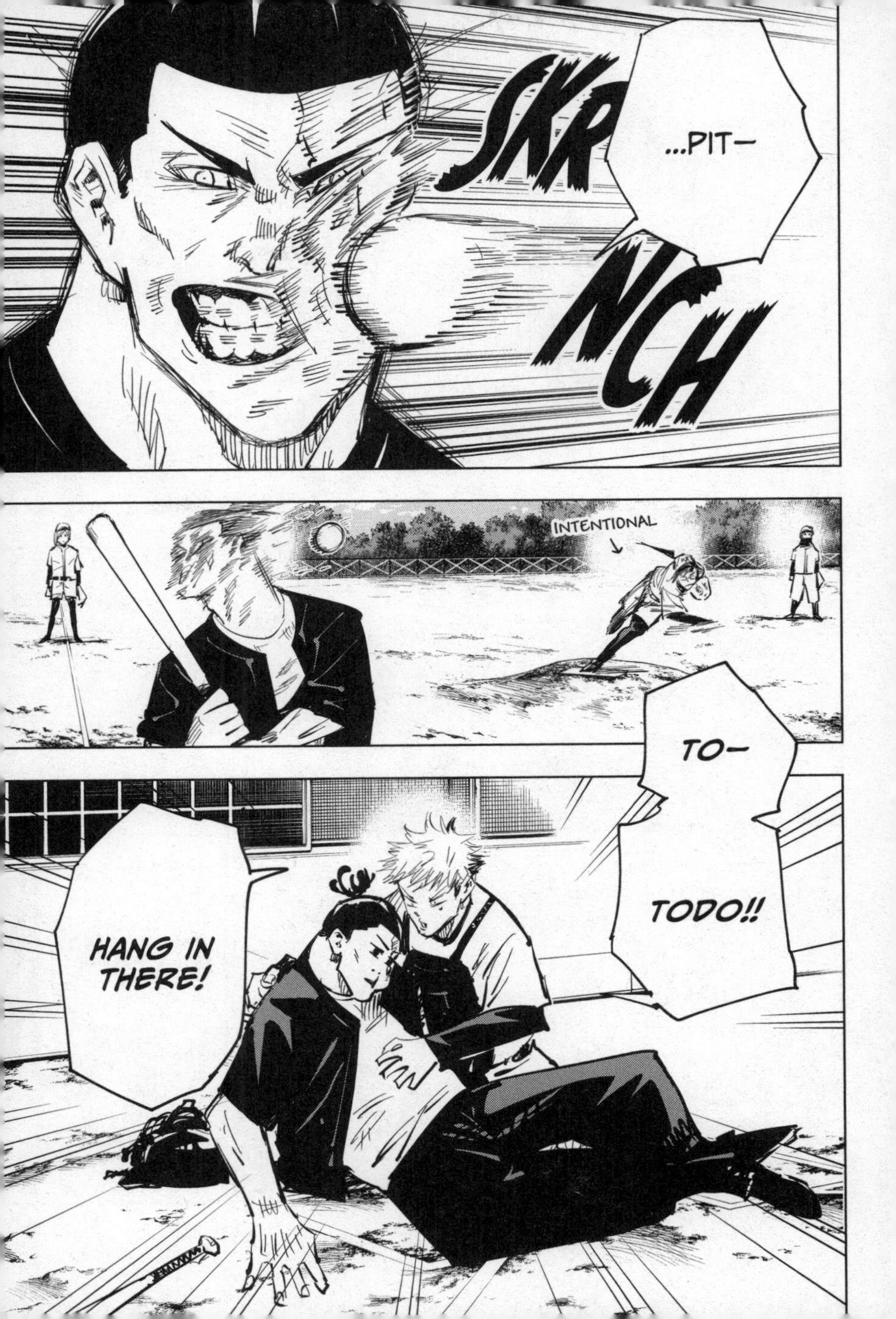
...PIT—
SKRNCH
INTENTIONAL
TO—
TODO!!
HANG IN THERE!

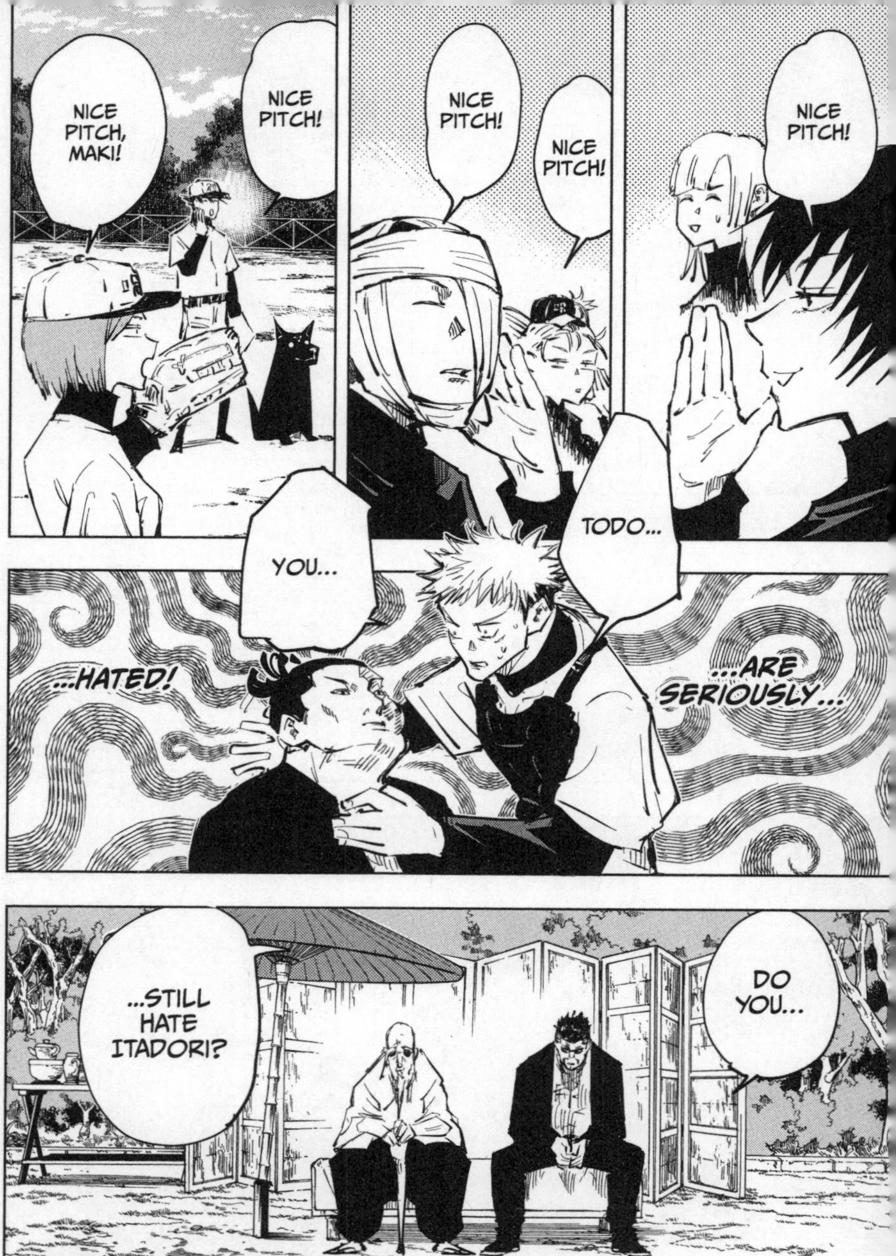
NICE PITCH!
NICE PITCH!
NICE PITCH!
NICE PITCH!
NICE PITCH, MAKI!
TODO...
YOU...
...ARE SERIOUSLY...
...HATED!
DO YOU...
...STILL HATE ITADORI?

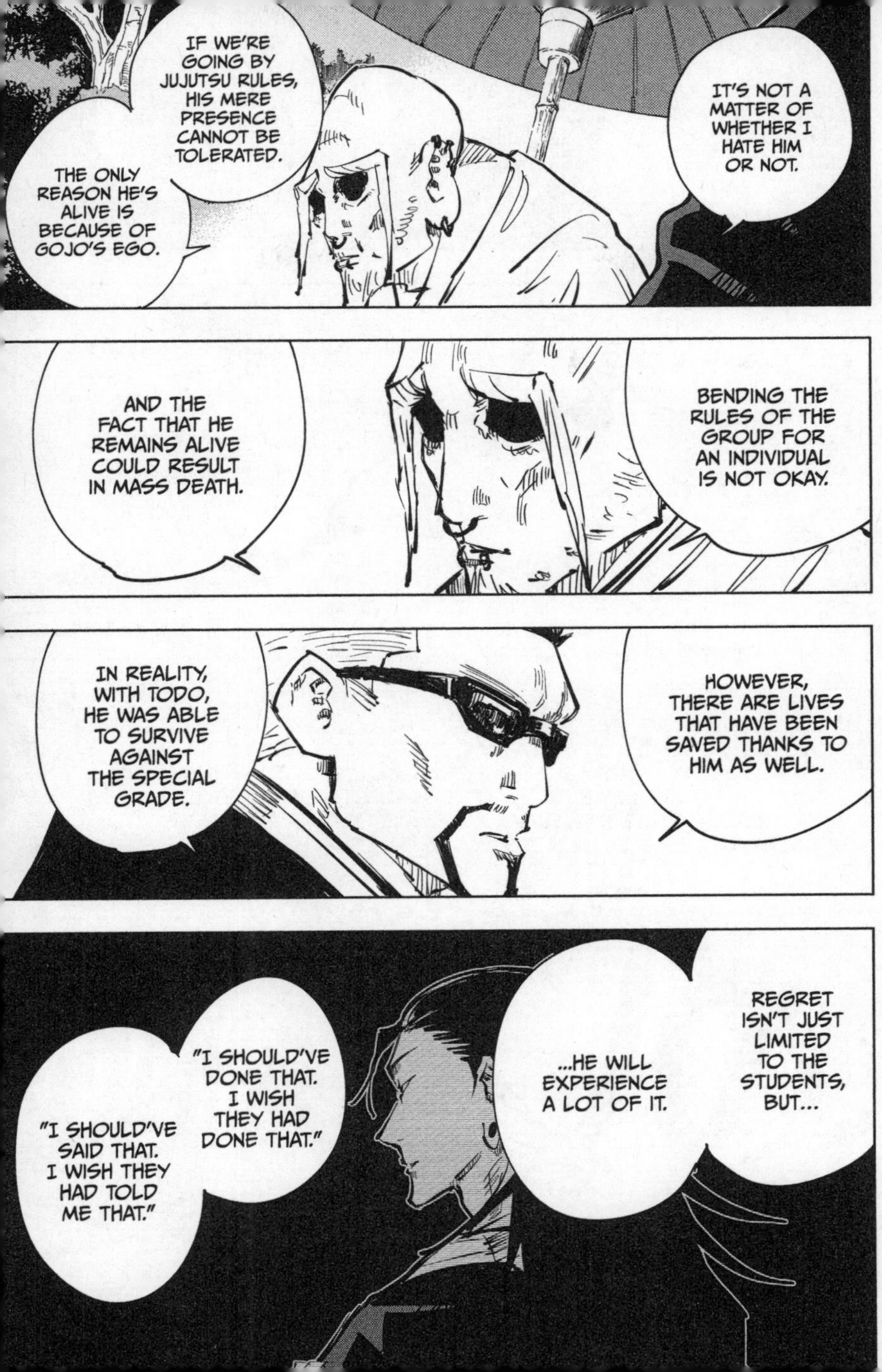
IT'S NOT A MATTER OF WHETHER I HATE HIM OR NOT.
IF WE'RE GOING BY JUJUTSU RULES, HIS MERE PRESENCE CANNOT BE TOLERATED.
THE ONLY REASON HE'S ALIVE IS BECAUSE OF GOJO'S EGO.
BENDING THE RULES OF THE GROUP FOR AN INDIVIDUAL IS NOT OKAY.
AND THE FACT THAT HE REMAINS ALIVE COULD RESULT IN MASS DEATH.
HOWEVER, THERE ARE LIVES THAT HAVE BEEN SAVED THANKS TO HIM AS WELL.
IN REALITY, WITH TODO, HE WAS ABLE TO SURVIVE AGAINST THE SPECIAL GRADE.
REGRET ISN'T JUST LIMITED TO THE STUDENTS, BUT...
...HE WILL EXPERIENCE A LOT OF IT.
"I SHOULD'VE DONE THAT. I WISH THEY HAD DONE THAT."
"I SHOULD'VE SAID THAT. I WISH THEY HAD TOLD ME THAT."

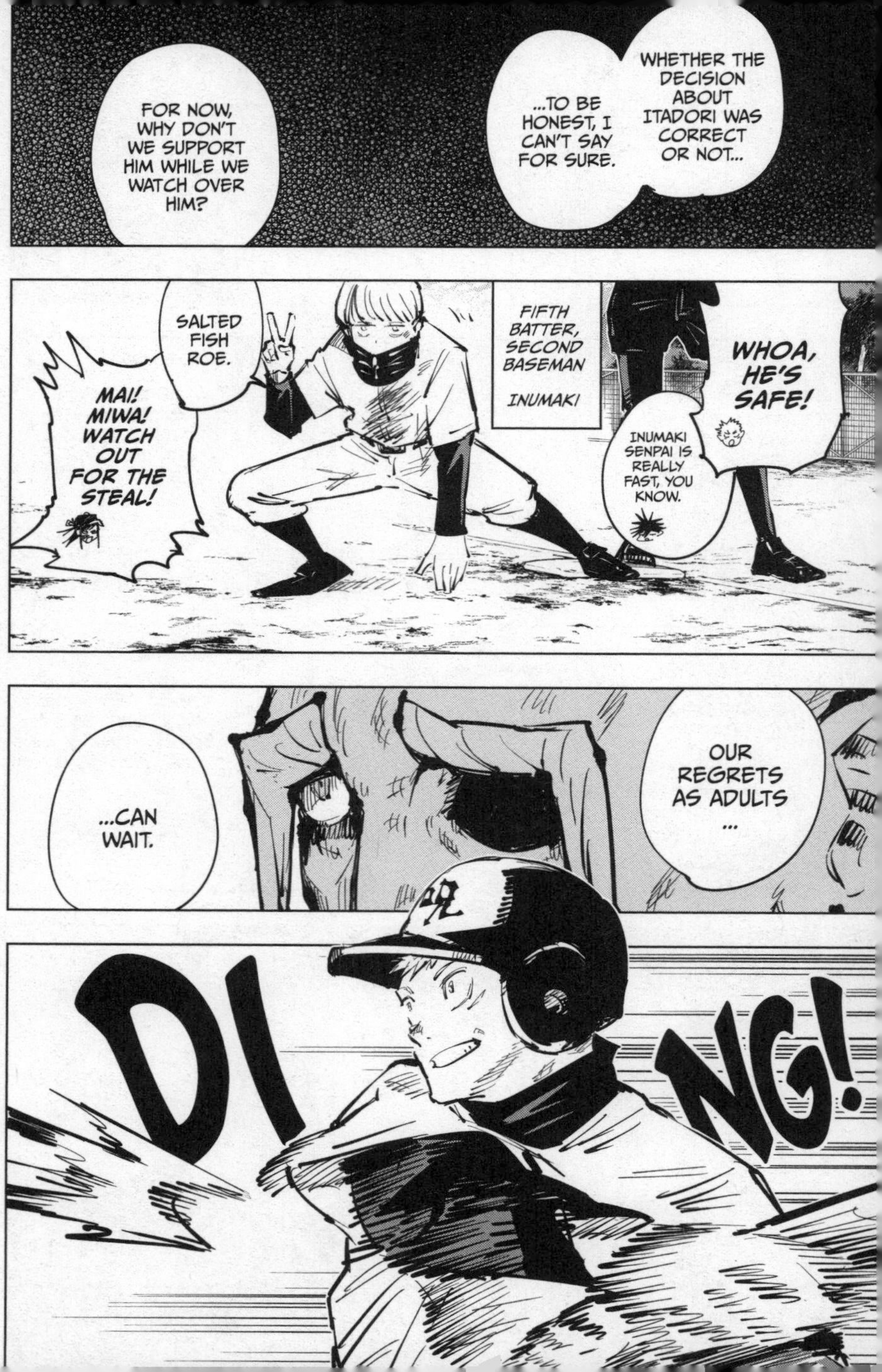
WHETHER THE DECISION ABOUT ITADORI WAS CORRECT OR NOT...
...TO BE HONEST, I CAN'T SAY FOR SURE.
FOR NOW, WHY DON'T WE SUPPORT HIM WHILE WE WATCH OVER HIM?
WHOA, HE'S SAFE!
INUMAKI SENPAI IS REALLY FAST, YOU KNOW.
FIFTH BATTER, SECOND BASEMAN
INUMAKI
SALTED FISH ROE.
MAI! MIWA! WATCH OUT FOR THE STEAL!
OUR REGRETS AS ADULTS ...
...CAN WAIT.
DING!

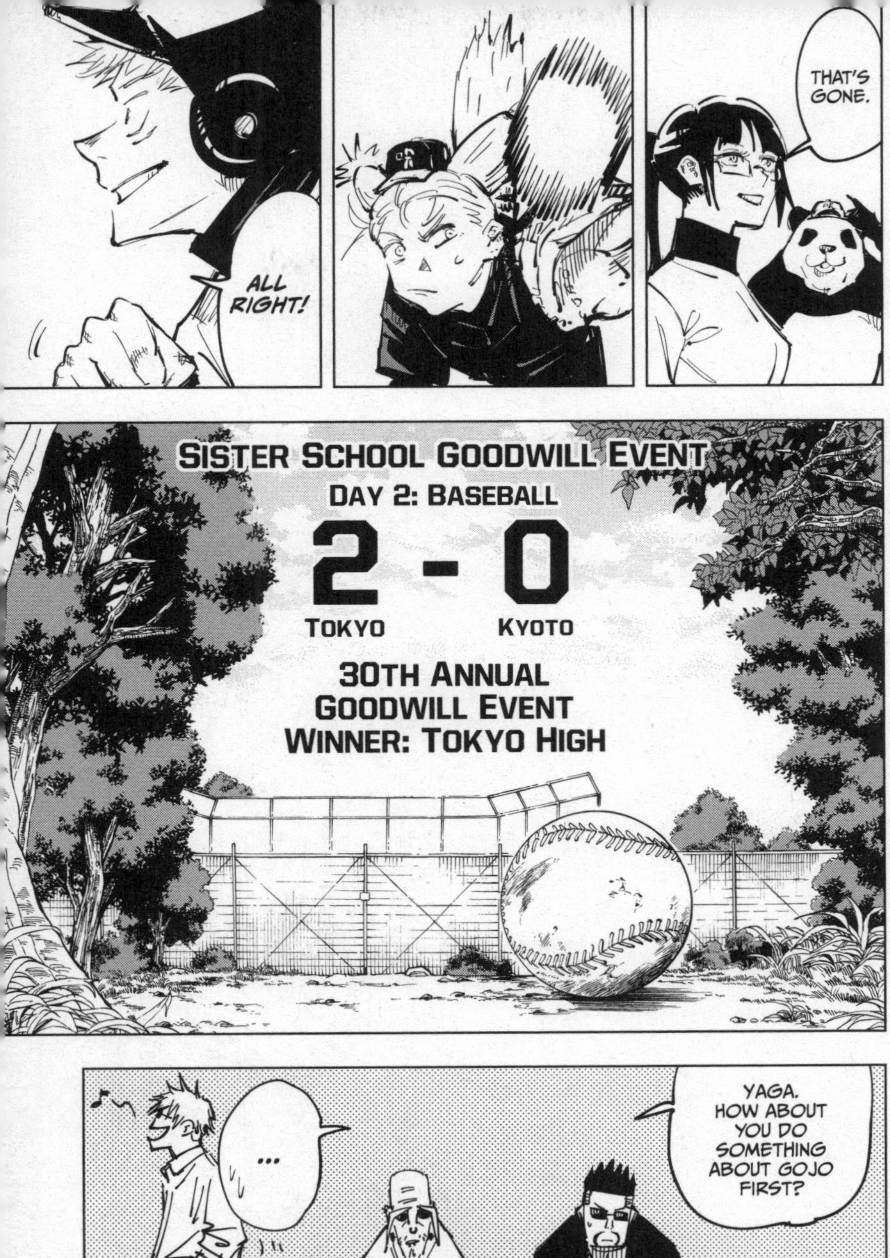
THAT'S GONE.
ALL RIGHT!
SISTER SCHOOL GOODWILL EVENT
DAY 2: BASEBALL
2 - 0
TOKYO
KYOTO
30TH ANNUAL GOODWILL EVENT WINNER: TOKYO HIGH
YAGA. HOW ABOUT YOU DO SOMETHING ABOUT GOJO FIRST?
...

Q: DIDN'T YOU YELL, "PLAY BALL!" TWICE?

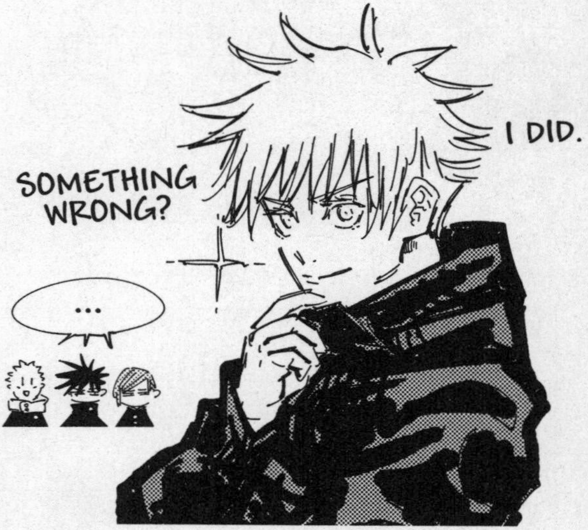
I DID.
SOMETHING WRONG?
...

Chapter 55: The Origin of Obedience

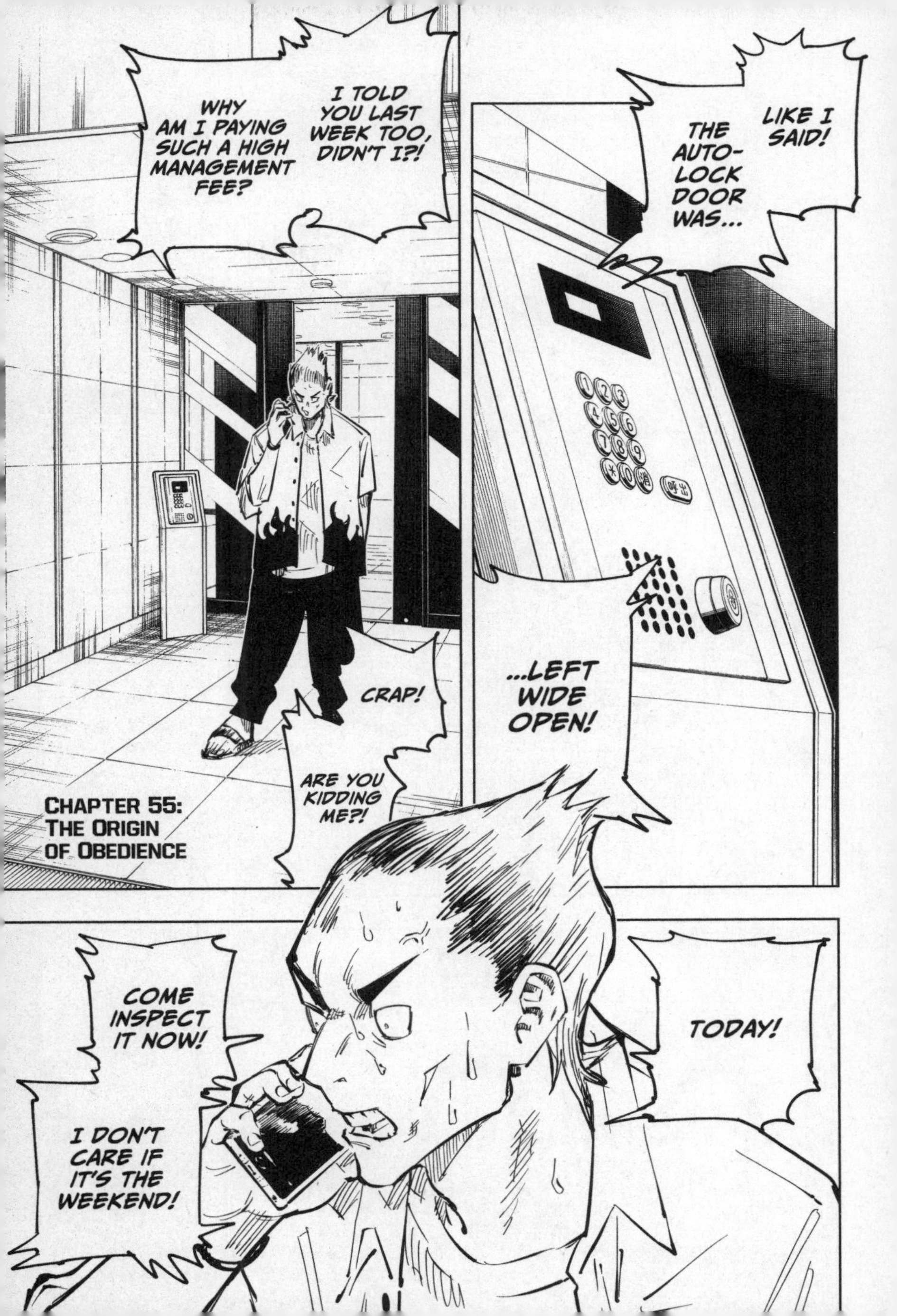
LIKE I SAID!
THE AUTO-LOCK DOOR WAS...
...LEFT WIDE OPEN!
I TOLD YOU LAST WEEK TOO, DIDN'T I?!
WHY AM I PAYING SUCH A HIGH MANAGEMENT FEE?
CRAP!
ARE YOU KIDDING ME?!
TODAY!
COME INSPECT IT NOW!
I DON'T CARE IF IT'S THE WEEKEND!

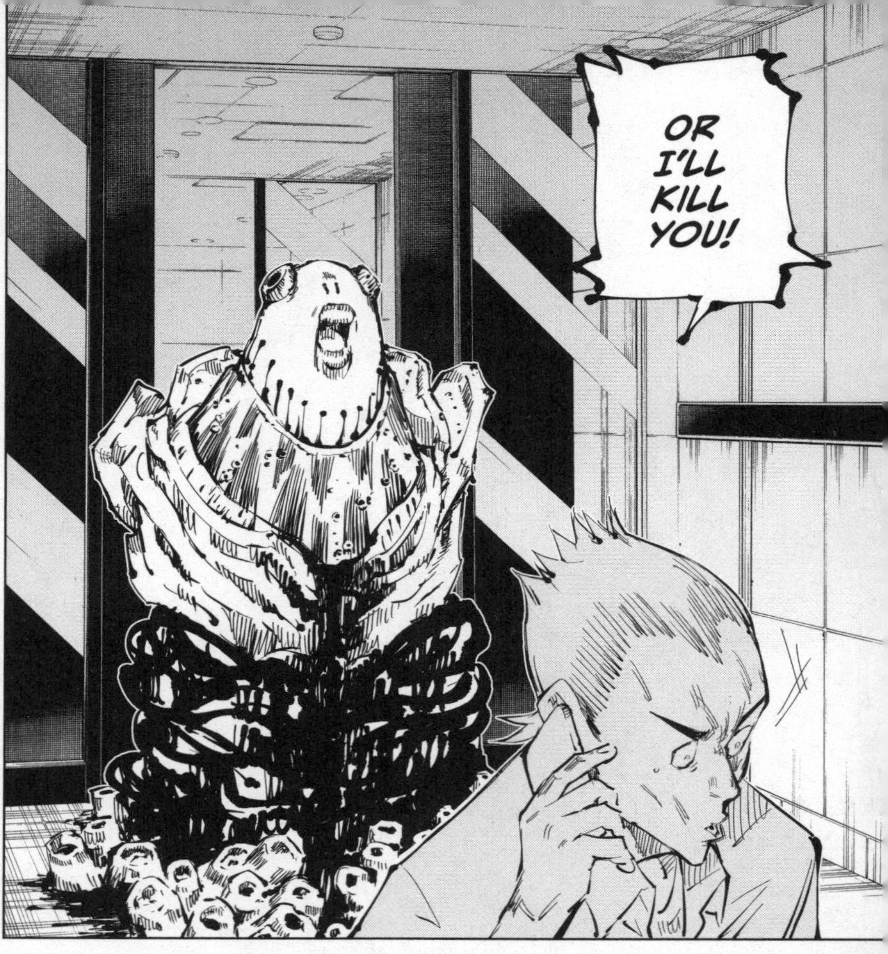
OR I'LL KILL YOU!
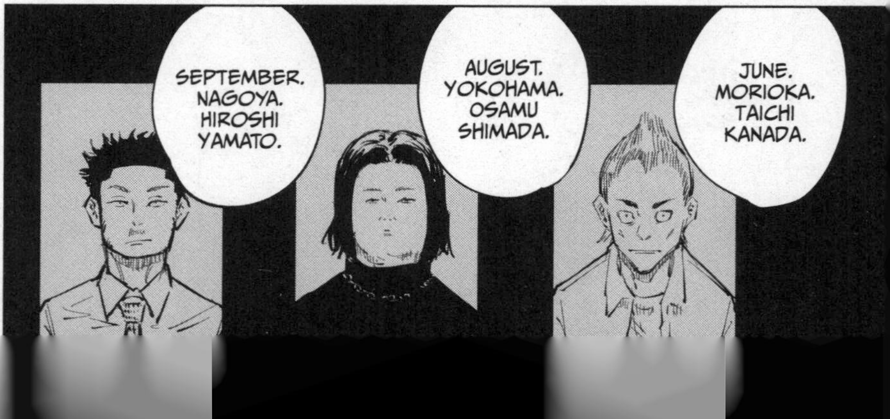
JUNE. MORIOKA. TAICHI KANADA.
AUGUST. YOKOHAMA. OSAMU SHIMADA.
SEPTEMBER. NAGOYA. HIROSHI YAMATO.

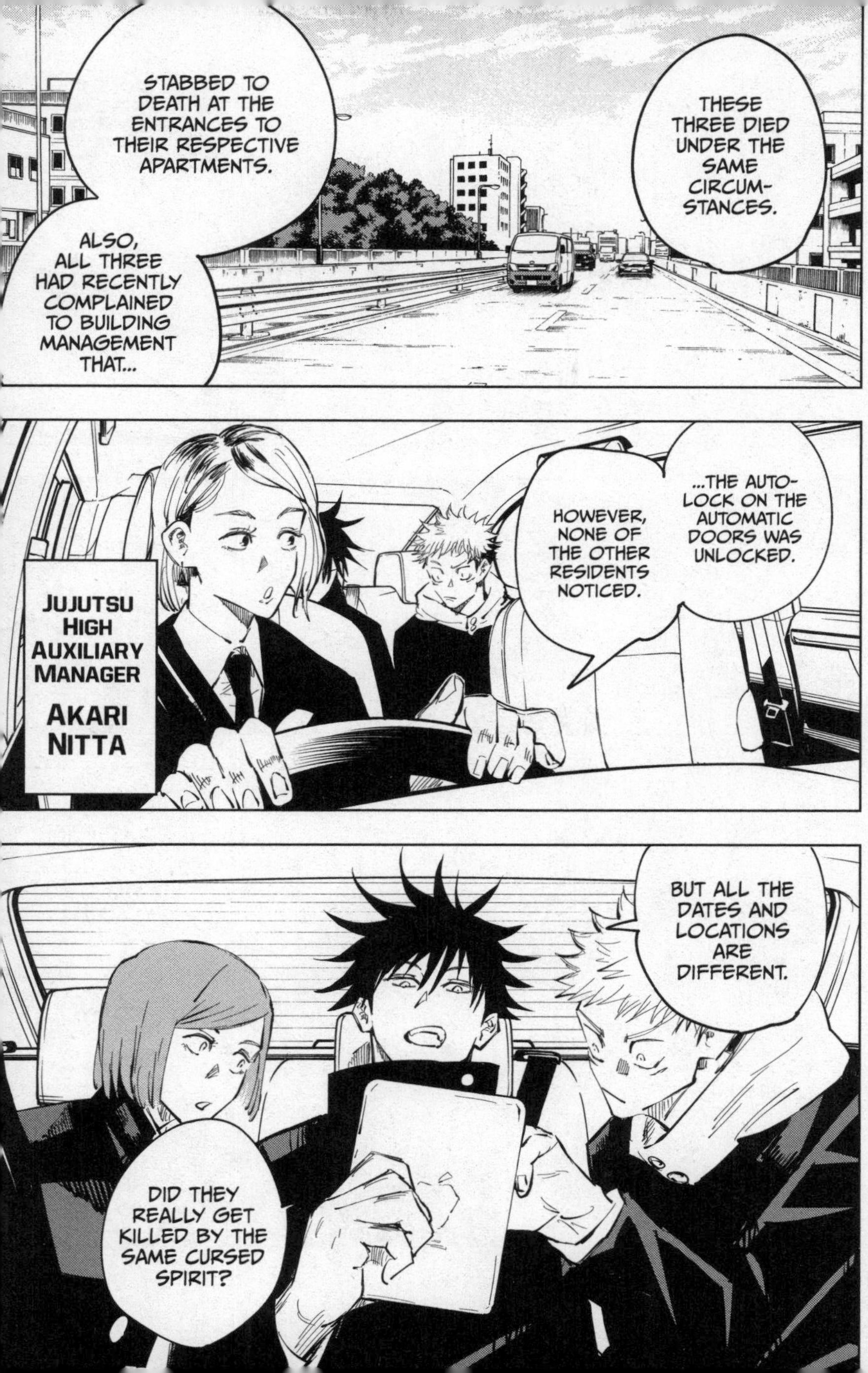
THESE THREE DIED UNDER THE SAME CIRCUM-STANCES.
STABBED TO DEATH AT THE ENTRANCES TO THEIR RESPECTIVE APARTMENTS.
ALSO, ALL THREE HAD RECENTLY COMPLAINED TO BUILDING MANAGEMENT THAT...
...THE AUTO-LOCK ON THE AUTOMATIC DOORS WAS UNLOCKED.
HOWEVER, NONE OF THE OTHER RESIDENTS NOTICED.
JUJUTSU HIGH AUXILIARY MANAGER
AKARI NITTA
BUT ALL THE DATES AND LOCATIONS ARE DIFFERENT.
DID THEY REALLY GET KILLED BY THE SAME CURSED SPIRIT?

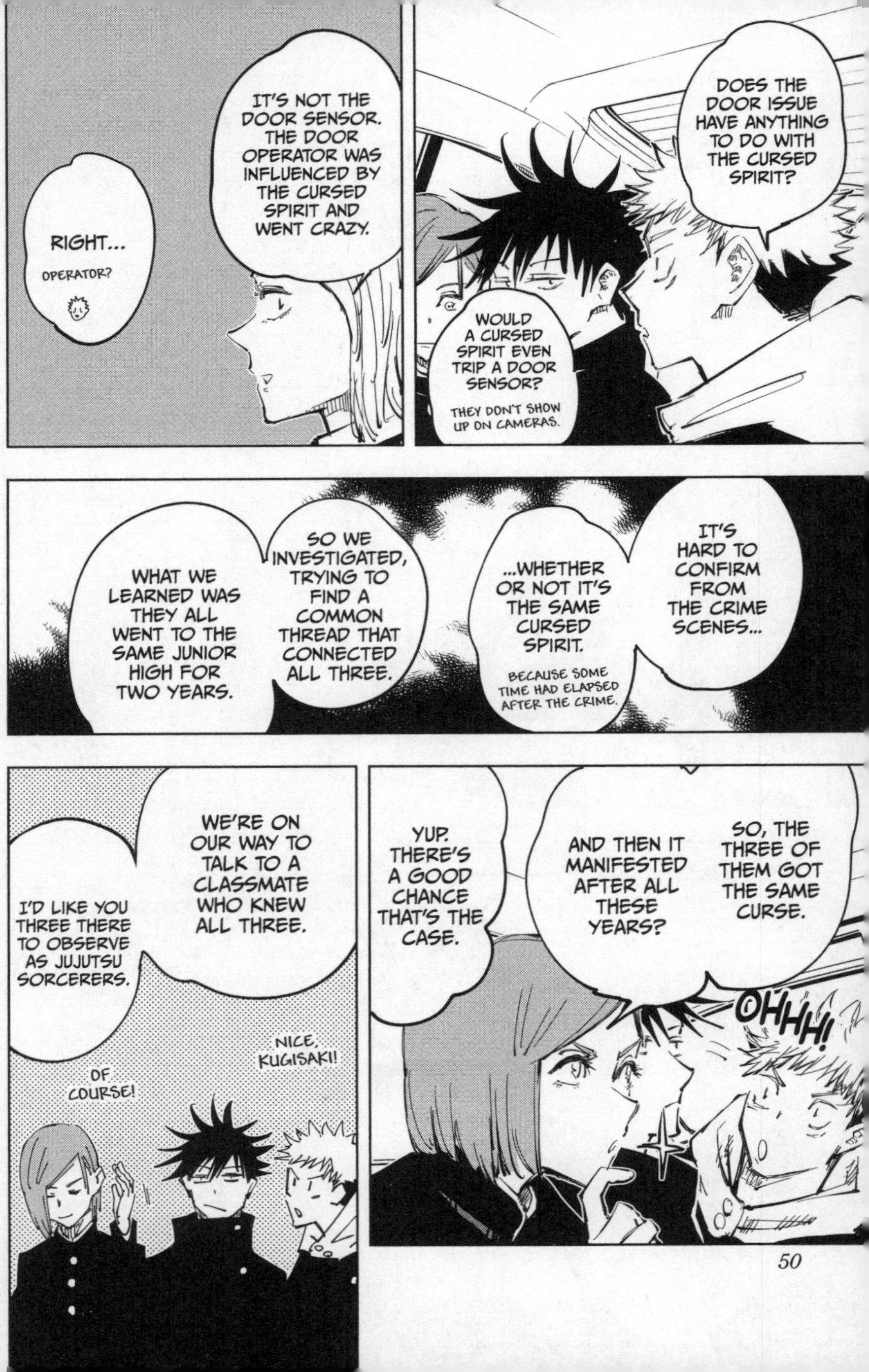
DOES THE DOOR ISSUE HAVE ANYTHING TO DO WITH THE CURSED SPIRIT?
WOULD A CURSED SPIRIT EVEN TRIP A DOOR SENSOR?
THEY DON'T SHOW UP ON CAMERAS.
IT'S NOT THE DOOR SENSOR. THE DOOR OPERATOR WAS INFLUENCED BY THE CURSED SPIRIT AND WENT CRAZY.
RIGHT...
OPERATOR?
IT'S HARD TO CONFIRM FROM THE CRIME SCENES...
...WHETHER OR NOT IT'S THE SAME CURSED SPIRIT.
BECAUSE SOME TIME HAD ELAPSED AFTER THE CRIME.
SO WE INVESTIGATED, TRYING TO FIND A COMMON THREAD THAT CONNECTED ALL THREE.
WHAT WE LEARNED WAS THEY ALL WENT TO THE SAME JUNIOR HIGH FOR TWO YEARS.
SO, THE THREE OF THEM GOT THE SAME CURSE.
AND THEN IT MANIFESTED AFTER ALL THESE YEARS?
YUP. THERE'S A GOOD CHANCE THAT'S THE CASE.
OHHH!
WE'RE ON OUR WAY TO TALK TO A CLASSMATE WHO KNEW ALL THREE.
I'D LIKE YOU THREE THERE TO OBSERVE AS JUJUTSU SORCERERS.
NICE, KUGISAKI!
OF COURSE!

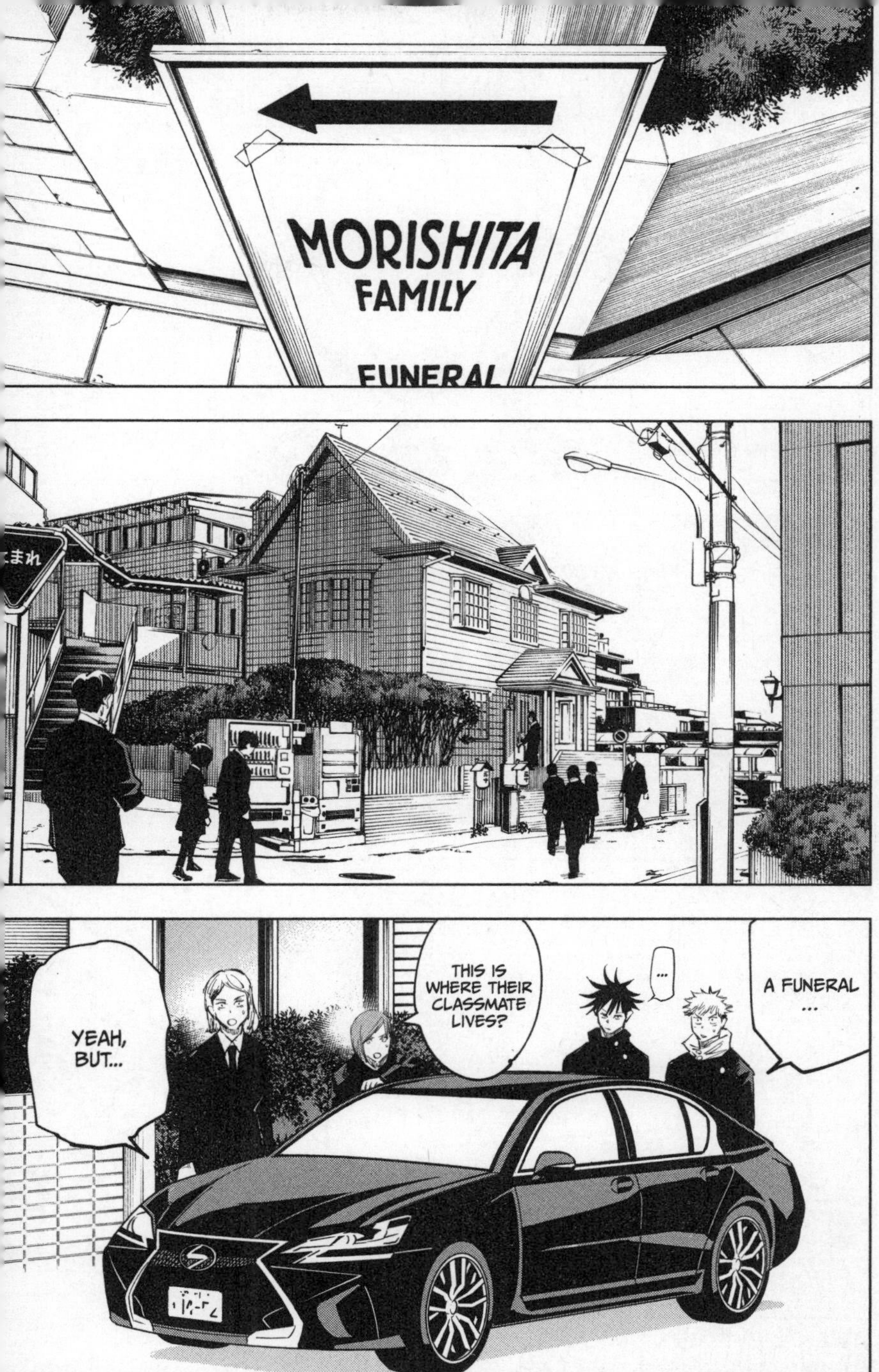
MORISHITA
FAMILY
FUNERAL
A FUNERAL ...
...
THIS IS WHERE THEIR CLASSMATE LIVES?
YEAH, BUT...

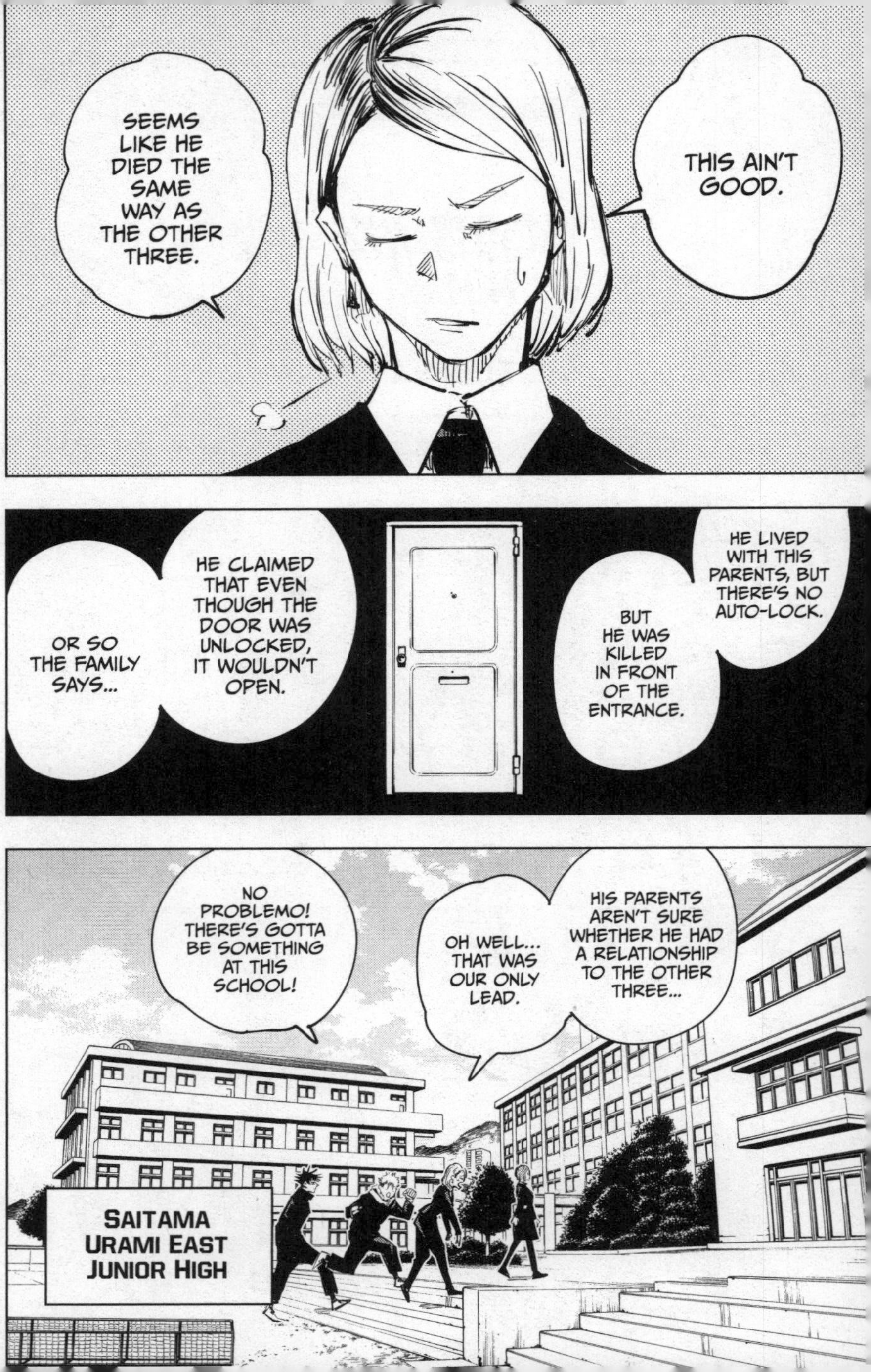
THIS AIN'T GOOD.
SEEMS LIKE HE DIED THE SAME WAY AS THE OTHER THREE.
HE LIVED WITH THIS PARENTS, BUT THERE'S NO AUTO-LOCK.
BUT HE WAS KILLED IN FRONT OF THE ENTRANCE.
HE CLAIMED THAT EVEN THOUGH THE DOOR WAS UNLOCKED, IT WOULDN'T OPEN.
OR SO THE FAMILY SAYS...
HIS PARENTS AREN'T SURE WHETHER HE HAD A RELATIONSHIP TO THE OTHER THREE...
OH WELL... THAT WAS OUR ONLY LEAD.
NO PROBLEMO! THERE'S GOTTA BE SOMETHING AT THIS SCHOOL!
SAITAMA URAMI EAST JUNIOR HIGH

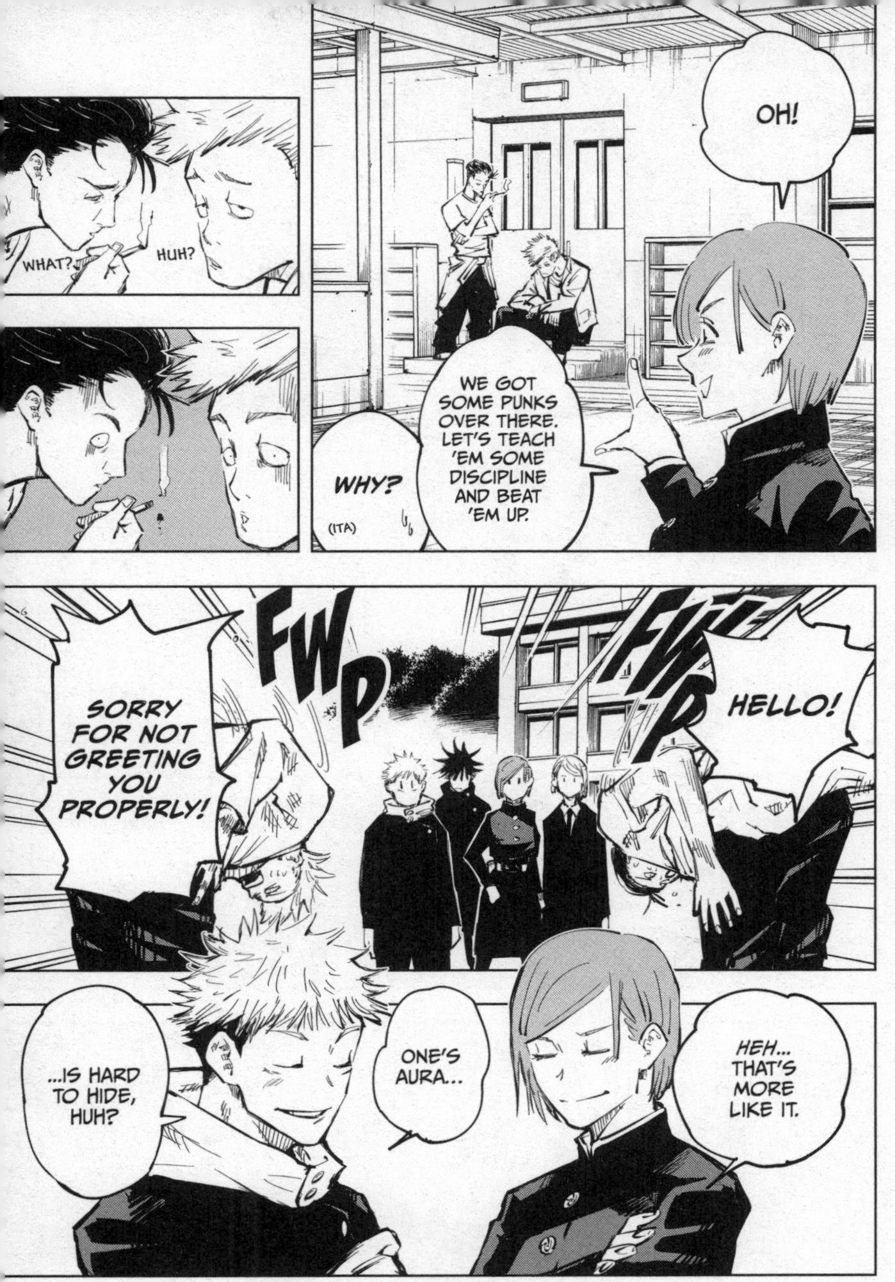
OH!
WE GOT SOME PUNKS OVER THERE. LET'S TEACH 'EM SOME DISCIPLINE AND BEAT 'EM UP.
WHY?
(ITA)
HUH?
WHAT?
HELLO!
FWP
FWP
SORRY FOR NOT GREETING YOU PROPERLY!
HEH... THAT'S MORE LIKE IT.
ONE'S AURA...
...IS HARD TO HIDE, HUH?

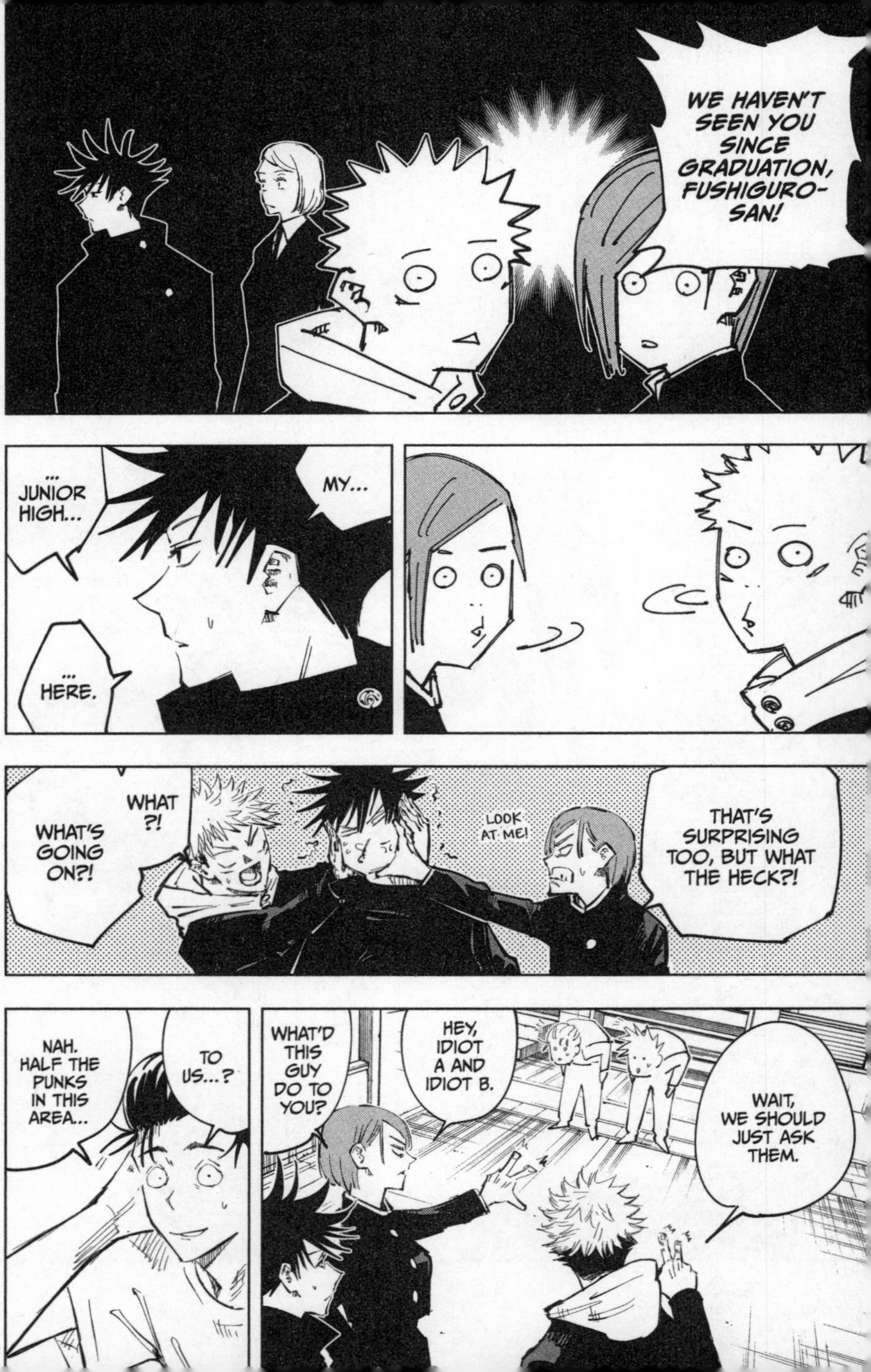

WE HAVEN'T SEEN YOU SINCE GRADUATION, FUSHIGURO-SAN!
MY...
...JUNIOR HIGH...
...HERE.
THAT'S SURPRISING TOO, BUT WHAT THE HECK?!
LOOK AT ME!
WHAT ?!
WHAT'S GOING ON?!
WAIT, WE SHOULD JUST ASK THEM.
HEY, IDIOT A AND IDIOT B.
WHAT'D THIS GUY DO TO YOU?
TO US...?
NAH. HALF THE PUNKS IN THIS AREA...

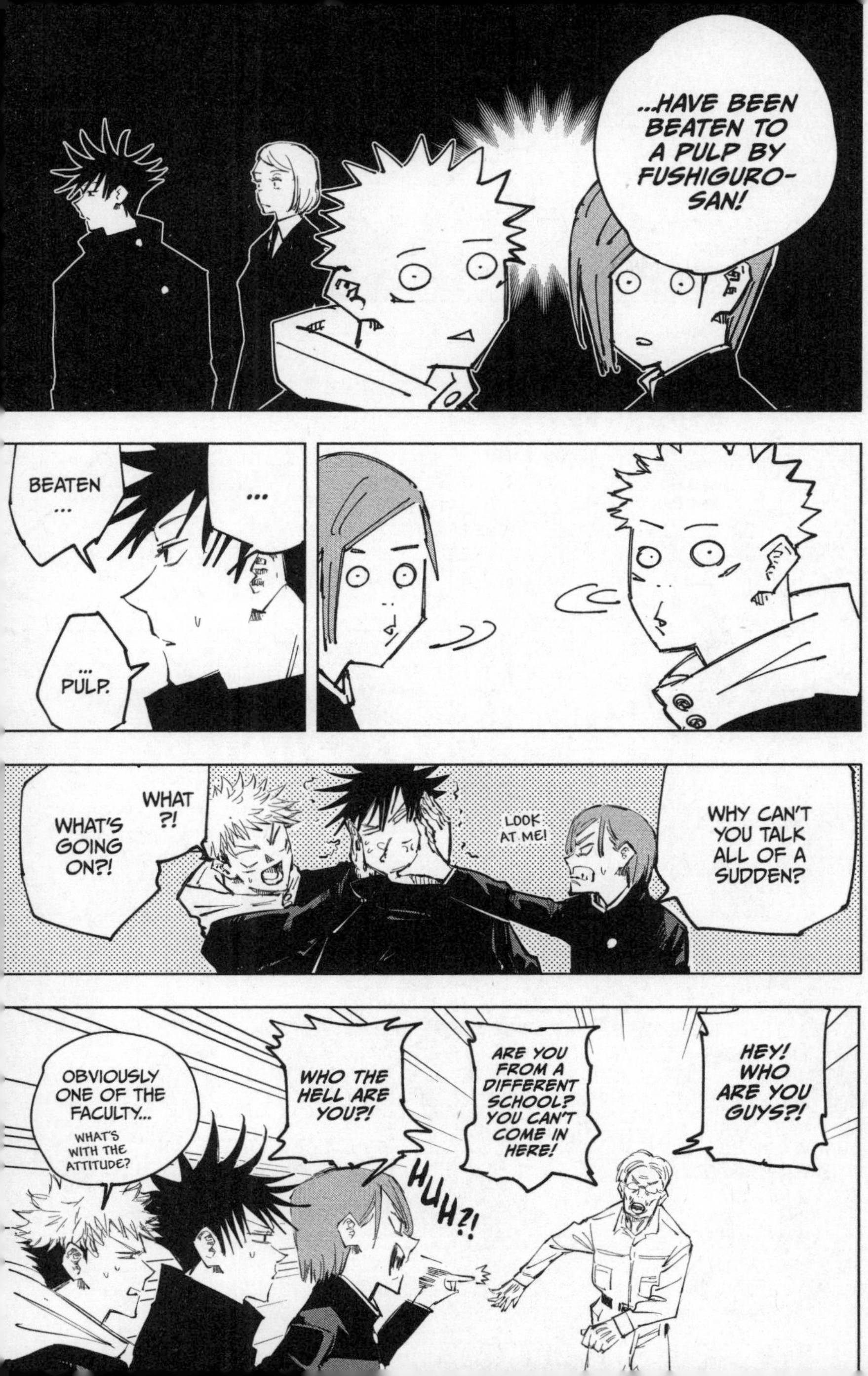
...HAVE BEEN BEATEN TO A PULP BY FUSHIGURO-SAN!
...
BEATEN ...
... PULP.
WHY CAN'T YOU TALK ALL OF A SUDDEN?
LOOK AT ME!
WHAT ?!
WHAT'S GOING ON?!
HEY! WHO ARE YOU GUYS?!
ARE YOU FROM A DIFFERENT SCHOOL? YOU CAN'T COME IN HERE!
WHO THE HELL ARE YOU?!
HUH?!
OBVIOUSLY ONE OF THE FACULTY...
WHAT'S WITH THE ATTITUDE?

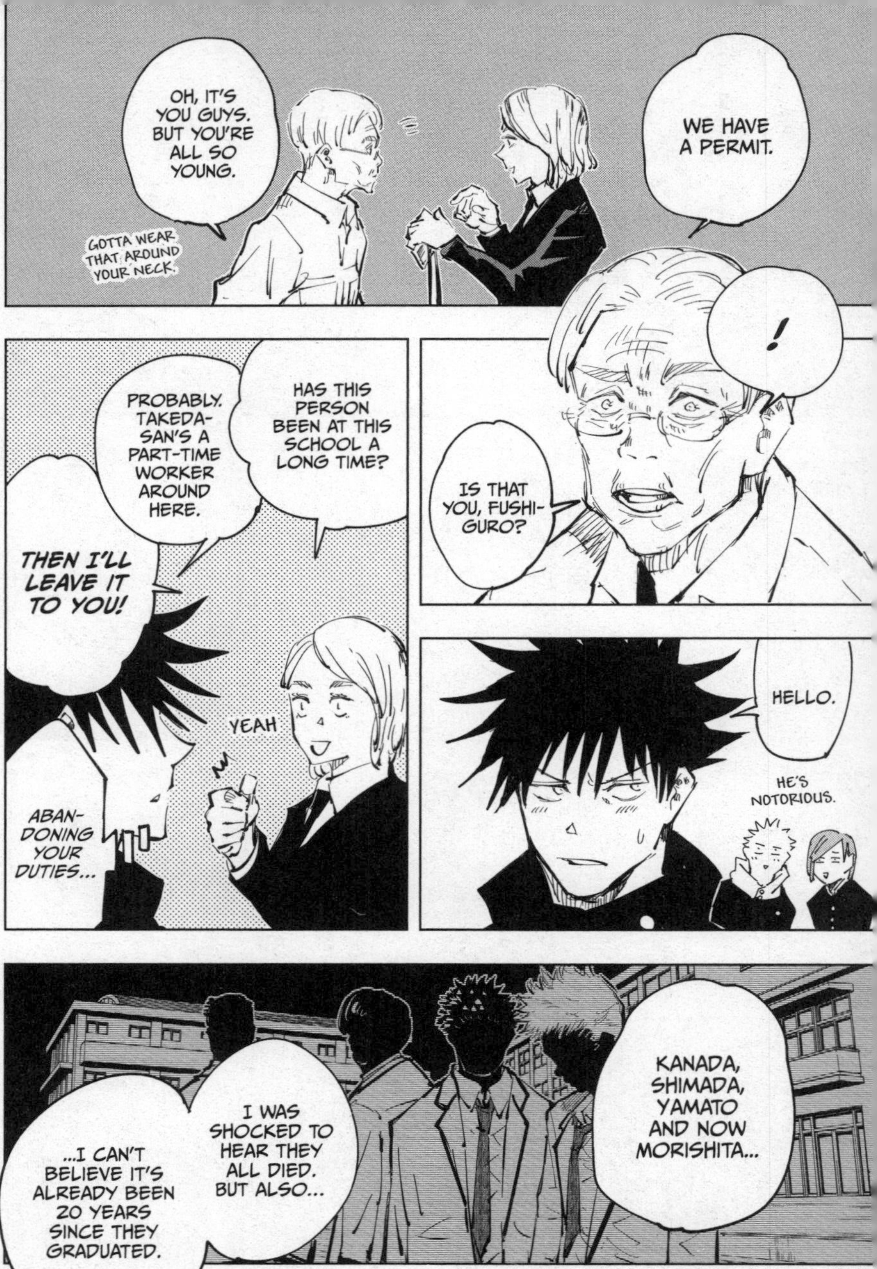
WE HAVE A PERMIT.
OH, IT'S YOU GUYS. BUT YOU'RE ALL SO YOUNG.
GOTTA WEAR THAT AROUND YOUR NECK.
!
IS THAT YOU, FUSHIGURO?
HELLO.
HE'S NOTORIOUS.
HAS THIS PERSON BEEN AT THIS SCHOOL A LONG TIME?
PROBABLY. TAKEDA-SAN'S A PART-TIME WORKER AROUND HERE.
THEN I'LL LEAVE IT TO YOU!
YEAH
ABANDONING YOUR DUTIES...
KANADA, SHIMADA, YAMATO AND NOW MORISHITA...
I WAS SHOCKED TO HEAR THEY ALL DIED. BUT ALSO...
...I CAN'T BELIEVE IT'S ALREADY BEEN 20 YEARS SINCE THEY GRADUATED.

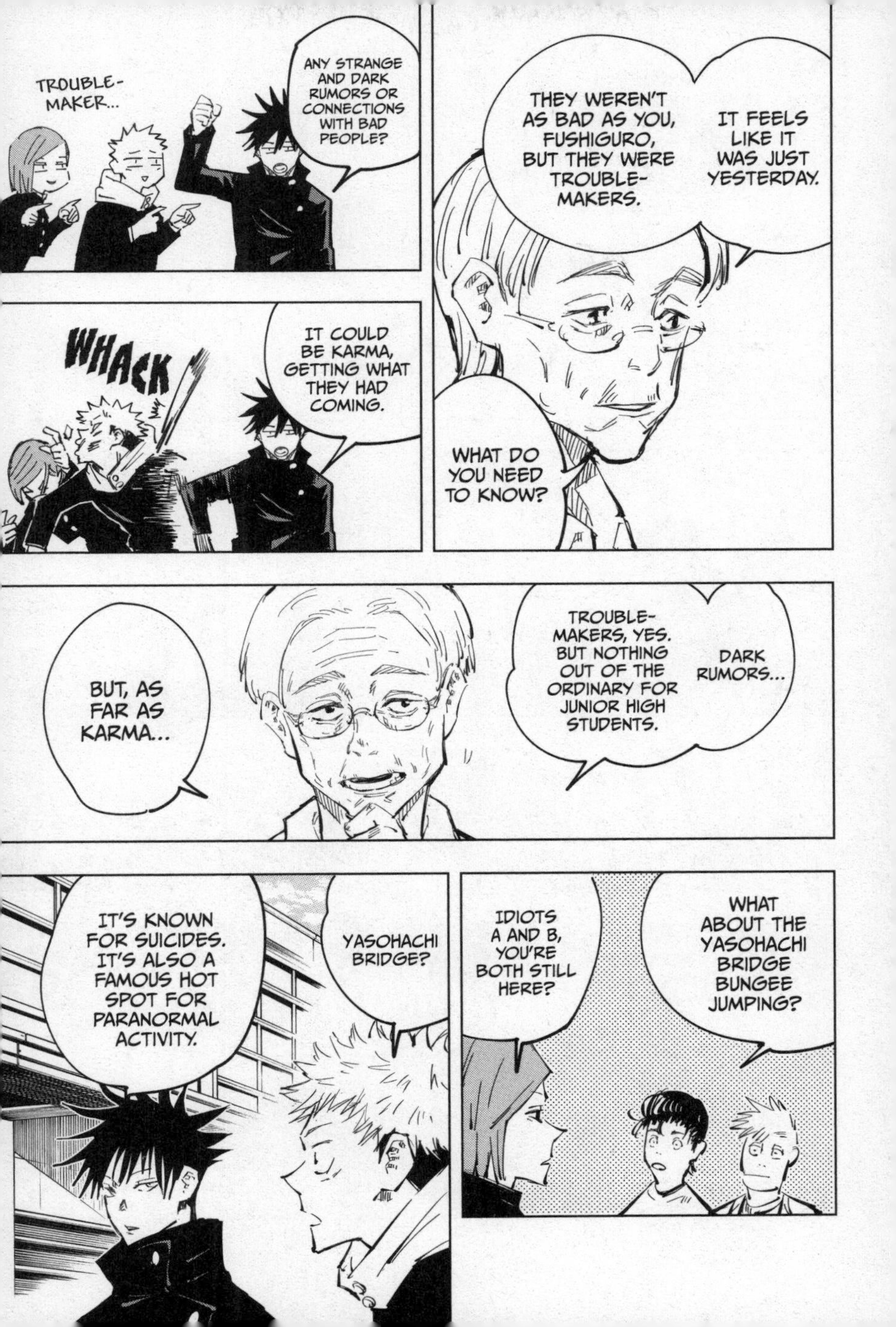
IT FEELS LIKE IT WAS JUST YESTERDAY.
THEY WEREN'T AS BAD AS YOU, FUSHIGURO, BUT THEY WERE TROUBLE-MAKERS.
WHAT DO YOU NEED TO KNOW?
ANY STRANGE AND DARK RUMORS OR CONNECTIONS WITH BAD PEOPLE?
TROUBLE-MAKER...
IT COULD BE KARMA, GETTING WHAT THEY HAD COMING.
WHACK
DARK RUMORS...
TROUBLE-MAKERS, YES. BUT NOTHING OUT OF THE ORDINARY FOR JUNIOR HIGH STUDENTS.
BUT, AS FAR AS KARMA...
WHAT ABOUT THE YASOHACHI BRIDGE BUNGEE JUMPING?
IDIOTS A AND B, YOU'RE BOTH STILL HERE?
YASOHACHI BRIDGE?
IT'S KNOWN FOR SUICIDES. IT'S ALSO A FAMOUS HOT SPOT FOR PARANORMAL ACTIVITY.

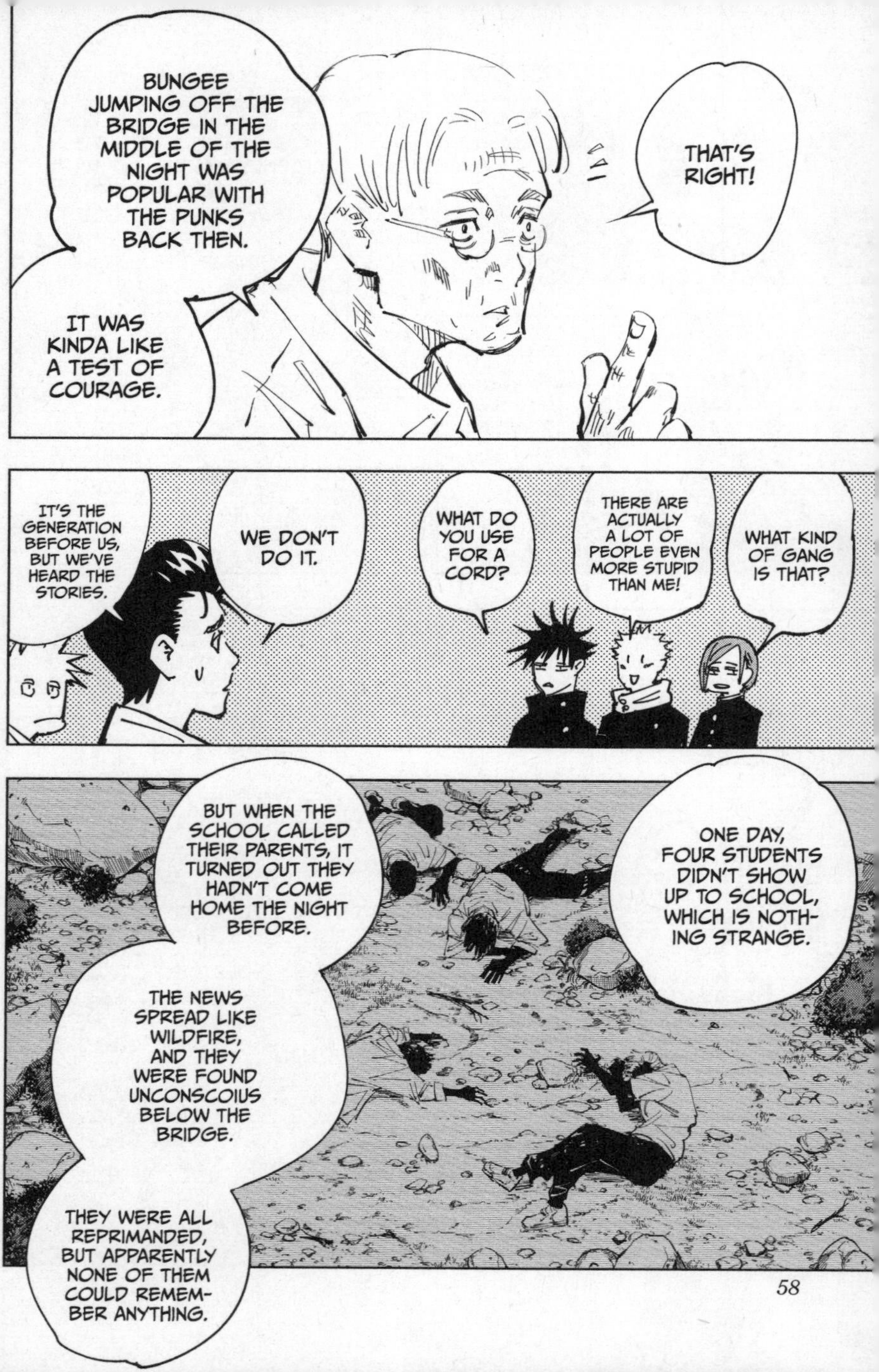
THAT'S RIGHT!
BUNGEE JUMPING OFF THE BRIDGE IN THE MIDDLE OF THE NIGHT WAS POPULAR WITH THE PUNKS BACK THEN.
IT WAS KINDA LIKE A TEST OF COURAGE.
WHAT KIND OF GANG IS THAT?
THERE ARE ACTUALLY A LOT OF PEOPLE EVEN MORE STUPID THAN ME!
WHAT DO YOU USE FOR A CORD?
WE DON'T DO IT.
IT'S THE GENERATION BEFORE US, BUT WE'VE HEARD THE STORIES.
ONE DAY, FOUR STUDENTS DIDN'T SHOW UP TO SCHOOL, WHICH IS NOTHING STRANGE.
BUT WHEN THE SCHOOL CALLED THEIR PARENTS, IT TURNED OUT THEY HADN'T COME HOME THE NIGHT BEFORE.
THE NEWS SPREAD LIKE WILDFIRE, AND THEY WERE FOUND UNCONSCOIUS BELOW THE BRIDGE.
THEY WERE ALL REPRIMANDED, BUT APPARENTLY NONE OF THEM COULD REMEMBER ANYTHING.

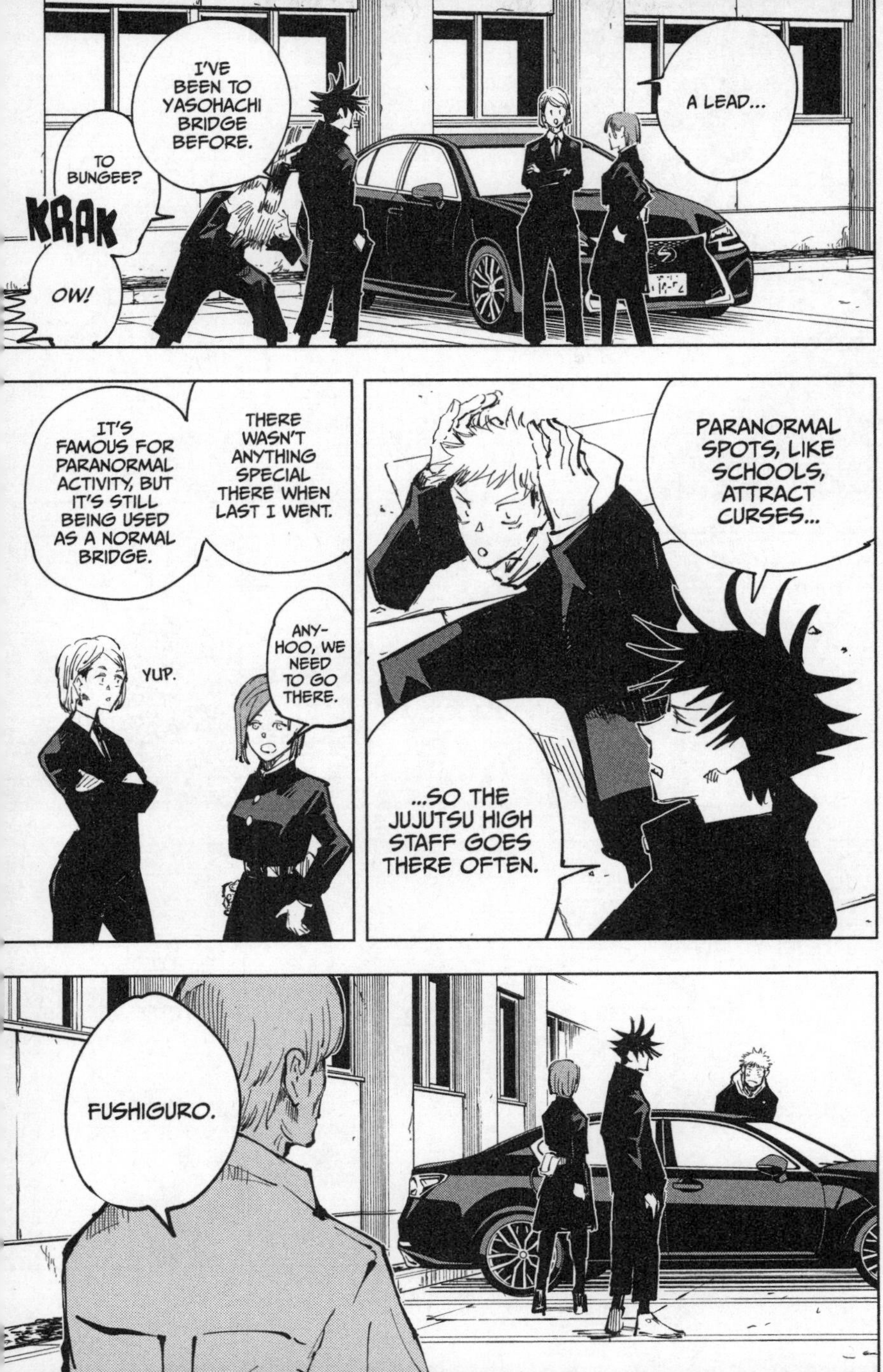
A LEAD...
I'VE BEEN TO YASOHACHI BRIDGE BEFORE.
TO BUNGEE?
KRAK
OW!
PARANORMAL SPOTS, LIKE SCHOOLS, ATTRACT CURSES...
...SO THE JUJUTSU HIGH STAFF GOES THERE OFTEN.
THERE WASN'T ANYTHING SPECIAL THERE WHEN LAST I WENT.
IT'S FAMOUS FOR PARANORMAL ACTIVITY, BUT IT'S STILL BEING USED AS A NORMAL BRIDGE.
ANY-HOO, WE NEED TO GO THERE.
YUP.
FUSHIGURO.

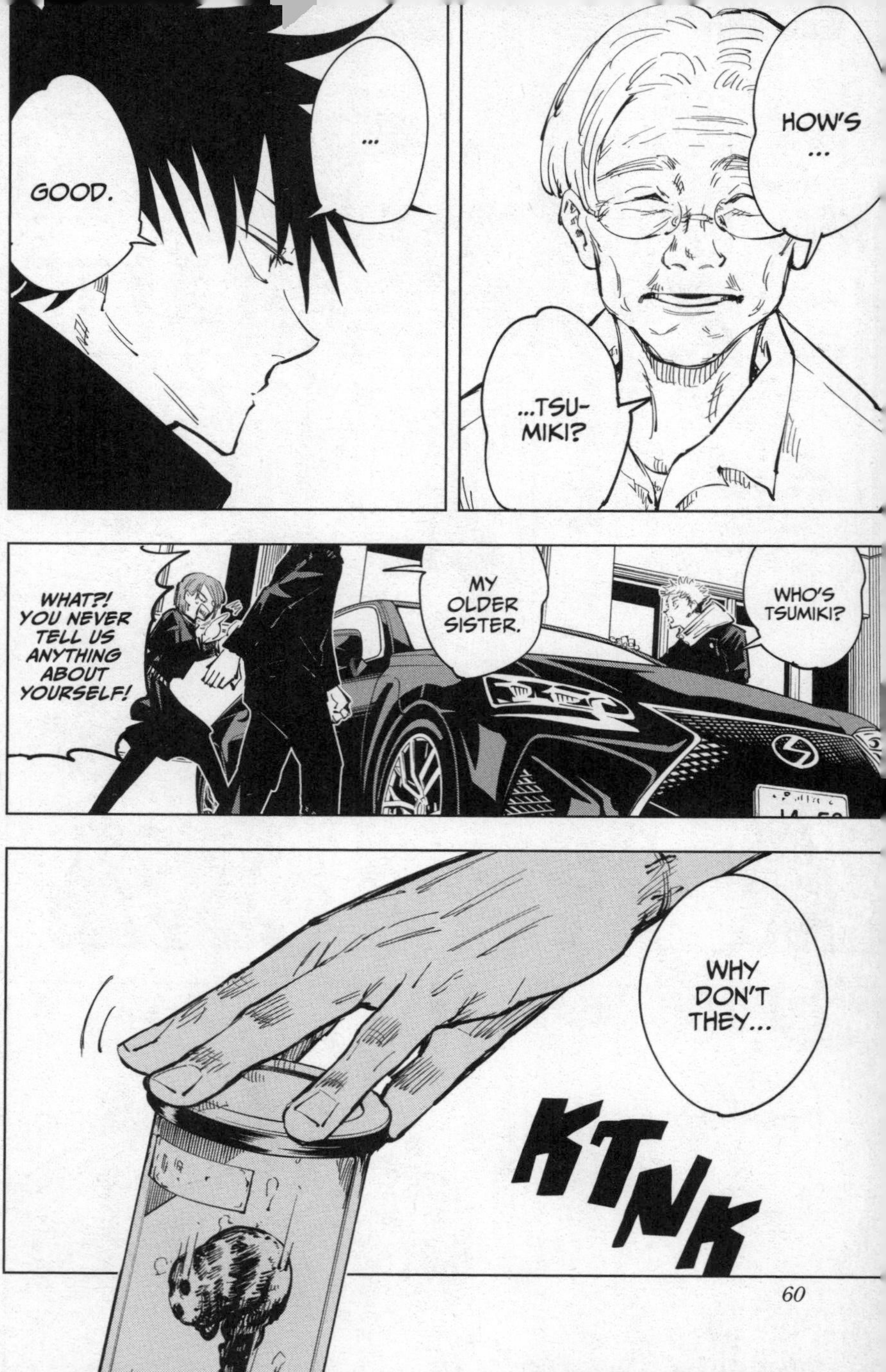
HOW'S ...
...TSUMIKI?
...
GOOD.
WHO'S TSUMIKI?
MY OLDER SISTER.
WHAT?! YOU NEVER TELL US ANYTHING ABOUT YOURSELF!
WHY DON'T THEY...
KTNK

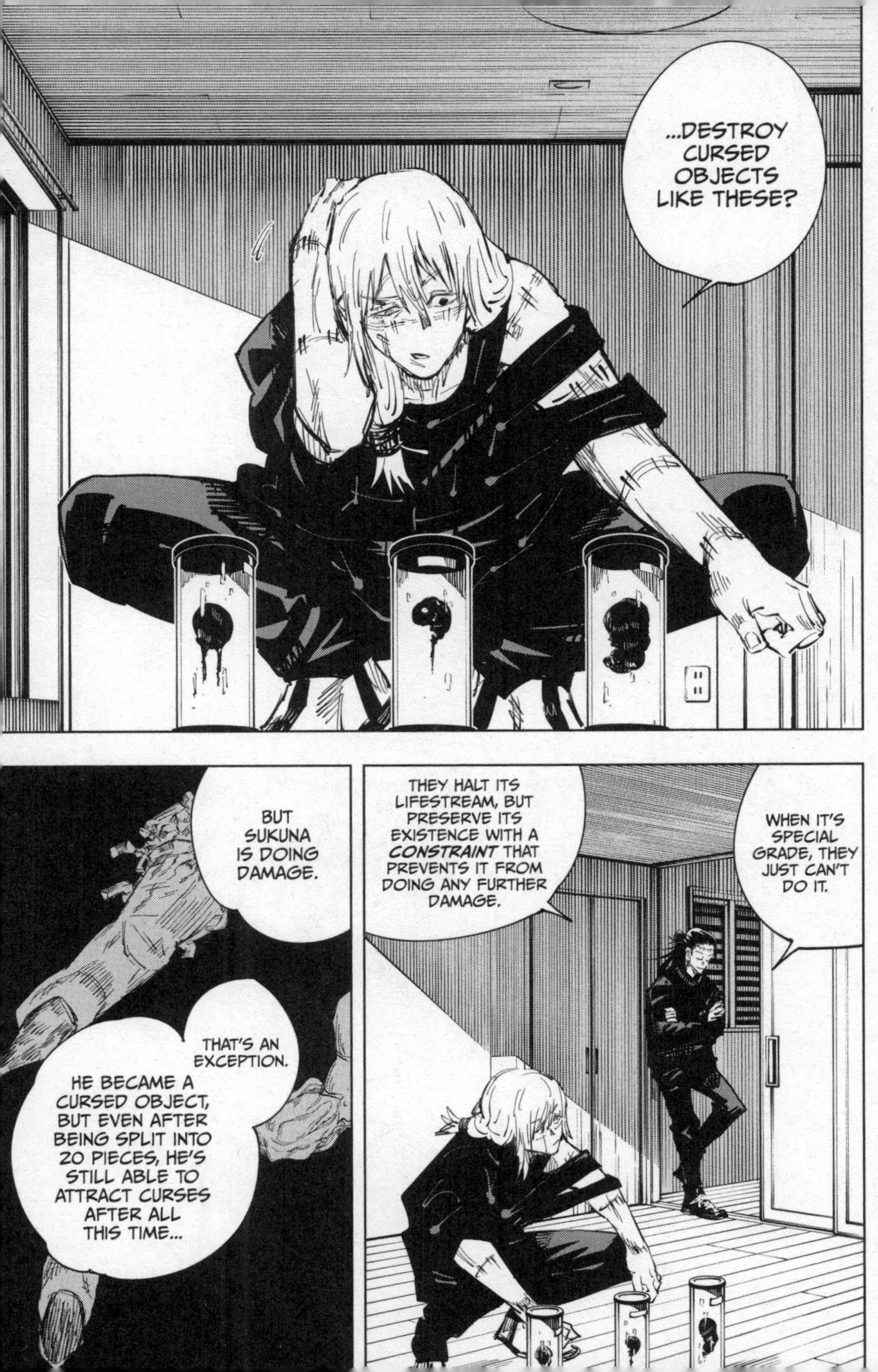
...DESTROY CURSED OBJECTS LIKE THESE?
WHEN IT'S SPECIAL GRADE, THEY JUST CAN'T DO IT.
THEY HALT ITS LIFESTREAM, BUT PRESERVE ITS EXISTENCE WITH A *CONSTRAINT* THAT PREVENTS IT FROM DOING ANY FURTHER DAMAGE.
BUT SUKUNA IS DOING DAMAGE.
THAT'S AN EXCEPTION.
HE BECAME A CURSED OBJECT, BUT EVEN AFTER BEING SPLIT INTO 20 PIECES, HE'S STILL ABLE TO ATTRACT CURSES AFTER ALL THIS TIME...

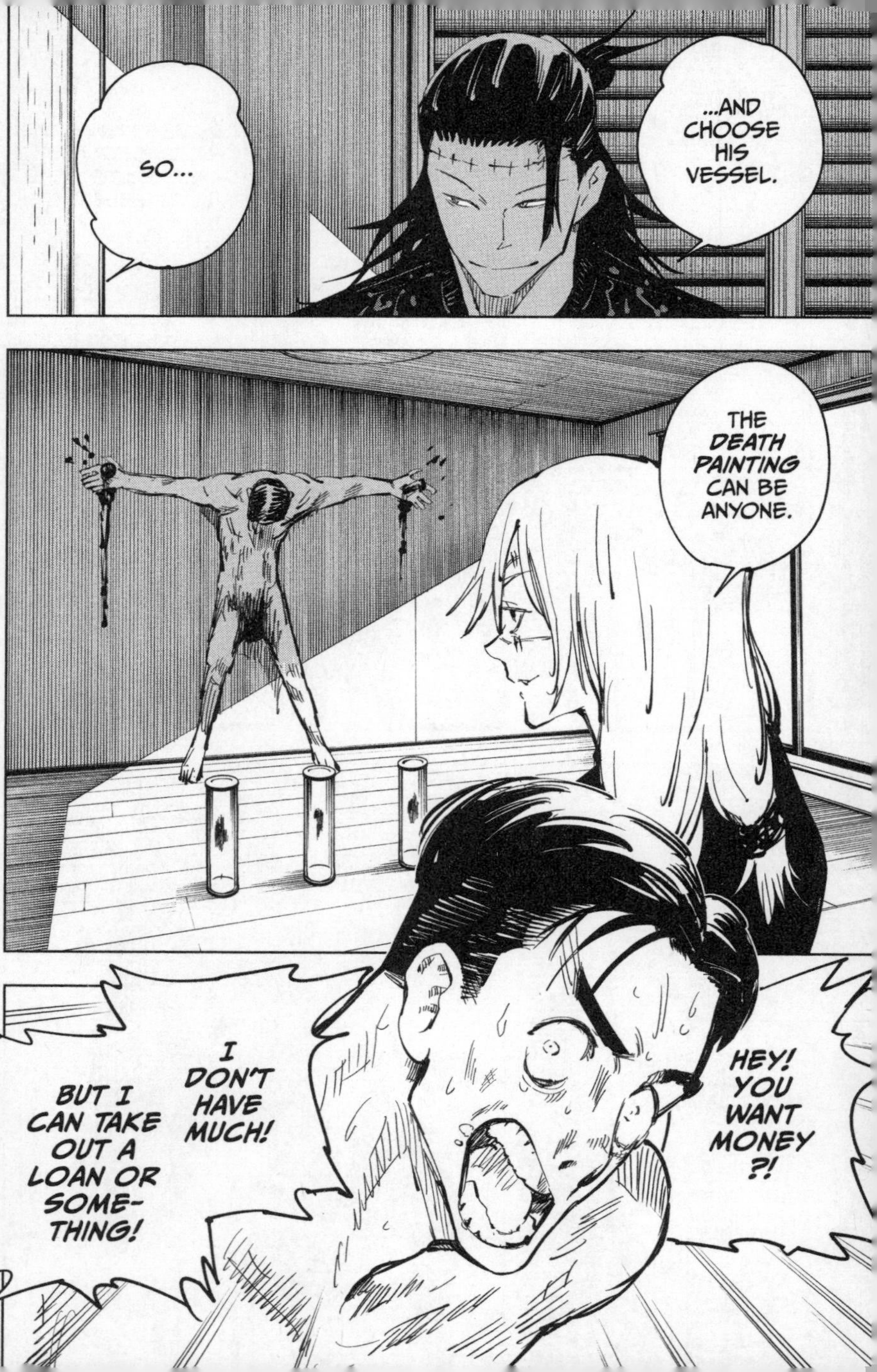
...AND CHOOSE HIS VESSEL.
SO...
THE *DEATH PAINTING* CAN BE ANYONE.
HEY! YOU WANT MONEY?!
I DON'T HAVE MUCH!
BUT I CAN TAKE OUT A LOAN OR SOME-THING!

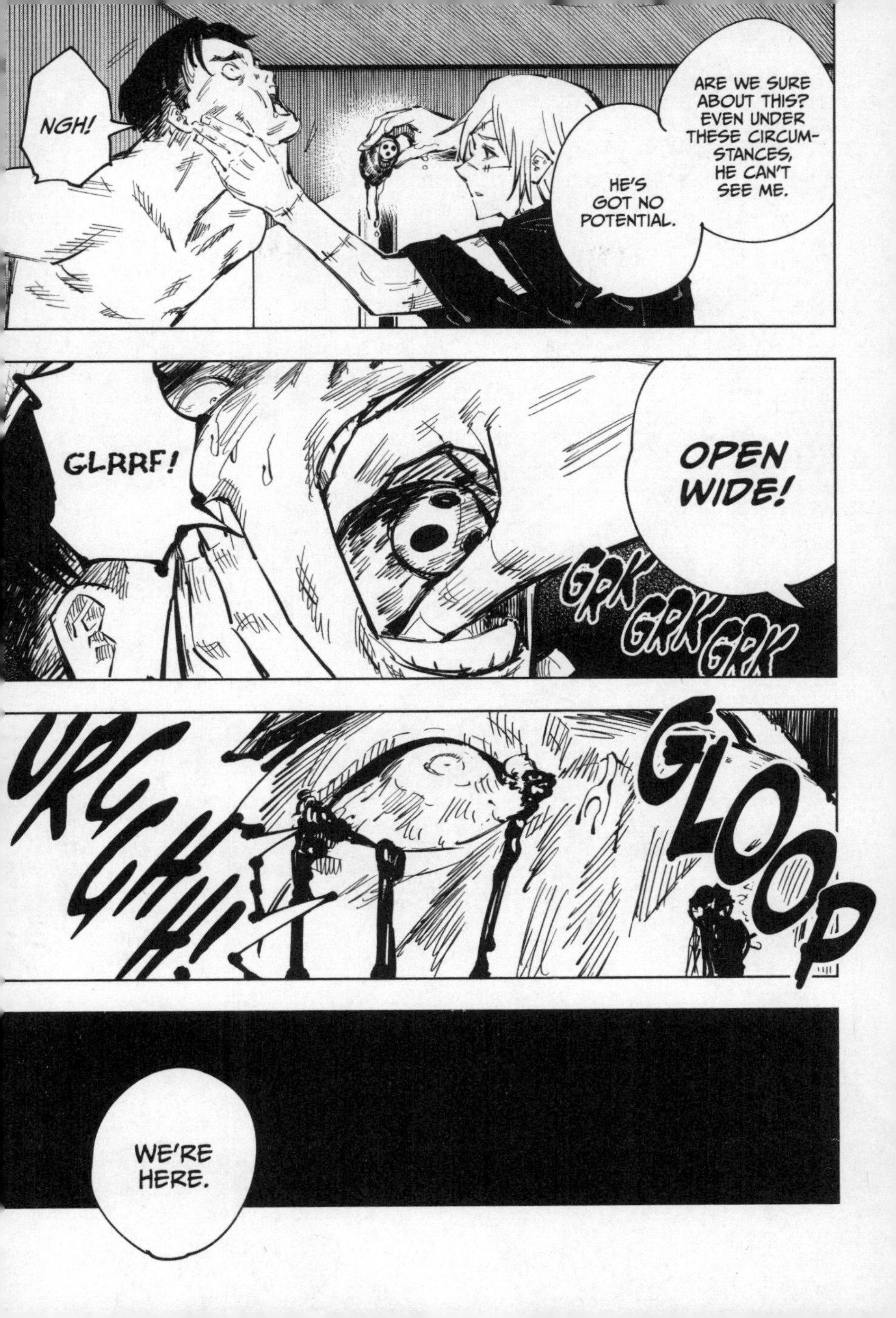
ARE WE SURE ABOUT THIS? EVEN UNDER THESE CIRCUM- STANCES, HE CAN'T SEE ME.
HE'S GOT NO POTENTIAL.
NGH!
OPEN WIDE!
GRK GRK GRK
GLRRF!
GLOOP
URGGHH!
WE'RE HERE.

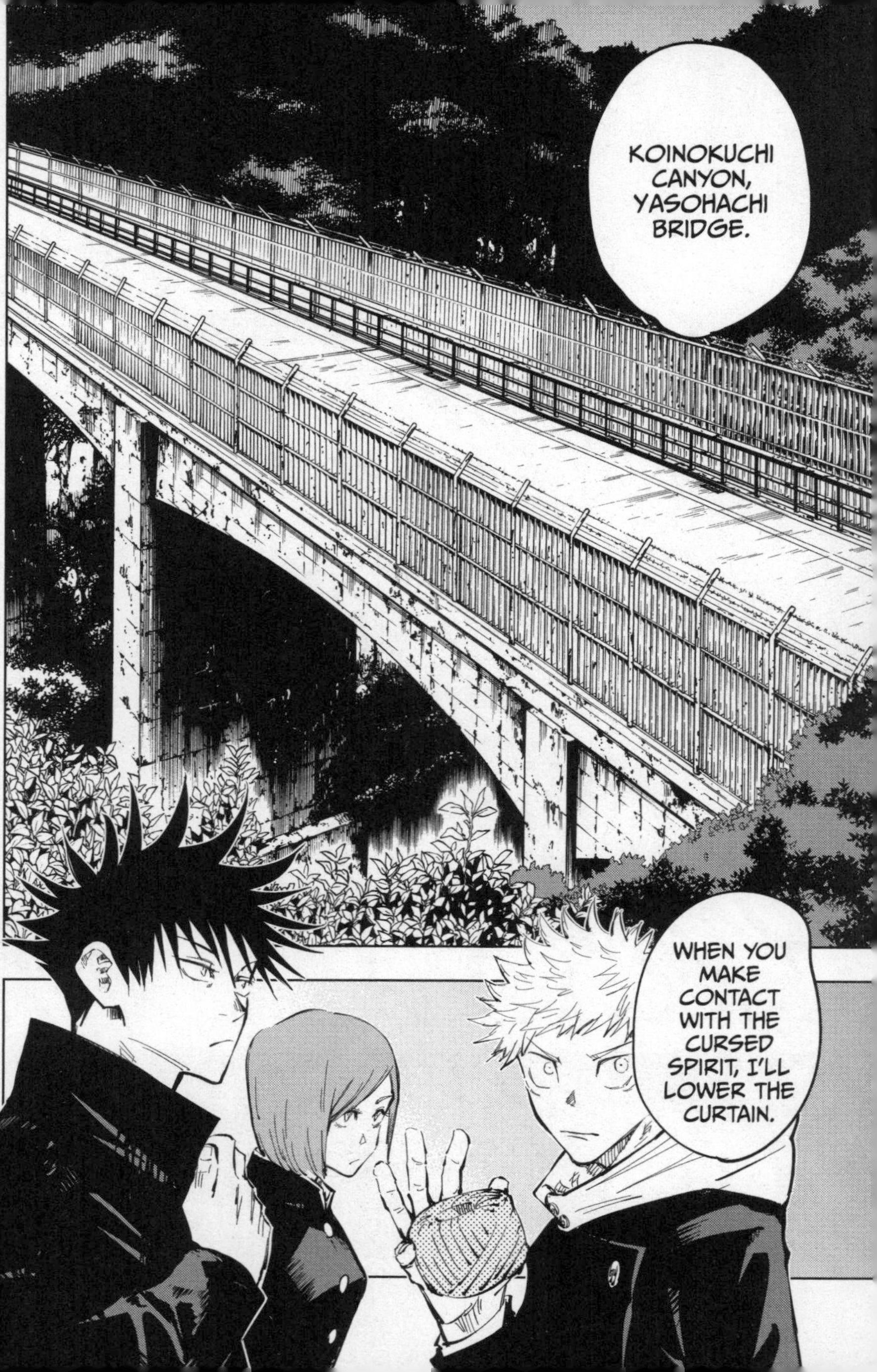
KOINOKUCHI CANYON, YASOHACHI BRIDGE.
WHEN YOU MAKE CONTACT WITH THE CURSED SPIRIT, I'LL LOWER THE CURTAIN.

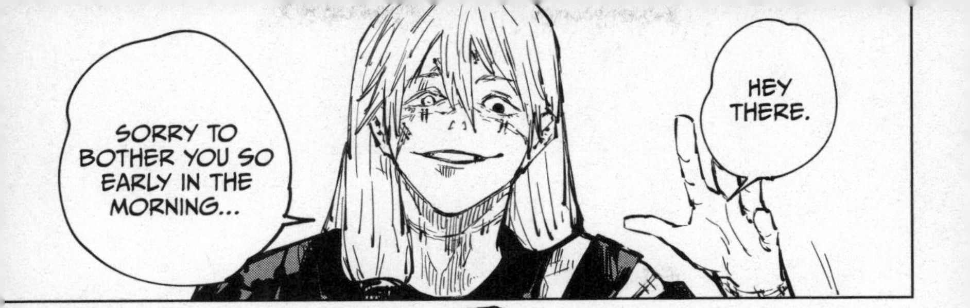
HEY THERE.
SORRY TO BOTHER YOU SO EARLY IN THE MORNING...

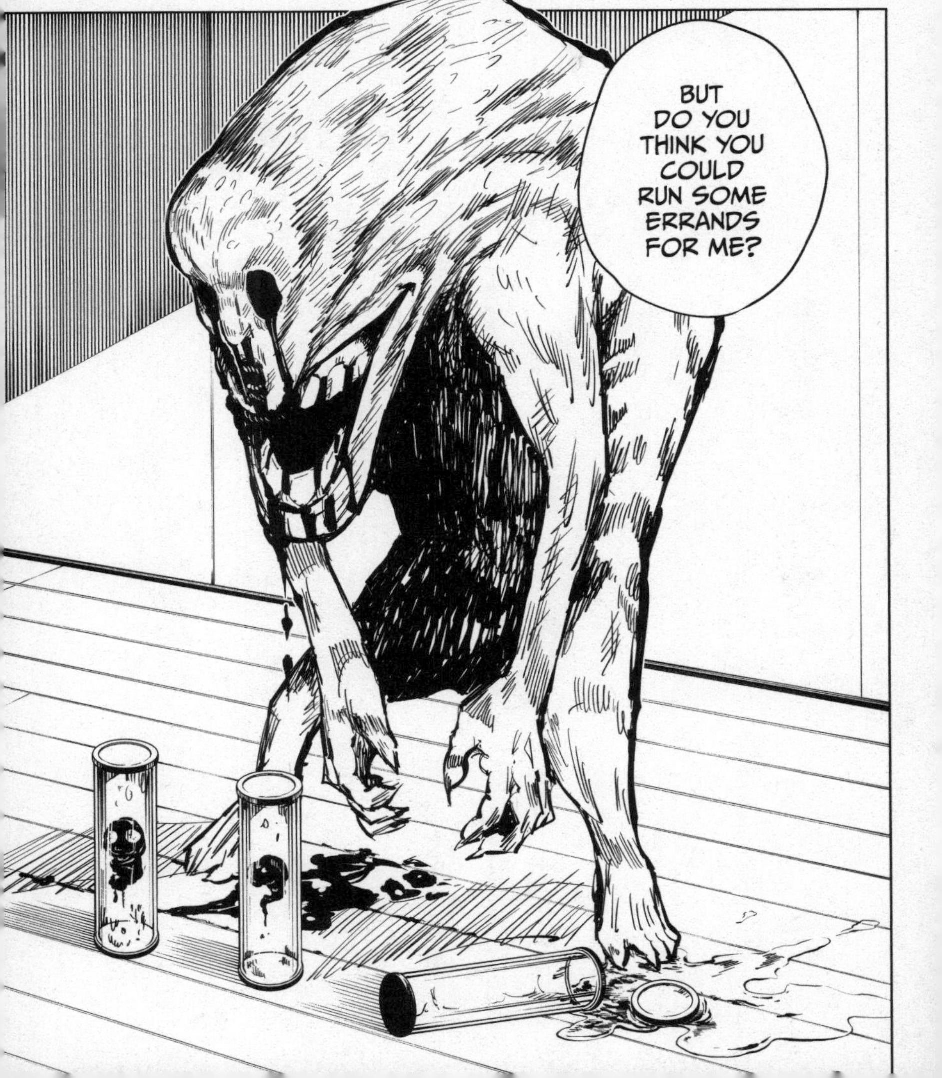
BUT DO YOU THINK YOU COULD RUN SOME ERRANDS FOR ME?

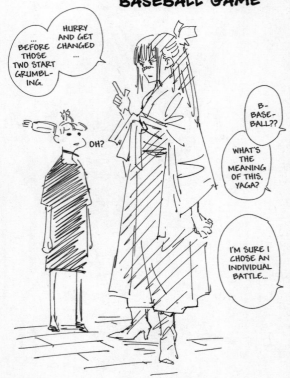

**UTAHIME-
THE ONE WHO WAS
MOST INTO THE
BASEBALL GAME**

HURRY AND GET CHANGED...
...BEFORE THOSE TWO START GRUMBLING.
OH?
B-BASEBALL??
WHAT'S THE MEANING OF THIS, YAGA?
I'M SURE I CHOSE AN INDIVIDUAL BATTLE...

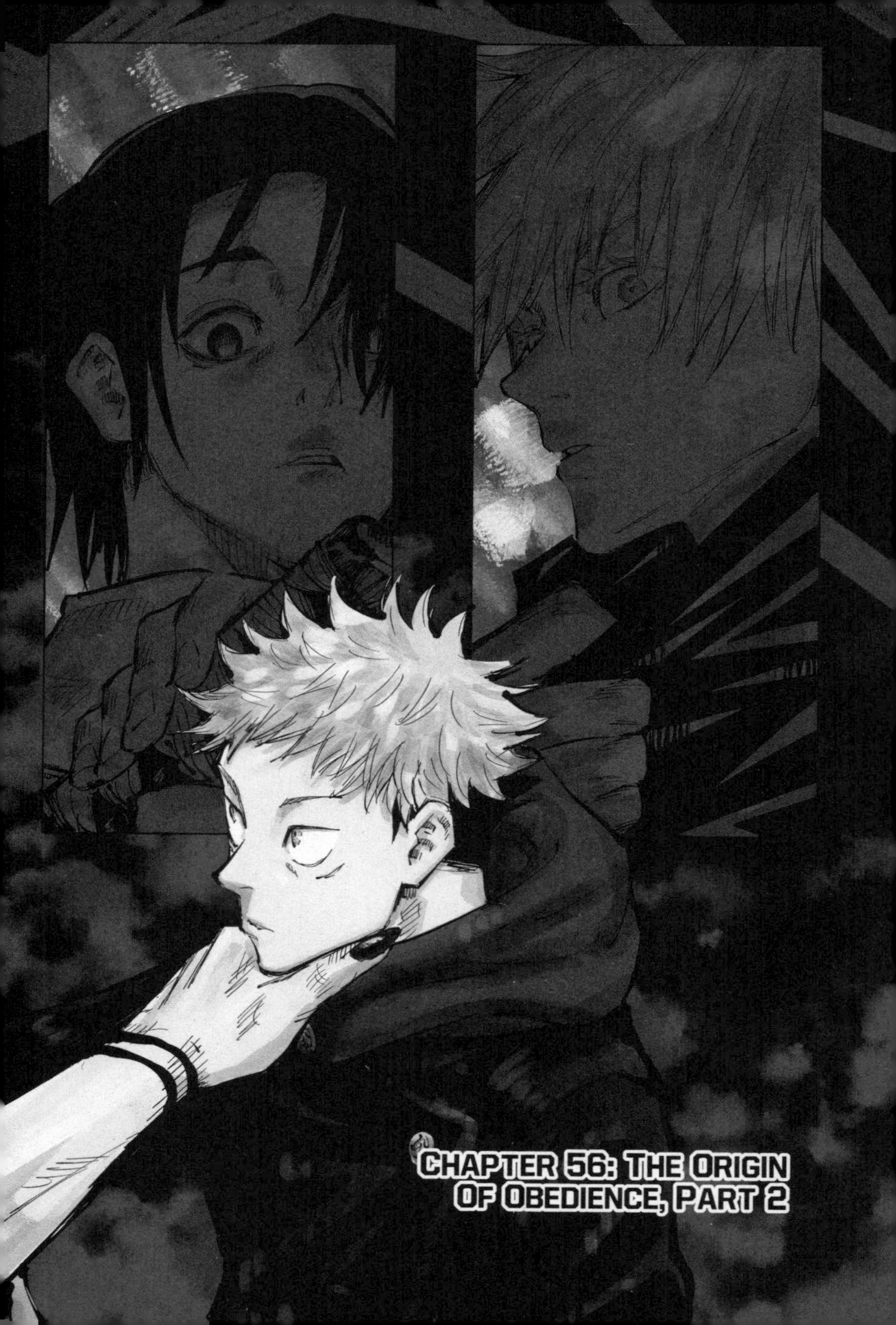

CHAPTER 56: THE ORIGIN OF OBEDIENCE, PART 2

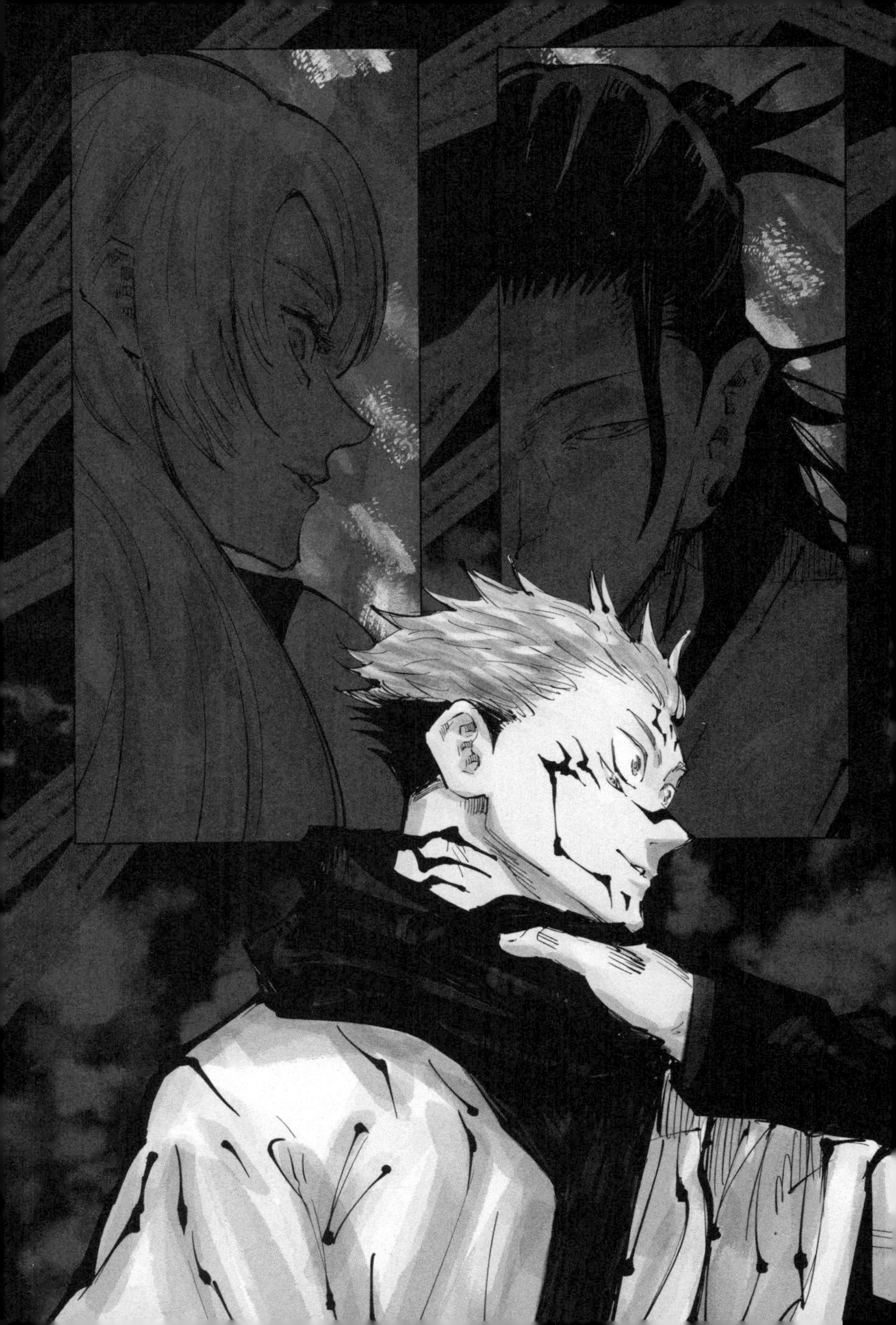

JUJUTSU KAISEN

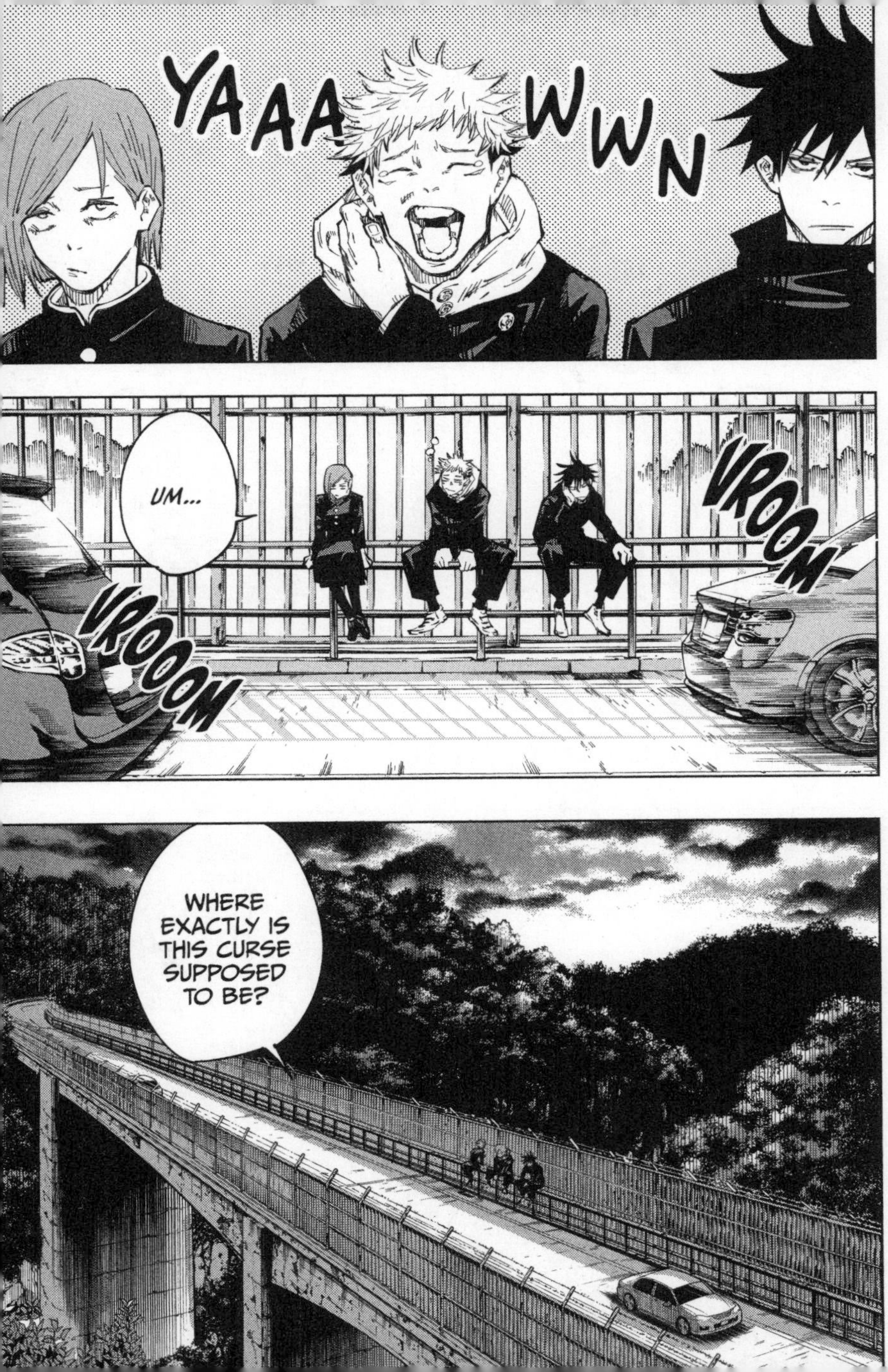
YAAAWWN
VROOM
UM...
VROOOM
WHERE EXACTLY IS THIS CURSE SUPPOSED TO BE?

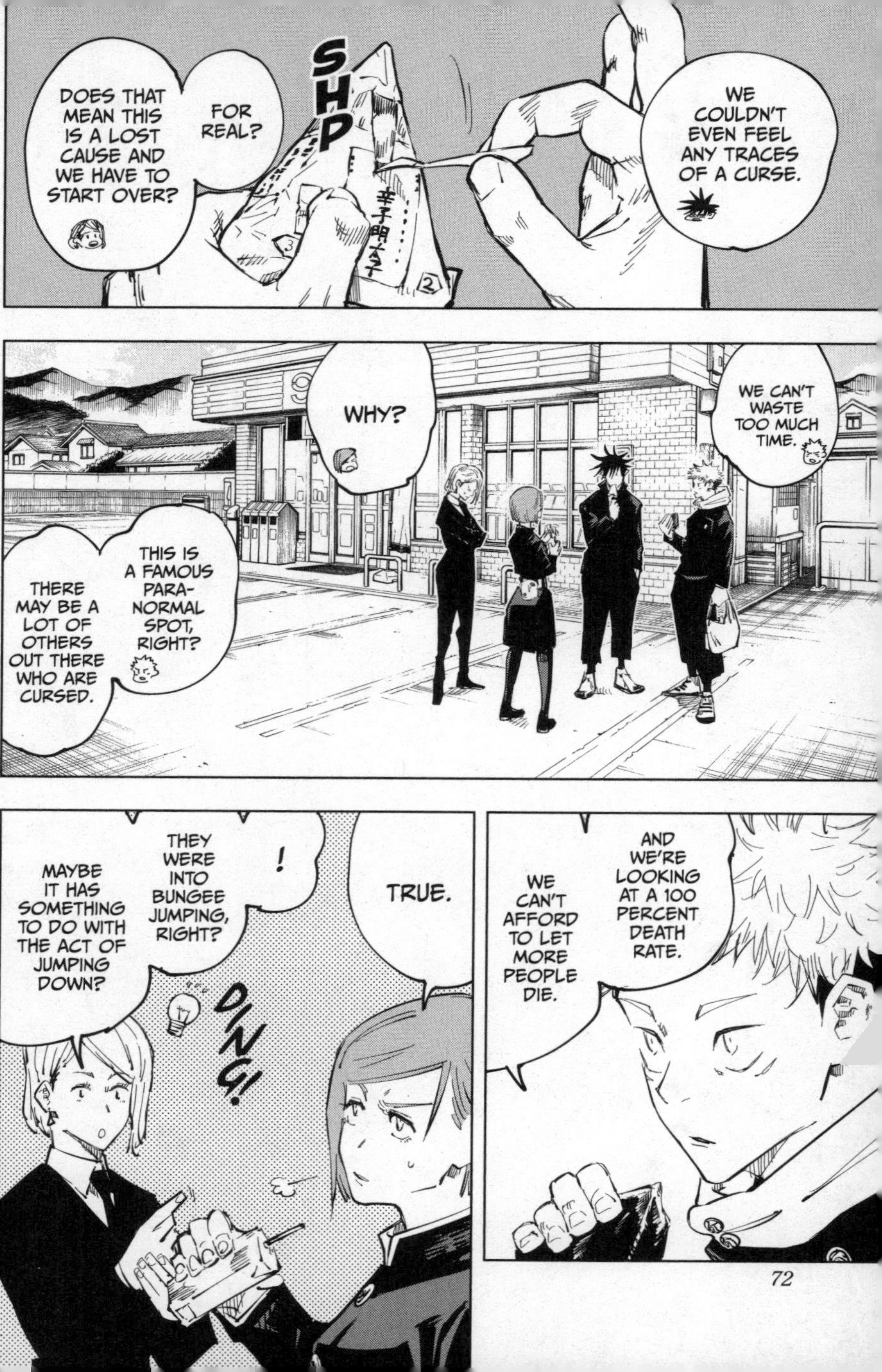
WE COULDN'T EVEN FEEL ANY TRACES OF A CURSE.
SHP
FOR REAL?
DOES THAT MEAN THIS IS A LOST CAUSE AND WE HAVE TO START OVER?
WE CAN'T WASTE TOO MUCH TIME.
WHY?
THIS IS A FAMOUS PARA-NORMAL SPOT, RIGHT?
THERE MAY BE A LOT OF OTHERS OUT THERE WHO ARE CURSED.
AND WE'RE LOOKING AT A 100 PERCENT DEATH RATE.
WE CAN'T AFFORD TO LET MORE PEOPLE DIE.
TRUE.
!
THEY WERE INTO BUNGEE JUMPING, RIGHT?
MAYBE IT HAS SOMETHING TO DO WITH THE ACT OF JUMPING DOWN?
DING!

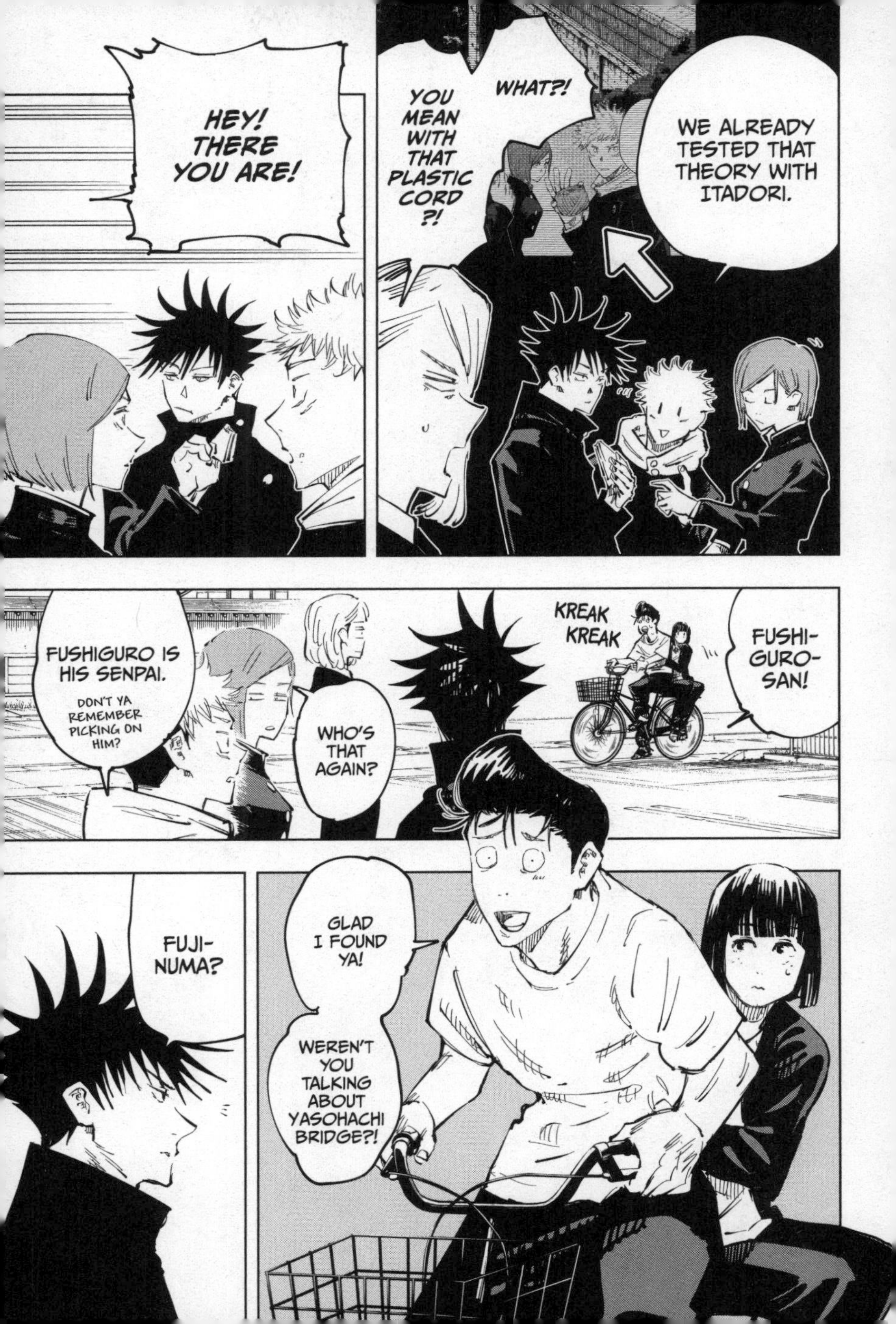
WE ALREADY TESTED THAT THEORY WITH ITADORI.
WHAT?!
YOU MEAN WITH THAT PLASTIC CORD?!
HEY! THERE YOU ARE!
FUSHIGURO-SAN!
KREAK KREAK
WHO'S THAT AGAIN?
FUSHIGURO IS HIS SENPAI.
DON'T YA REMEMBER PICKING ON HIM?
GLAD I FOUND YA!
WEREN'T YOU TALKING ABOUT YASOHACHI BRIDGE?!
FUJI-NUMA?

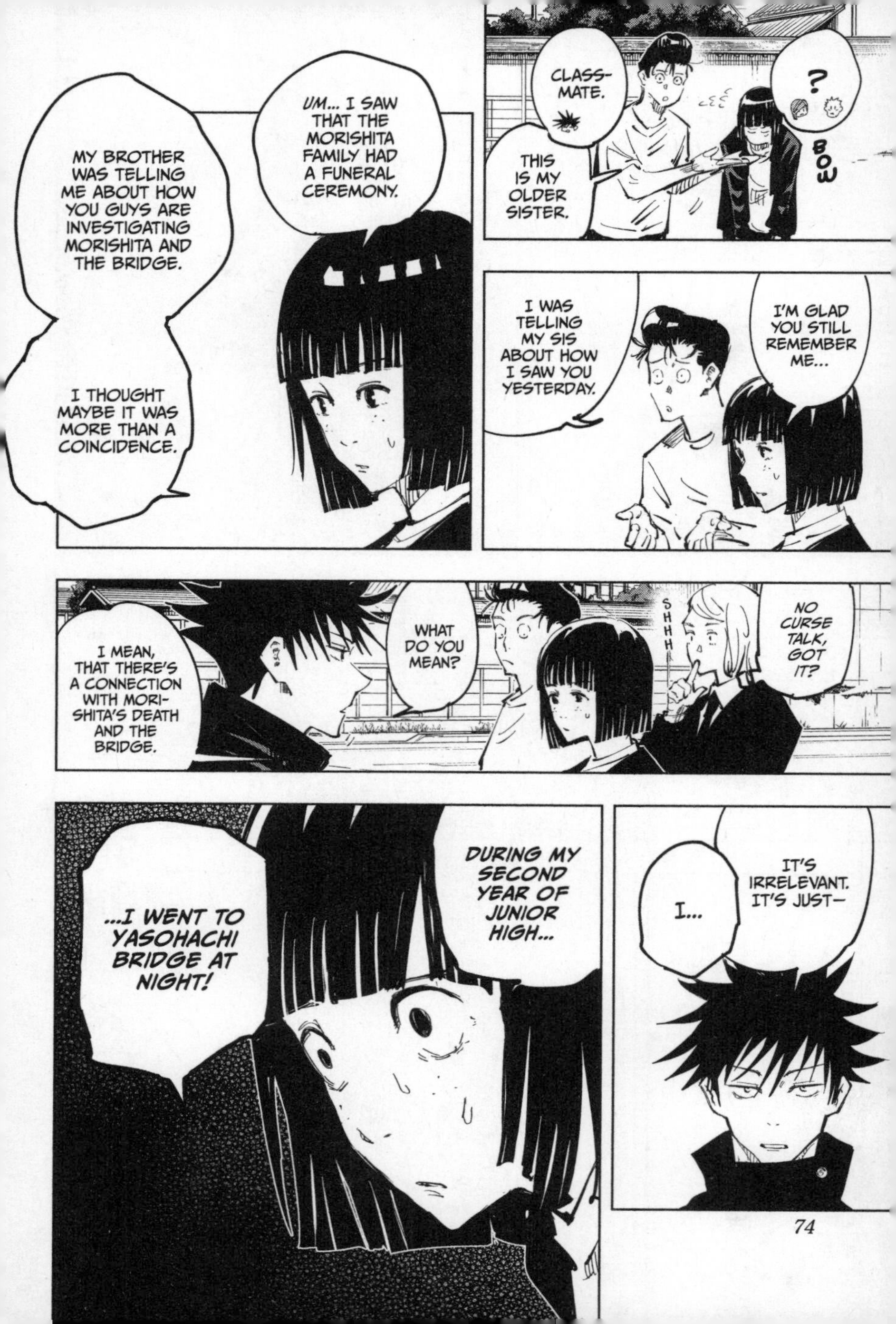
?
CLASS-MATE.
THIS IS MY OLDER SISTER.
BOW
I'M GLAD YOU STILL REMEMBER ME...
I WAS TELLING MY SIS ABOUT HOW I SAW YOU YESTERDAY.
UM... I SAW THAT THE MORISHITA FAMILY HAD A FUNERAL CEREMONY.
MY BROTHER WAS TELLING ME ABOUT HOW YOU GUYS ARE INVESTIGATING MORISHITA AND THE BRIDGE.
I THOUGHT MAYBE IT WAS MORE THAN A COINCIDENCE.
NO CURSE TALK, GOT IT?
SHHH
WHAT DO YOU MEAN?
I MEAN, THAT THERE'S A CONNECTION WITH MORI-SHITA'S DEATH AND THE BRIDGE.
IT'S IRRELEVANT. IT'S JUST—
I...
DURING MY SECOND YEAR OF JUNIOR HIGH...
...I WENT TO YASOHACHI BRIDGE AT NIGHT!

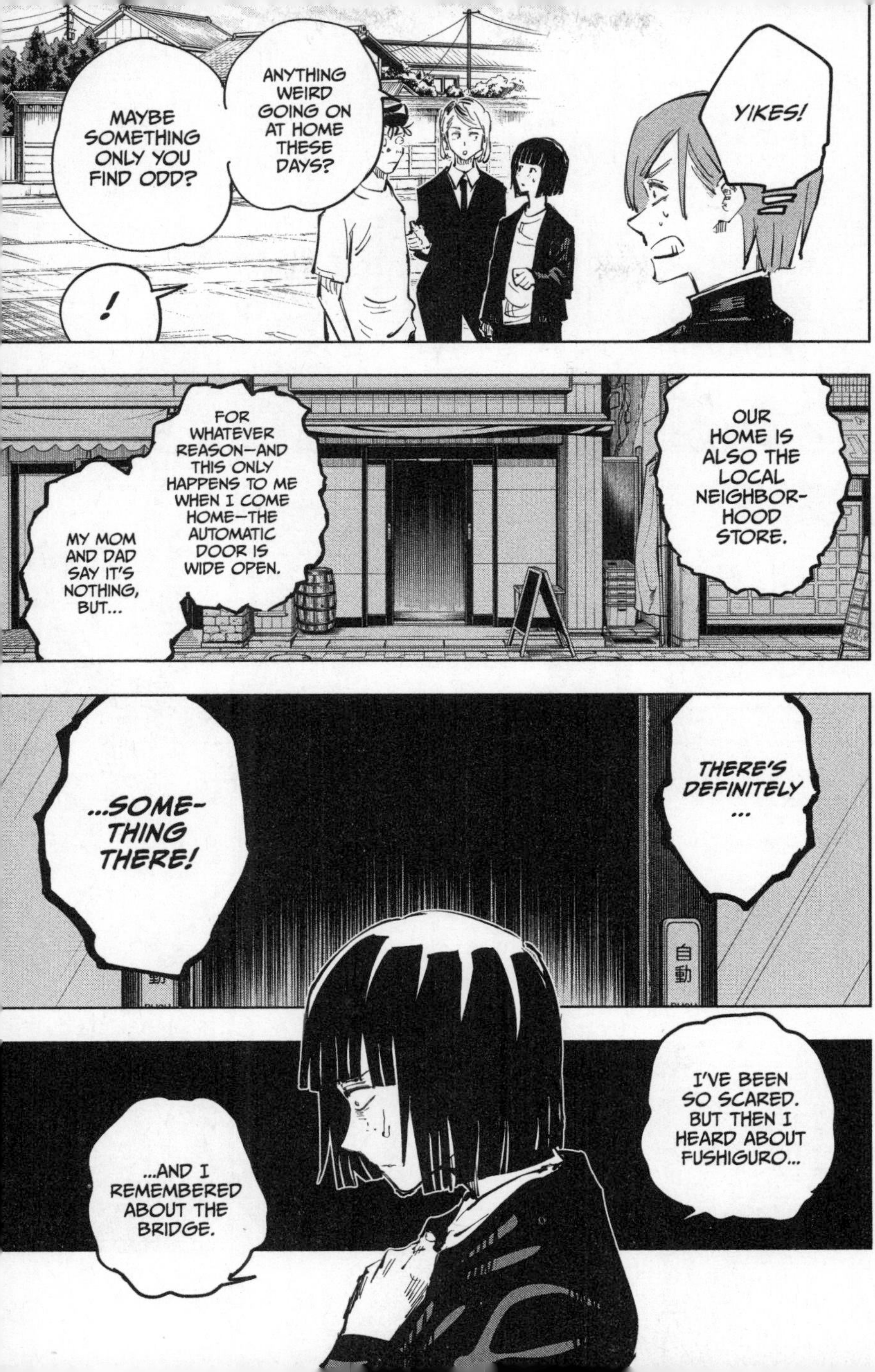
YIKES!
ANYTHING WEIRD GOING ON AT HOME THESE DAYS?
MAYBE SOMETHING ONLY YOU FIND ODD?
!
OUR HOME IS ALSO THE LOCAL NEIGHBOR-HOOD STORE.
FOR WHATEVER REASON—AND THIS ONLY HAPPENS TO ME WHEN I COME HOME—THE AUTOMATIC DOOR IS WIDE OPEN.
MY MOM AND DAD SAY IT'S NOTHING, BUT...
THERE'S DEFINITELY...
...SOME-THING THERE!
自動
I'VE BEEN SO SCARED. BUT THEN I HEARD ABOUT FUSHIGURO...
...AND I REMEMBERED ABOUT THE BRIDGE.

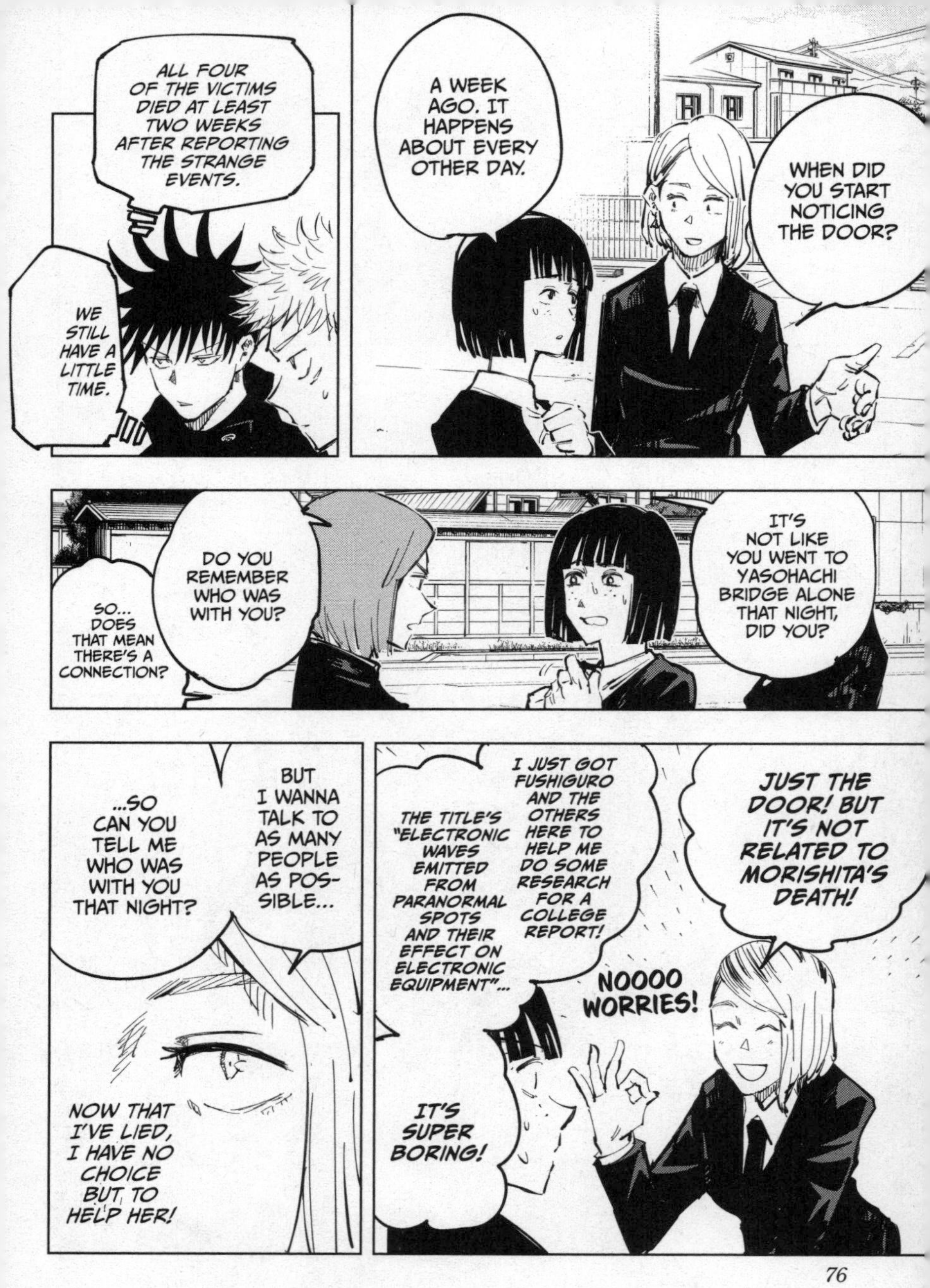
WHEN DID YOU START NOTICING THE DOOR?
A WEEK AGO. IT HAPPENS ABOUT EVERY OTHER DAY.
ALL FOUR OF THE VICTIMS DIED AT LEAST TWO WEEKS AFTER REPORTING THE STRANGE EVENTS.
WE STILL HAVE A LITTLE TIME.
IT'S NOT LIKE YOU WENT TO YASOHACHI BRIDGE ALONE THAT NIGHT, DID YOU?
DO YOU REMEMBER WHO WAS WITH YOU?
SO... DOES THAT MEAN THERE'S A CONNECTION?
JUST THE DOOR! BUT IT'S NOT RELATED TO MORISHITA'S DEATH!
I JUST GOT FUSHIGURO AND THE OTHERS HERE TO HELP ME DO SOME RESEARCH FOR A COLLEGE REPORT!
THE TITLE'S "ELECTRONIC WAVES EMITTED FROM PARANORMAL SPOTS AND THEIR EFFECT ON ELECTRONIC EQUIPMENT"...
NOOOO WORRIES!
IT'S SUPER BORING!
BUT I WANNA TALK TO AS MANY PEOPLE AS POSSIBLE...
...SO CAN YOU TELL ME WHO WAS WITH YOU THAT NIGHT?
NOW THAT I'VE LIED, I HAVE NO CHOICE BUT TO HELP HER!

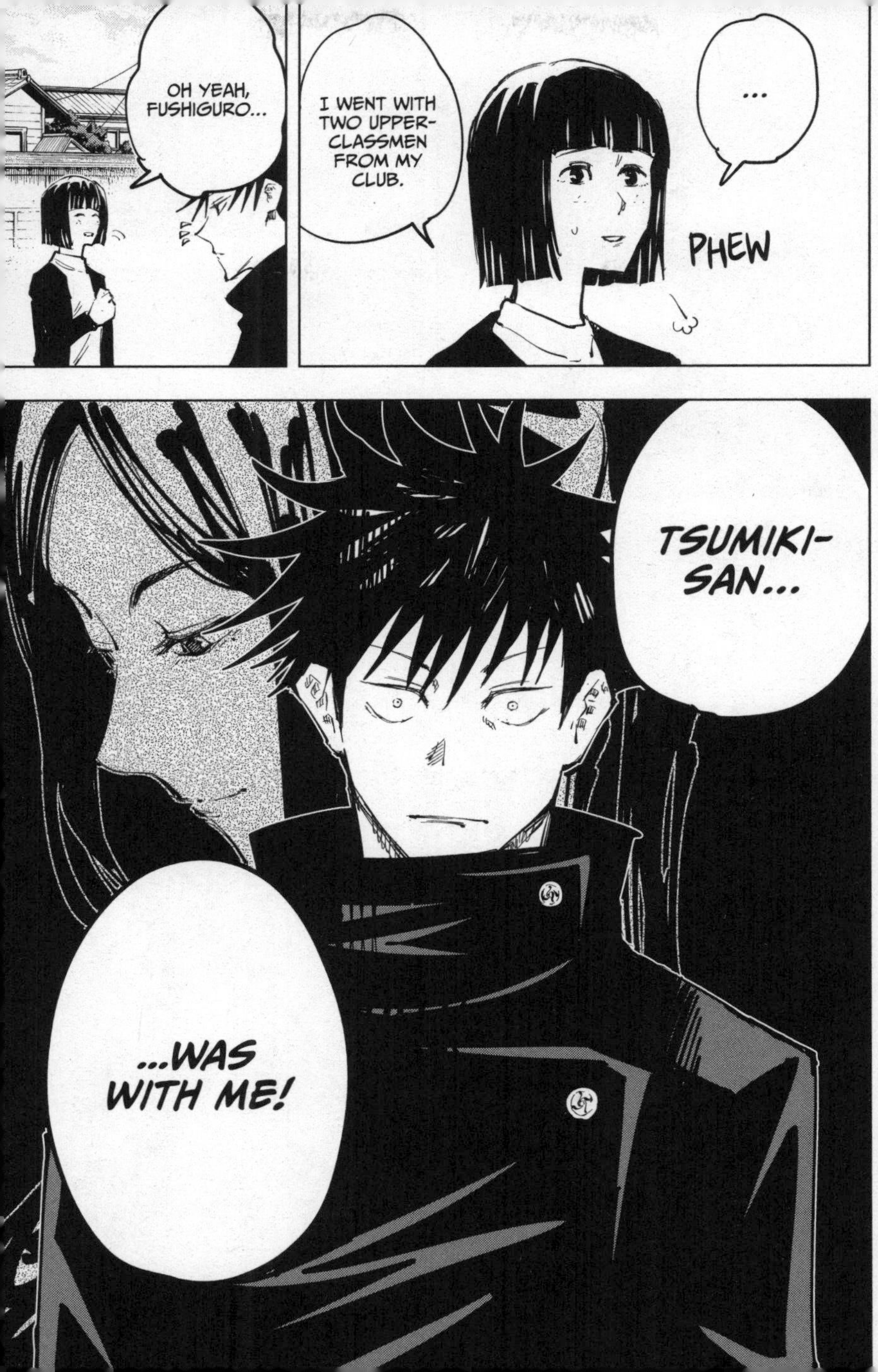
...
I WENT WITH TWO UPPER-CLASSMEN FROM MY CLUB.
PHEW
OH YEAH, FUSHIGURO...
TSUMIKI-SAN...
...WAS WITH ME!

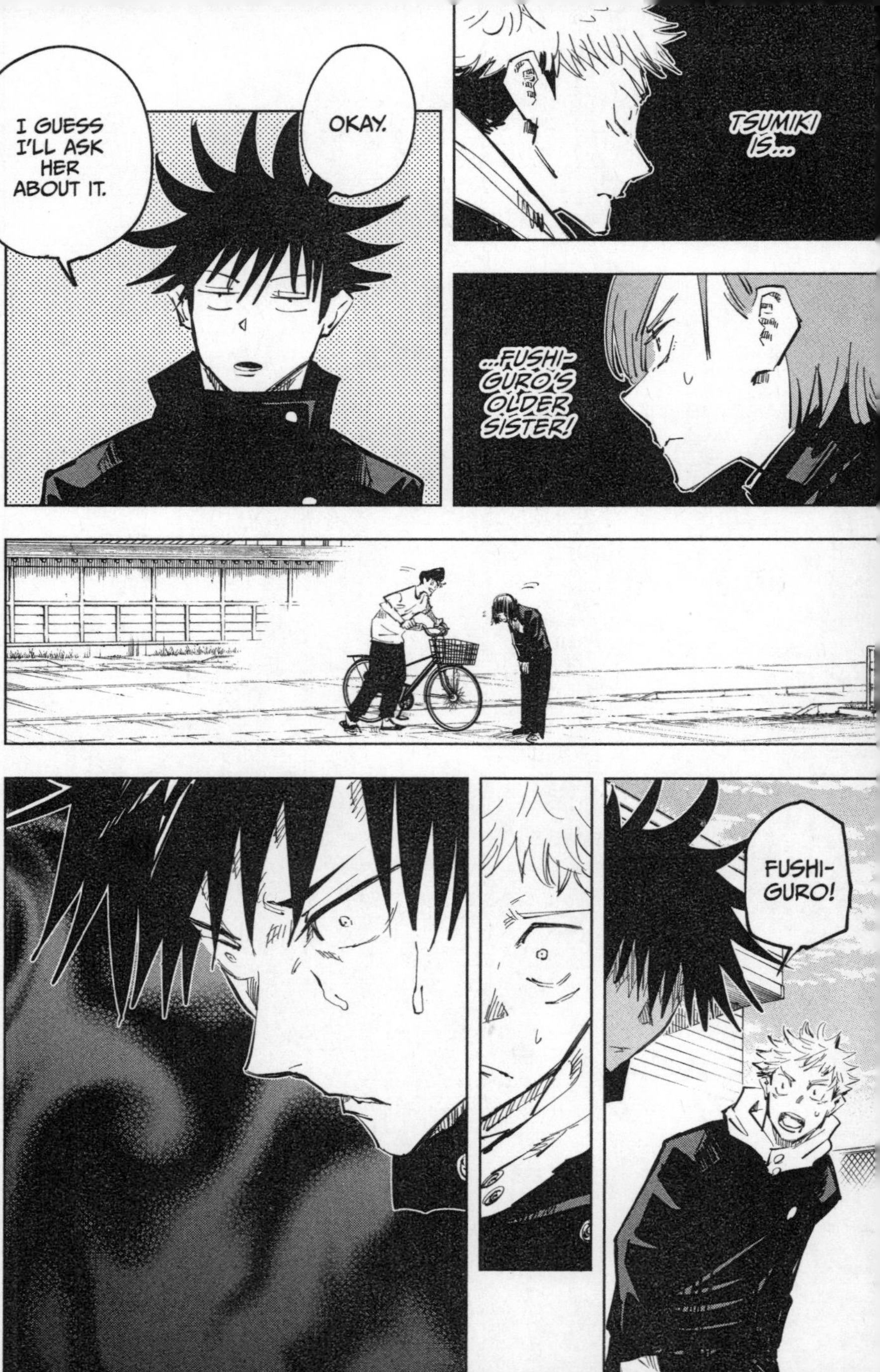
TSUMIKI IS...
...FUSHIGURO'S OLDER SISTER!
OKAY.
I GUESS I'LL ASK HER ABOUT IT.
FUSHIGURO!

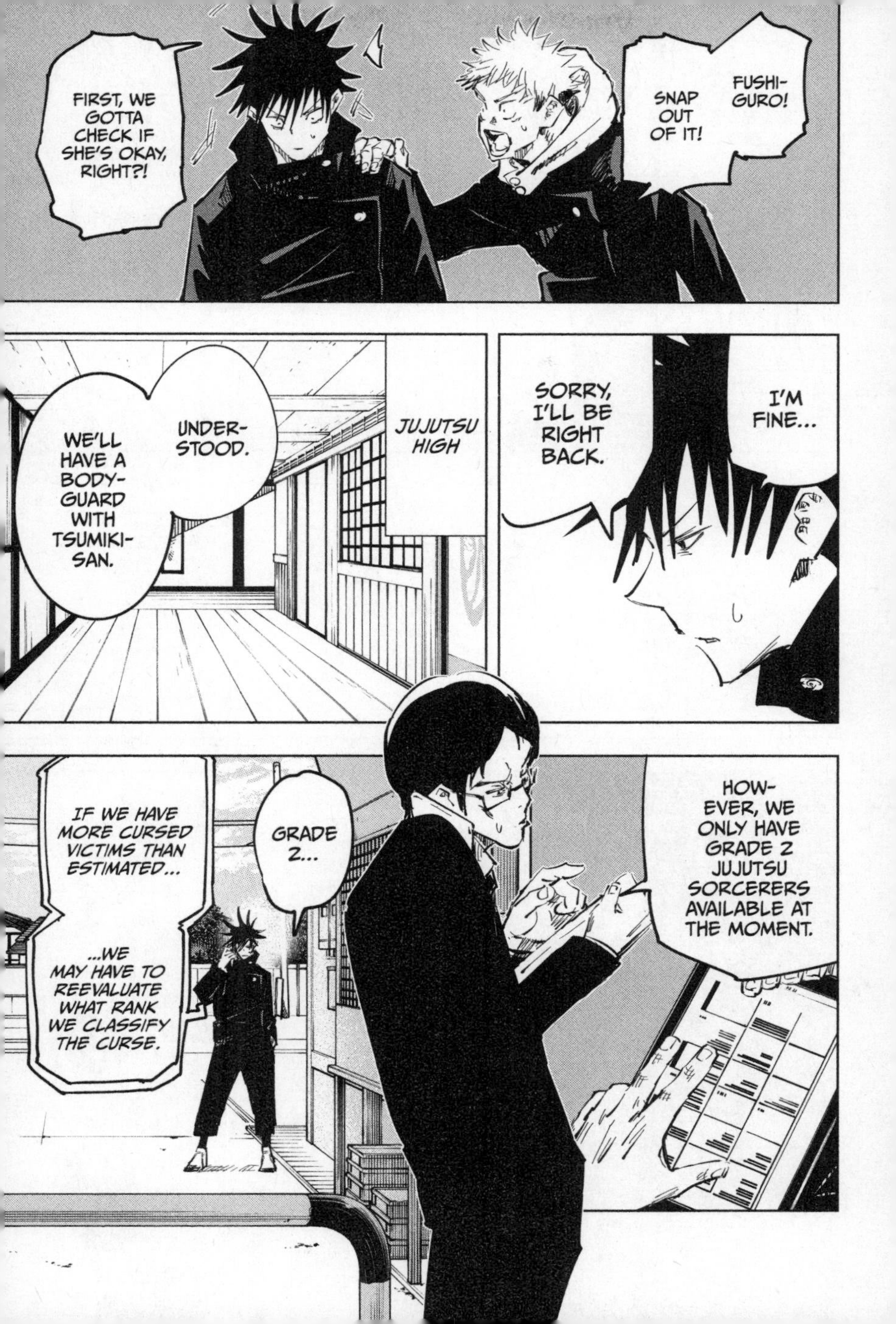
FUSHI-GURO!
SNAP OUT OF IT!
FIRST, WE GOTTA CHECK IF SHE'S OKAY, RIGHT?!
I'M FINE...
SORRY, I'LL BE RIGHT BACK.
JUJUTSU HIGH
UNDER-STOOD.
WE'LL HAVE A BODY-GUARD WITH TSUMIKI-SAN.
HOW-EVER, WE ONLY HAVE GRADE 2 JUJUTSU SORCERERS AVAILABLE AT THE MOMENT.
GRADE 2...
IF WE HAVE MORE CURSED VICTIMS THAN ESTIMATED...
...WE MAY HAVE TO REEVALUATE WHAT RANK WE CLASSIFY THE CURSE.

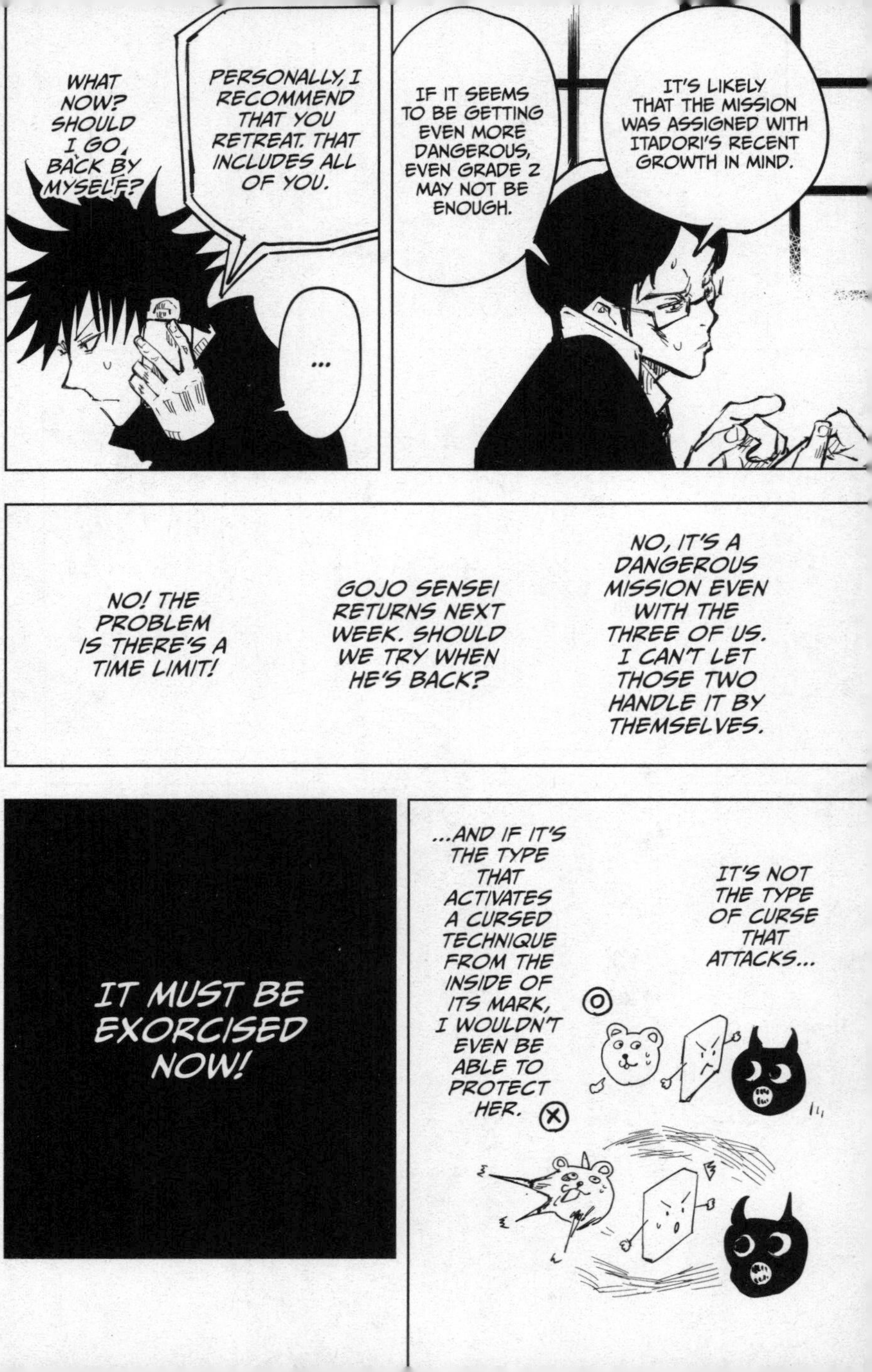
IT'S LIKELY THAT THE MISSION WAS ASSIGNED WITH ITADORI'S RECENT GROWTH IN MIND.
IF IT SEEMS TO BE GETTING EVEN MORE DANGEROUS, EVEN GRADE 2 MAY NOT BE ENOUGH.
PERSONALLY, I RECOMMEND THAT YOU RETREAT. THAT INCLUDES ALL OF YOU.
...
WHAT NOW? SHOULD I GO BACK BY MYSELF?
NO, IT'S A DANGEROUS MISSION EVEN WITH THE THREE OF US. I CAN'T LET THOSE TWO HANDLE IT BY THEMSELVES.
GOJO SENSEI RETURNS NEXT WEEK. SHOULD WE TRY WHEN HE'S BACK?
NO! THE PROBLEM IS THERE'S A TIME LIMIT!
IT'S NOT THE TYPE OF CURSE THAT ATTACKS...
...AND IF IT'S THE TYPE THAT ACTIVATES A CURSED TECHNIQUE FROM THE INSIDE OF ITS MARK, I WOULDN'T EVEN BE ABLE TO PROTECT HER.
IT MUST BE EXORCISED NOW!

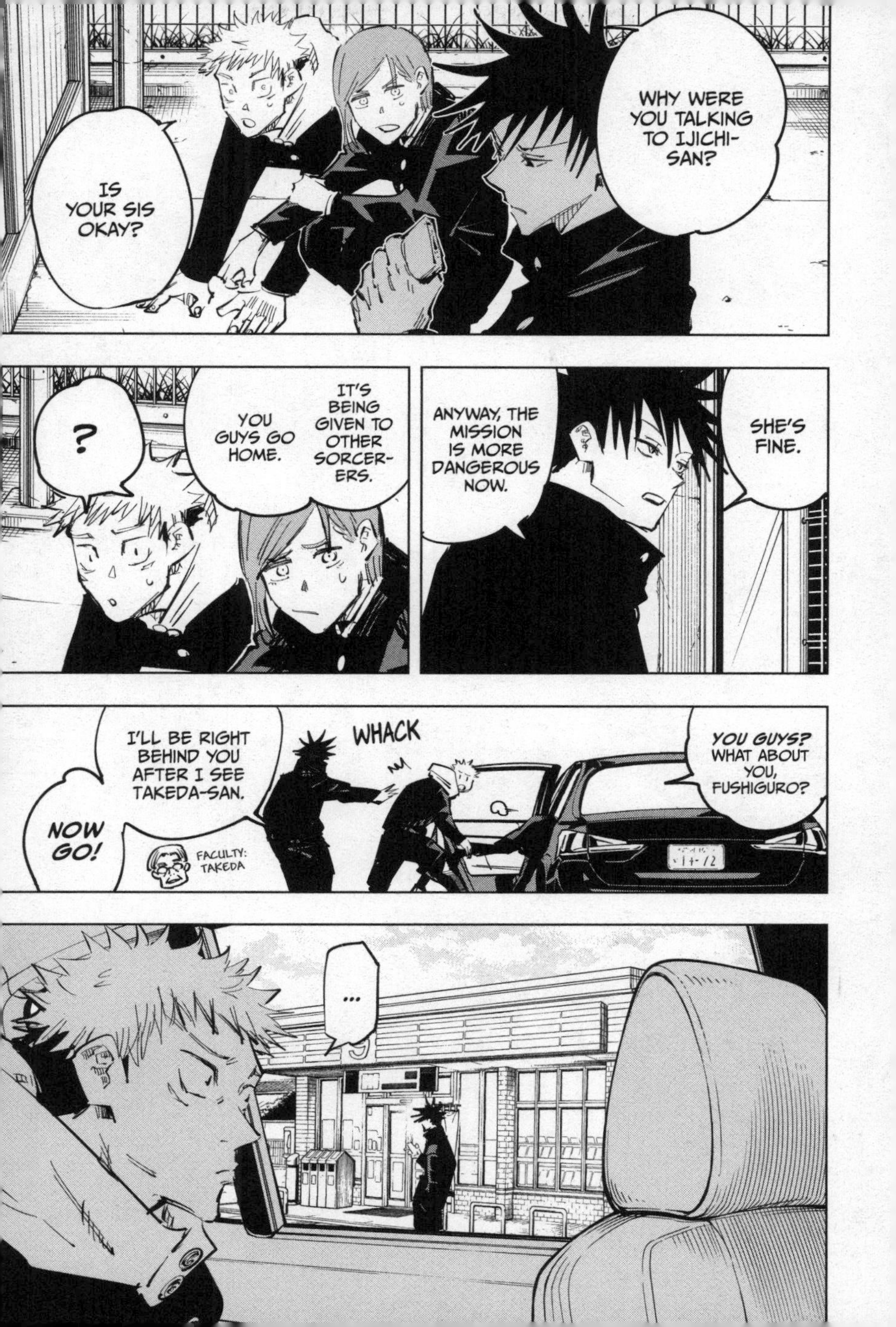

WHY WERE YOU TALKING TO IJICHI-SAN?
IS YOUR SIS OKAY?
SHE'S FINE.
ANYWAY, THE MISSION IS MORE DANGEROUS NOW.
IT'S BEING GIVEN TO OTHER SORCERERS.
YOU GUYS GO HOME.
?
YOU GUYS? WHAT ABOUT YOU, FUSHIGURO?
WHACK
I'LL BE RIGHT BEHIND YOU AFTER I SEE TAKEDA-SAN.
NOW GO!
FACULTY: TAKEDA
...

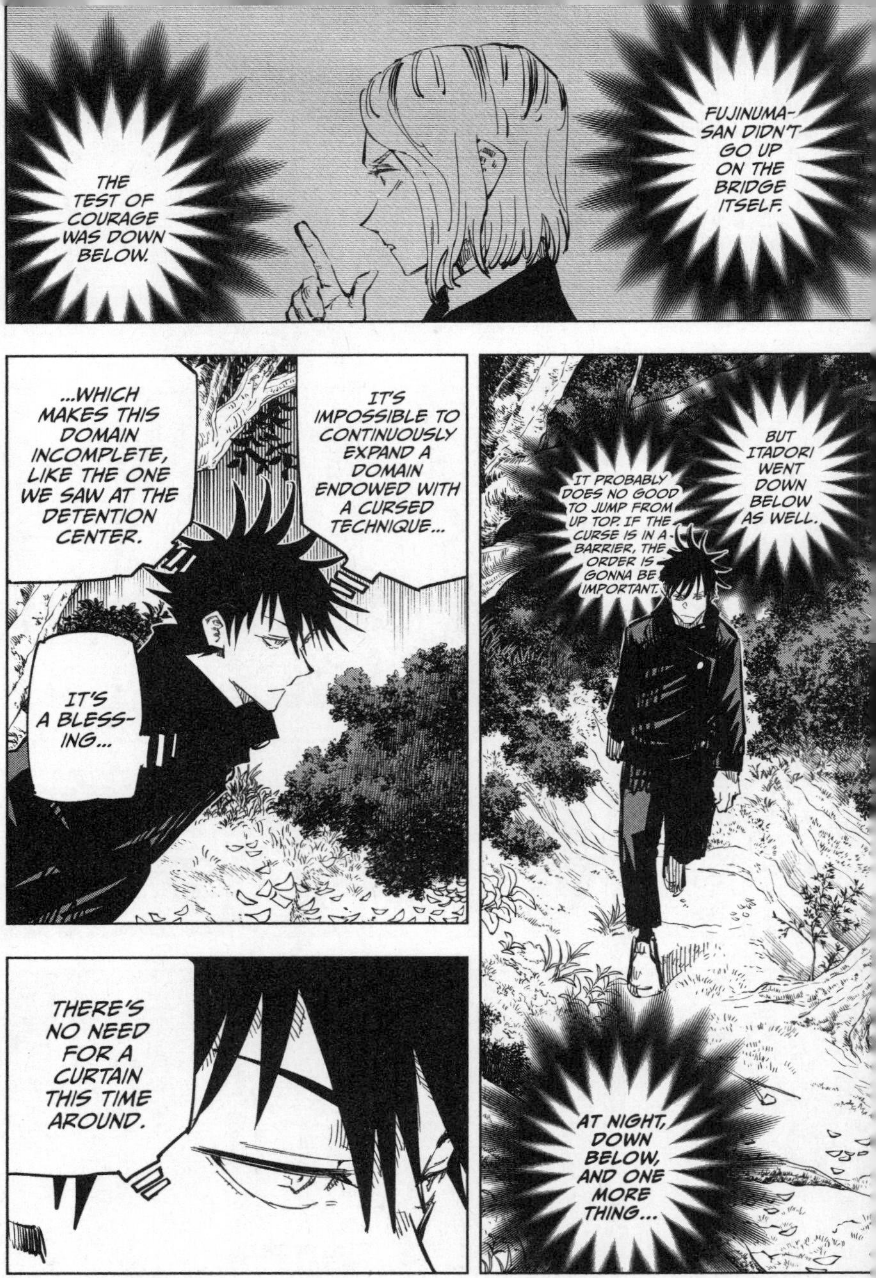
FUJINUMA-SAN DIDN'T GO UP ON THE BRIDGE ITSELF.
THE TEST OF COURAGE WAS DOWN BELOW.
BUT ITADORI WENT DOWN BELOW AS WELL.
IT PROBABLY DOES NO GOOD TO JUMP FROM UP TOP. IF THE CURSE IS IN A BARRIER, THE ORDER IS GONNA BE IMPORTANT.
AT NIGHT, DOWN BELOW, AND ONE MORE THING...
IT'S IMPOSSIBLE TO CONTINUOUSLY EXPAND A DOMAIN ENDOWED WITH A CURSED TECHNIQUE...
...WHICH MAKES THIS DOMAIN INCOMPLETE, LIKE THE ONE WE SAW AT THE DETENTION CENTER.
IT'S A BLESS-ING...
THERE'S NO NEED FOR A CURTAIN THIS TIME AROUND.

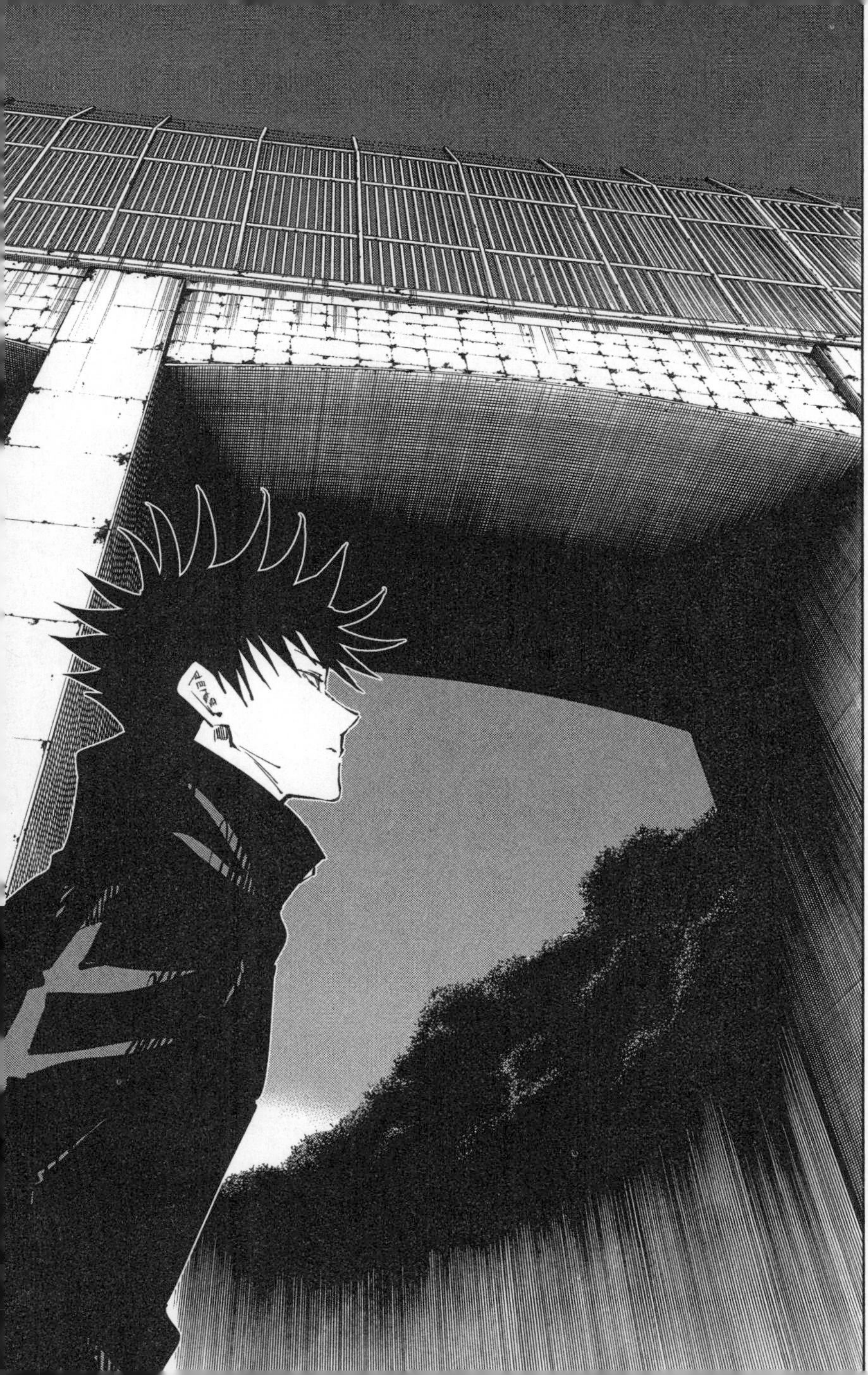

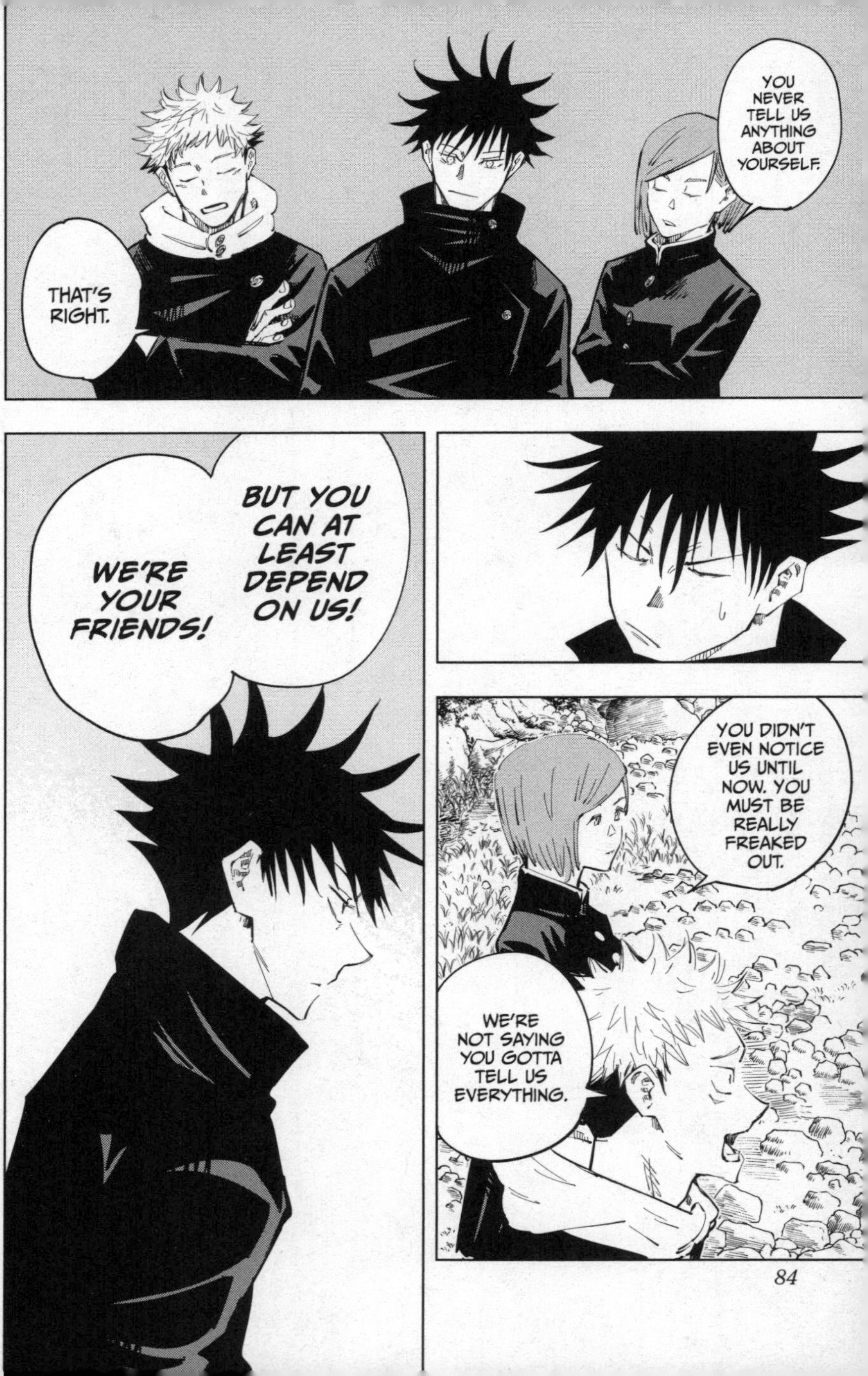

YOU NEVER TELL US ANYTHING ABOUT YOURSELF.
THAT'S RIGHT.
YOU DIDN'T EVEN NOTICE US UNTIL NOW. YOU MUST BE REALLY FREAKED OUT.
WE'RE NOT SAYING YOU GOTTA TELL US EVERYTHING.
BUT YOU CAN AT LEAST DEPEND ON US!
WE'RE YOUR FRIENDS!

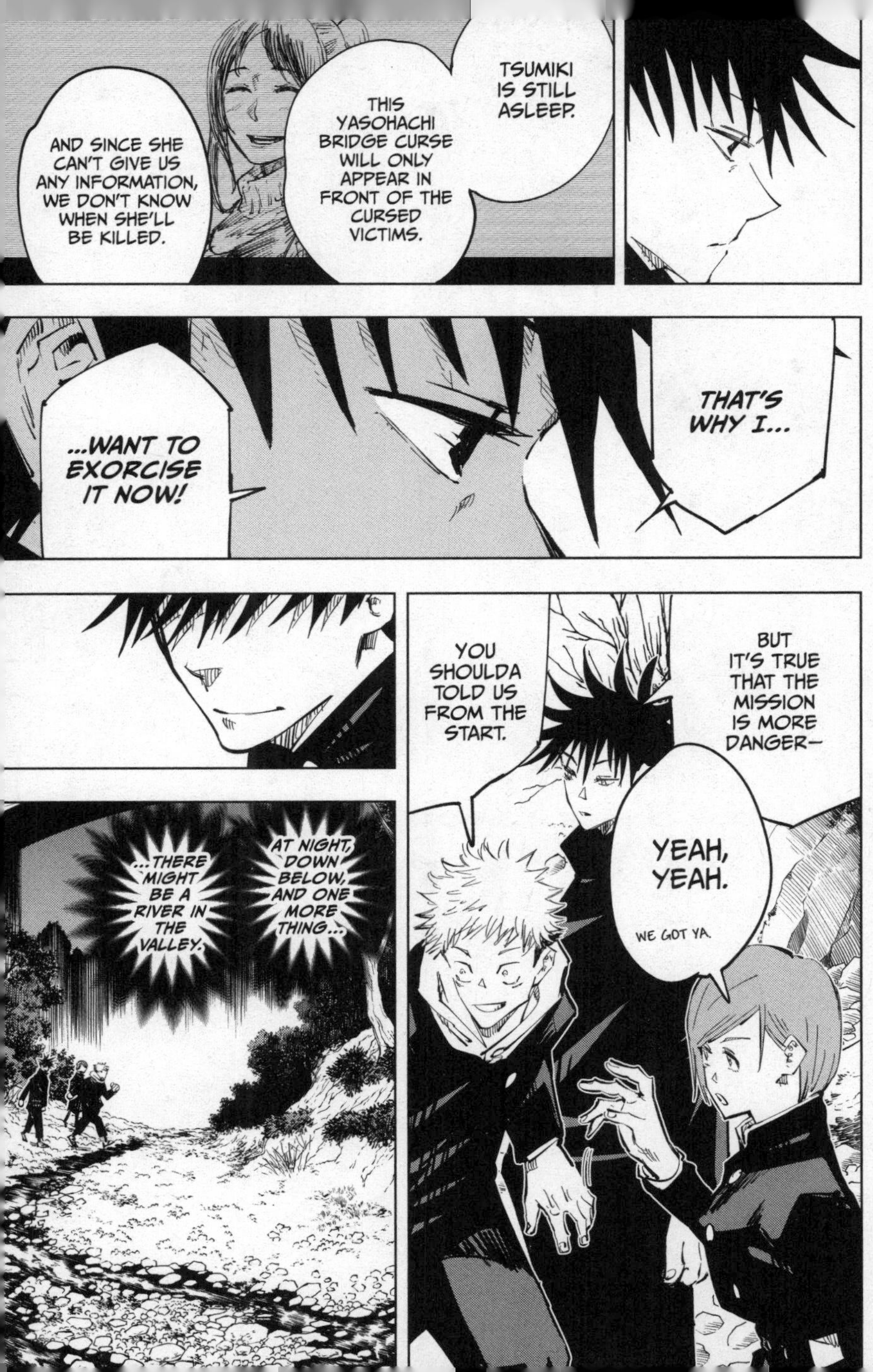
TSUMIKI IS STILL ASLEEP.
THIS YASOHACHI BRIDGE CURSE WILL ONLY APPEAR IN FRONT OF THE CURSED VICTIMS.
AND SINCE SHE CAN'T GIVE US ANY INFORMATION, WE DON'T KNOW WHEN SHE'LL BE KILLED.
THAT'S WHY I...
...WANT TO EXORCISE IT NOW!
BUT IT'S TRUE THAT THE MISSION IS MORE DANGER—
YOU SHOULDA TOLD US FROM THE START.
YEAH, YEAH.
WE GOT YA.
AT NIGHT, DOWN BELOW, AND ONE MORE THING...
...THERE MIGHT BE A RIVER IN THE VALLEY.

WOOO
MR

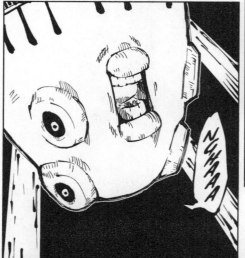

NGHAAAA

CROSSING A RIVER AND BARRIERS. JUST THAT ACT ALONE...

BZZT

...HAS SIGNIFICANT MEANING IN JUJUTSU.

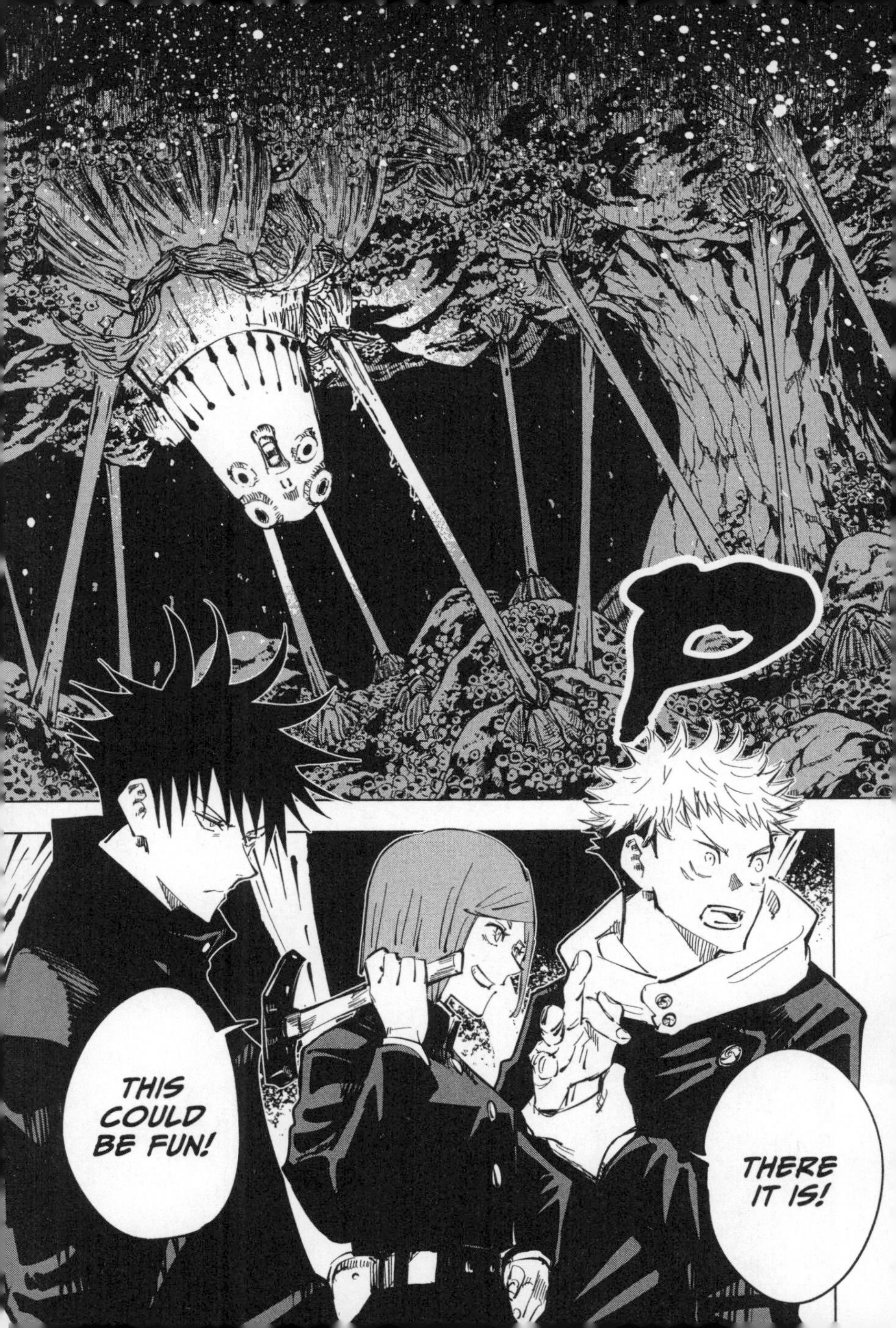
P
THERE IT IS!
THIS COULD BE FUN!

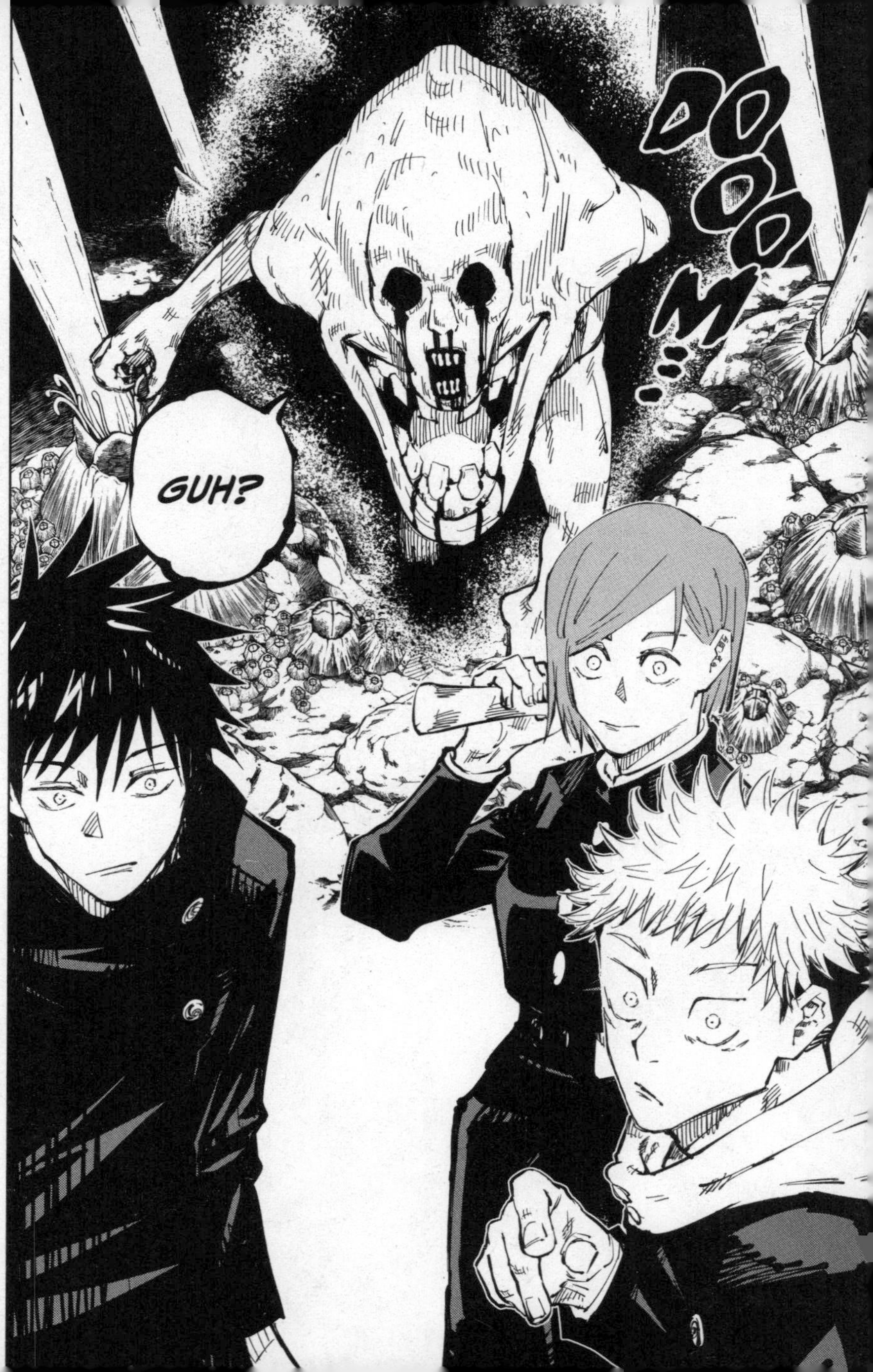
DOOOOM...
GUH?

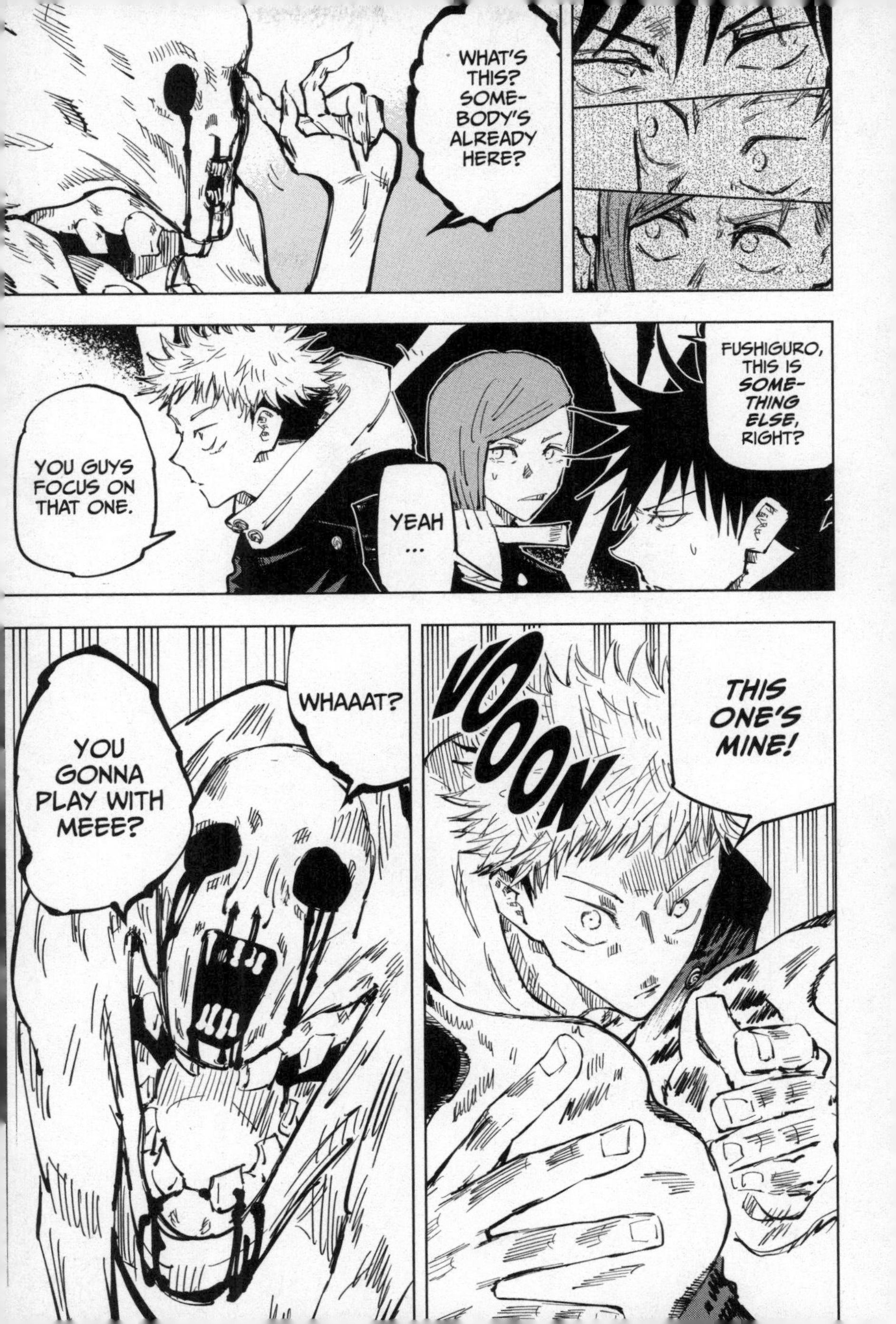
WHAT'S THIS? SOME-BODY'S ALREADY HERE?
FUSHIGURO, THIS IS SOME-THING ELSE, RIGHT?
YEAH ...
YOU GUYS FOCUS ON THAT ONE.
THIS ONE'S MINE!
VOOON
WHAAAT?
YOU GONNA PLAY WITH MEEE?

GOODWILL EVENT INJURY METER

HEAVY DAMAGE

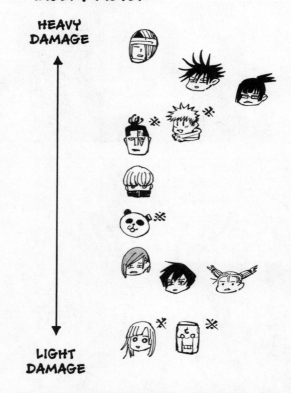

LIGHT DAMAGE

THOSE WITH AN ASTERISK DIDN'T RECEIVE TREATMENT FROM IEIRI.

I'M BEAT.

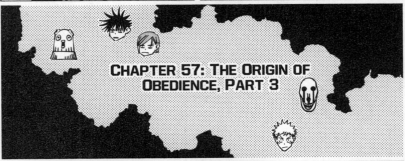

CHAPTER 57: THE ORIGIN OF OBEDIENCE, PART 3

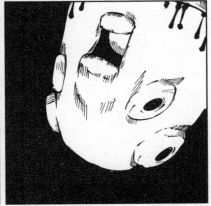

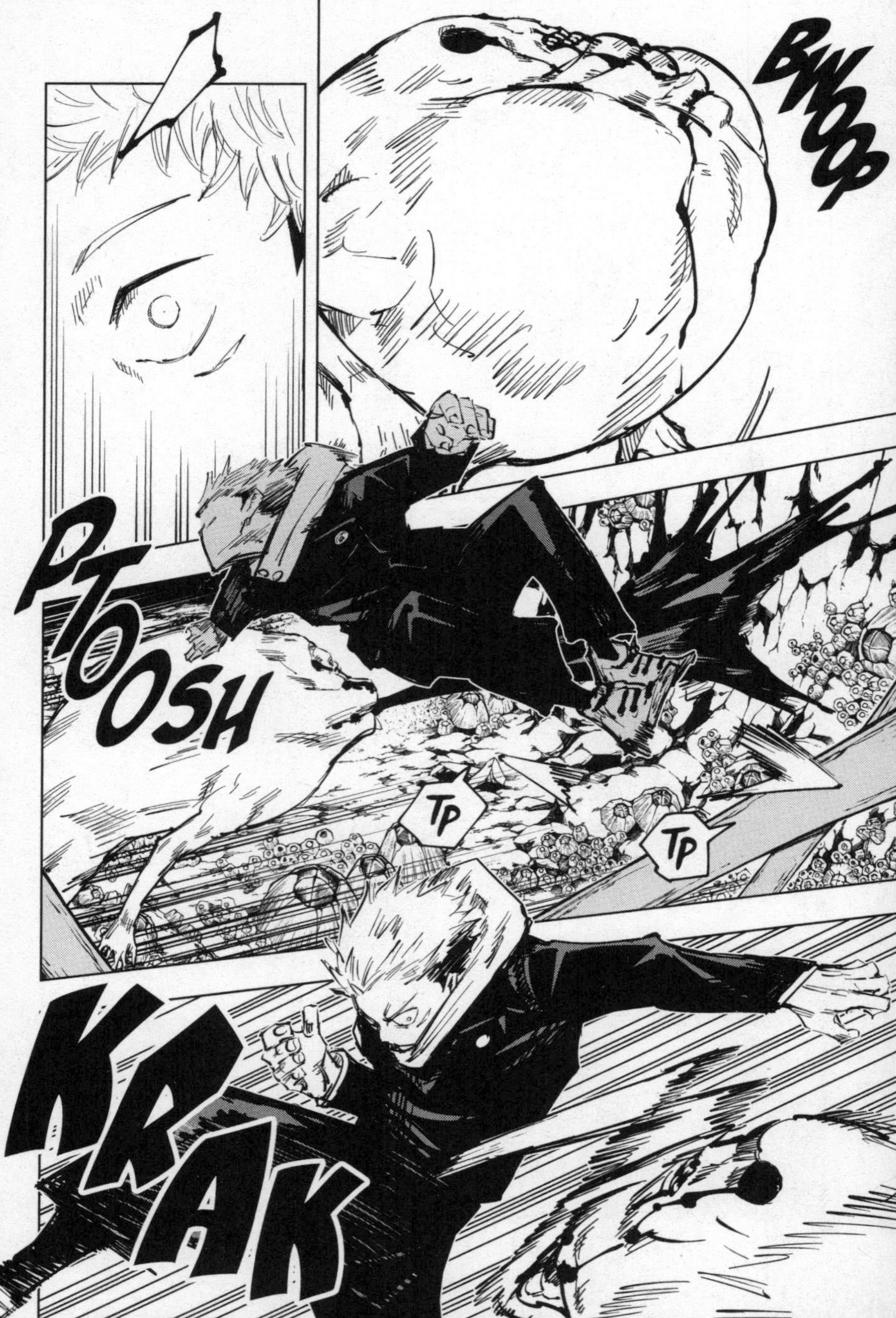
BWOOOP
PTOOSH
TP
TP
KRAK

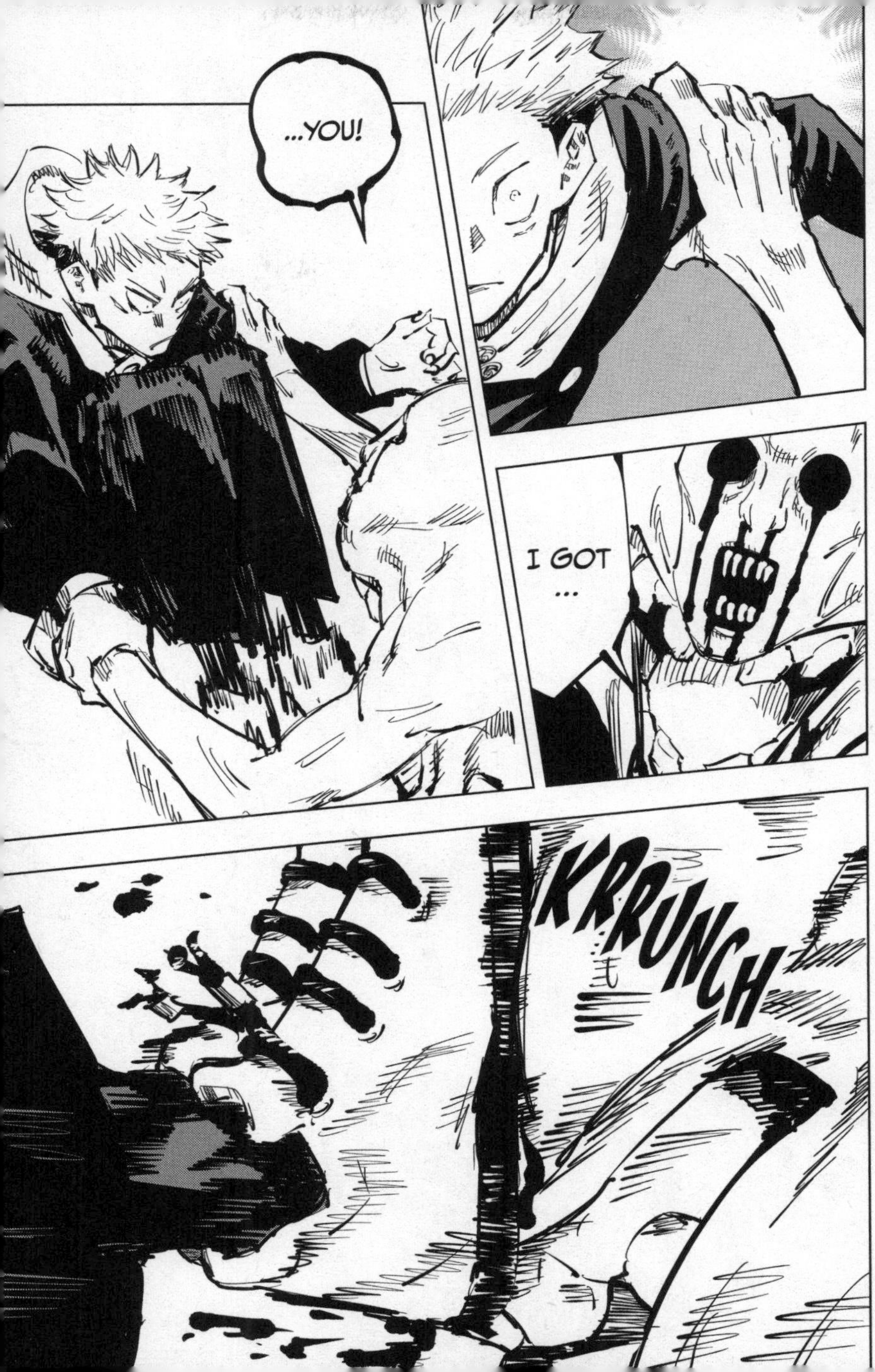
I GOT ...
...YOU!
KRRUNCH

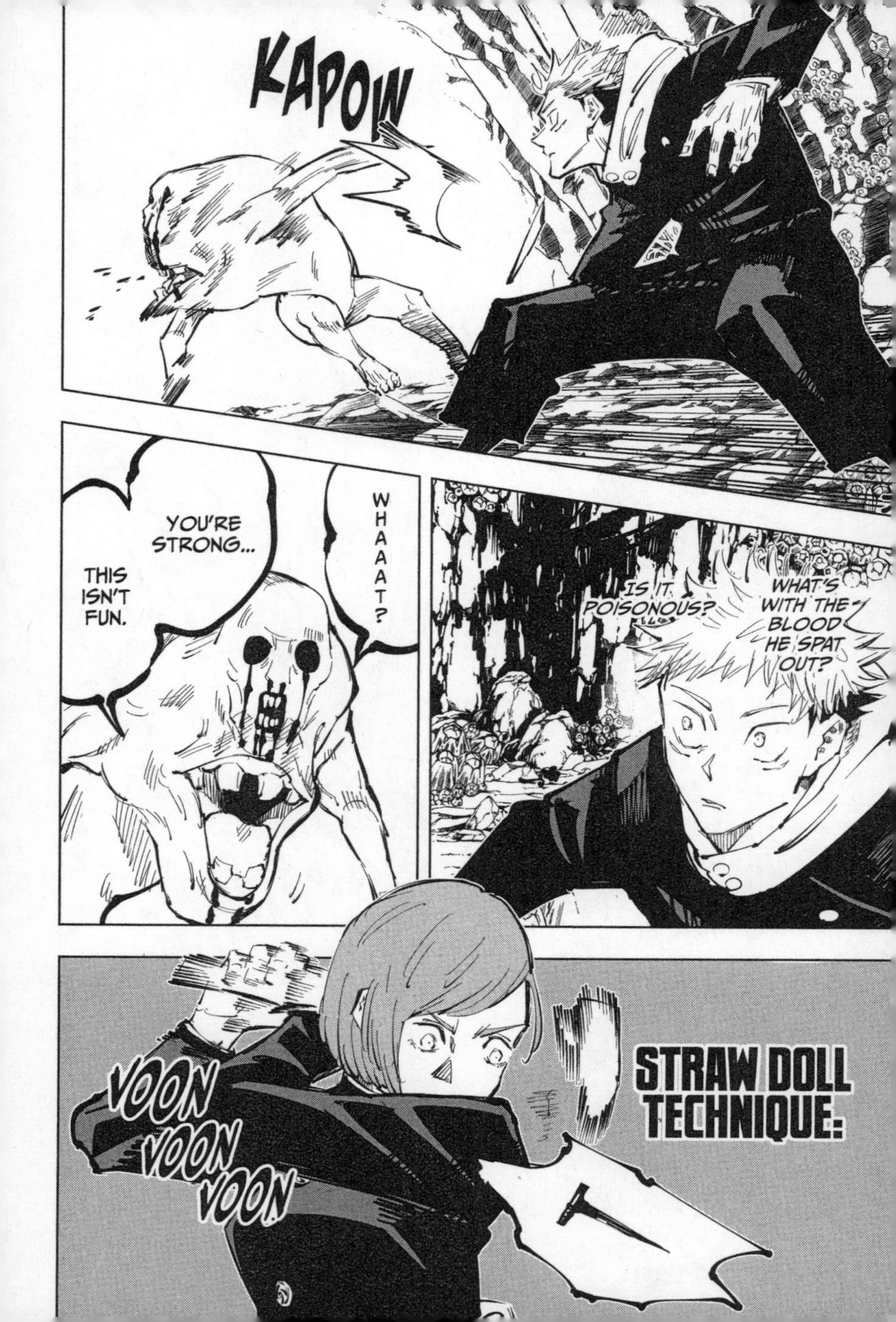
KAPOW
WHAT'S WITH THE BLOOD HE SPAT OUT?
IS IT POISONOUS?
WHAAAT?
YOU'RE STRONG...
THIS ISN'T FUN.
STRAW DOLL TECHNIQUE.
VOON VOON VOON

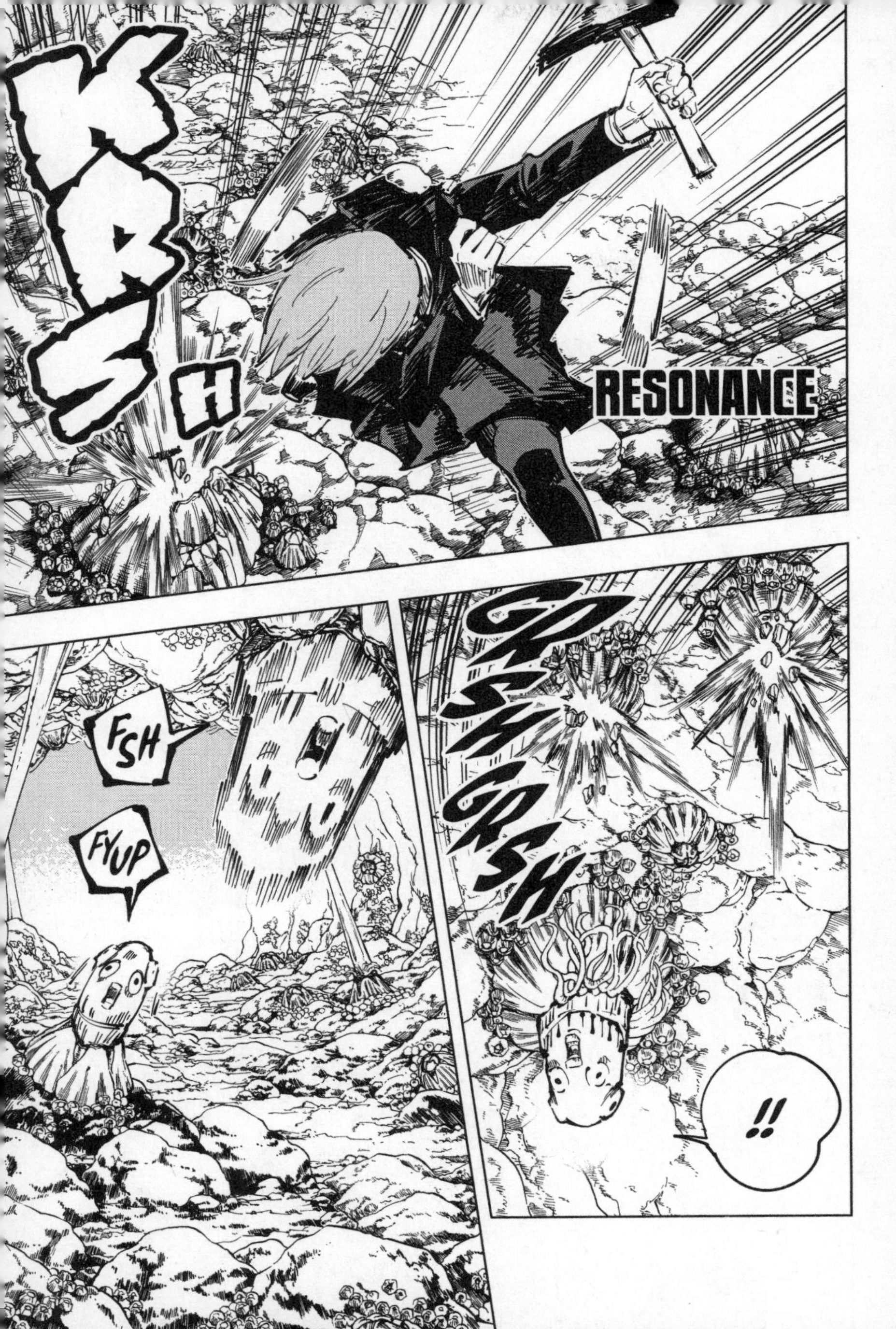
KRSH
RESONANCE
GRSH GRSH
!!
FSH
FYUP

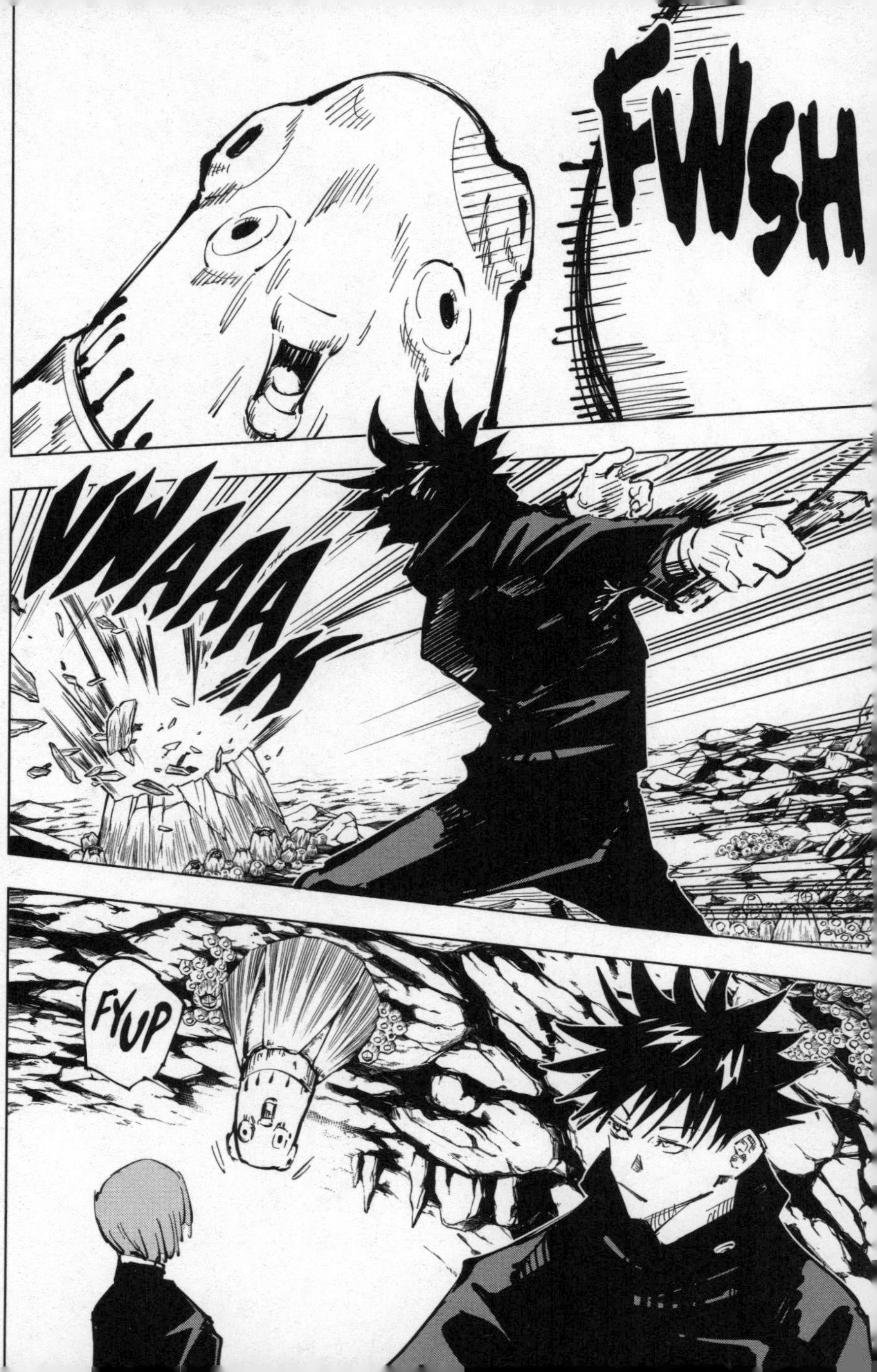
FWSH
VWAAAK
FYUP

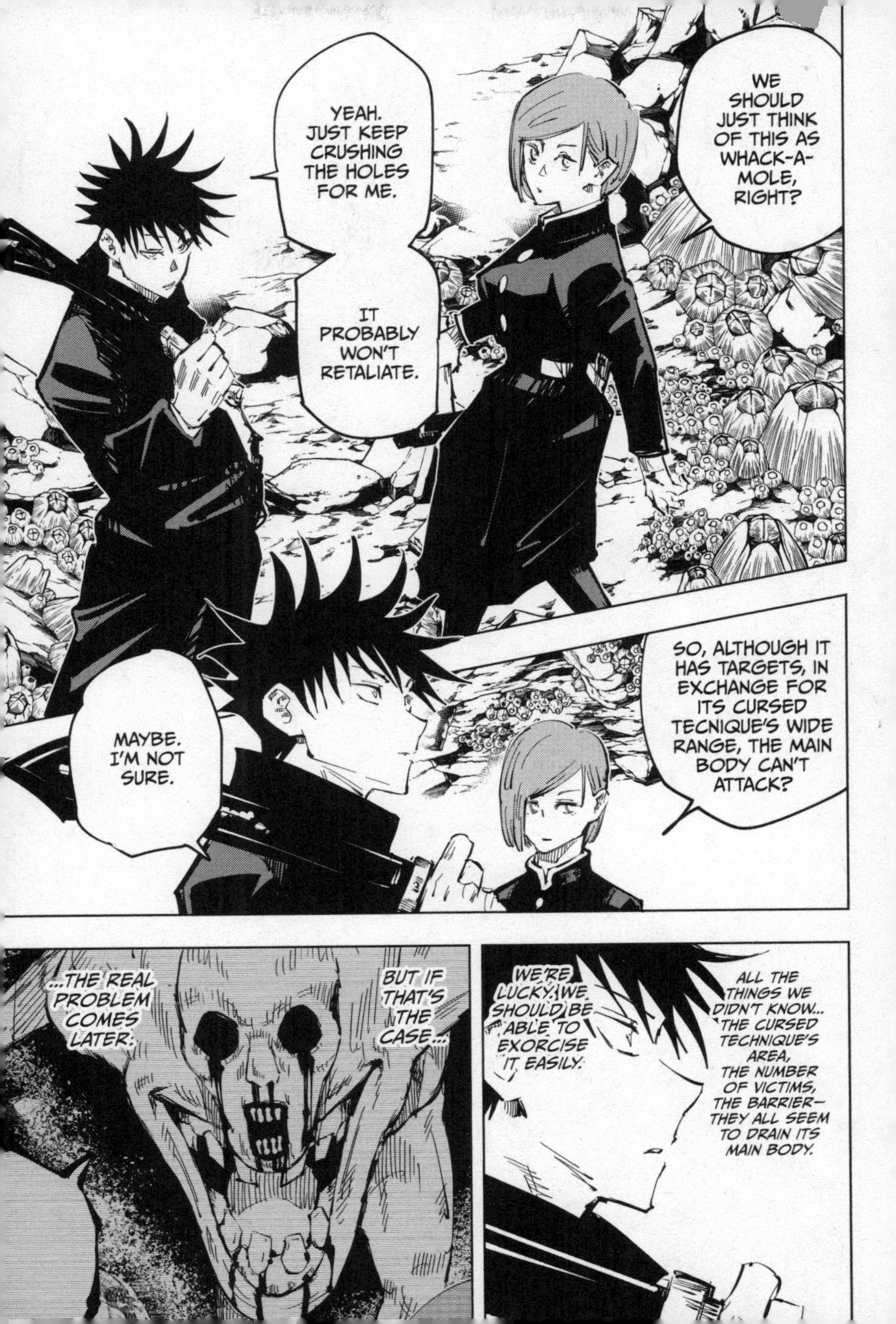
WE SHOULD JUST THINK OF THIS AS WHACK-A-MOLE, RIGHT?
YEAH. JUST KEEP CRUSHING THE HOLES FOR ME.
IT PROBABLY WON'T RETALIATE.
SO, ALTHOUGH IT HAS TARGETS, IN EXCHANGE FOR ITS CURSED TECNIQUE'S WIDE RANGE, THE MAIN BODY CAN'T ATTACK?
MAYBE. I'M NOT SURE.
ALL THE THINGS WE DIDN'T KNOW... THE CURSED TECHNIQUE'S AREA, THE NUMBER OF VICTIMS, THE BARRIER— THEY ALL SEEM TO DRAIN ITS MAIN BODY.
WE'RE LUCKY. WE SHOULD BE ABLE TO EXORCISE IT EASILY.
BUT IF THAT'S THE CASE...
...THE REAL PROBLEM COMES LATER.

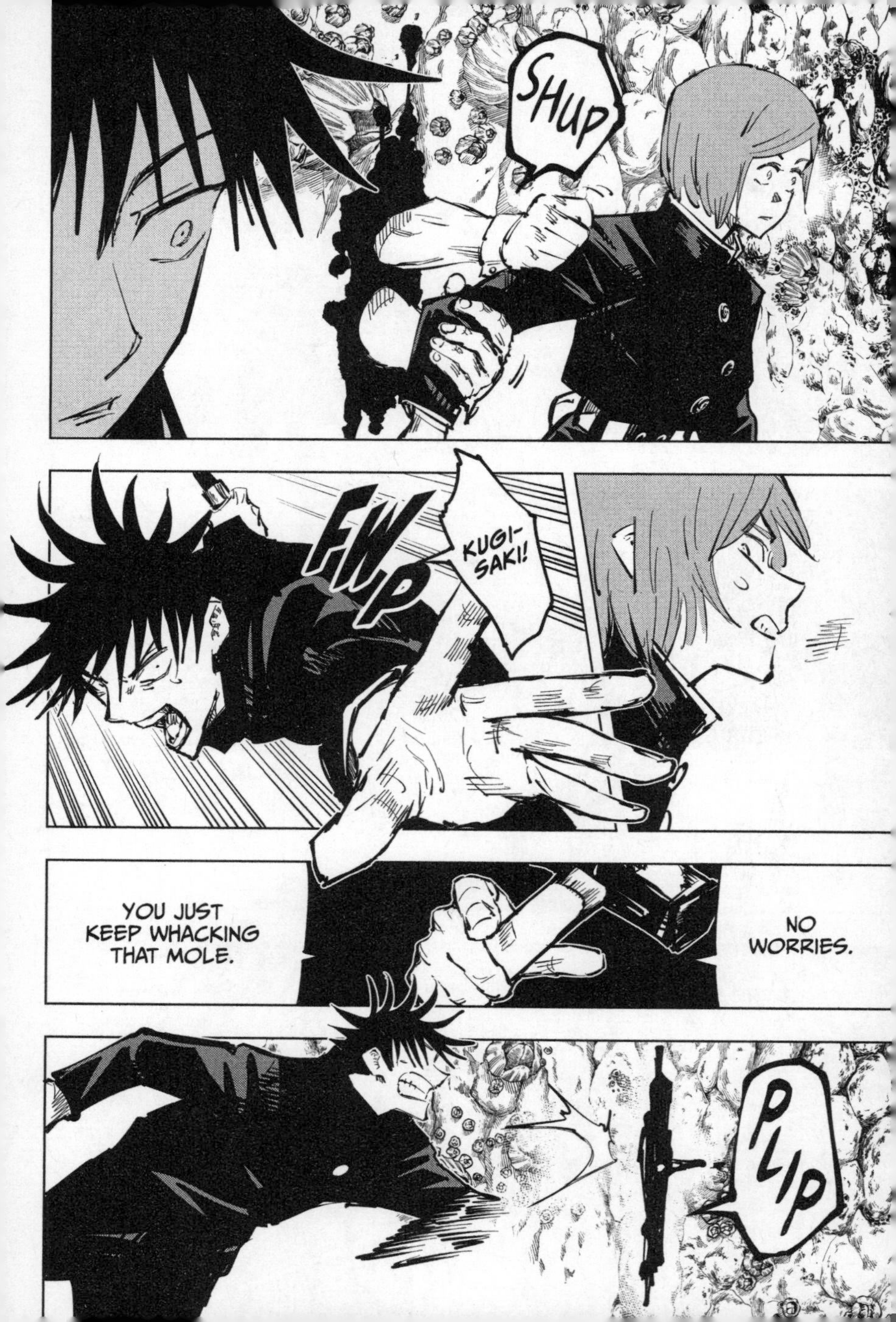
SHUP
FWP
KUGI-SAKI!
NO WORRIES.
YOU JUST KEEP WHACKING THAT MOLE.
PLIP

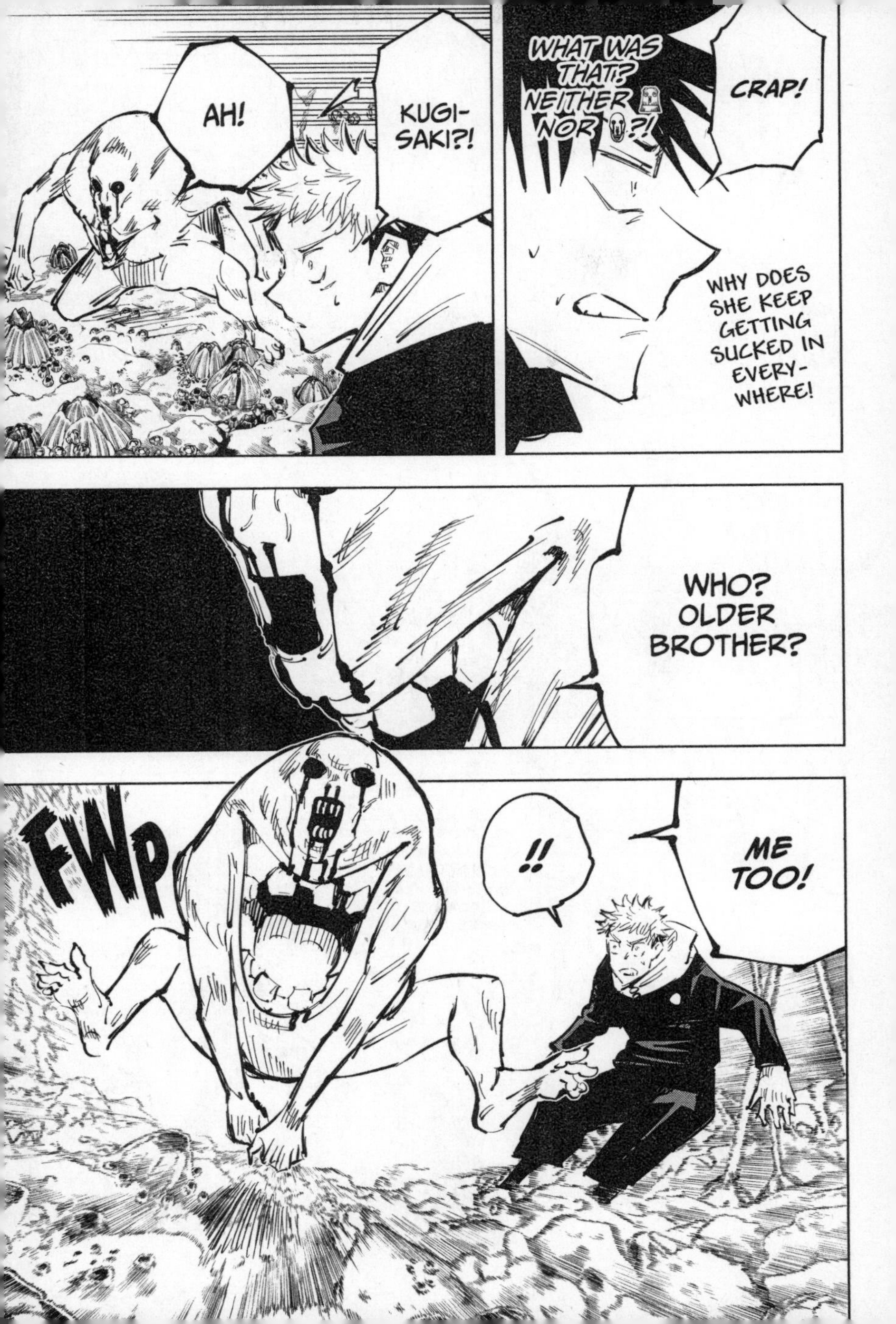
CRAP!
WHAT WAS THAT? NEITHER NOR ?!
WHY DOES SHE KEEP GETTING SUCKED IN EVERY-WHERE!
KUGI-SAKI?!
AH!
WHO? OLDER BROTHER?
ME TOO!
!!
FWP

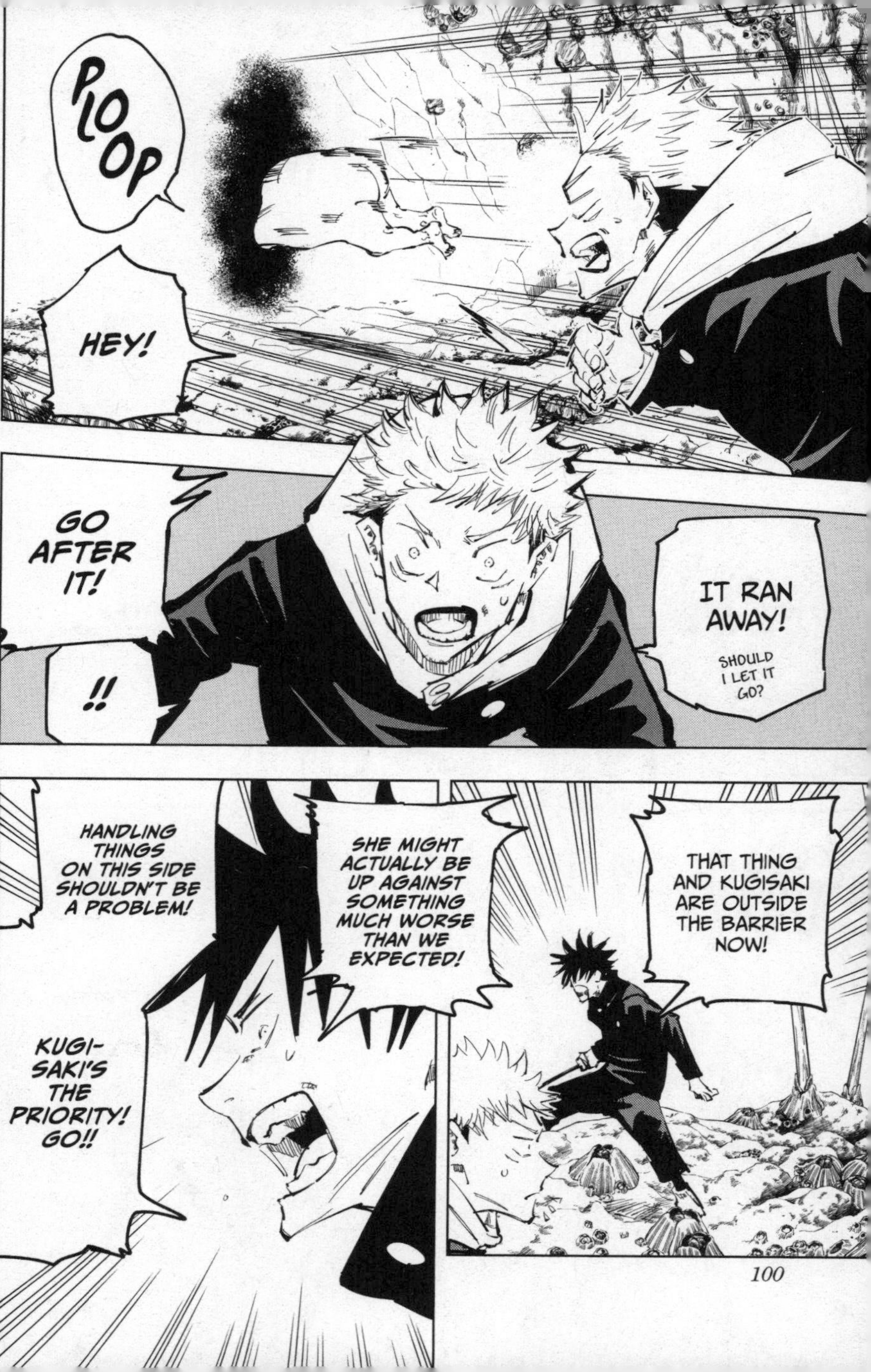
PLOOP
HEY!
IT RAN AWAY!
SHOULD I LET IT GO?
GO AFTER IT!
!!
THAT THING AND KUGISAKI ARE OUTSIDE THE BARRIER NOW!
SHE MIGHT ACTUALLY BE UP AGAINST SOMETHING MUCH WORSE THAN WE EXPECTED!
HANDLING THINGS ON THIS SIDE SHOULDN'T BE A PROBLEM!
KUGI-SAKI'S THE PRIORITY! GO!!

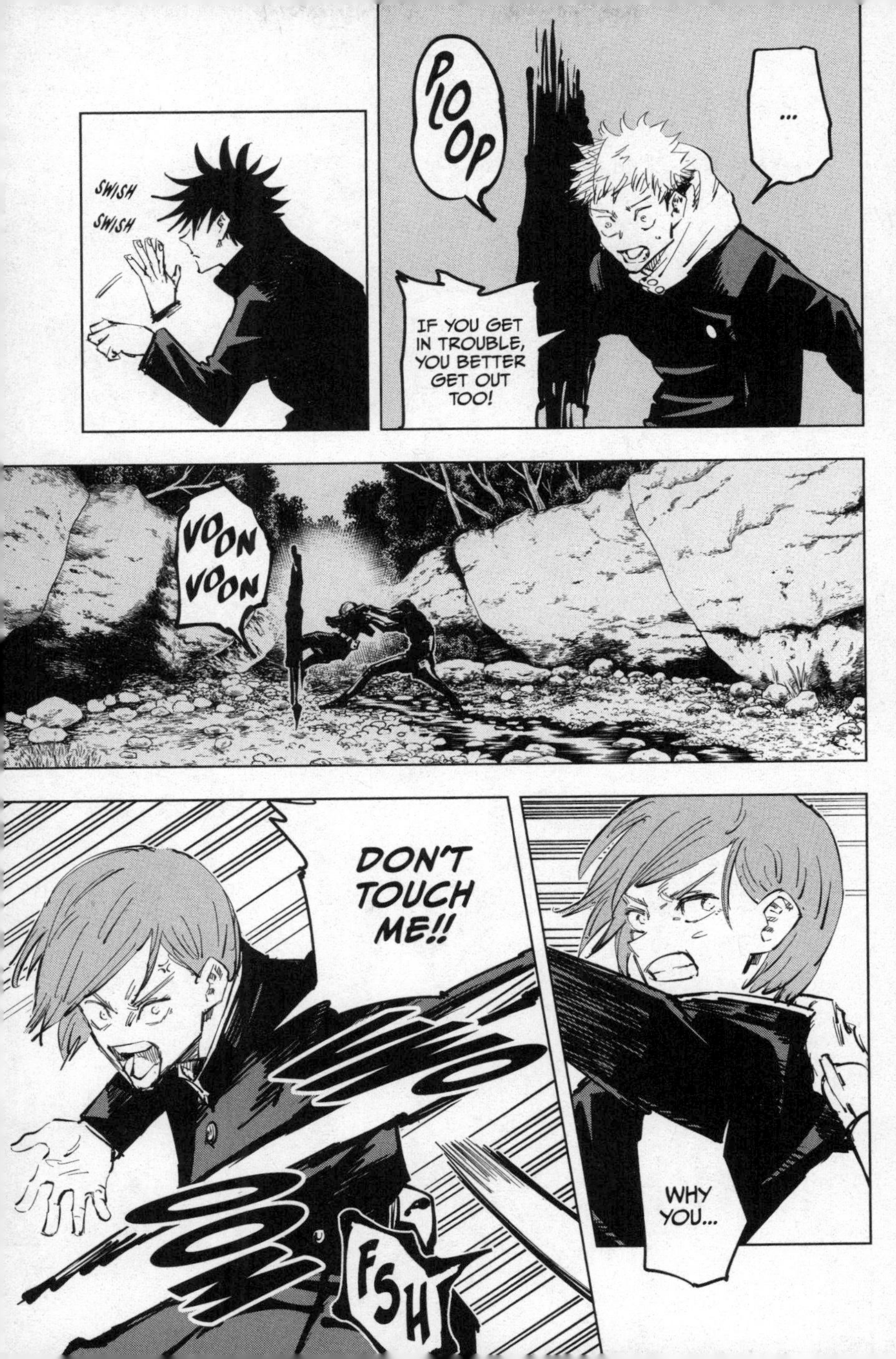
...
PLOOP
IF YOU GET IN TROUBLE, YOU BETTER GET OUT TOO!
SWISH
SWISH
VOON VOON
WHY YOU...
DON'T TOUCH ME!!
FSH

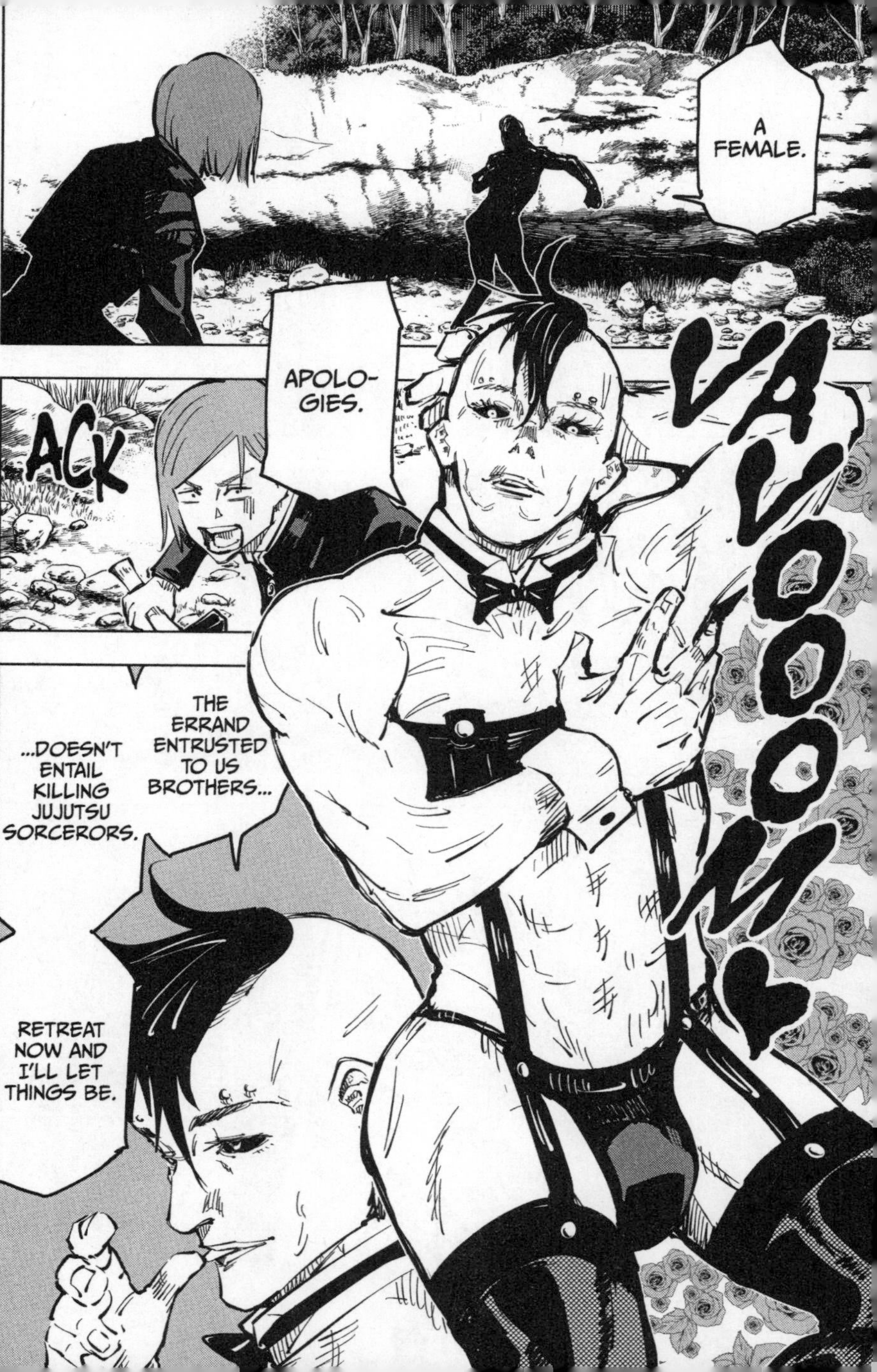
A FEMALE.
APOLO-GIES.
VAVOOOM
ACK
THE ERRAND ENTRUSTED TO US BROTHERS...
...DOESN'T ENTAIL KILLING JUJUTSU SORCERORS.
RETREAT NOW AND I'LL LET THINGS BE.

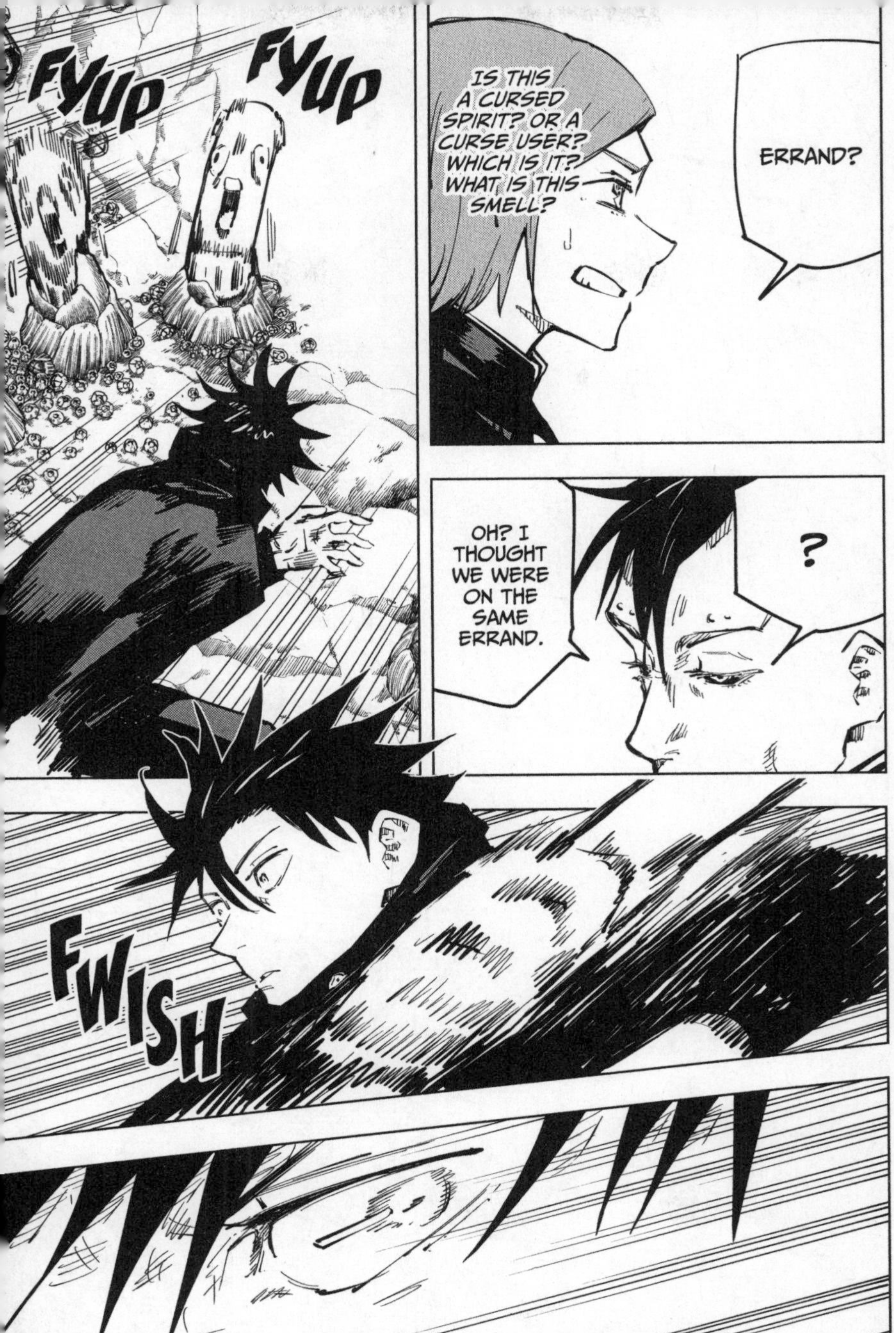
ERRAND?
IS THIS A CURSED SPIRIT? OR A CURSE USER? WHICH IS IT? WHAT IS THIS SMELL?
?
OH? I THOUGHT WE WERE ON THE SAME ERRAND.
FYUP
FYUP
FWISH

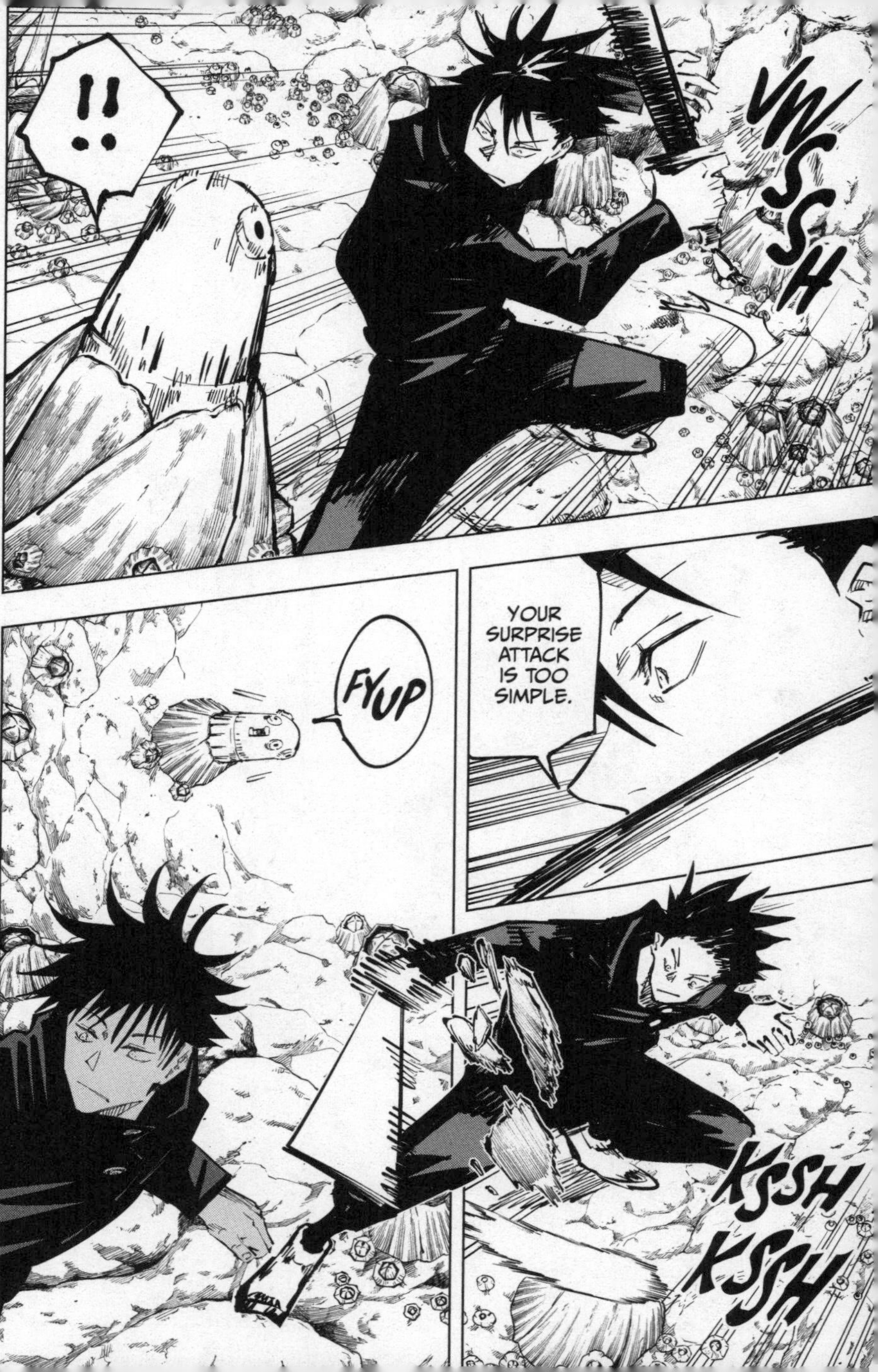
VWSSH
!!
YOUR SURPRISE ATTACK IS TOO SIMPLE.
KSH KSH
FYUP

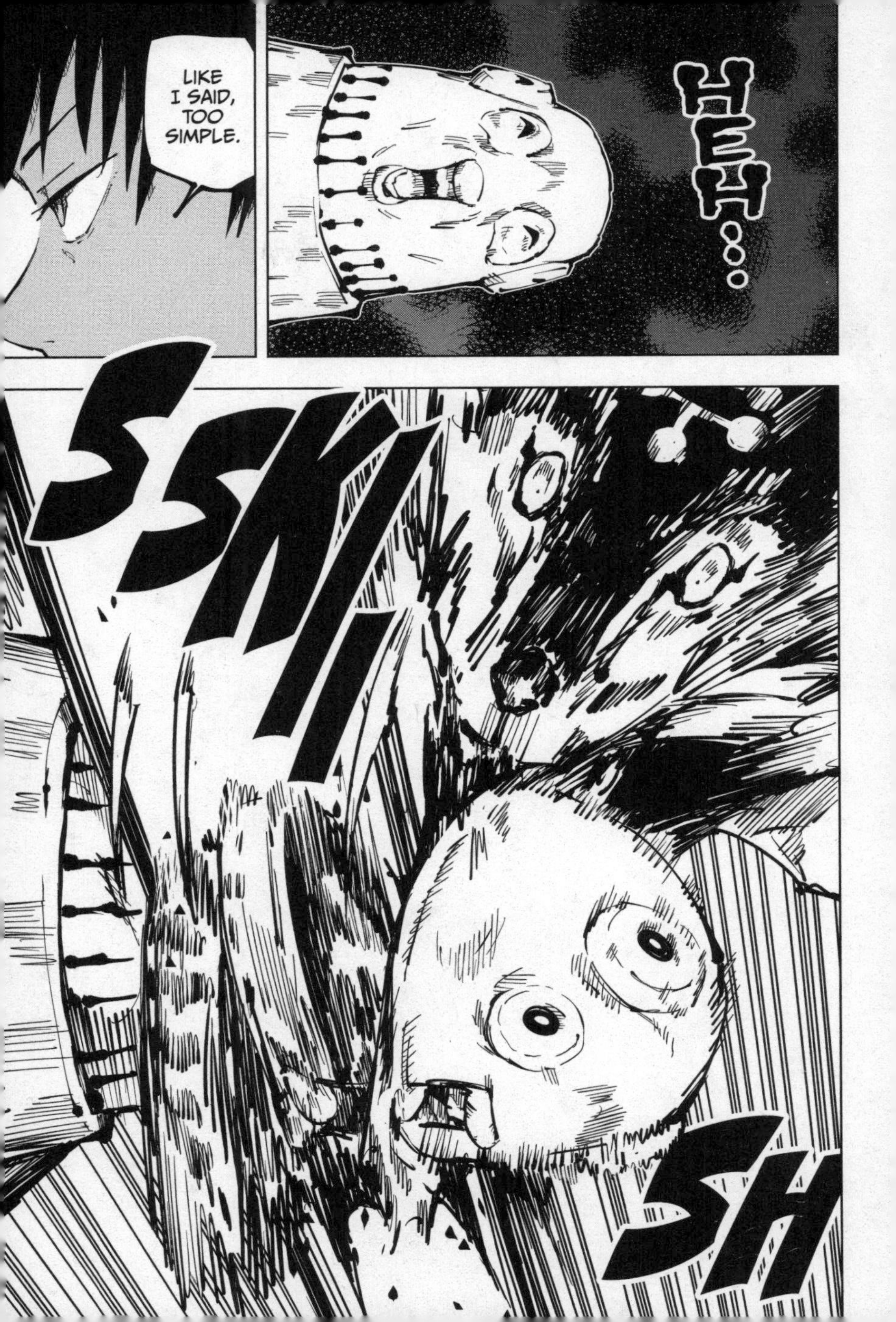
HEH...
LIKE I SAID, TOO SIMPLE.
SH

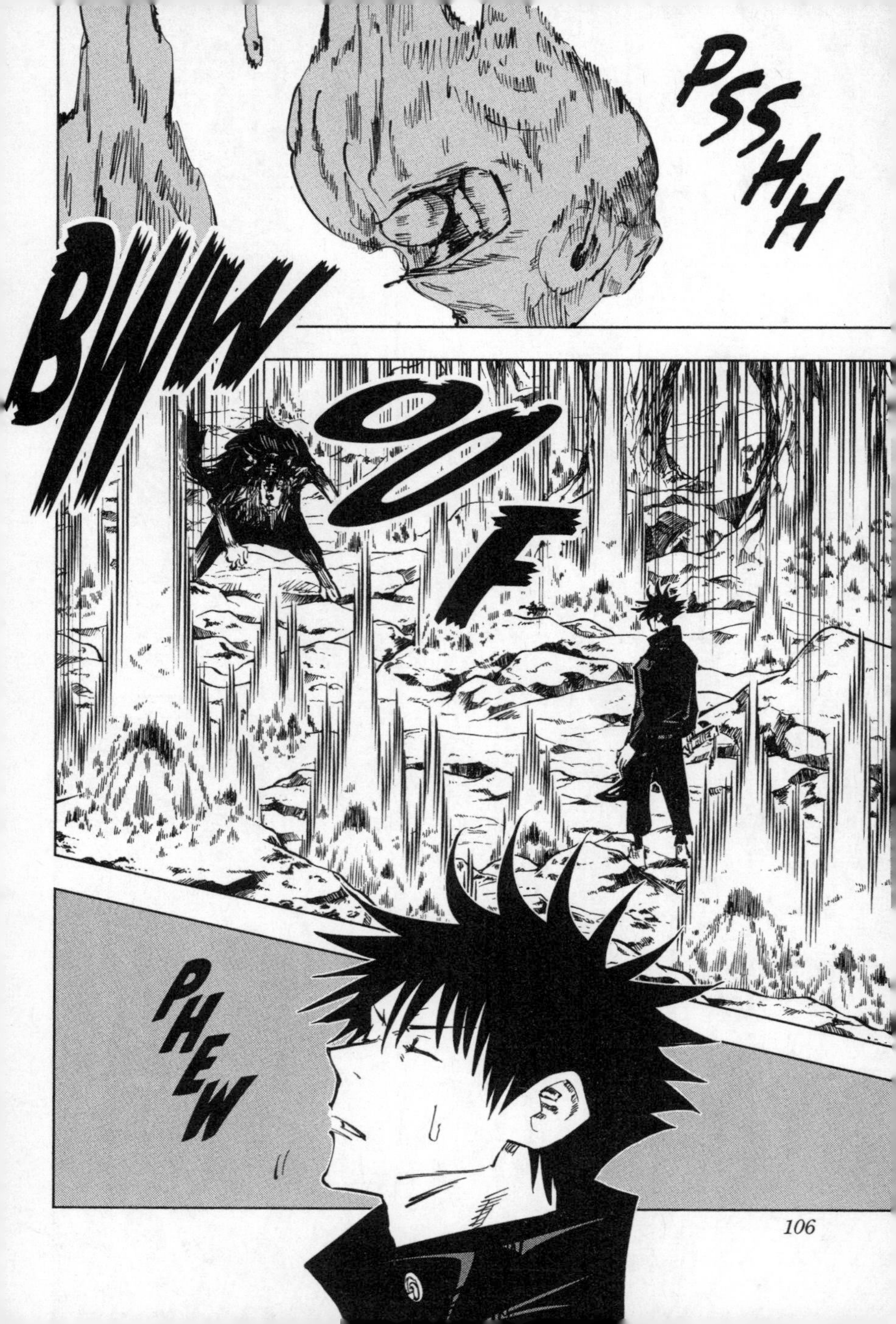
PSSHH
BWOOF
PHEW

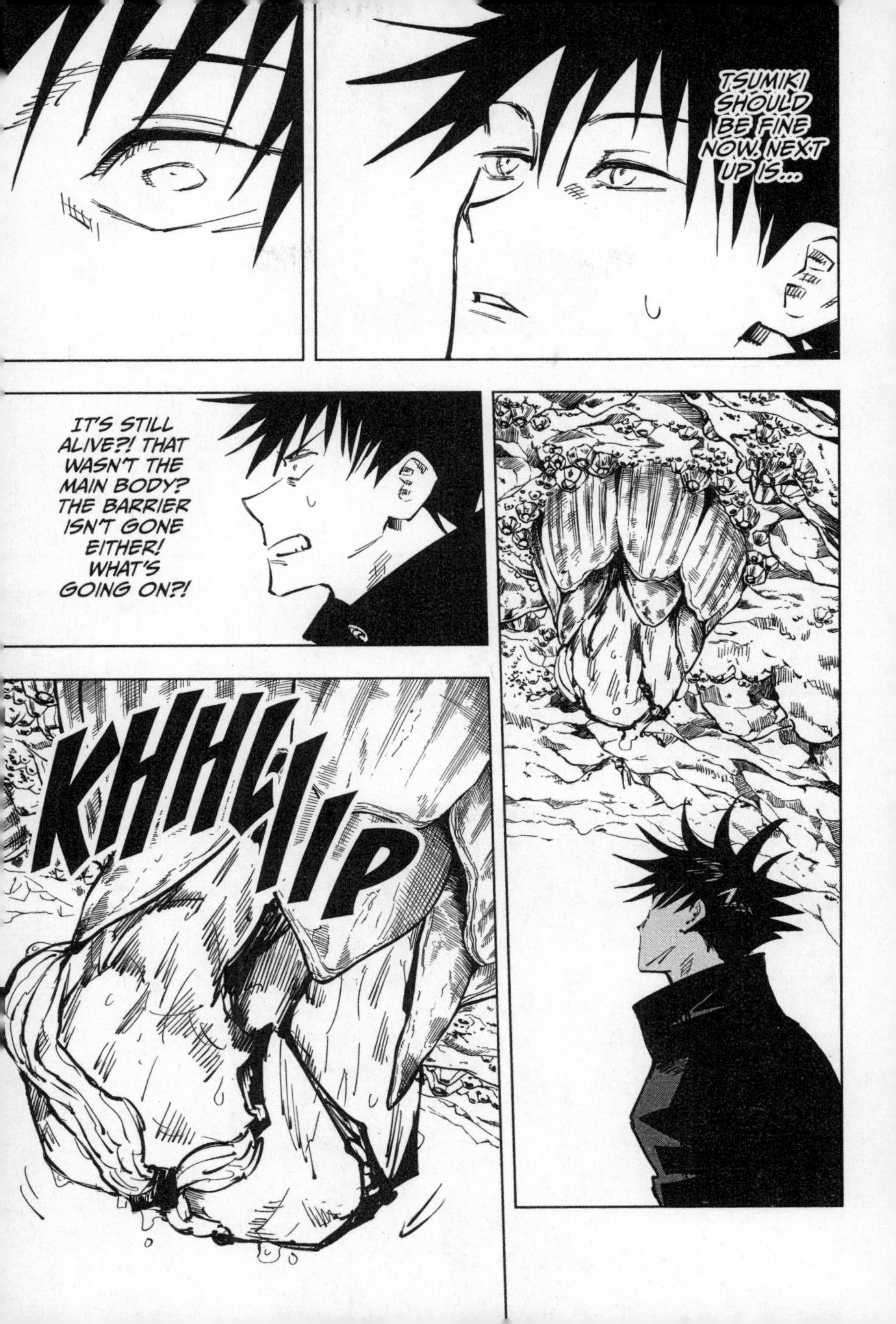
TSUMIKI SHOULD BE FINE NOW. NEXT UP IS...
IT'S STILL ALIVE?! THAT WASN'T THE MAIN BODY? THE BARRIER ISN'T GONE EITHER! WHAT'S GOING ON?!

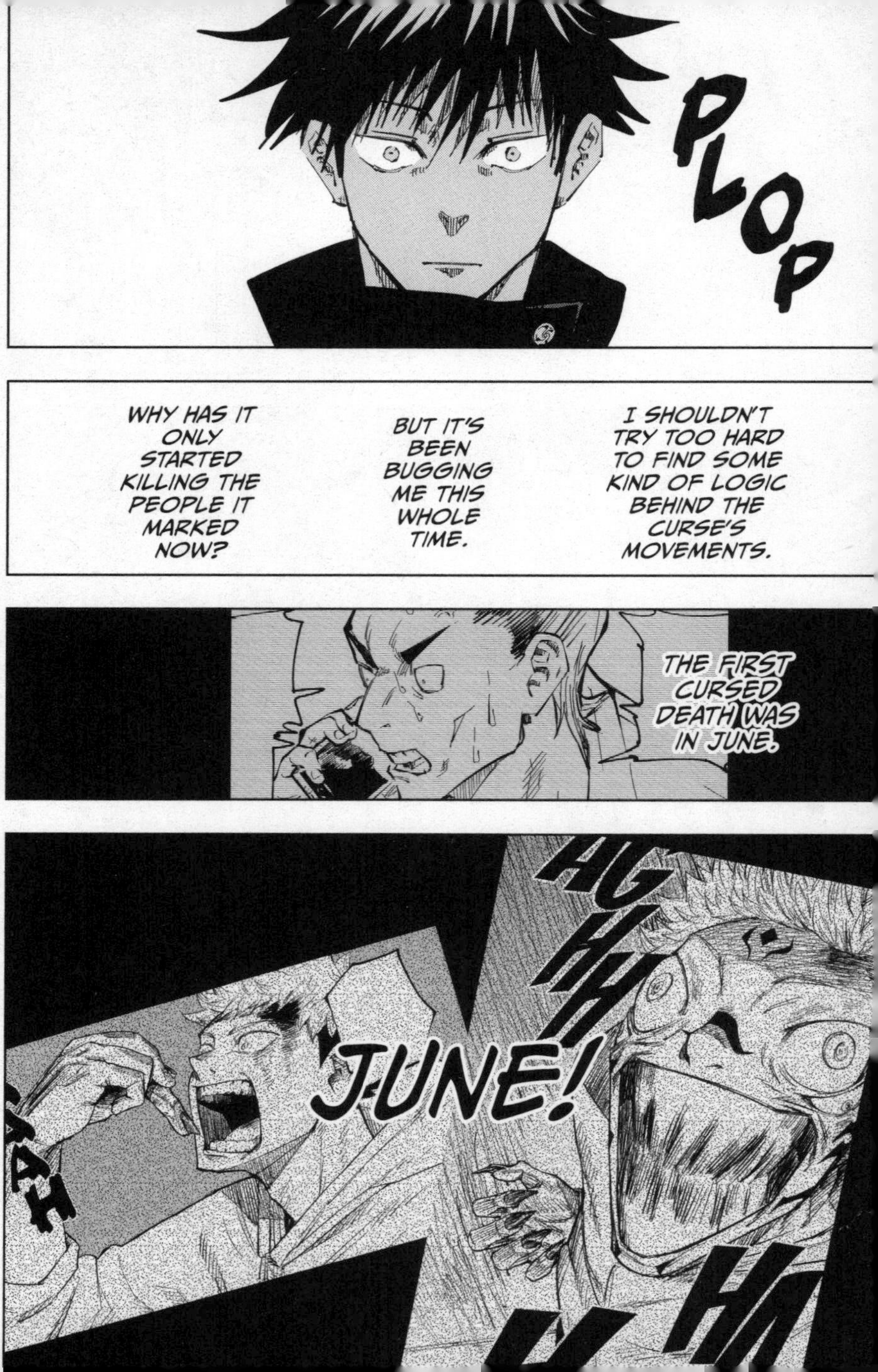
PLOP
I SHOULDN'T TRY TOO HARD TO FIND SOME KIND OF LOGIC BEHIND THE CURSE'S MOVEMENTS.
BUT IT'S BEEN BUGGING ME THIS WHOLE TIME.
WHY HAS IT ONLY STARTED KILLING THE PEOPLE IT MARKED NOW?
THE FIRST CURSED DEATH WAS IN JUNE.
JUNE!

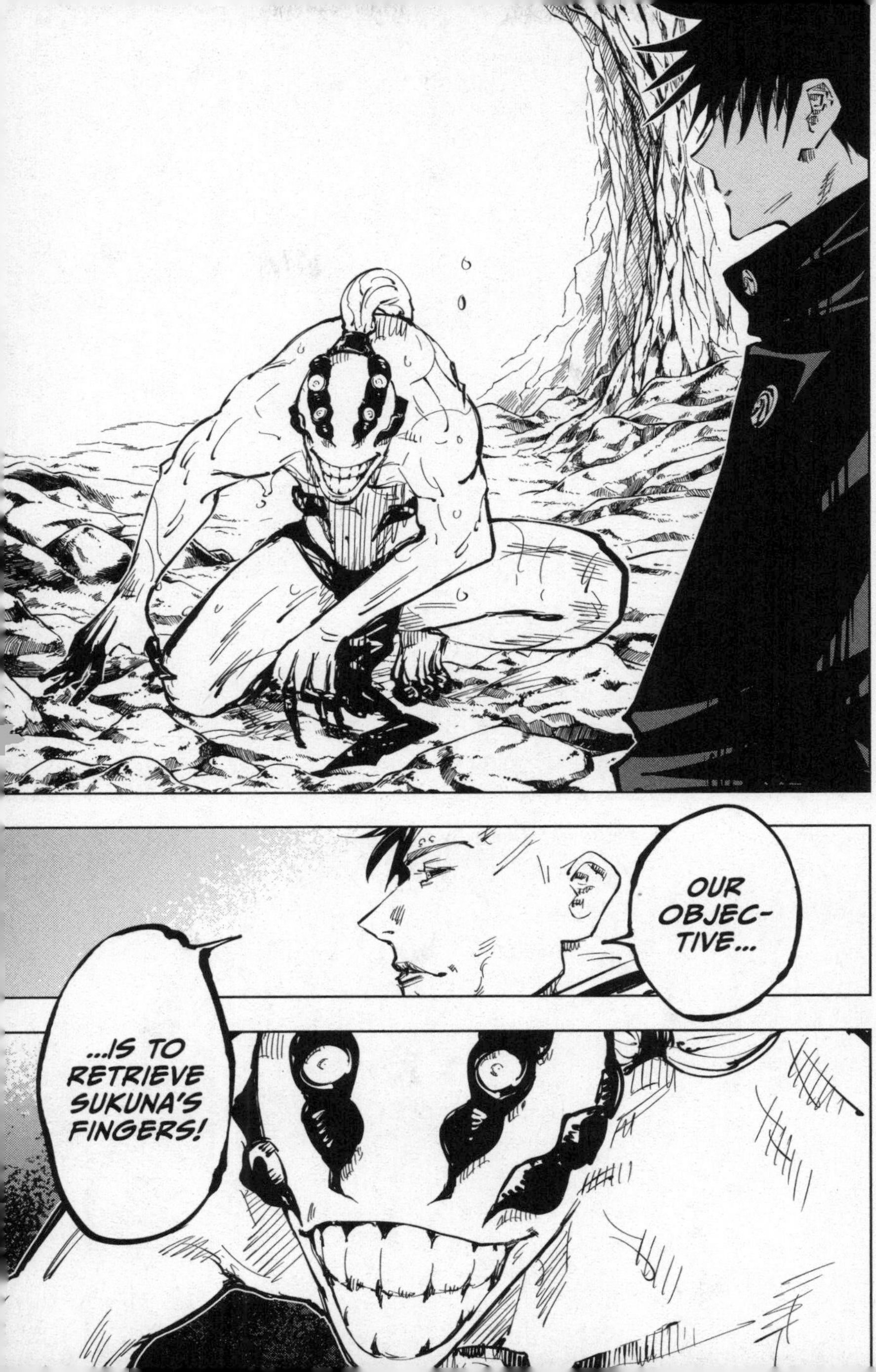
OUR OBJECTIVE...
...IS TO RETRIEVE SUKUNA'S FINGERS!

YOSHINOBU
GAKUGANJI (76 YEARS OLD)

- His mysterious eyebrows change in length depending on his mood.

- He loves Jimi Hendrix.

- He's looking for a drummer.

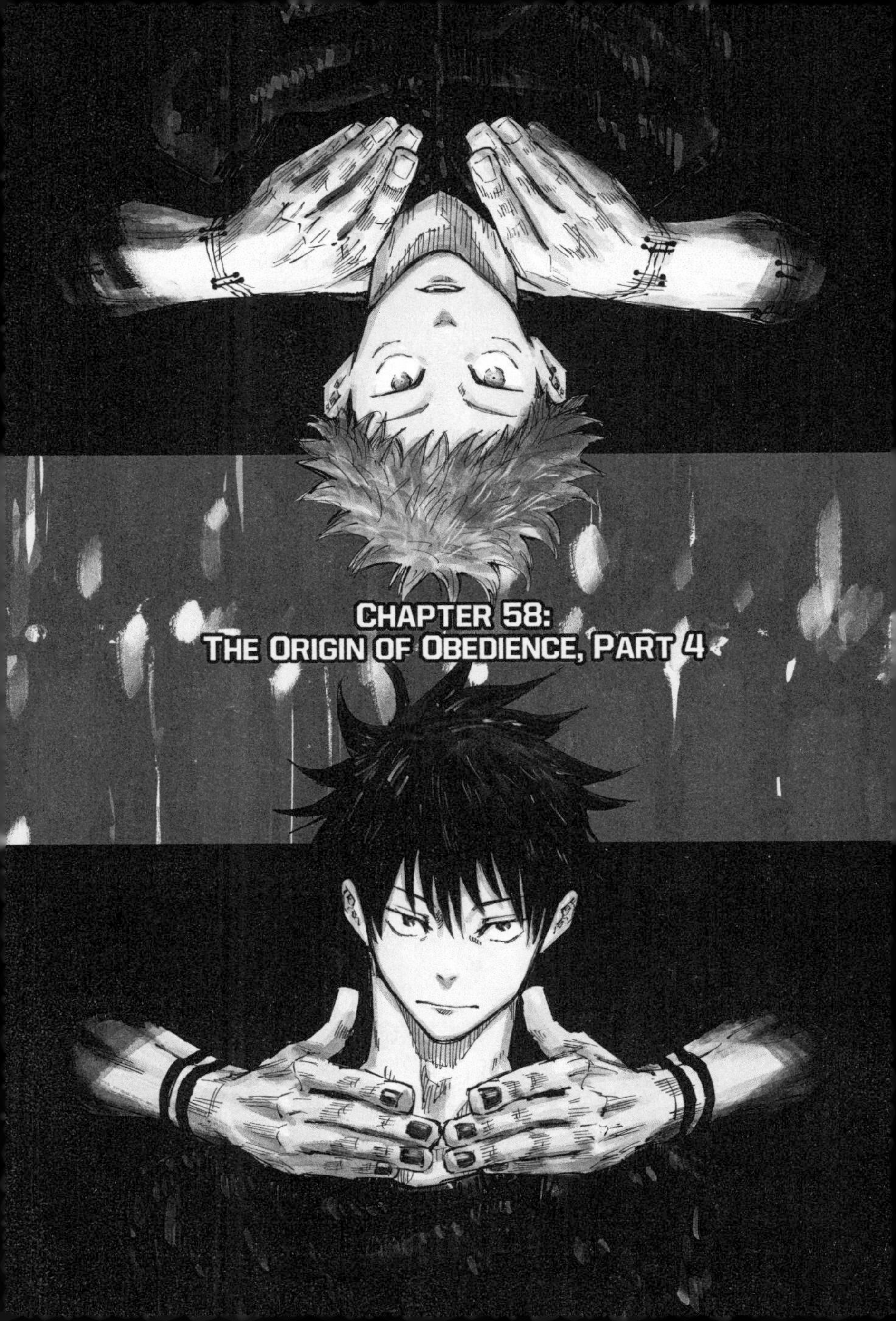
CHAPTER 58:
THE ORIGIN OF OBEDIENCE, PART 4

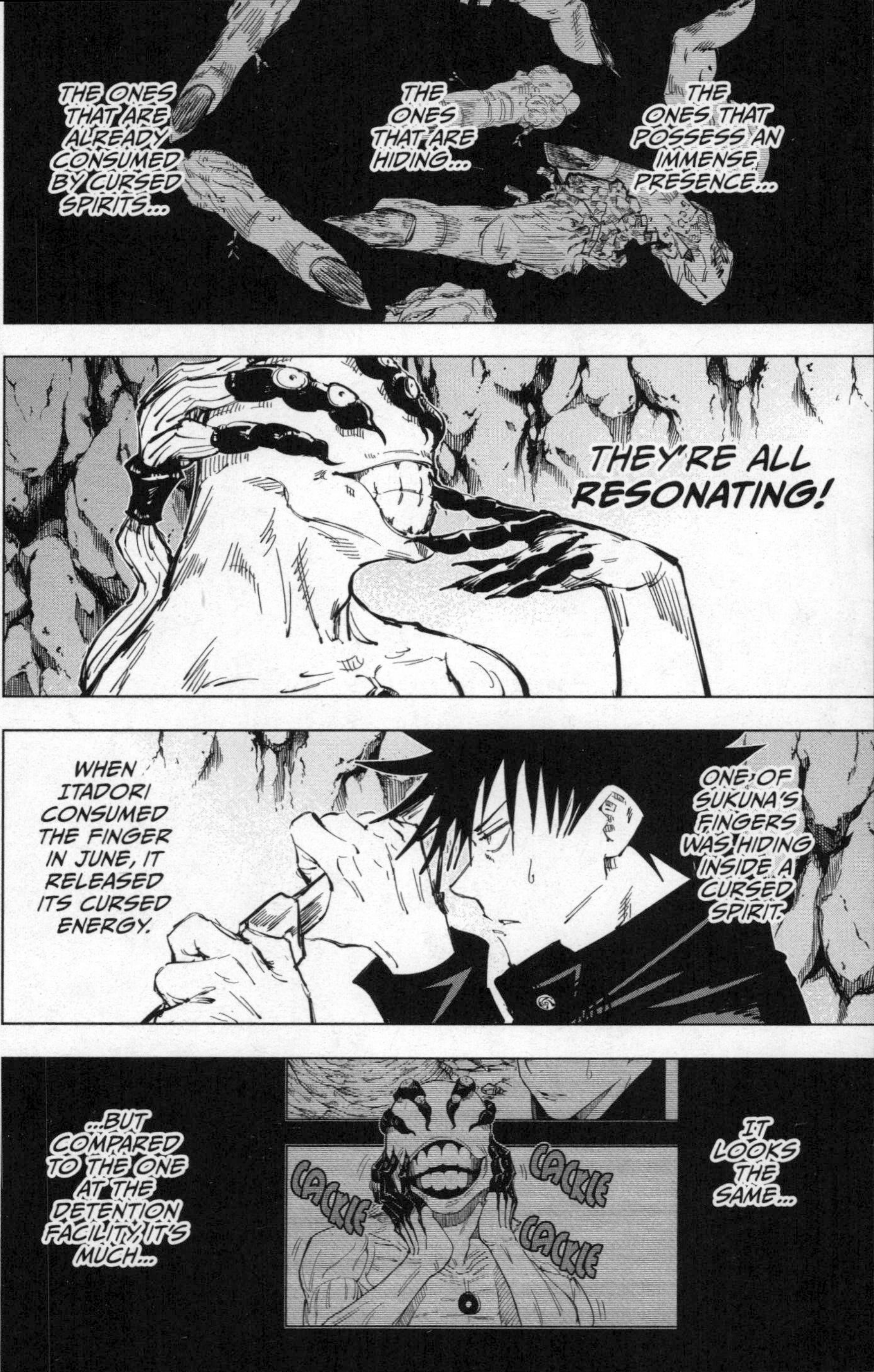
THE ONES THAT POSSESS AN IMMENSE PRESENCE...
THE ONES THAT ARE HIDING...
THE ONES THAT ARE ALREADY CONSUMED BY CURSED SPIRITS...
THEY'RE ALL RESONATING!
ONE OF SUKUNA'S FINGERS WAS HIDING INSIDE A CURSED SPIRIT.
WHEN ITADORI CONSUMED THE FINGER IN JUNE, IT RELEASED ITS CURSED ENERGY.
IT LOOKS THE SAME...
CACKLE
CACKLE
CACKLE
...BUT COMPARED TO THE ONE AT THE DETENTION FACILITY, IT'S MUCH...

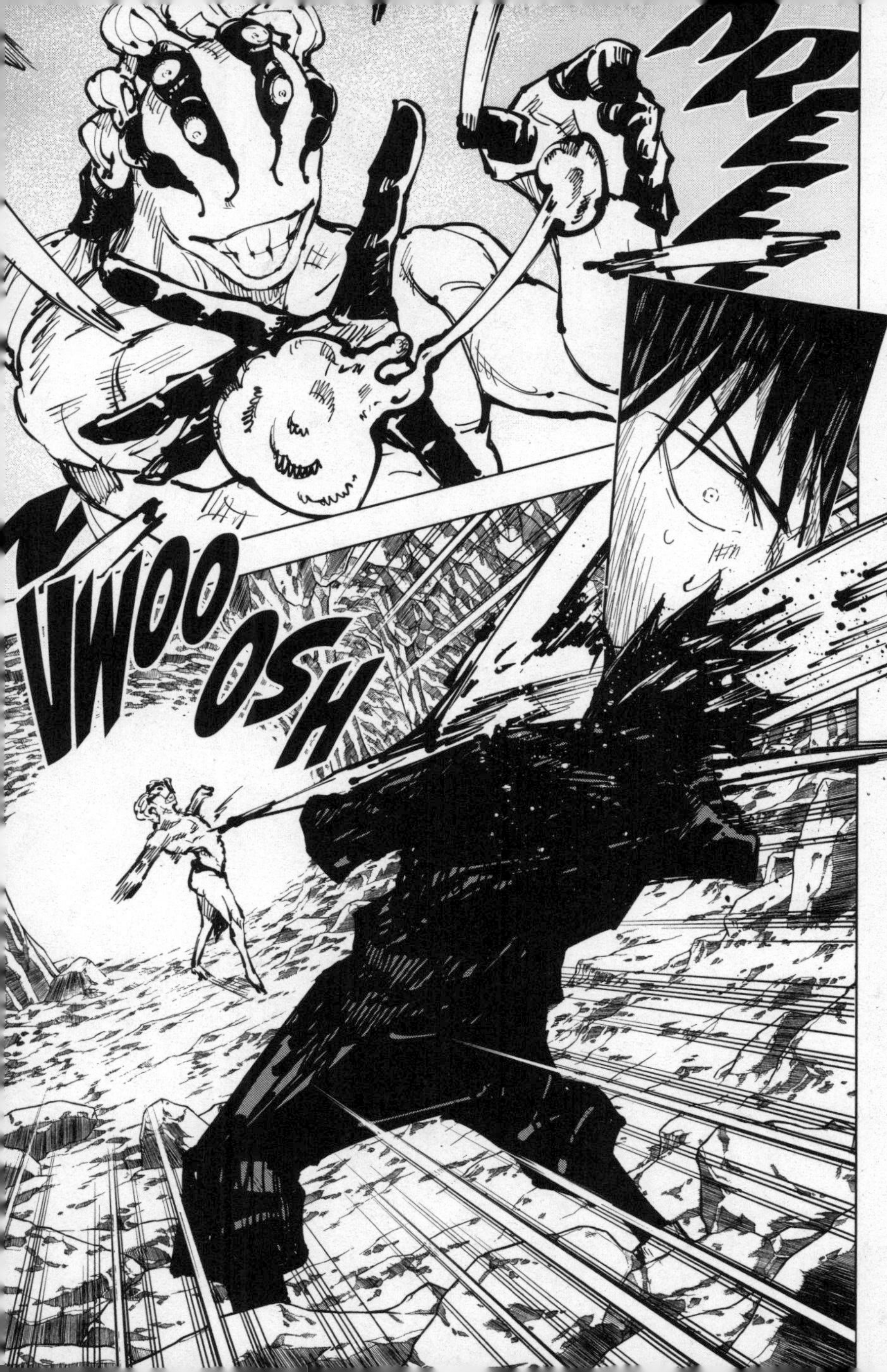
CREEE
WOOOSH

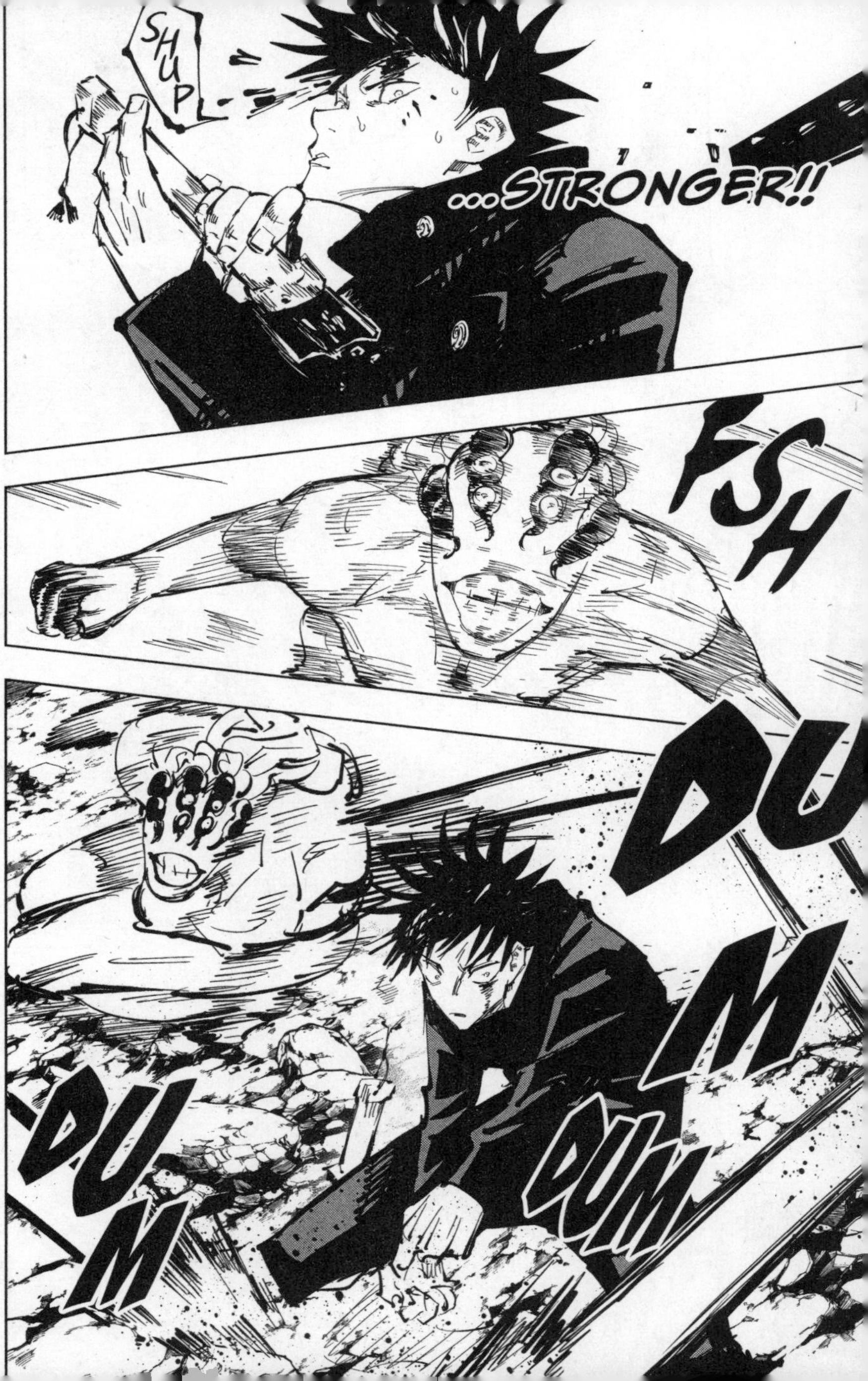
SHUP
...STRONGER!!
FSH
DUMM
DUM
DUM

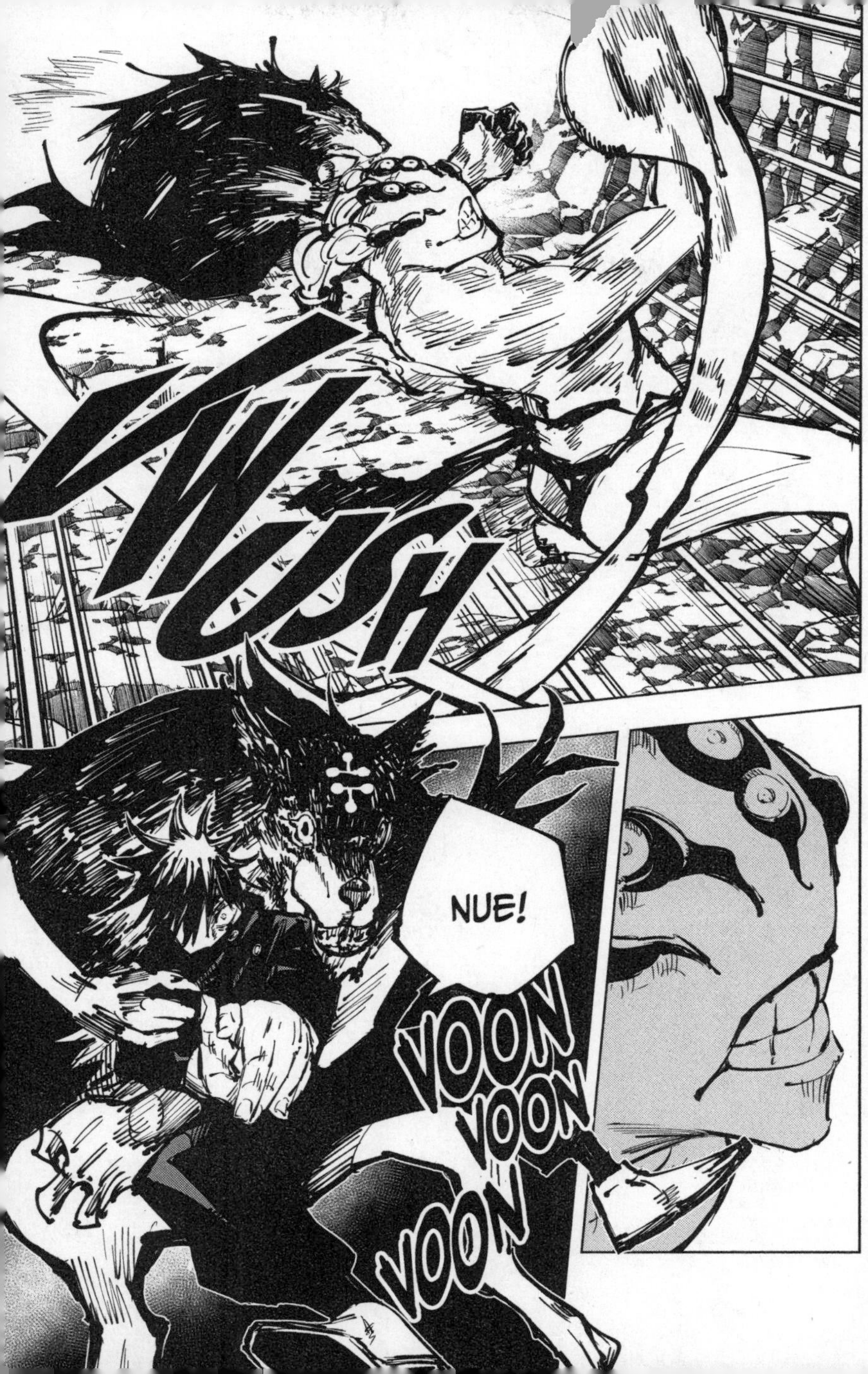
WHSH
NUE!
VOON
VOON
VOON

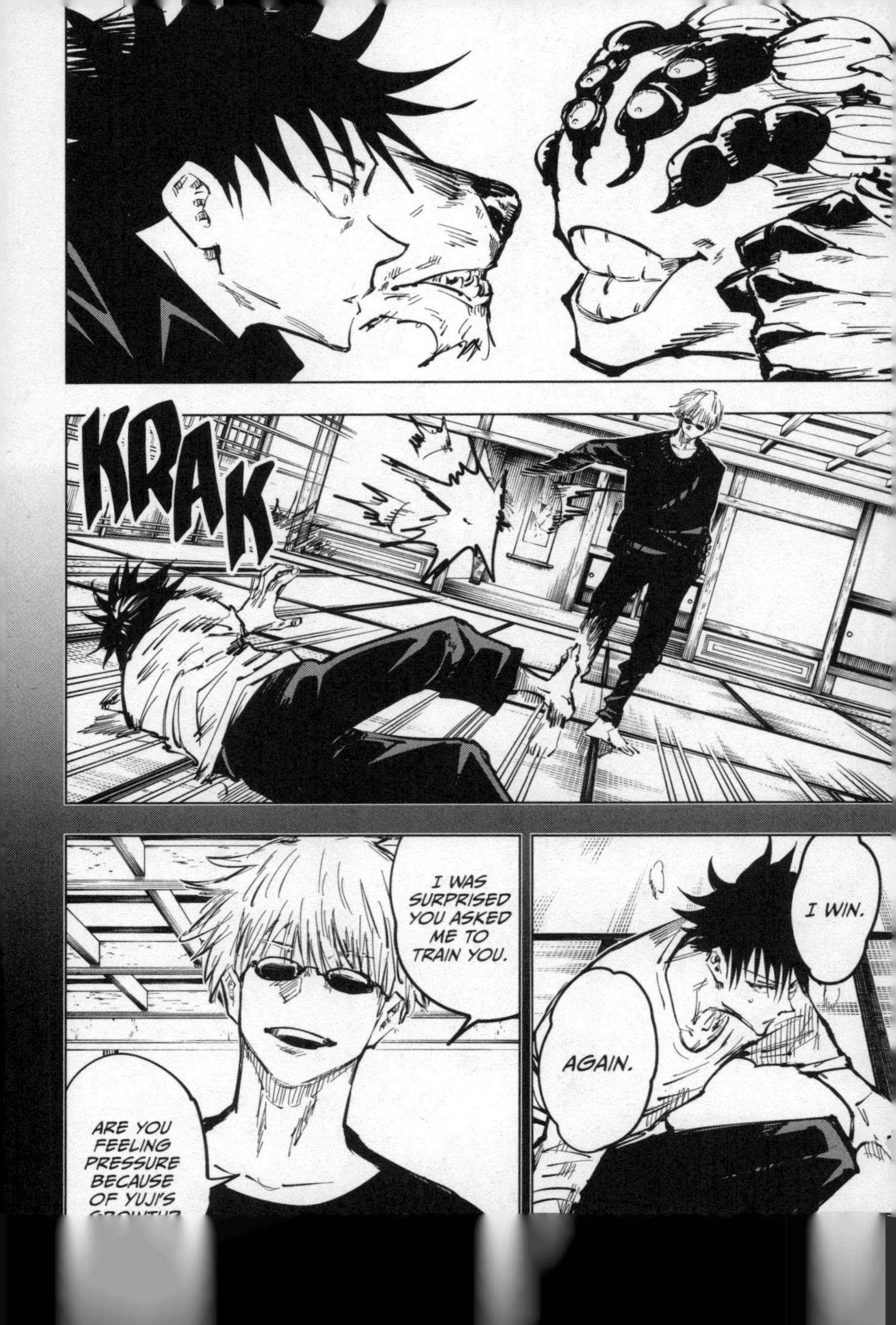
KRAK
I WIN.
AGAIN.
I WAS SURPRISED YOU ASKED ME TO TRAIN YOU.
ARE YOU FEELING PRESSURE BECAUSE OF YUJI'S

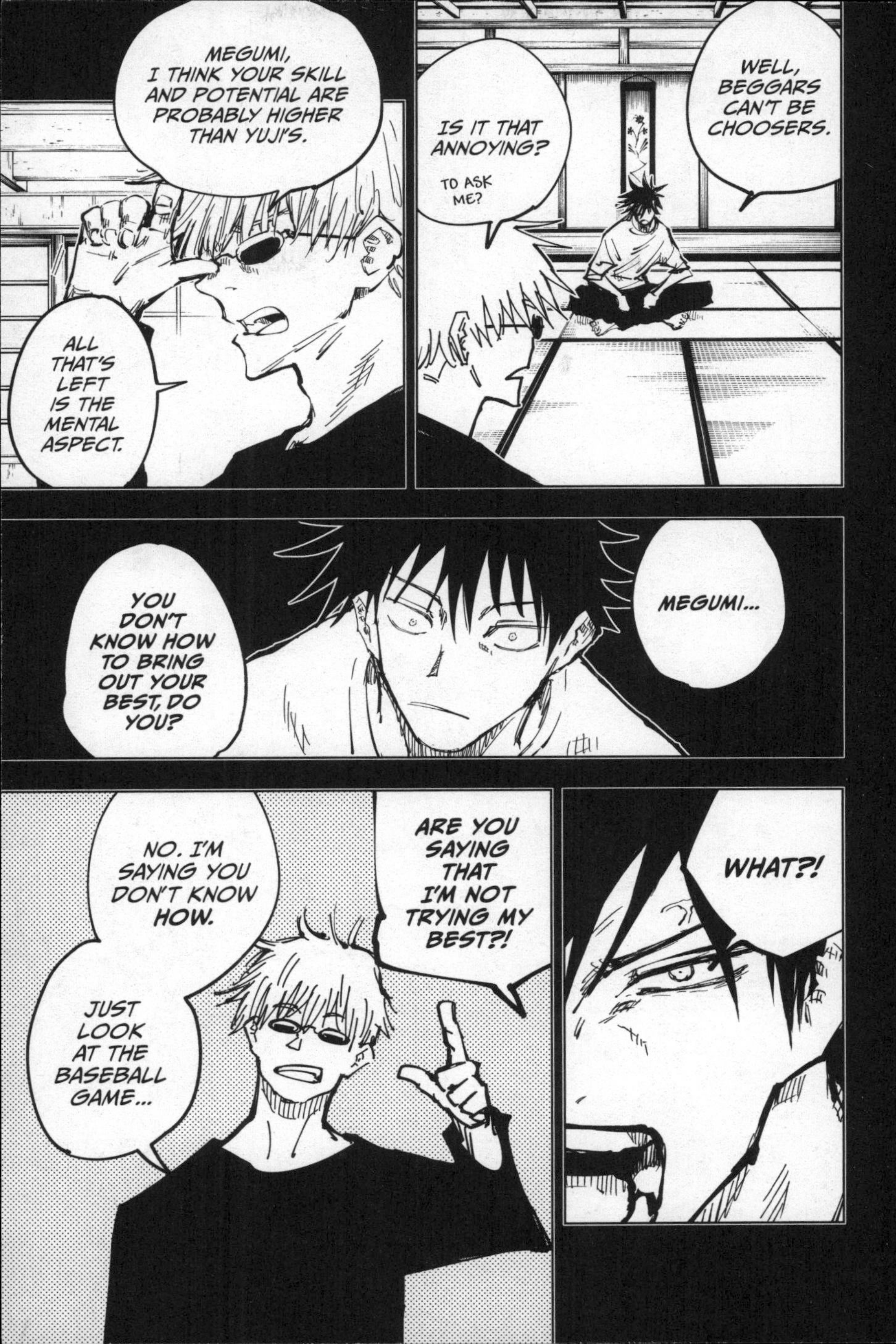
WELL, BEGGARS CAN'T BE CHOOSERS.
IS IT THAT ANNOYING?
TO ASK ME?
MEGUMI, I THINK YOUR SKILL AND POTENTIAL ARE PROBABLY HIGHER THAN YUJI'S.
ALL THAT'S LEFT IS THE MENTAL ASPECT.
MEGUMI...
YOU DON'T KNOW HOW TO BRING OUT YOUR BEST, DO YOU?
WHAT?!
ARE YOU SAYING THAT I'M NOT TRYING MY BEST?!
NO. I'M SAYING YOU DON'T KNOW HOW.
JUST LOOK AT THE BASEBALL GAME...

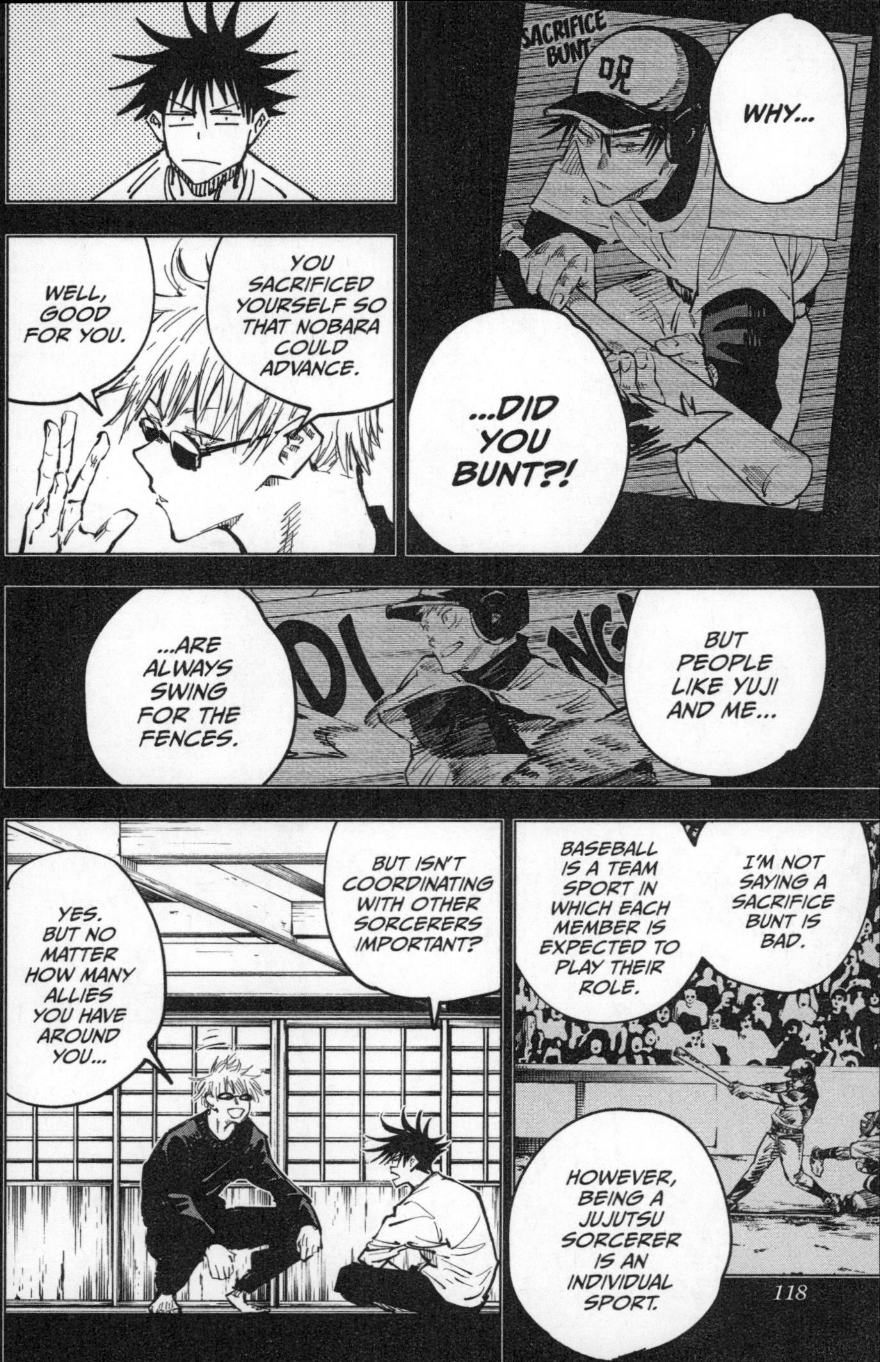
SACRIFICE BUNT
WHY...
...DID YOU BUNT?!
YOU SACRIFICED YOURSELF SO THAT NOBARA COULD ADVANCE.
WELL, GOOD FOR YOU.
BUT PEOPLE LIKE YUJI AND ME...
...ARE ALWAYS SWING FOR THE FENCES.
I'M NOT SAYING A SACRIFICE BUNT IS BAD.
BASEBALL IS A TEAM SPORT IN WHICH EACH MEMBER IS EXPECTED TO PLAY THEIR ROLE.
HOWEVER, BEING A JUJUTSU SORCERER IS AN INDIVIDUAL SPORT.
BUT ISN'T COORDINATING WITH OTHER SORCERERS IMPORTANT?
YES. BUT NO MATTER HOW MANY ALLIES YOU HAVE AROUND YOU...

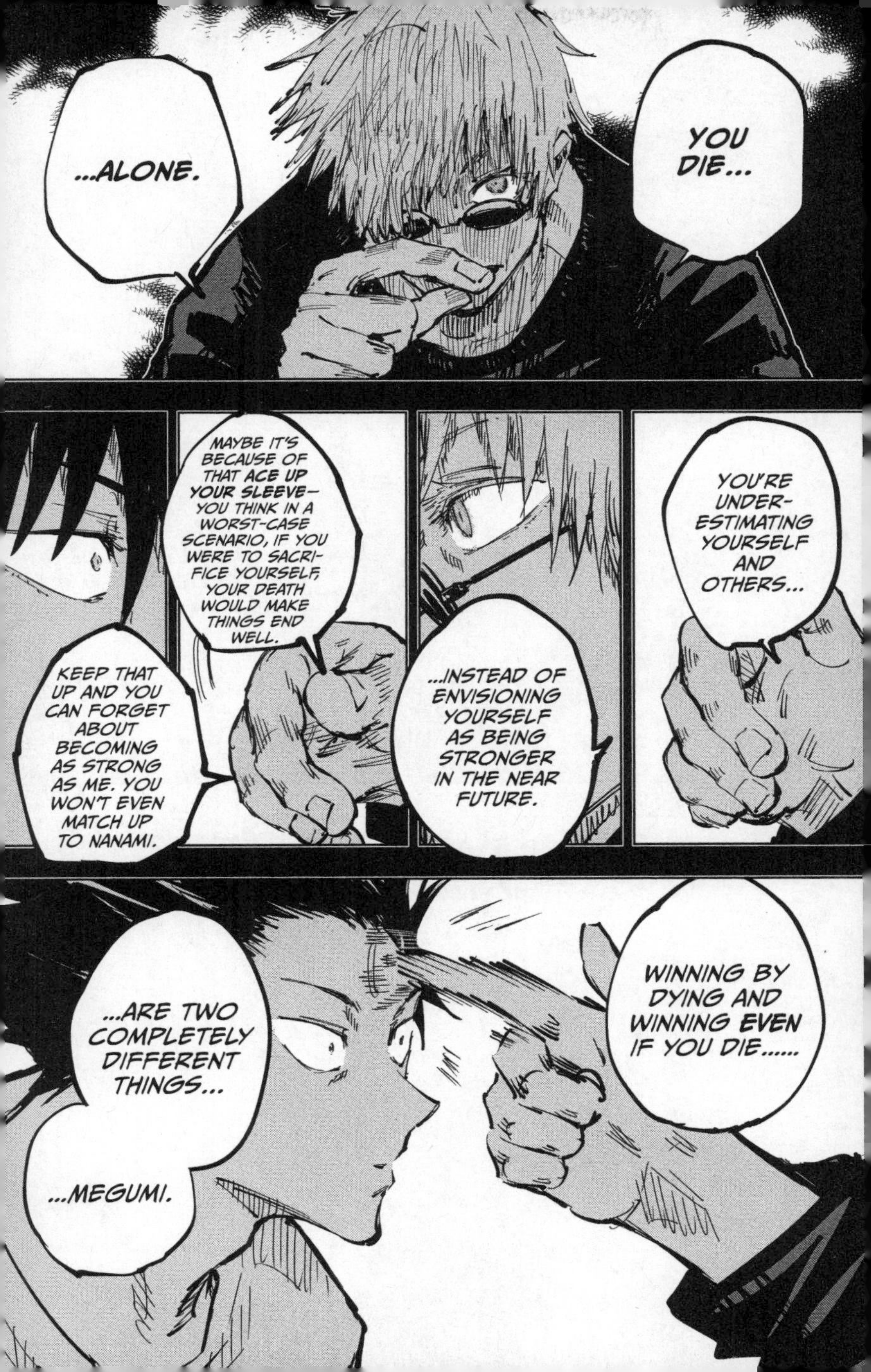
YOU DIE...
...ALONE.
YOU'RE UNDER-ESTIMATING YOURSELF AND OTHERS...
MAYBE IT'S BECAUSE OF THAT ACE UP YOUR SLEEVE—YOU THINK IN A WORST-CASE SCENARIO, IF YOU WERE TO SACRIFICE YOURSELF, YOUR DEATH WOULD MAKE THINGS END WELL.
...INSTEAD OF ENVISIONING YOURSELF AS BEING STRONGER IN THE NEAR FUTURE.
KEEP THAT UP AND YOU CAN FORGET ABOUT BECOMING AS STRONG AS ME. YOU WON'T EVEN MATCH UP TO NANAMI.
WINNING BY DYING AND WINNING EVEN IF YOU DIE......
...ARE TWO COMPLETELY DIFFERENT THINGS...
...MEGUMI.

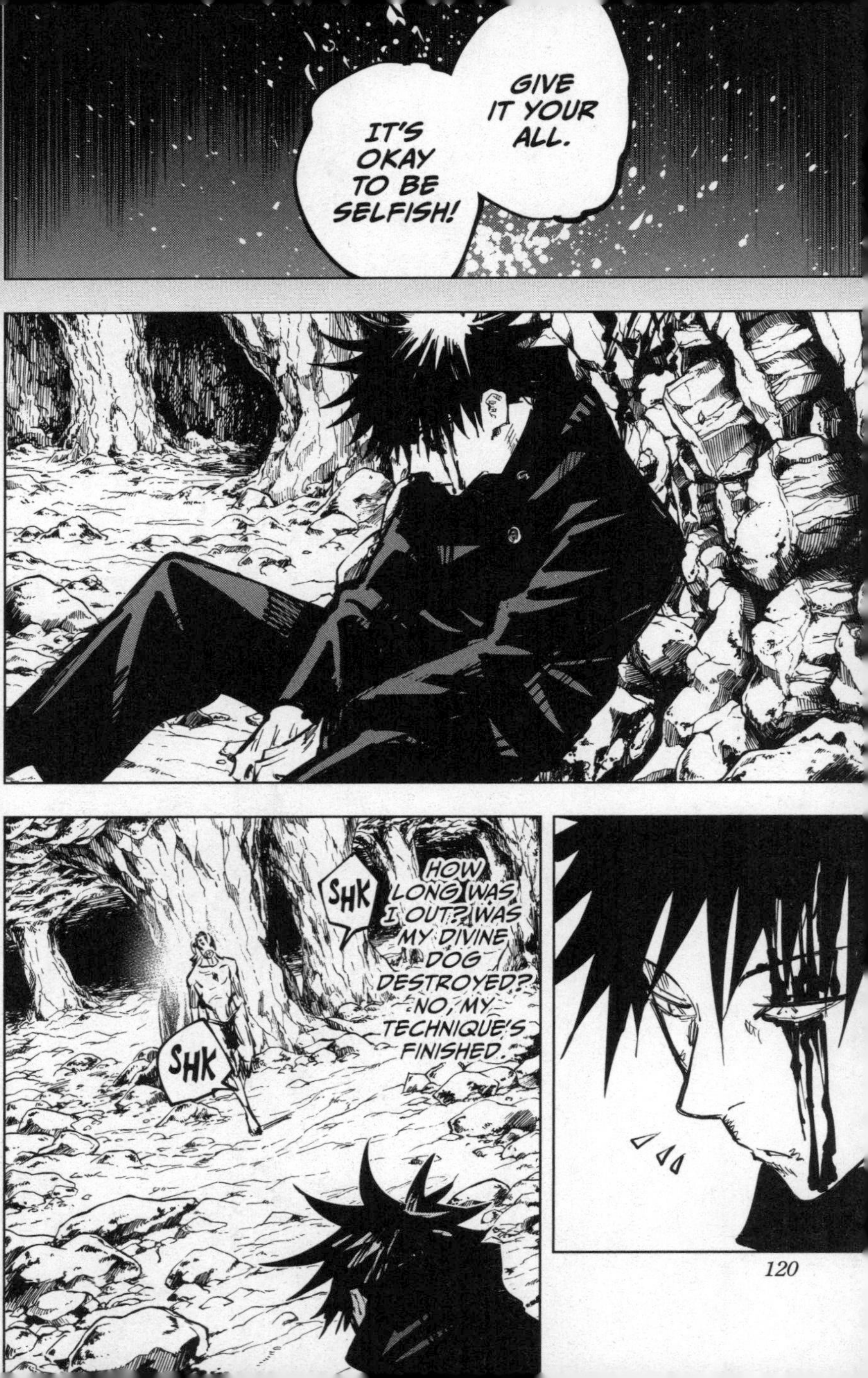
GIVE IT YOUR ALL.
IT'S OKAY TO BE SELFISH!
HOW LONG WAS I OUT? WAS MY DIVINE DOG DESTROYED? NO, MY TECHNIQUE'S FINISHED.
SHK
SHK

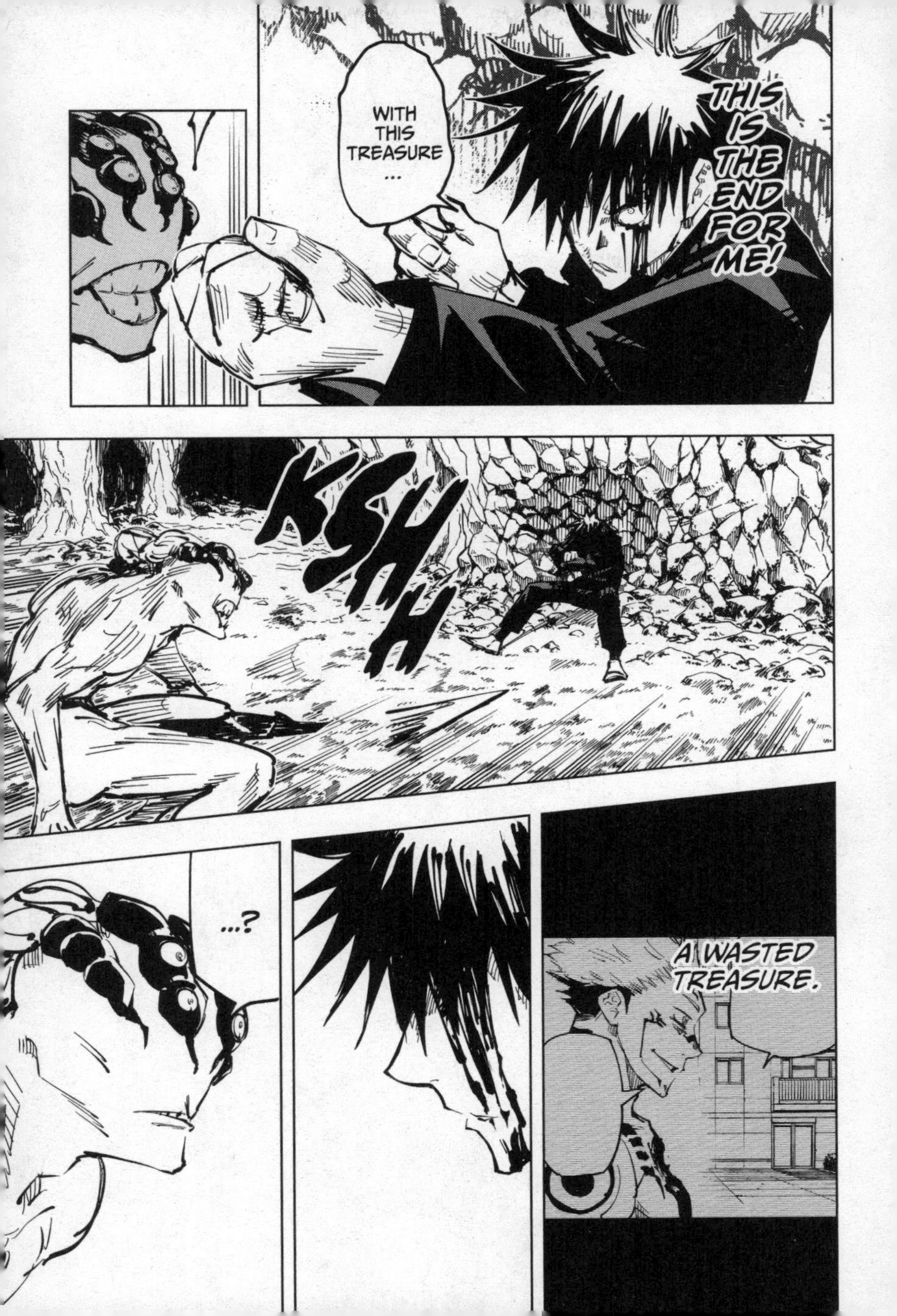
WITH THIS TREASURE ...
THIS IS THE END FOR ME!
KSHH
A WASTED TREASURE.
...?

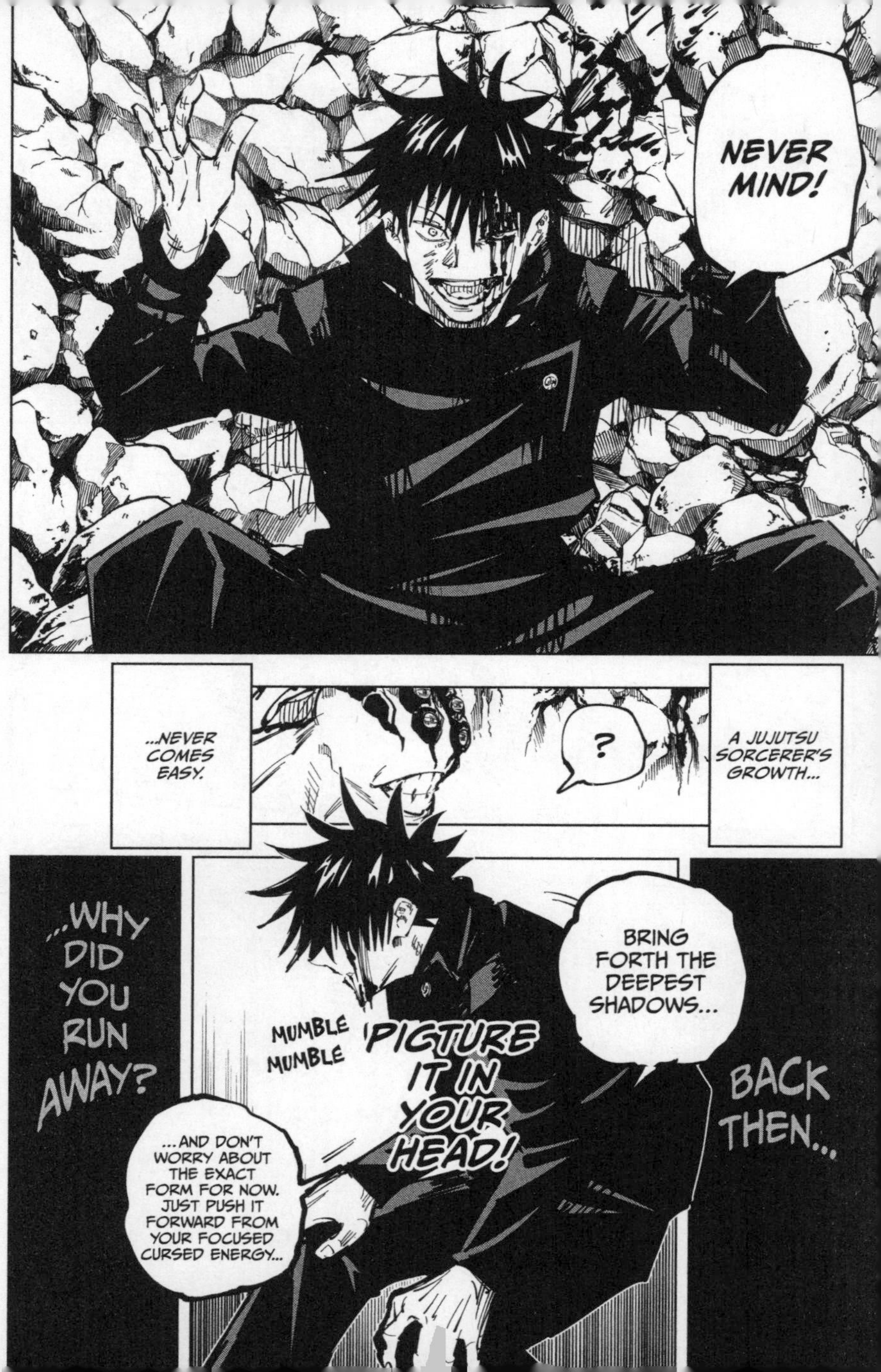
NEVER MIND!
A JUJUTSU SORCERER'S GROWTH...
?
...NEVER COMES EASY.
BACK THEN...
BRING FORTH THE DEEPEST SHADOWS...
PICTURE IT IN YOUR HEAD!
MUMBLE MUMBLE
...AND DON'T WORRY ABOUT THE EXACT FORM FOR NOW. JUST PUSH IT FORWARD FROM YOUR FOCUSED CURSED ENERGY...
...WHY DID YOU RUN AWAY?

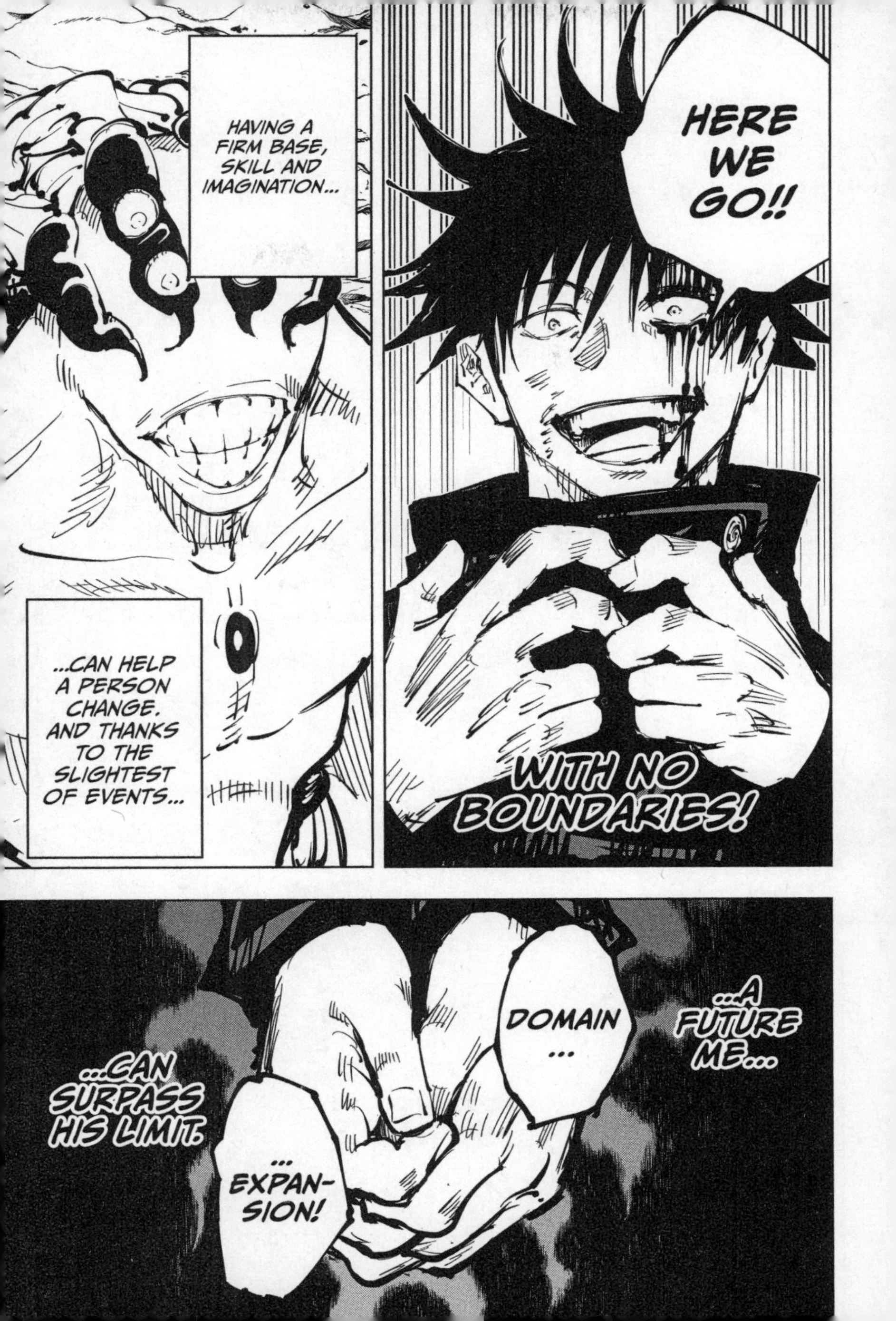
HERE WE GO!!
WITH NO BOUNDARIES!
HAVING A FIRM BASE, SKILL AND IMAGINATION...
...CAN HELP A PERSON CHANGE. AND THANKS TO THE SLIGHTEST OF EVENTS...
...A FUTURE ME...
DOMAIN ...
...CAN SURPASS HIS LIMIT.
... EXPANSION!

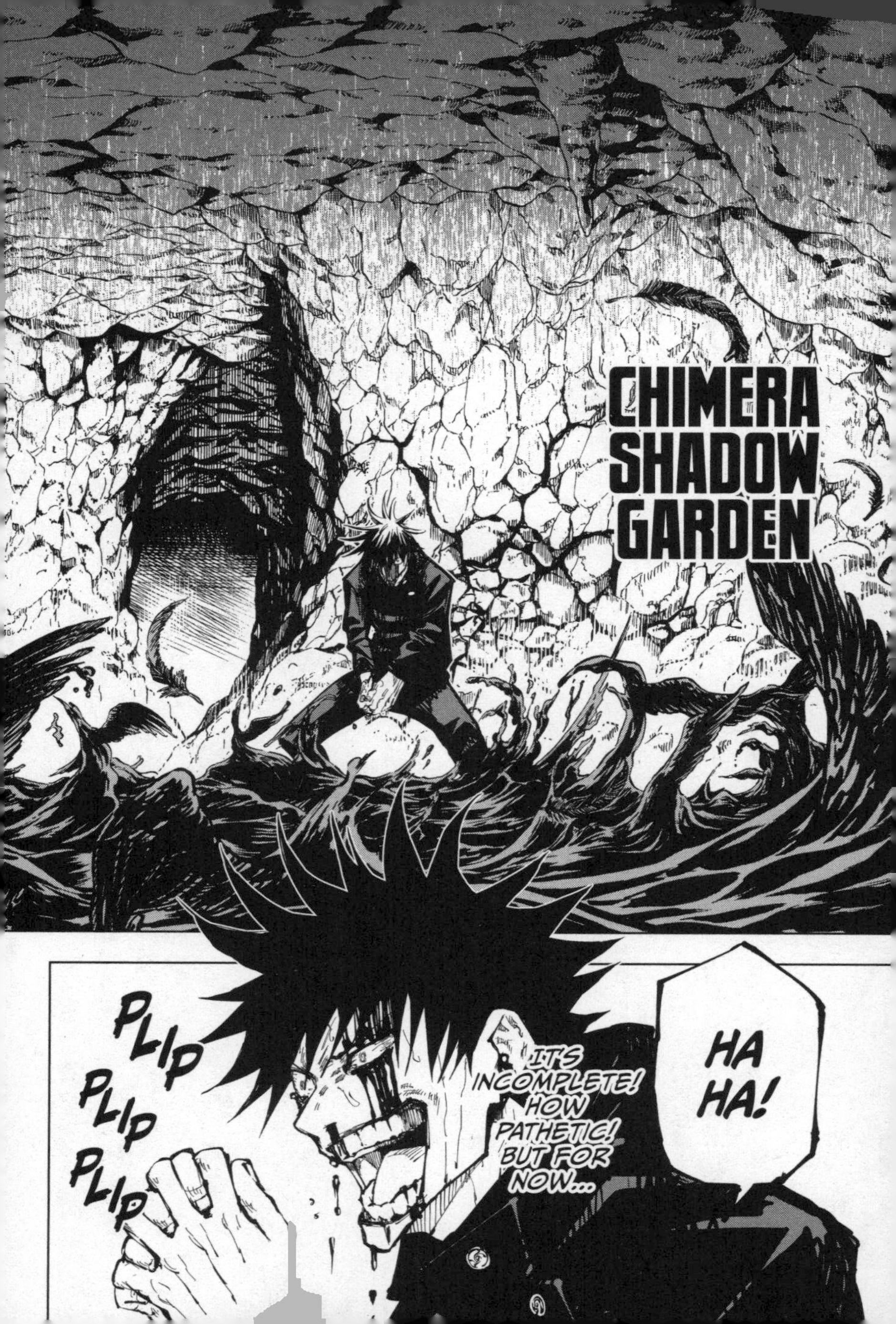
CHIMERA SHADOW GARDEN
HA HA!
IT'S INCOMPLETE! HOW PATHETIC! BUT FOR NOW...
PLIP PLIP PLIP PLIP

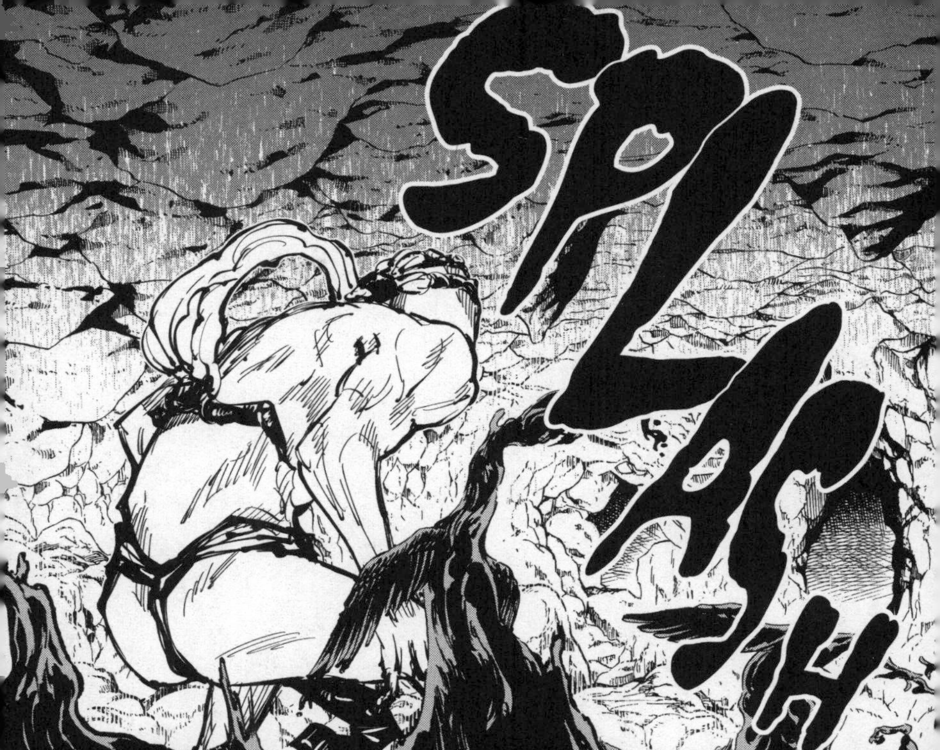
SPLASH
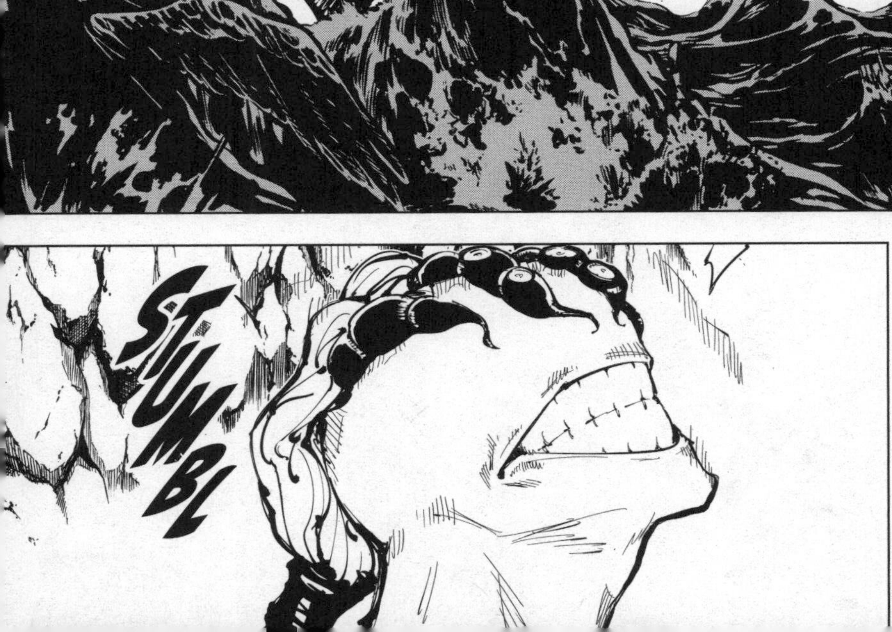
STUMBL

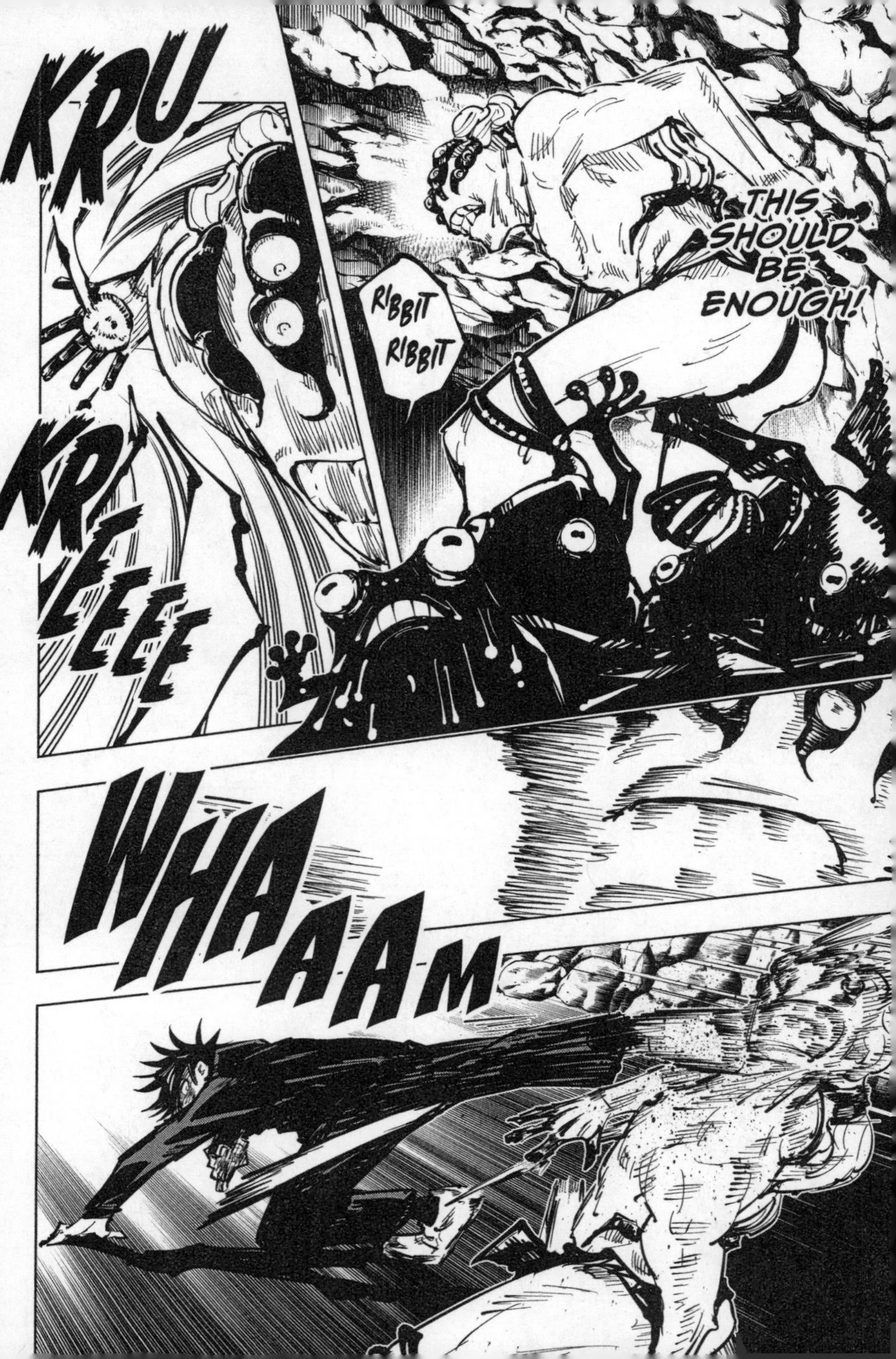
THIS SHOULD BE ENOUGH!
RIBBIT RIBBIT
KRU
KREEEE
WHAAAM

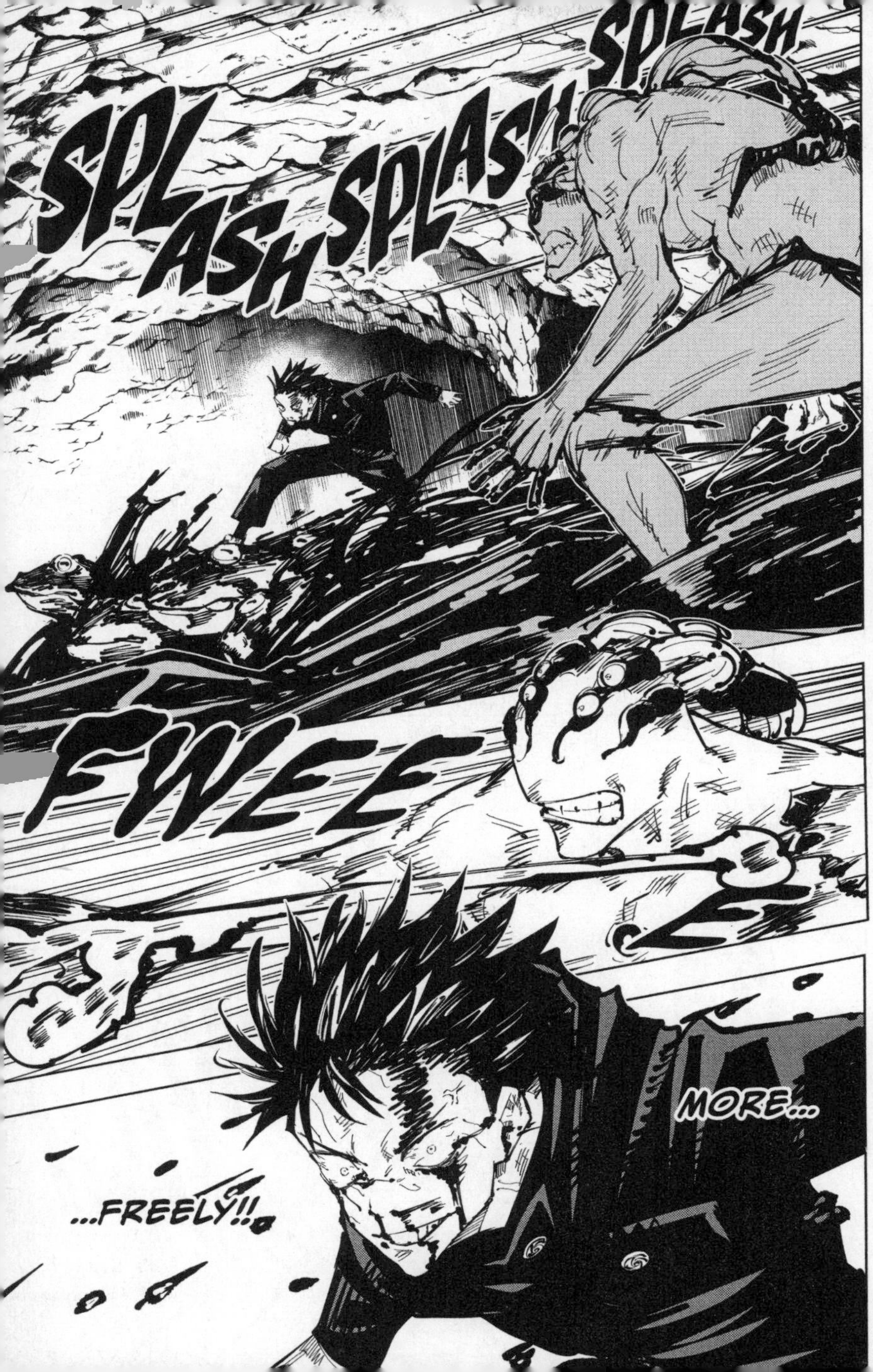
SPLASH
SPLASH
SPLASH
FWEE
MORE...
...FREELY!!

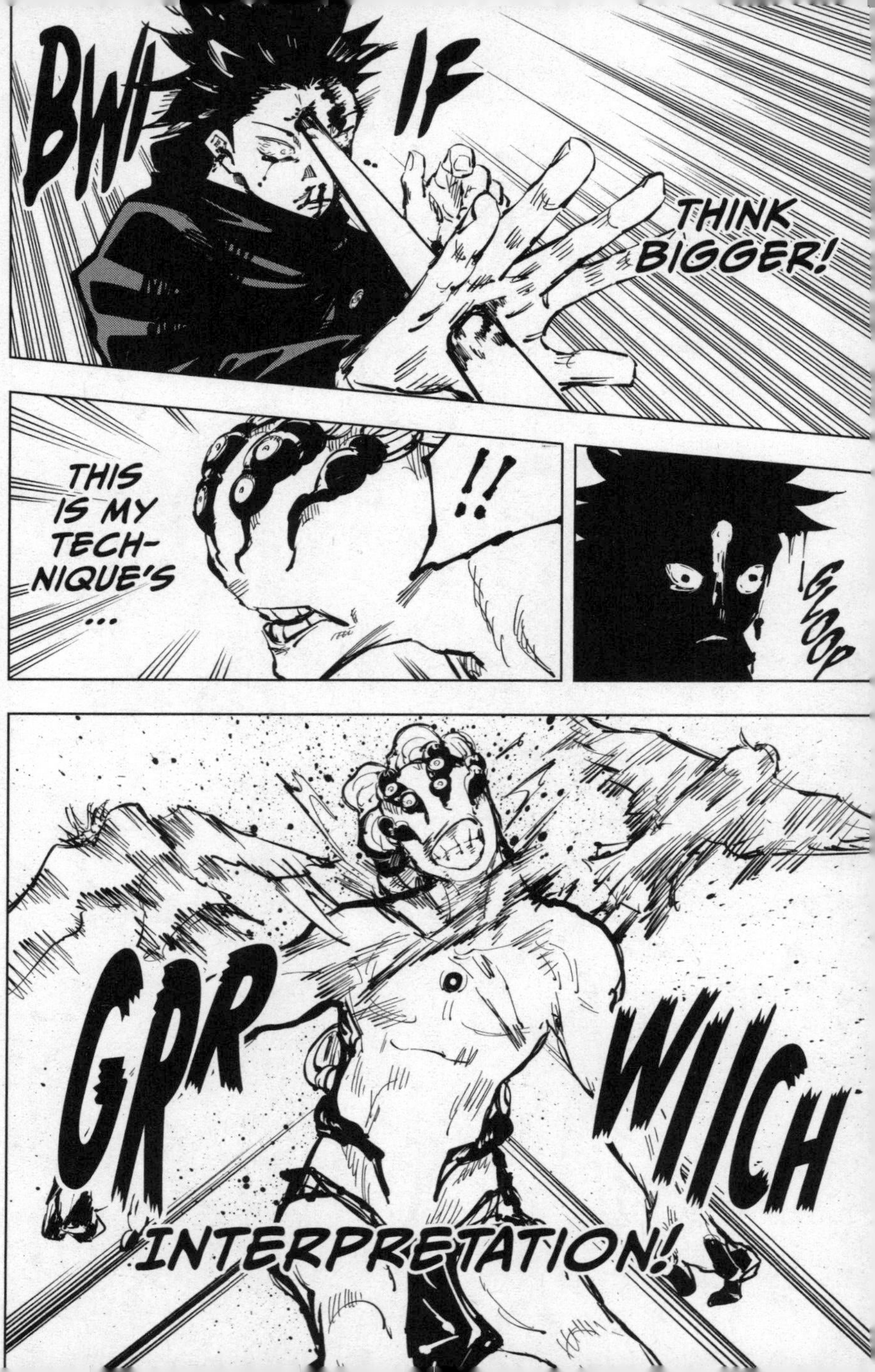
BW IF
THINK BIGGER!
GLOOP
!!
THIS IS MY TECH-NIQUE'S ...
GPR WICH
INTERPRETATION!

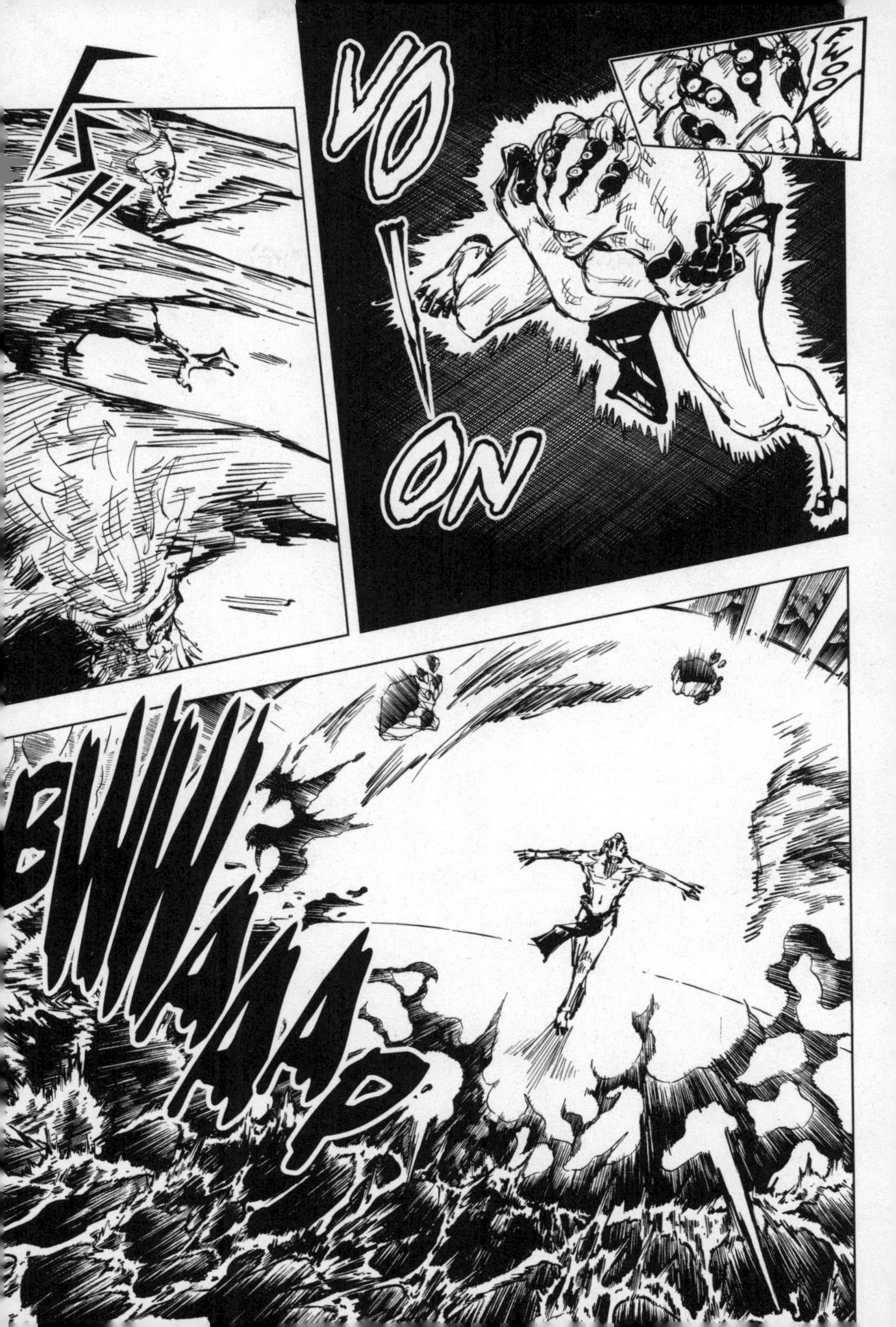
FWOO
VO—ON
FSSH
BWAAAAD

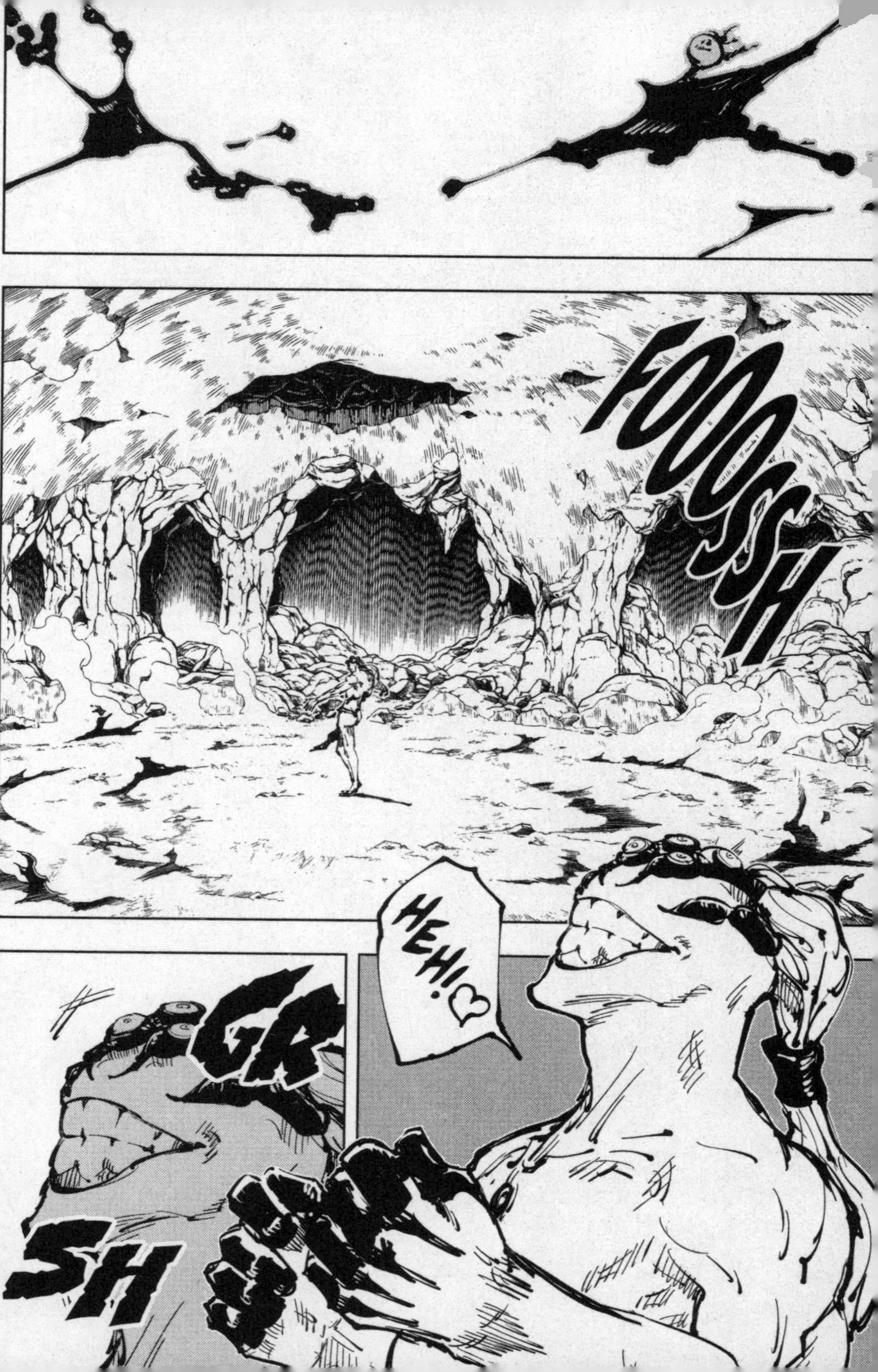
FOOOSH
HEHI!♡
GRSH

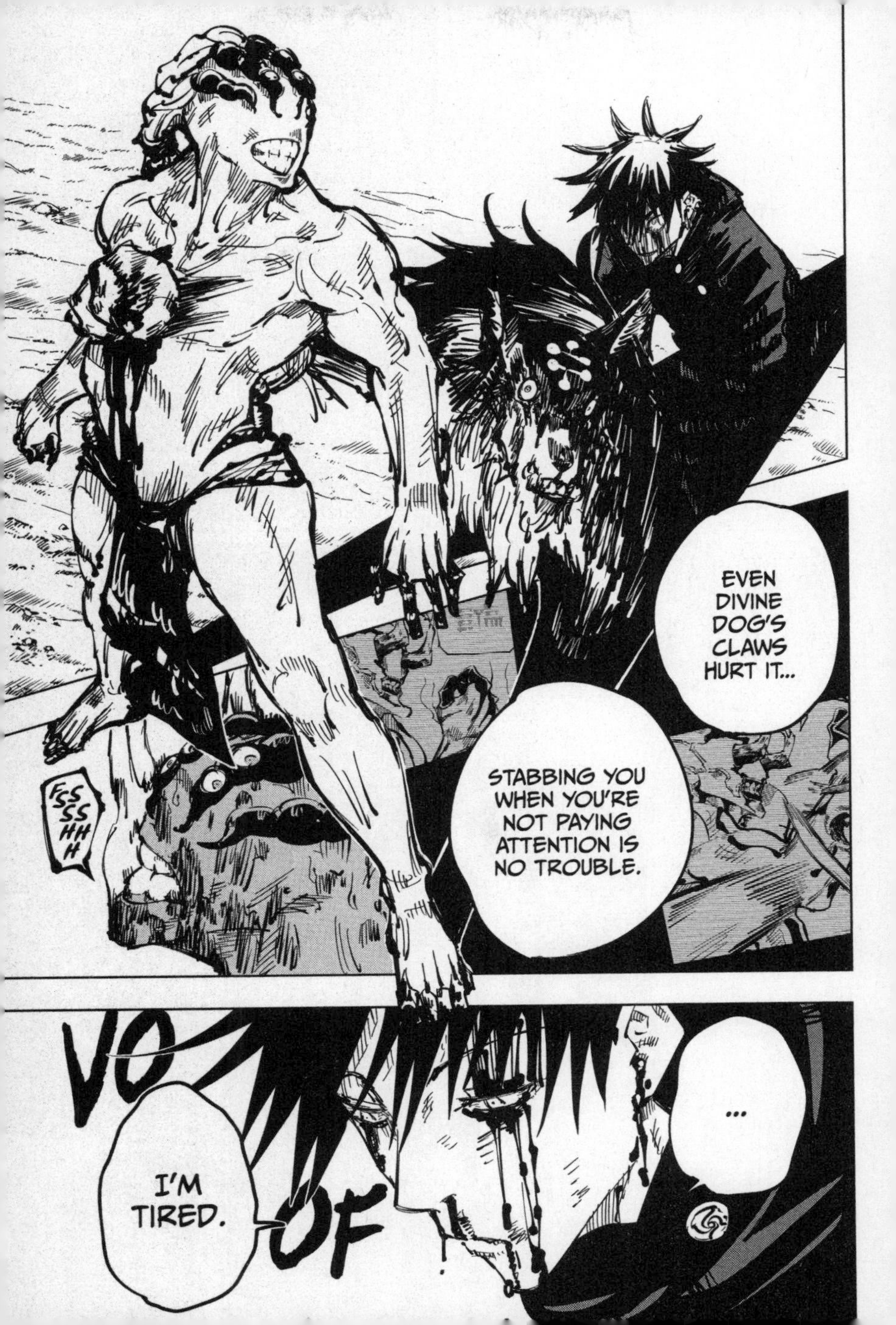
EVEN DIVINE DOG'S CLAWS HURT IT...
STABBING YOU WHEN YOU'RE NOT PAYING ATTENTION IS NO TROUBLE.
FSSSSHHH
...
VO
I'M TIRED.
OF

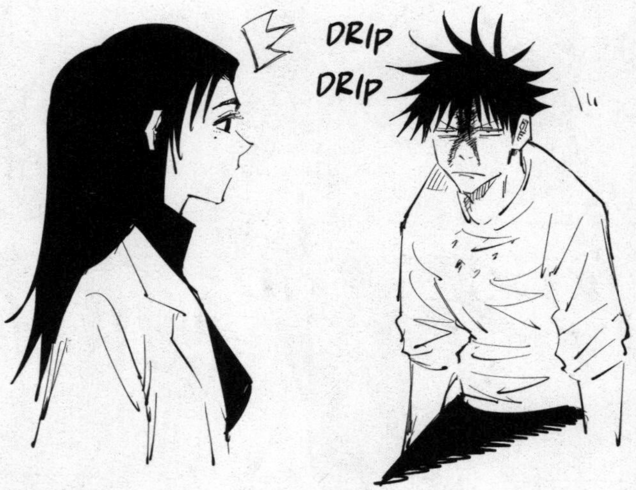
DRIP
DRIP

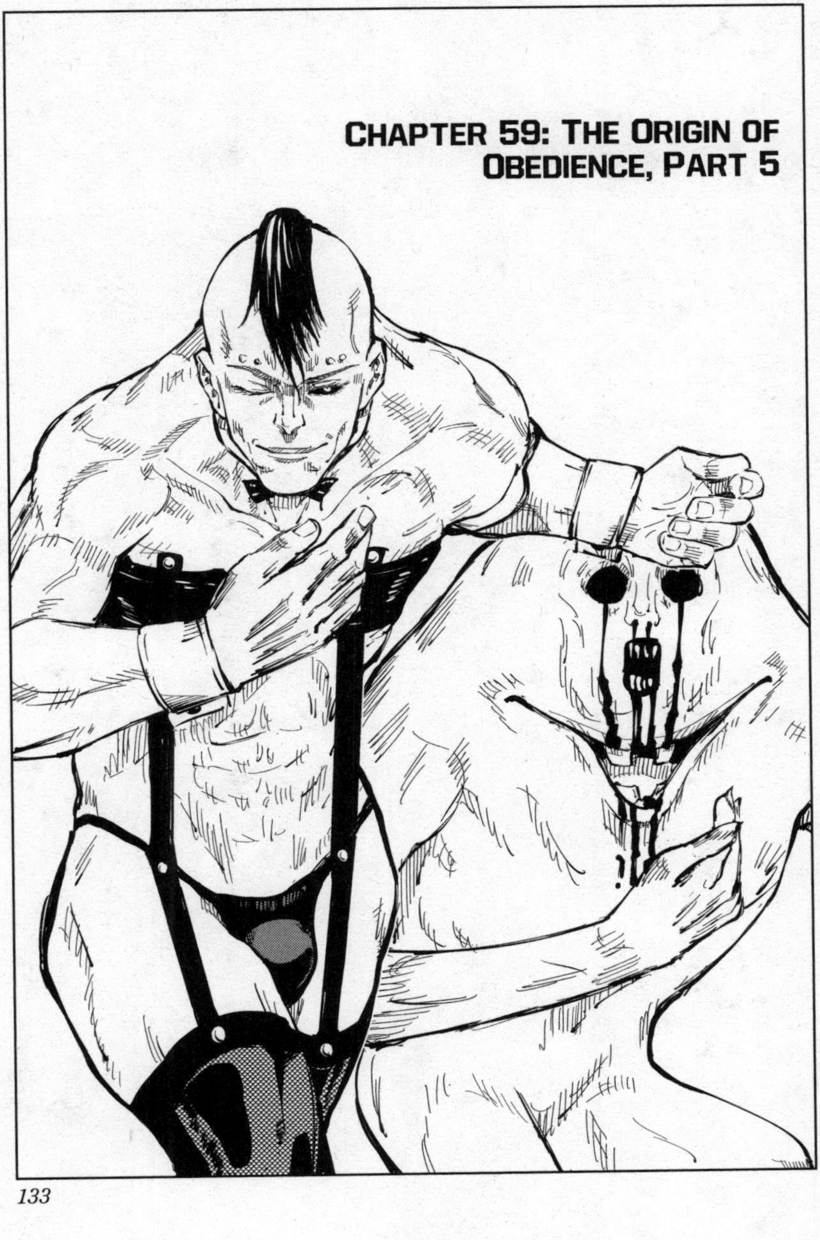
CHAPTER 59: THE ORIGIN OF OBEDIENCE, PART 5

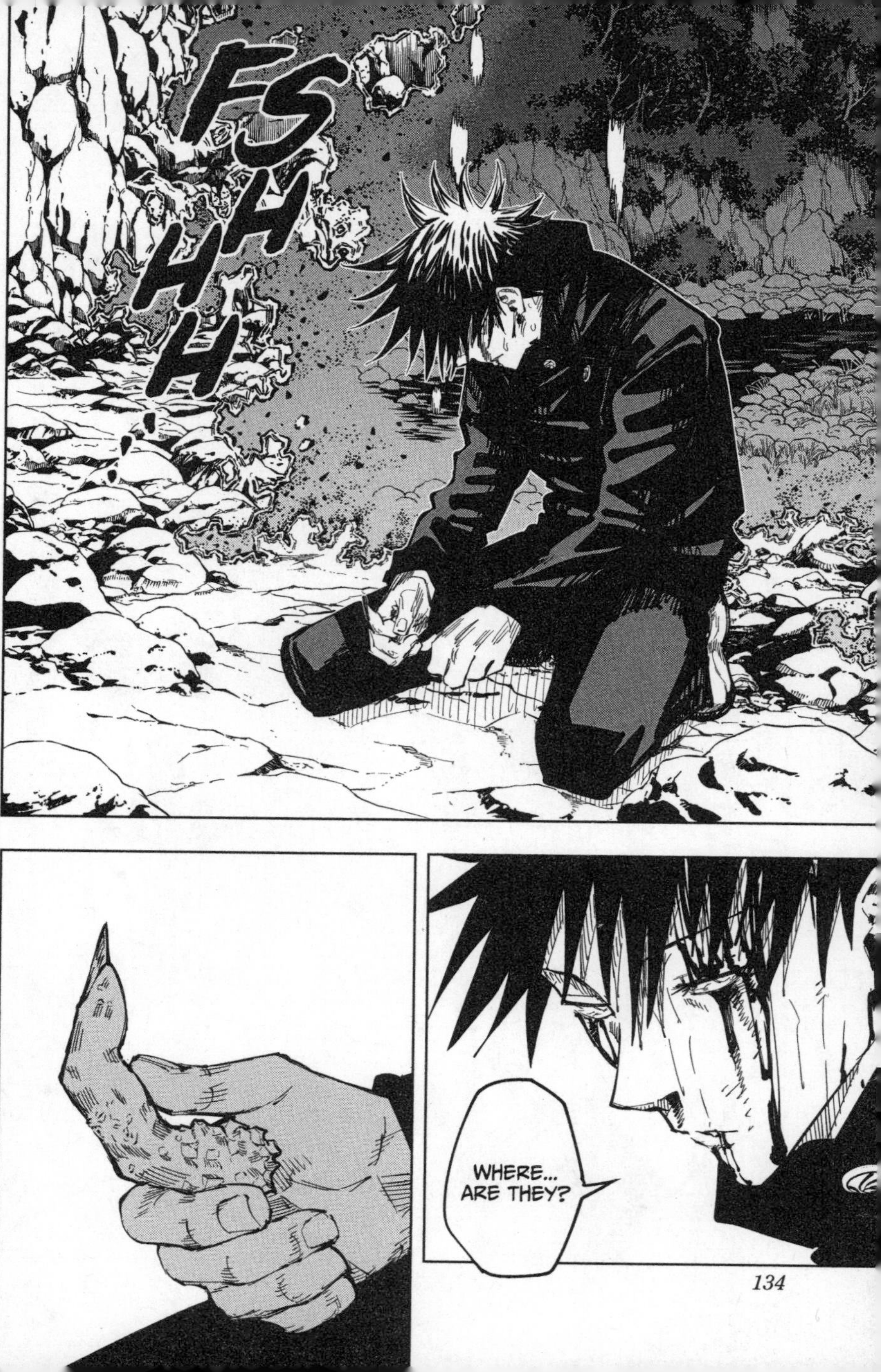
FSHHHH
WHERE... ARE THEY?

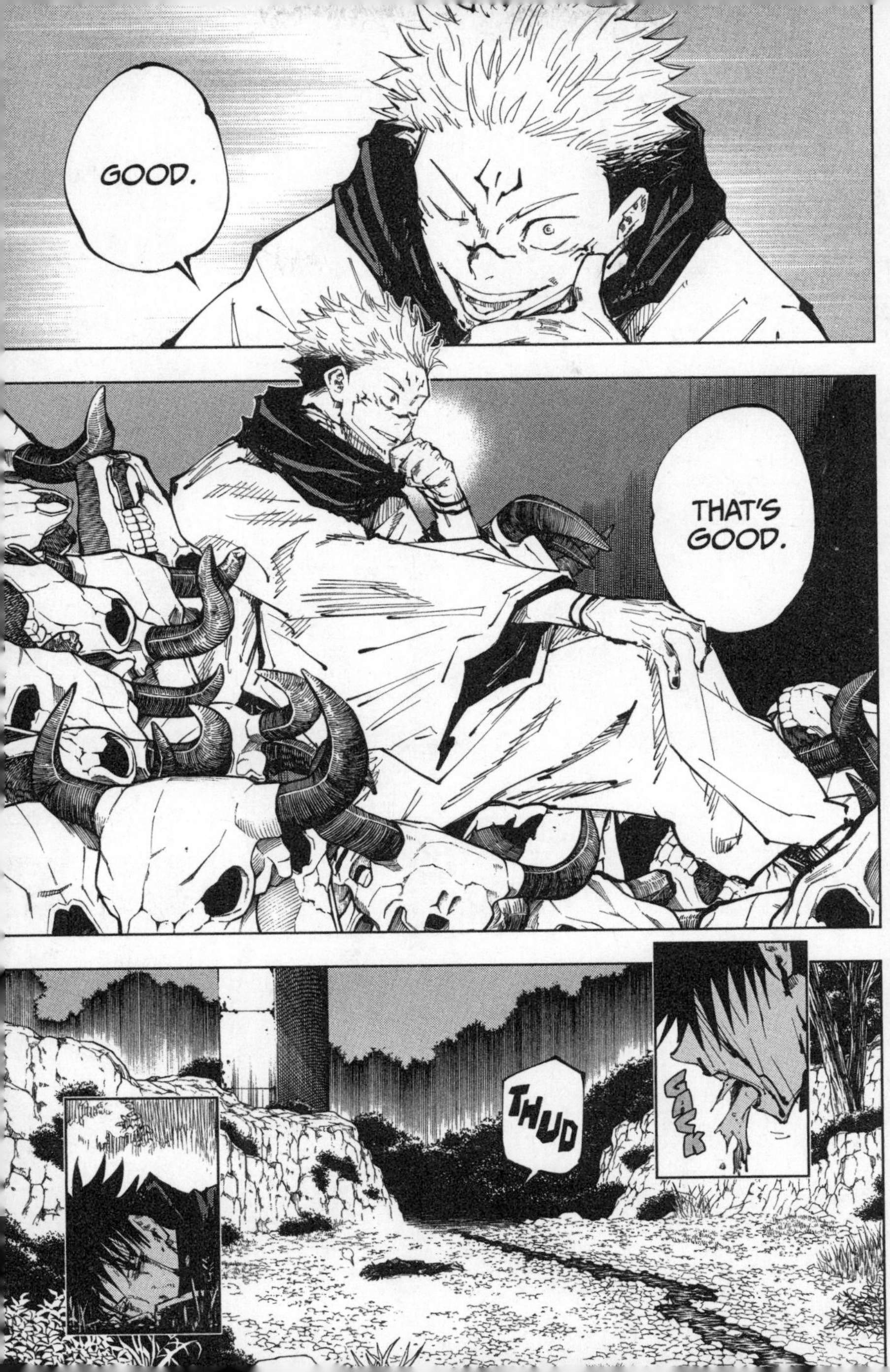
GOOD.
THAT'S GOOD.
GACK
THUD

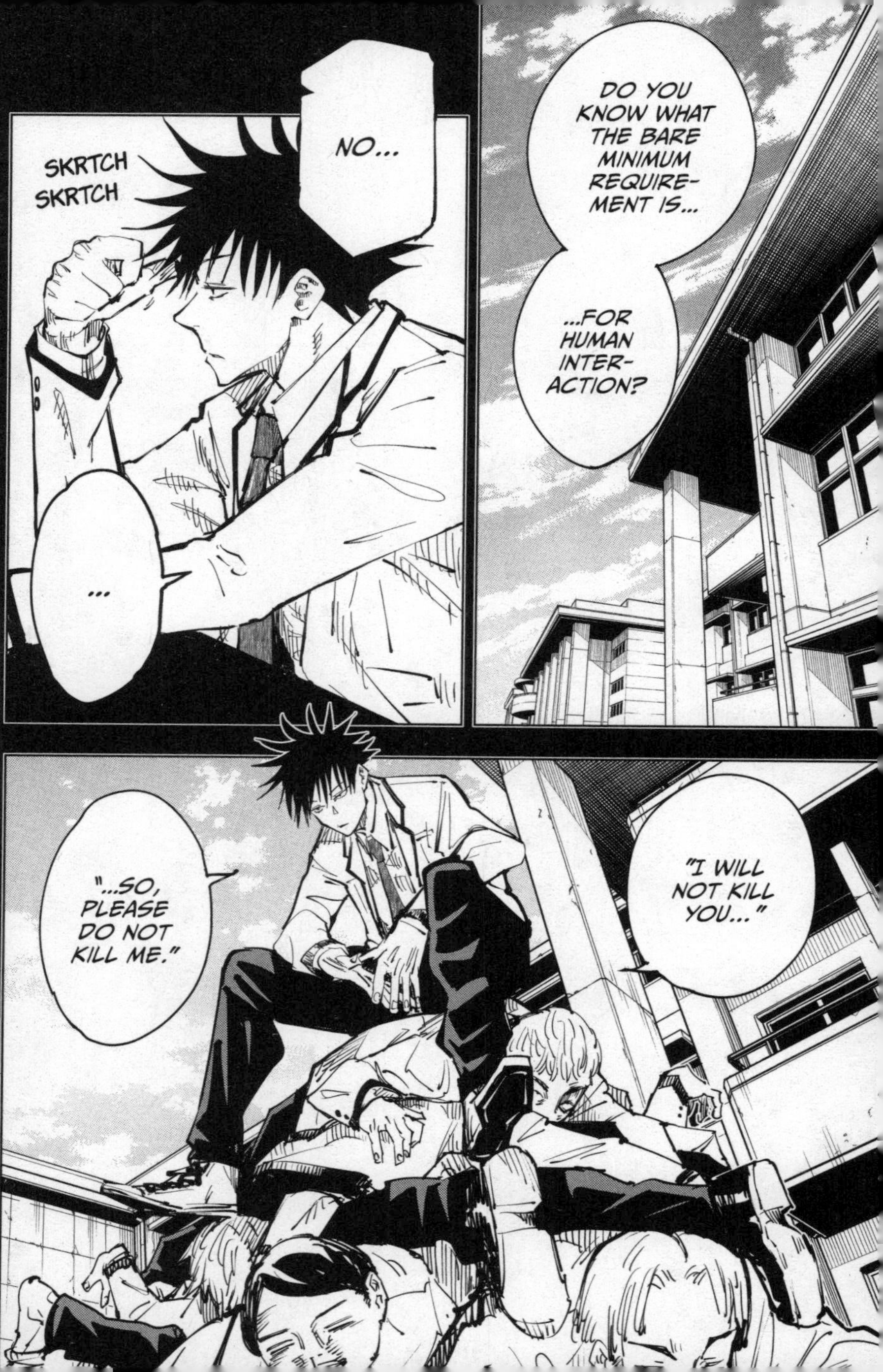
DO YOU KNOW WHAT THE BARE MINIMUM REQUIRE-MENT IS...
...FOR HUMAN INTER-ACTION?
NO...
SKRTCH SKRTCH
...
"I WILL NOT KILL YOU..."
"...SO, PLEASE DO NOT KILL ME."

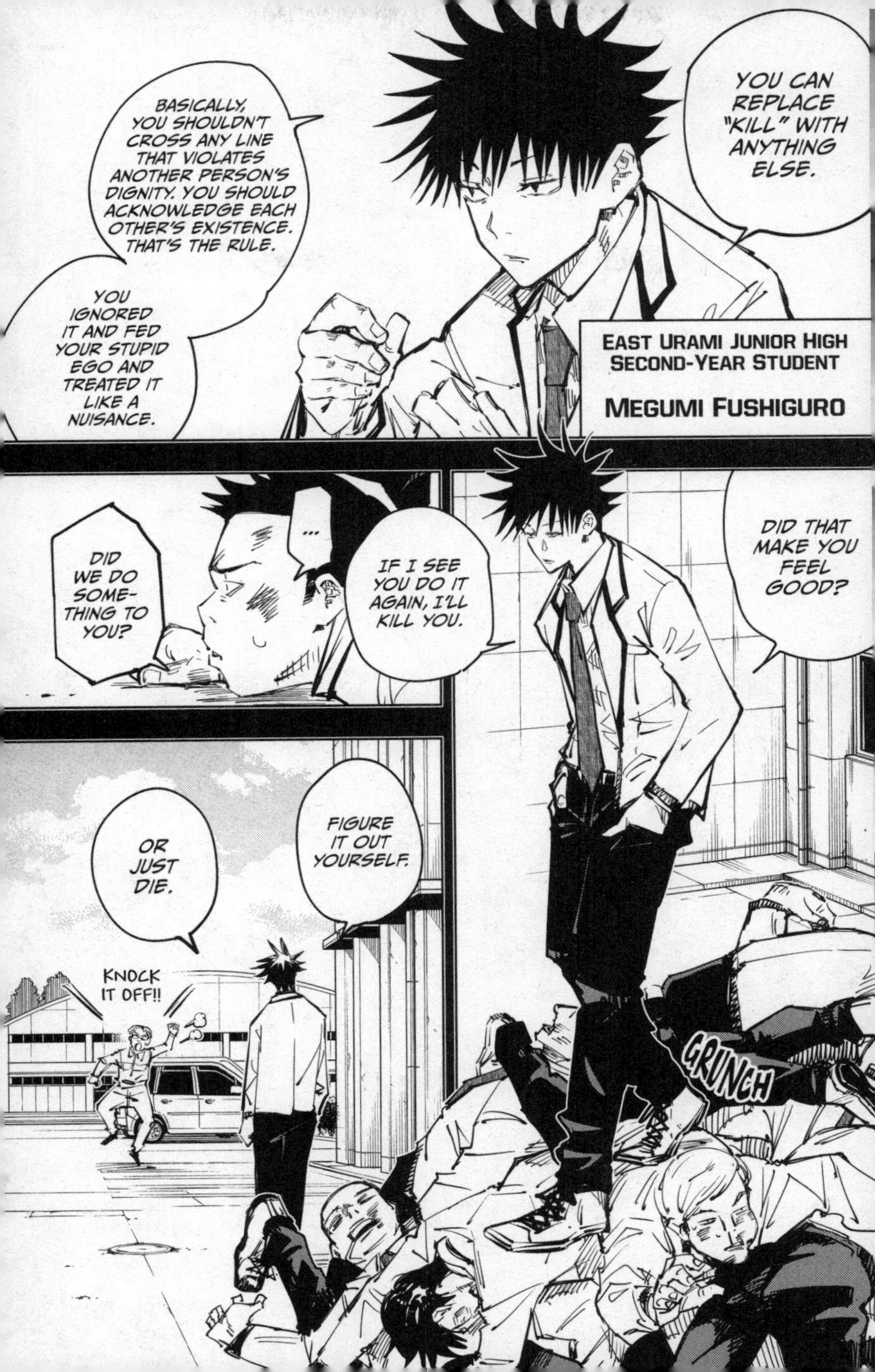
YOU CAN REPLACE "KILL" WITH ANYTHING ELSE.
EAST URAMI JUNIOR HIGH SECOND-YEAR STUDENT
MEGUMI FUSHIGURO
BASICALLY, YOU SHOULDN'T CROSS ANY LINE THAT VIOLATES ANOTHER PERSON'S DIGNITY. YOU SHOULD ACKNOWLEDGE EACH OTHER'S EXISTENCE. THAT'S THE RULE.
YOU IGNORED IT AND FED YOUR STUPID EGO AND TREATED IT LIKE A NUISANCE.
DID THAT MAKE YOU FEEL GOOD?
GRUNCH
...
IF I SEE YOU DO IT AGAIN, I'LL KILL YOU.
DID WE DO SOME-THING TO YOU?
FIGURE IT OUT YOURSELF.
OR JUST DIE.
KNOCK IT OFF!!

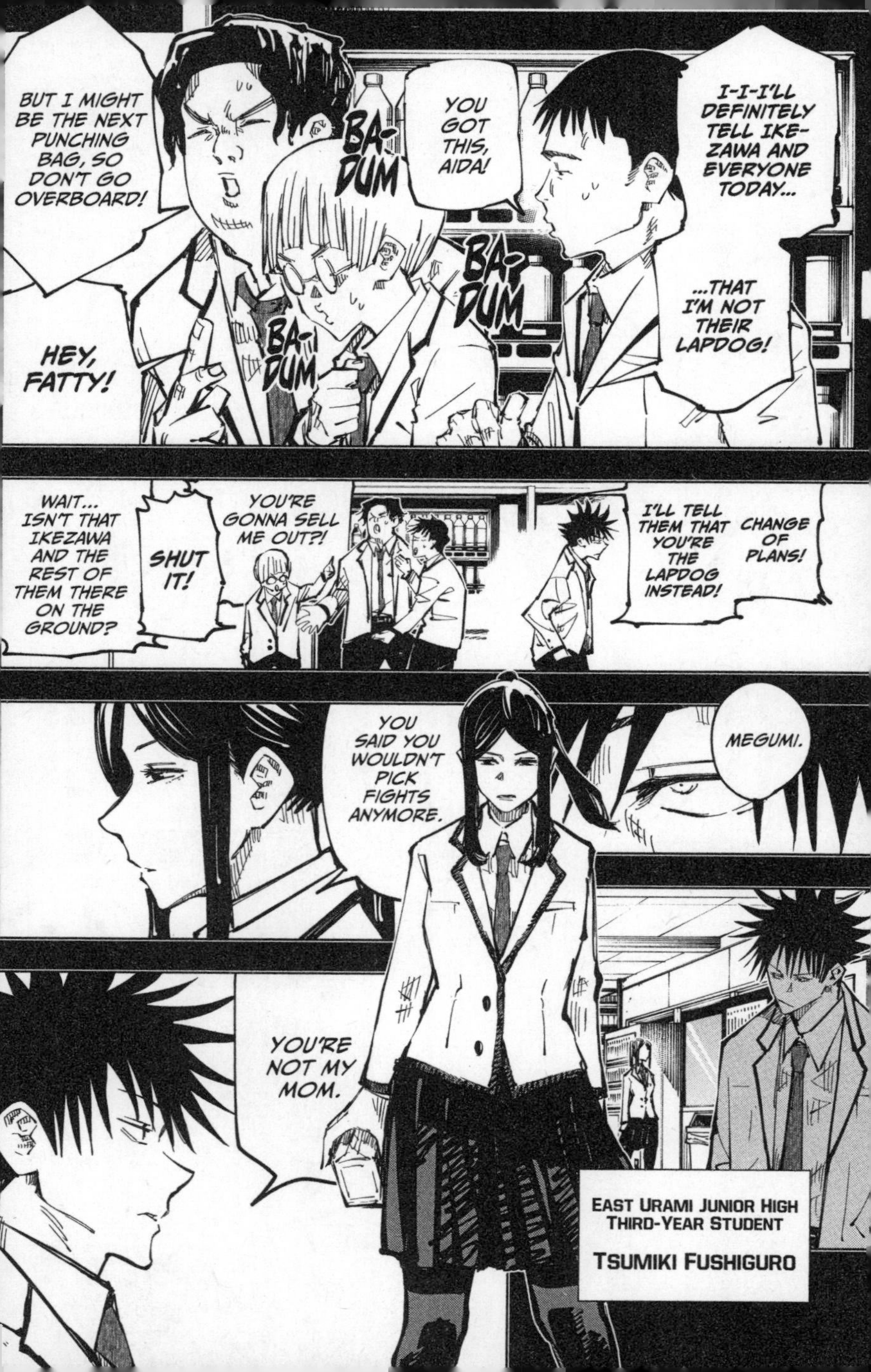
I-I-I'LL DEFINITELY TELL IKE-ZAWA AND EVERYONE TODAY...
...THAT I'M NOT THEIR LAPDOG!
BA-DUM
YOU GOT THIS, AIDA!
BA-DUM
BA-DUM
BUT I MIGHT BE THE NEXT PUNCHING BAG, SO DON'T GO OVERBOARD!
HEY, FATTY!
CHANGE OF PLANS!
I'LL TELL THEM THAT YOU'RE THE LAPDOG INSTEAD!
YOU'RE GONNA SELL ME OUT?!
SHUT IT!
WAIT... ISN'T THAT IKEZAWA AND THE REST OF THEM THERE ON THE GROUND?
MEGUMI.
YOU SAID YOU WOULDN'T PICK FIGHTS ANYMORE.
YOU'RE NOT MY MOM.
EAST URAMI JUNIOR HIGH THIRD-YEAR STUDENT
TSUMIKI FUSHIGURO

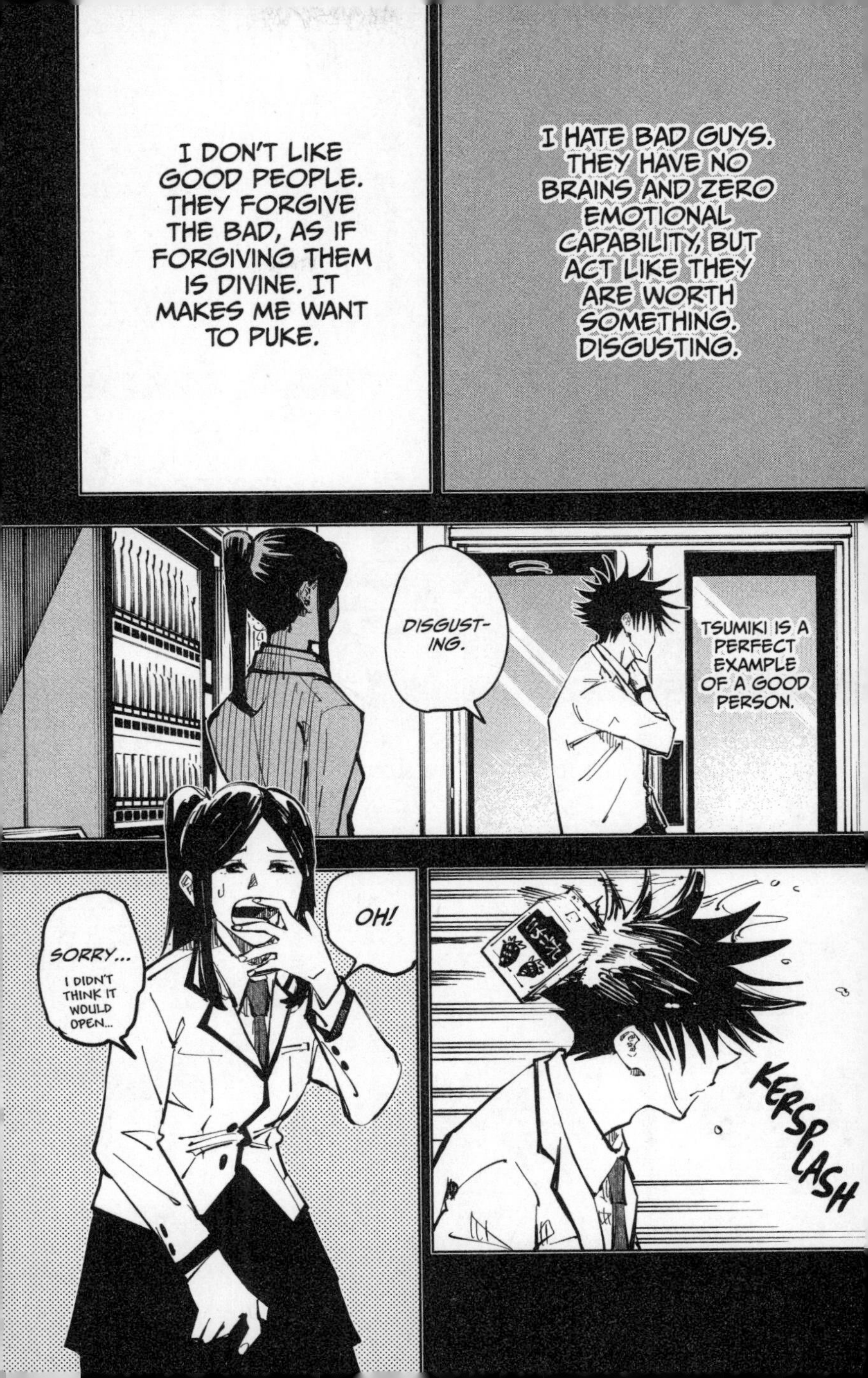
I HATE BAD GUYS. THEY HAVE NO BRAINS AND ZERO EMOTIONAL CAPABILITY, BUT ACT LIKE THEY ARE WORTH SOMETHING. DISGUSTING.
I DON'T LIKE GOOD PEOPLE. THEY FORGIVE THE BAD, AS IF FORGIVING THEM IS DIVINE. IT MAKES ME WANT TO PUKE.
TSUMIKI IS A PERFECT EXAMPLE OF A GOOD PERSON.
DISGUSTING.
KERSPLASH
OH!
SORRY... I DIDN'T THINK IT WOULD OPEN...

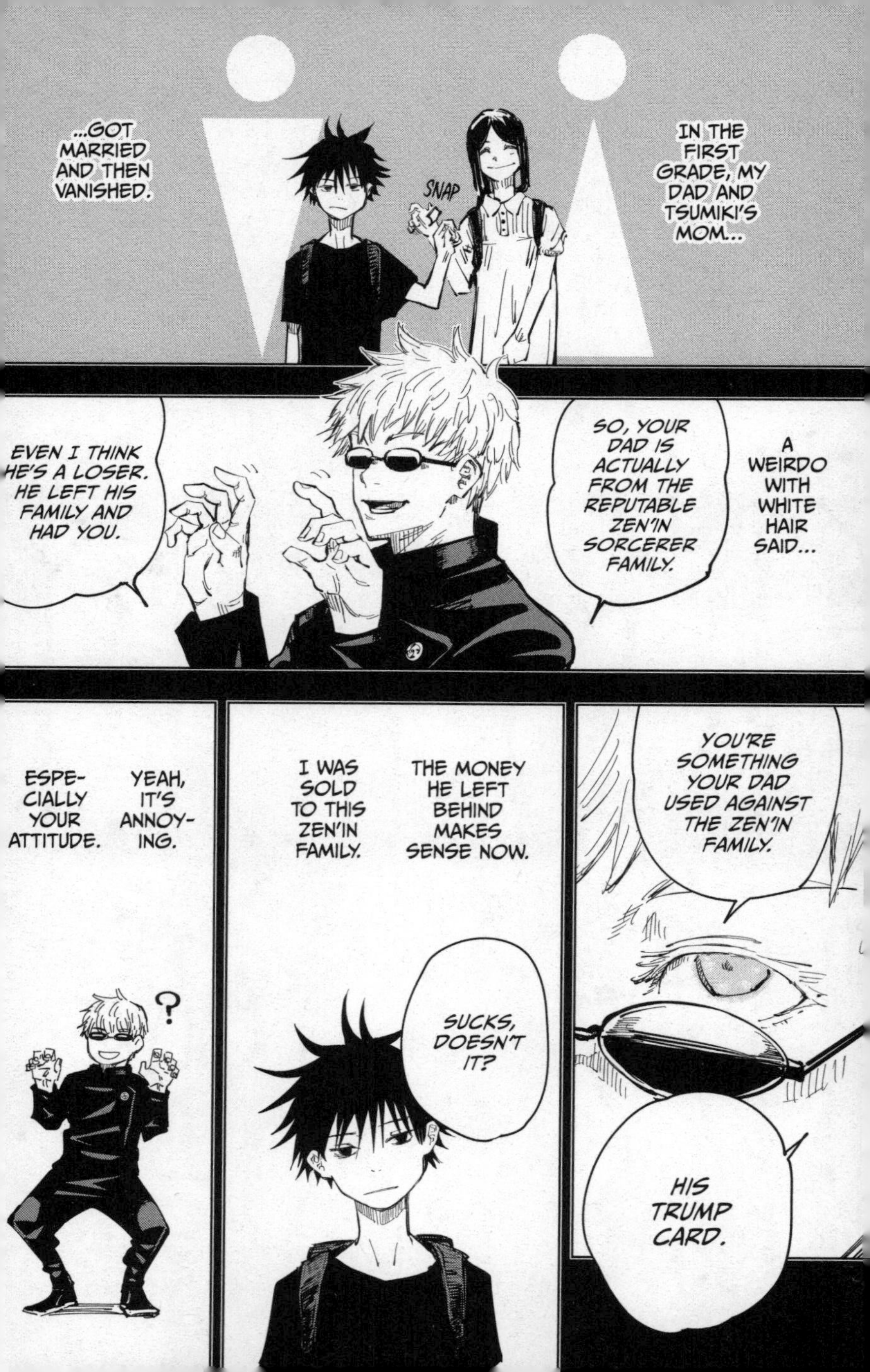
IN THE FIRST GRADE, MY DAD AND TSUMIKI'S MOM...
SNAP
...GOT MARRIED AND THEN VANISHED.
A WEIRDO WITH WHITE HAIR SAID...
SO, YOUR DAD IS ACTUALLY FROM THE REPUTABLE ZEN'IN SORCERER FAMILY.
EVEN I THINK HE'S A LOSER. HE LEFT HIS FAMILY AND HAD YOU.
YOU'RE SOMETHING YOUR DAD USED AGAINST THE ZEN'IN FAMILY.
HIS TRUMP CARD.
THE MONEY HE LEFT BEHIND MAKES SENSE NOW.
I WAS SOLD TO THIS ZEN'IN FAMILY.
SUCKS, DOESN'T IT?
YEAH, IT'S ANNOY-ING.
ESPE-CIALLY YOUR ATTITUDE.
?

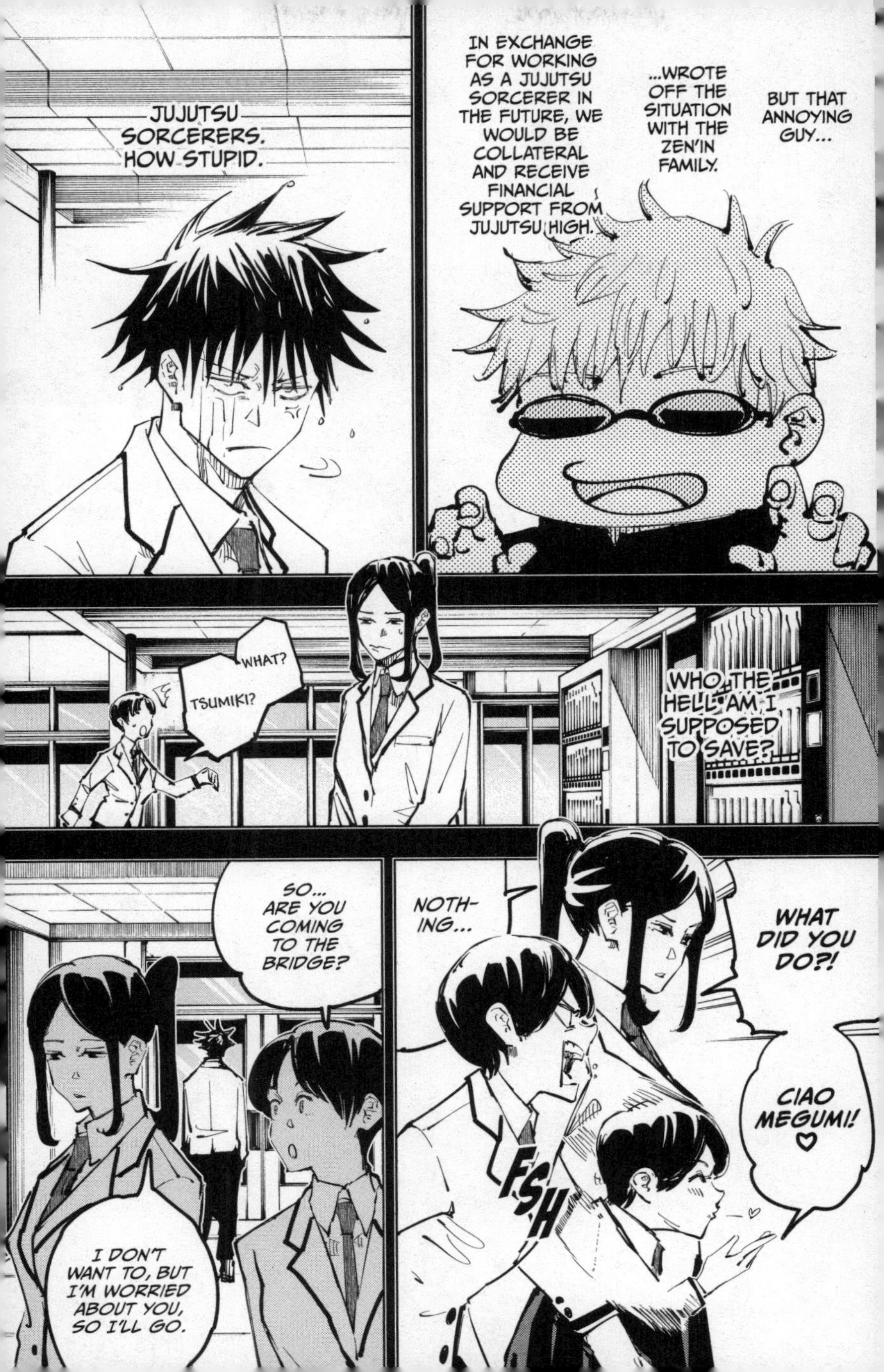
BUT THAT ANNOYING GUY...
...WROTE OFF THE SITUATION WITH THE ZEN'IN FAMILY.
IN EXCHANGE FOR WORKING AS A JUJUTSU SORCERER IN THE FUTURE, WE WOULD BE COLLATERAL AND RECEIVE FINANCIAL SUPPORT FROM JUJUTSU HIGH.
JUJUTSU SORCERERS. HOW STUPID.
WHO THE HELL AM I SUPPOSED TO SAVE?
WHAT?
TSUMIKI?
WHAT DID YOU DO?!
NOTH-ING...
CIAO MEGUMI! ♡
FSH
SO... ARE YOU COMING TO THE BRIDGE?
I DON'T WANT TO, BUT I'M WORRIED ABOUT YOU, SO I'LL GO.

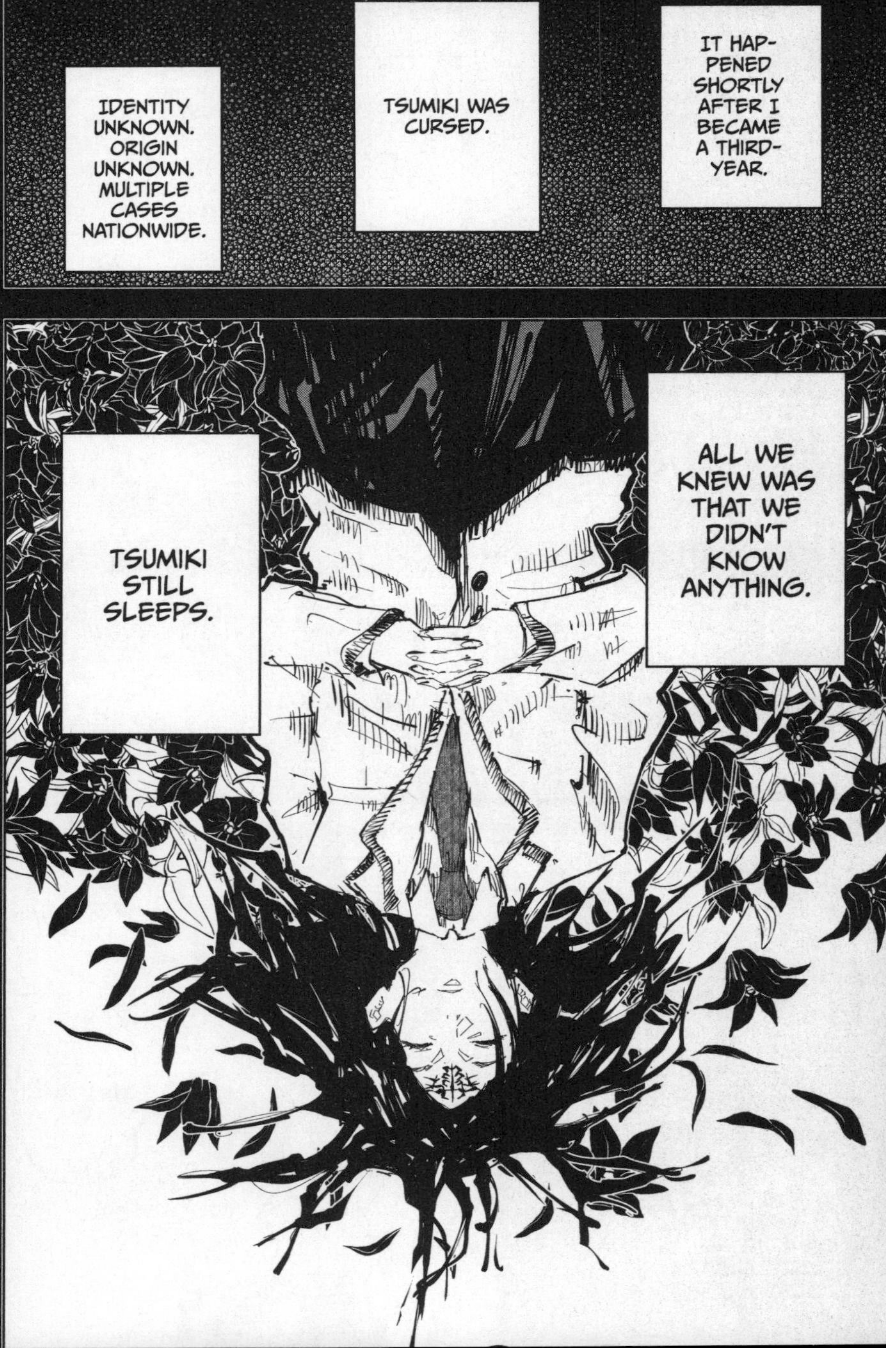
IT HAP-PENED SHORTLY AFTER I BECAME A THIRD-YEAR.
TSUMIKI WAS CURSED.
IDENTITY UNKNOWN. ORIGIN UNKNOWN. MULTIPLE CASES NATIONWIDE.
ALL WE KNEW WAS THAT WE DIDN'T KNOW ANYTHING.
TSUMIKI STILL SLEEPS.

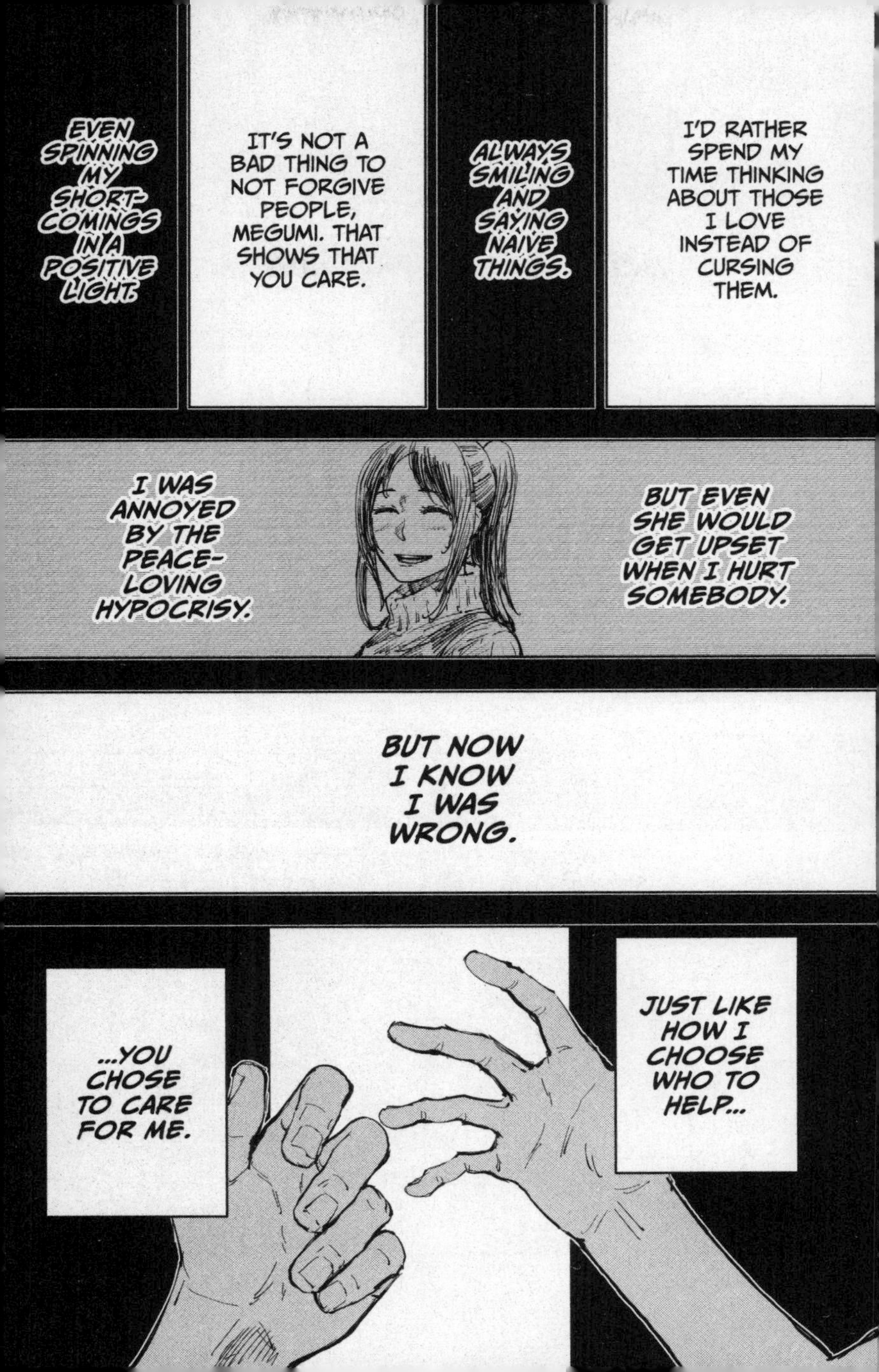
I'D RATHER SPEND MY TIME THINKING ABOUT THOSE I LOVE INSTEAD OF CURSING THEM.
ALWAYS SMILING AND SAYING NAIVE THINGS.
IT'S NOT A BAD THING TO NOT FORGIVE PEOPLE, MEGUMI. THAT SHOWS THAT YOU CARE.
EVEN SPINNING MY SHORT-COMINGS IN A POSITIVE LIGHT.
BUT EVEN SHE WOULD GET UPSET WHEN I HURT SOMEBODY.
I WAS ANNOYED BY THE PEACE-LOVING HYPOCRISY.
BUT NOW I KNOW I WAS WRONG.
JUST LIKE HOW I CHOOSE WHO TO HELP...
...YOU CHOSE TO CARE FOR ME.

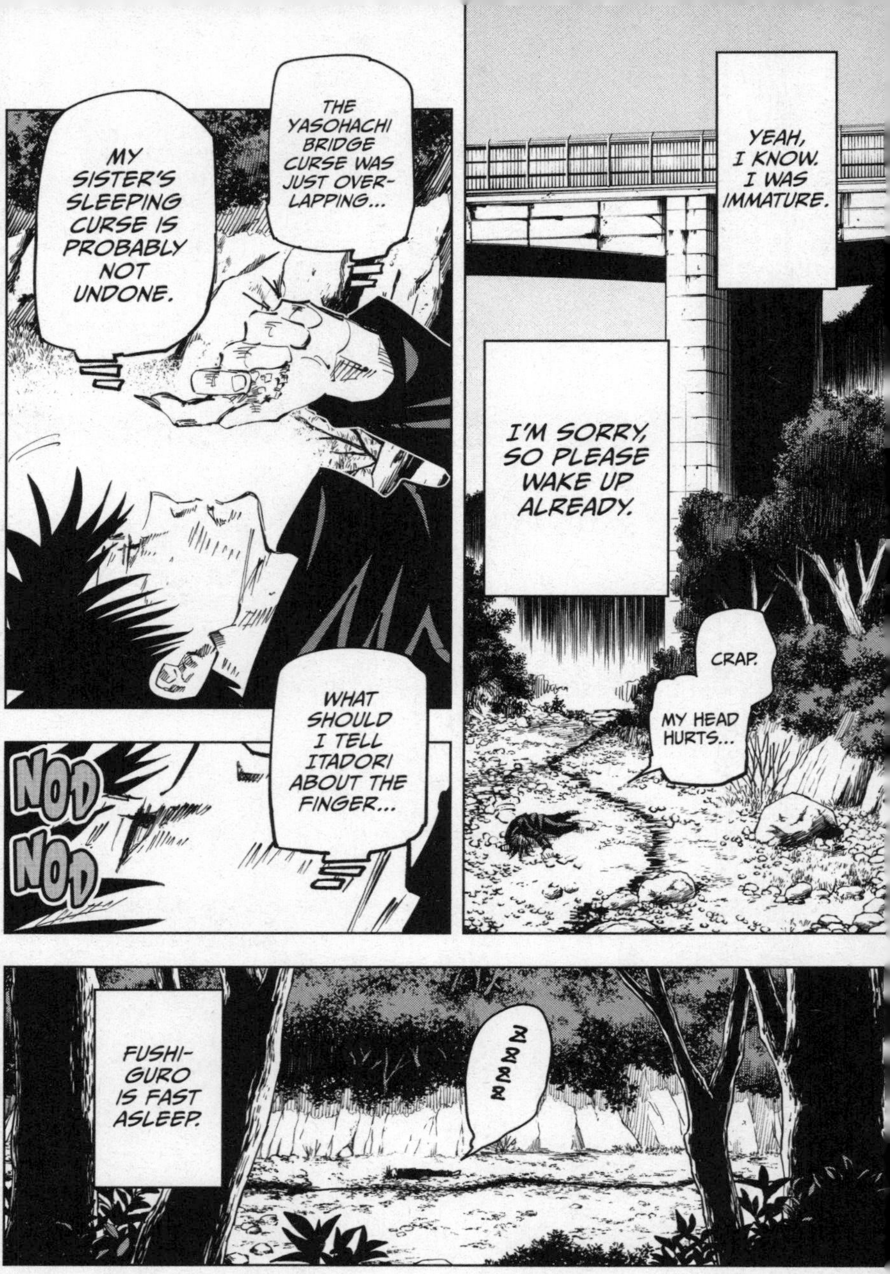
YEAH, I KNOW. I WAS IMMATURE.
I'M SORRY, SO PLEASE WAKE UP ALREADY.
CRAP.
MY HEAD HURTS...
THE YASOHACHI BRIDGE CURSE WAS JUST OVER-LAPPING...
MY SISTER'S SLEEPING CURSE IS PROBABLY NOT UNDONE.
WHAT SHOULD I TELL ITADORI ABOUT THE FINGER...
NOD NOD
FUSHIGURO IS FAST ASLEEP.

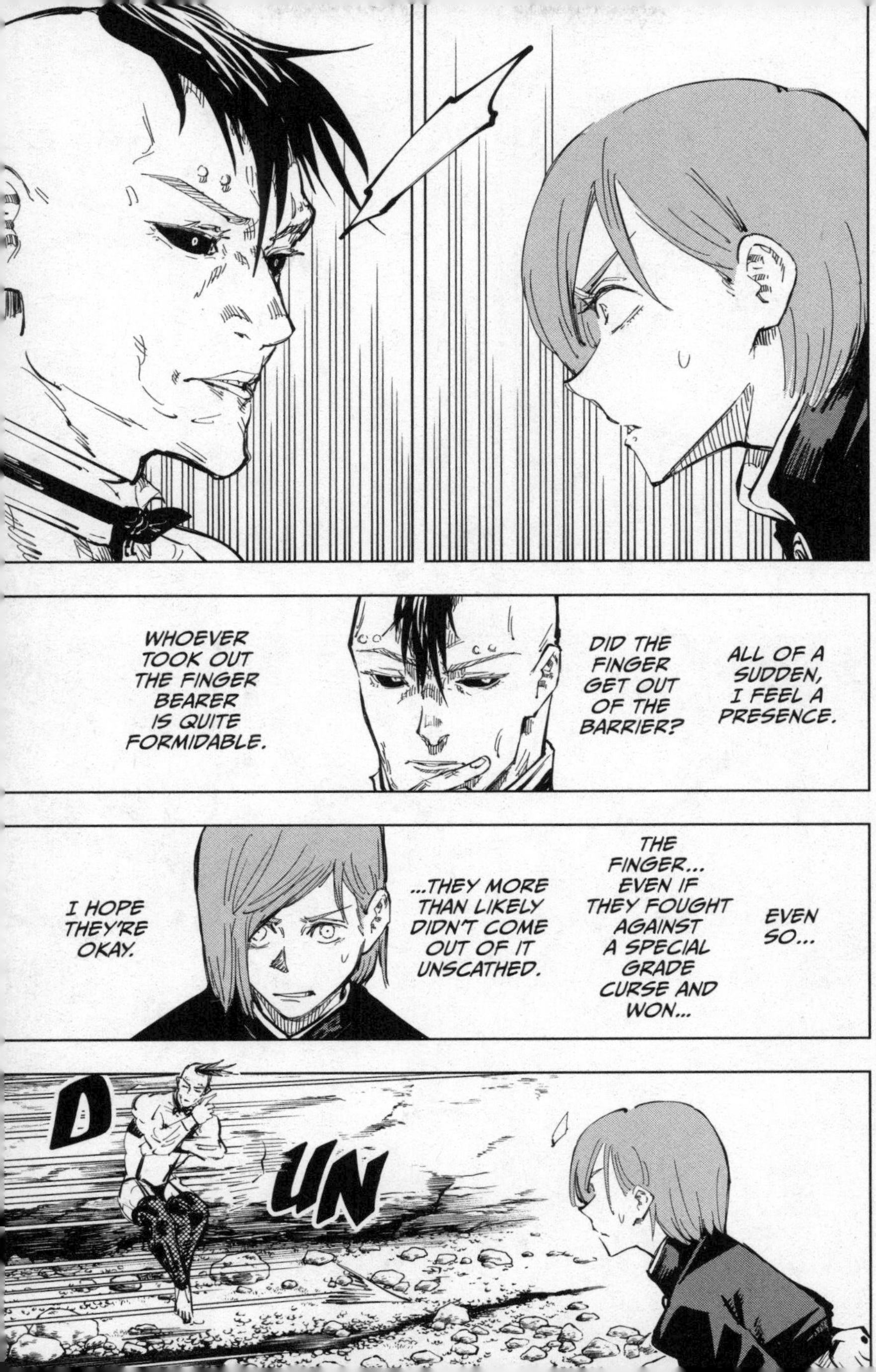
ALL OF A SUDDEN, I FEEL A PRESENCE.
DID THE FINGER GET OUT OF THE BARRIER?
WHOEVER TOOK OUT THE FINGER BEARER IS QUITE FORMIDABLE.
EVEN SO...
THE FINGER... EVEN IF THEY FOUGHT AGAINST A SPECIAL GRADE CURSE AND WON...
...THEY MORE THAN LIKELY DIDN'T COME OUT OF IT UNSCATHED.
I HOPE THEY'RE OKAY.
D
UN

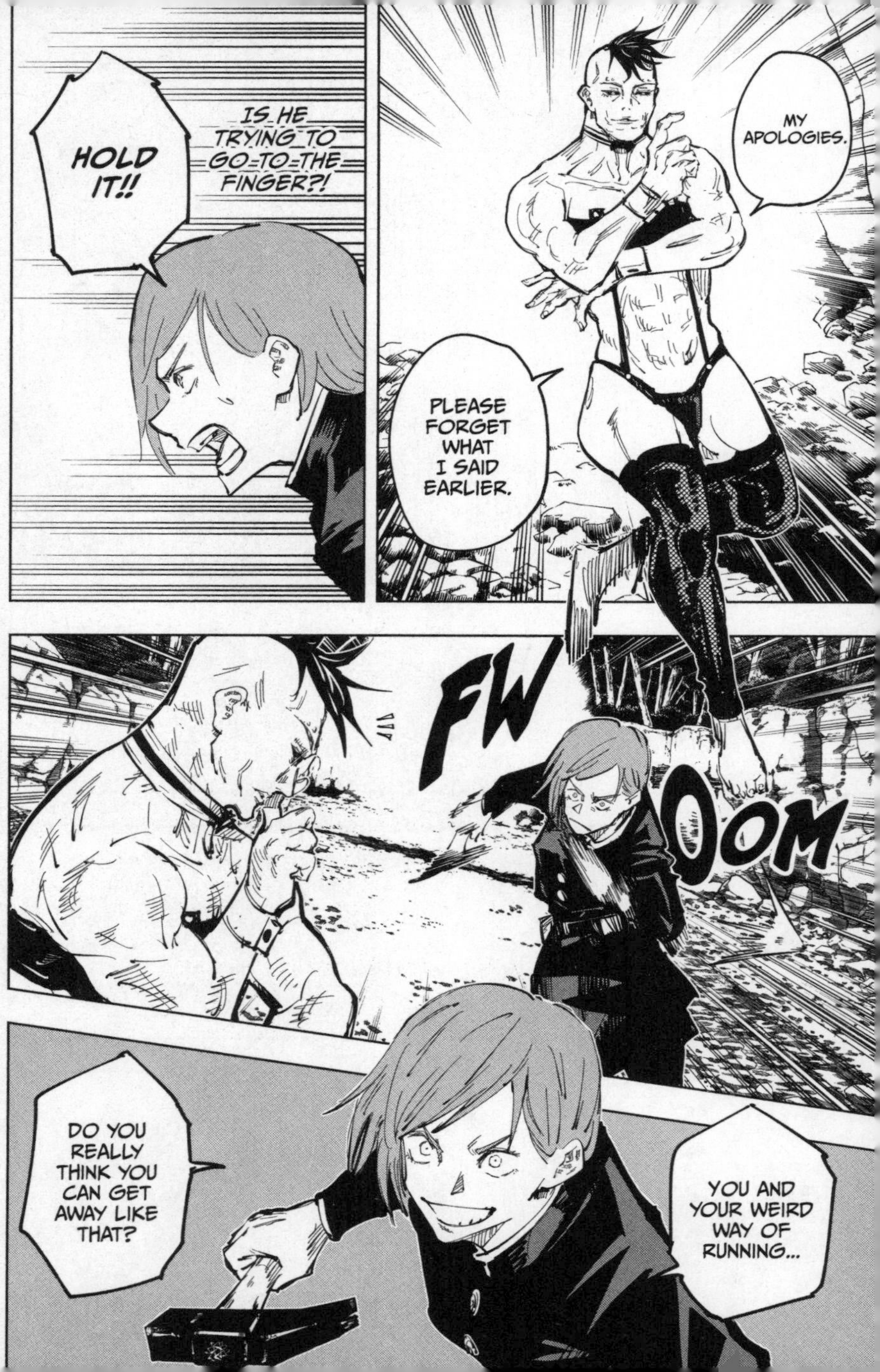
MY APOLOGIES.
PLEASE FORGET WHAT I SAID EARLIER.
HOLD IT!!
IS HE TRYING TO GO TO THE FINGER?!
FWOOM
YOU AND YOUR WEIRD WAY OF RUNNING...
DO YOU REALLY THINK YOU CAN GET AWAY LIKE THAT?

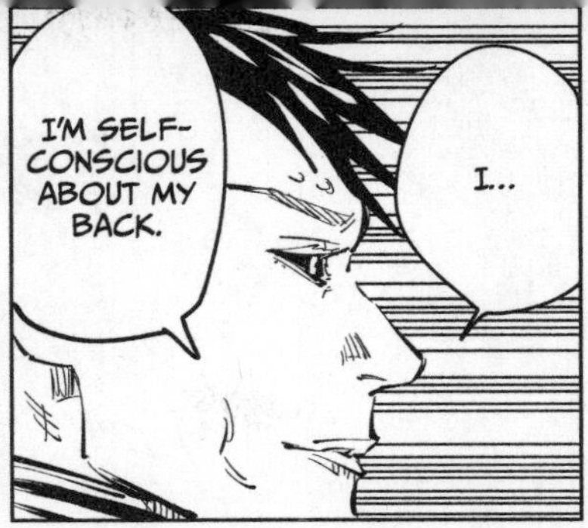
I...
I'M SELF-CONSCIOUS ABOUT MY BACK.
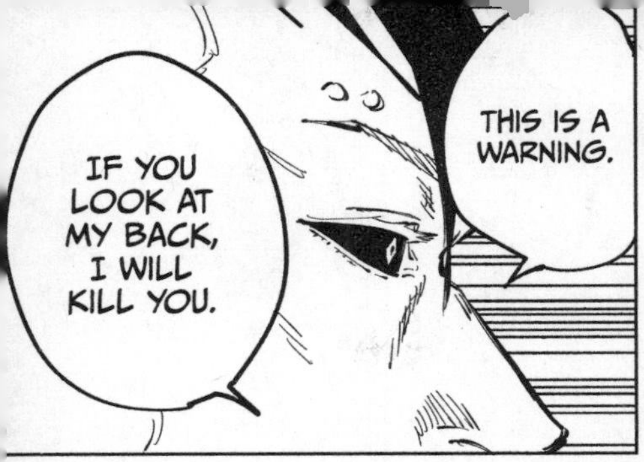
THIS IS A WARNING.
IF YOU LOOK AT MY BACK, I WILL KILL YOU.
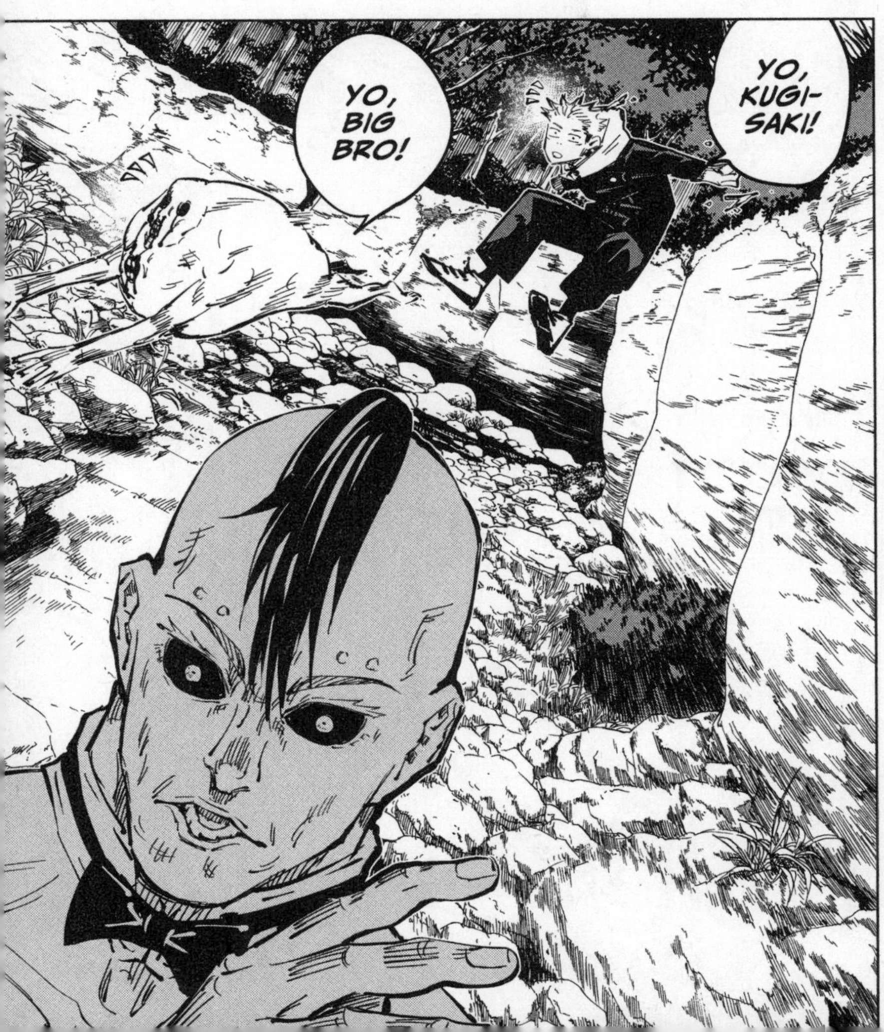
YO, KUGI-SAKI!
YO, BIG BRO!

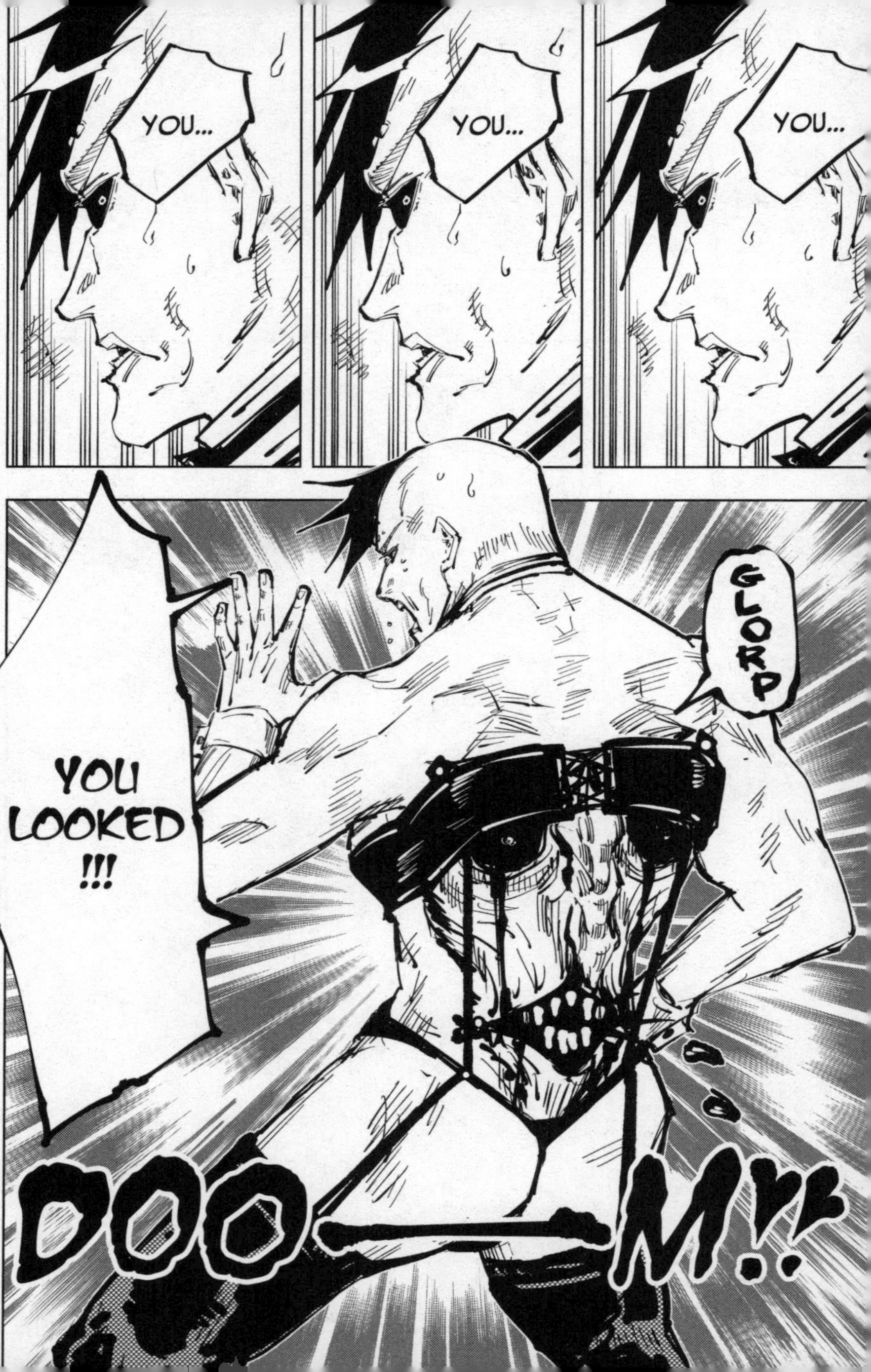
YOU...
YOU...
YOU...
GLORP
YOU LOOKED !!!
DOO—M!!

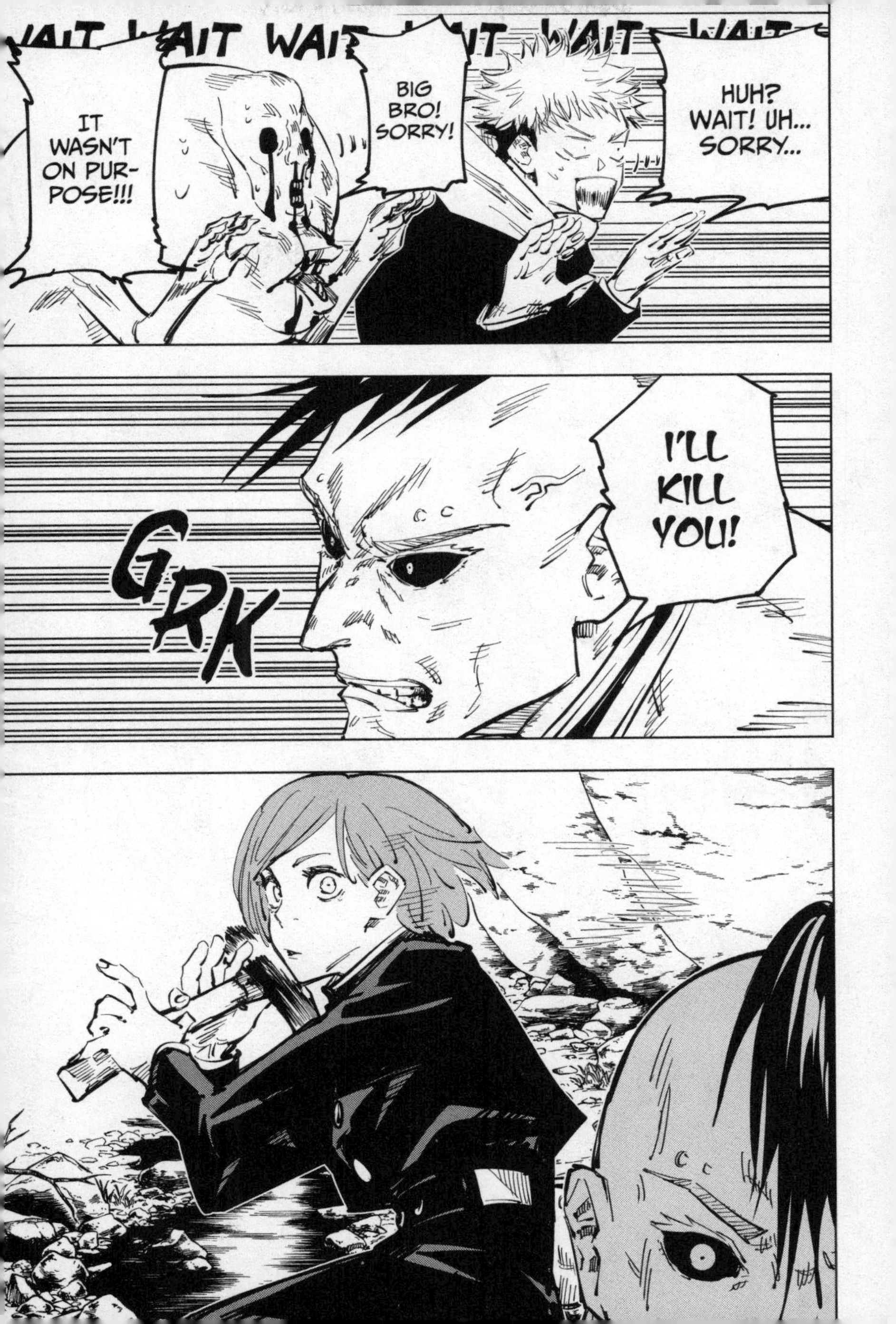
WAIT WAIT
HUH? WAIT! UH... SORRY...
BIG BRO! SORRY!
IT WASN'T ON PUR-POSE!!!
I'LL KILL YOU!
GRK

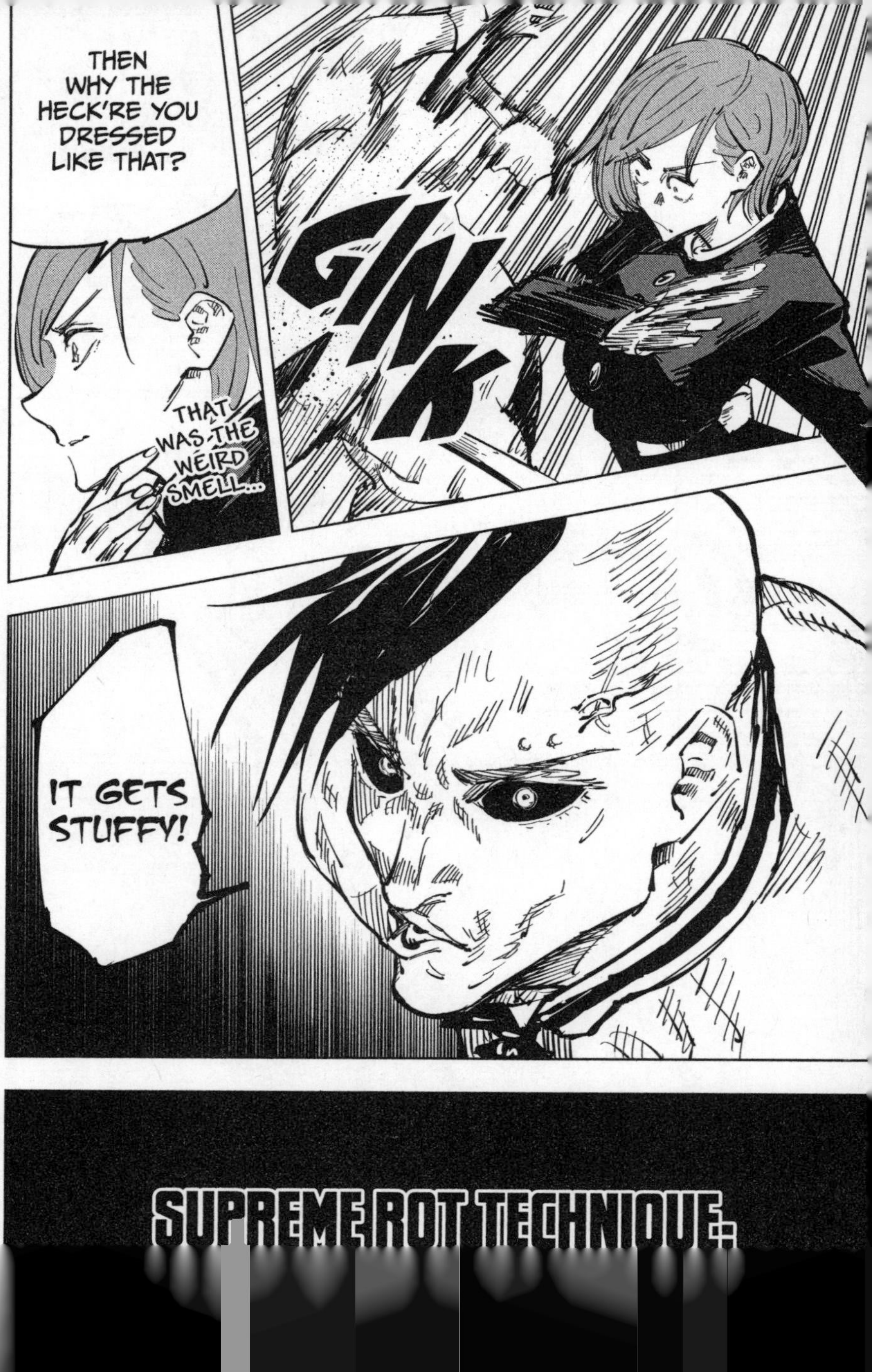
GNK
THEN WHY THE HECK'RE YOU DRESSED LIKE THAT?
THAT WAS THE WEIRD SMELL...
IT GETS STUFFY!
SUPREME ROT TECHNIQUE:

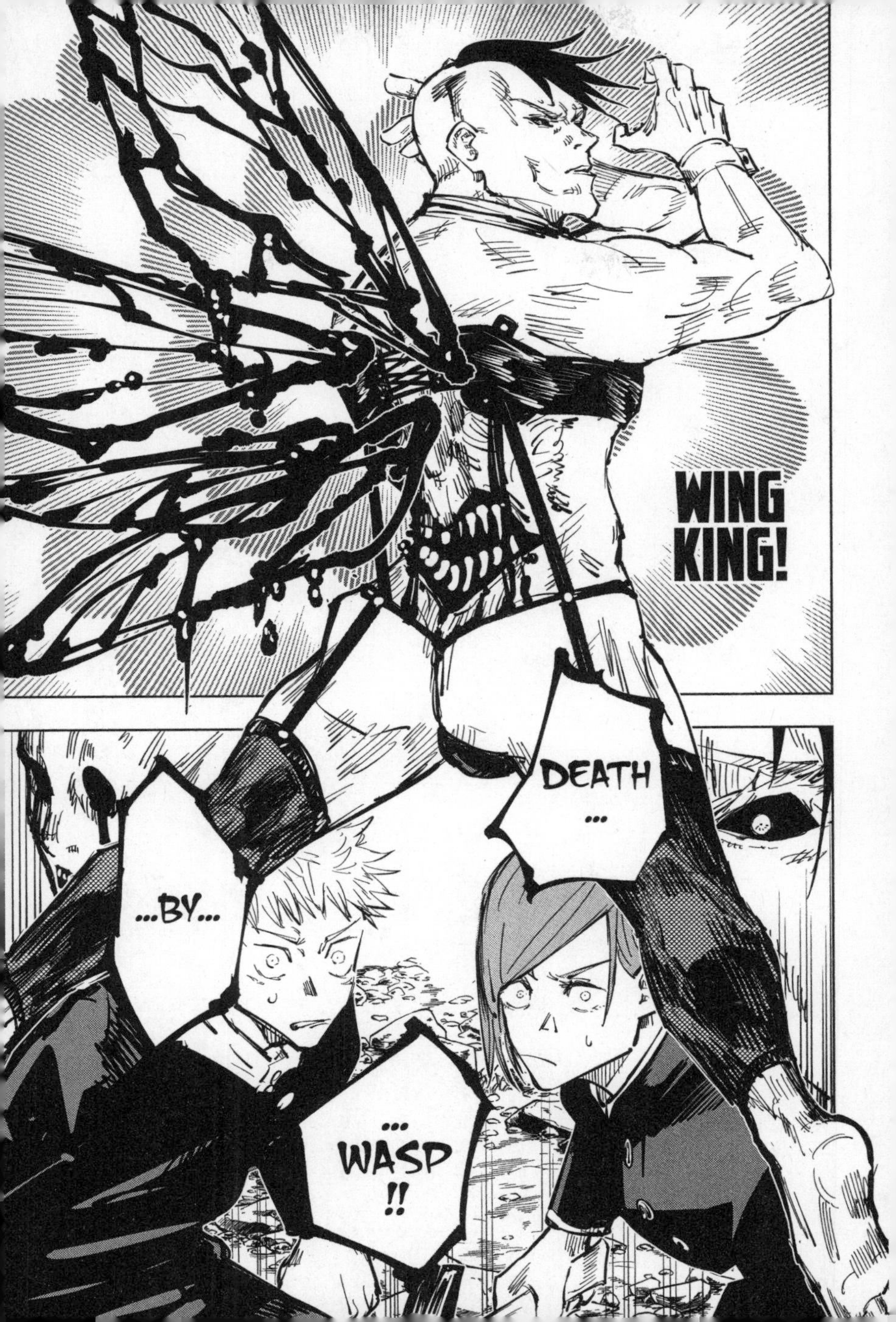
WING KING!
DEATH ...
...BY...
... WASP !!

Q: WHAT IS "DEATH BY WASP"?

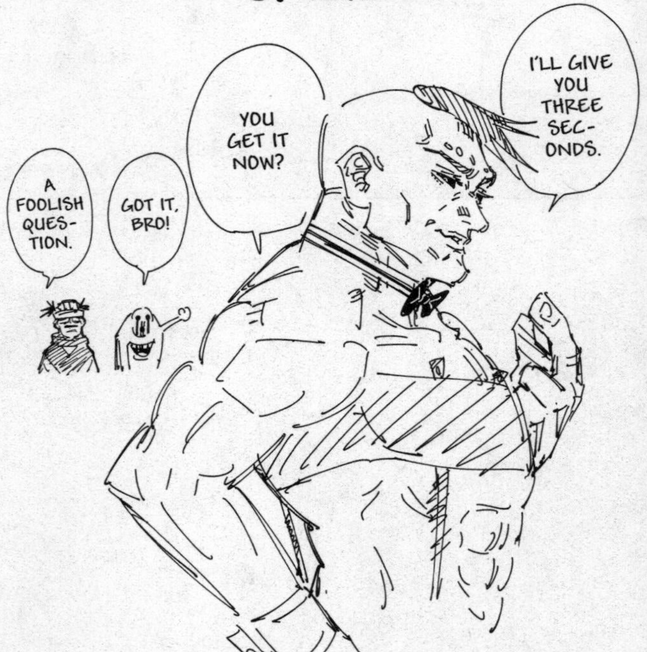
I'LL GIVE YOU THREE SEC-ONDS.
YOU GET IT NOW?
GOT IT, BRO!
A FOOLISH QUES-TION.

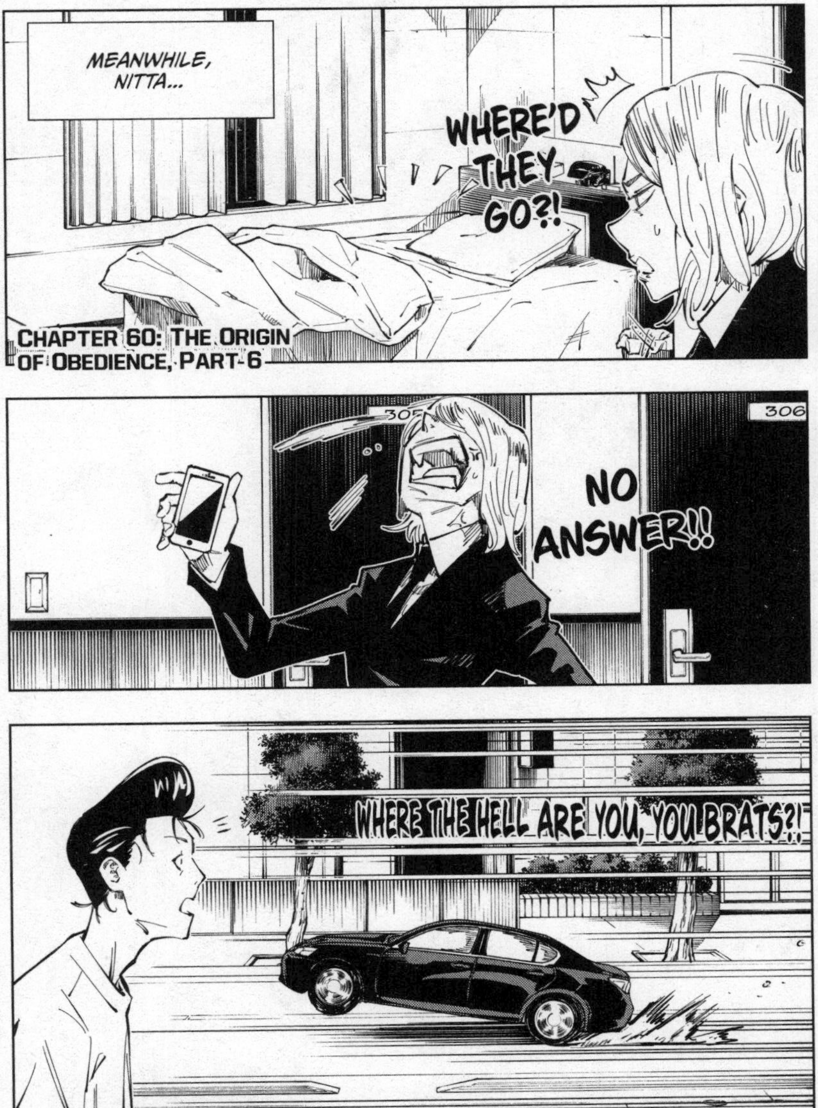
MEANWHILE, NITTA...
WHERE'D THEY GO?!
CHAPTER 60: THE ORIGIN OF OBEDIENCE, PART 6
306
NO ANSWER!!
WHERE THE HELL ARE YOU, YOU BRATS?!

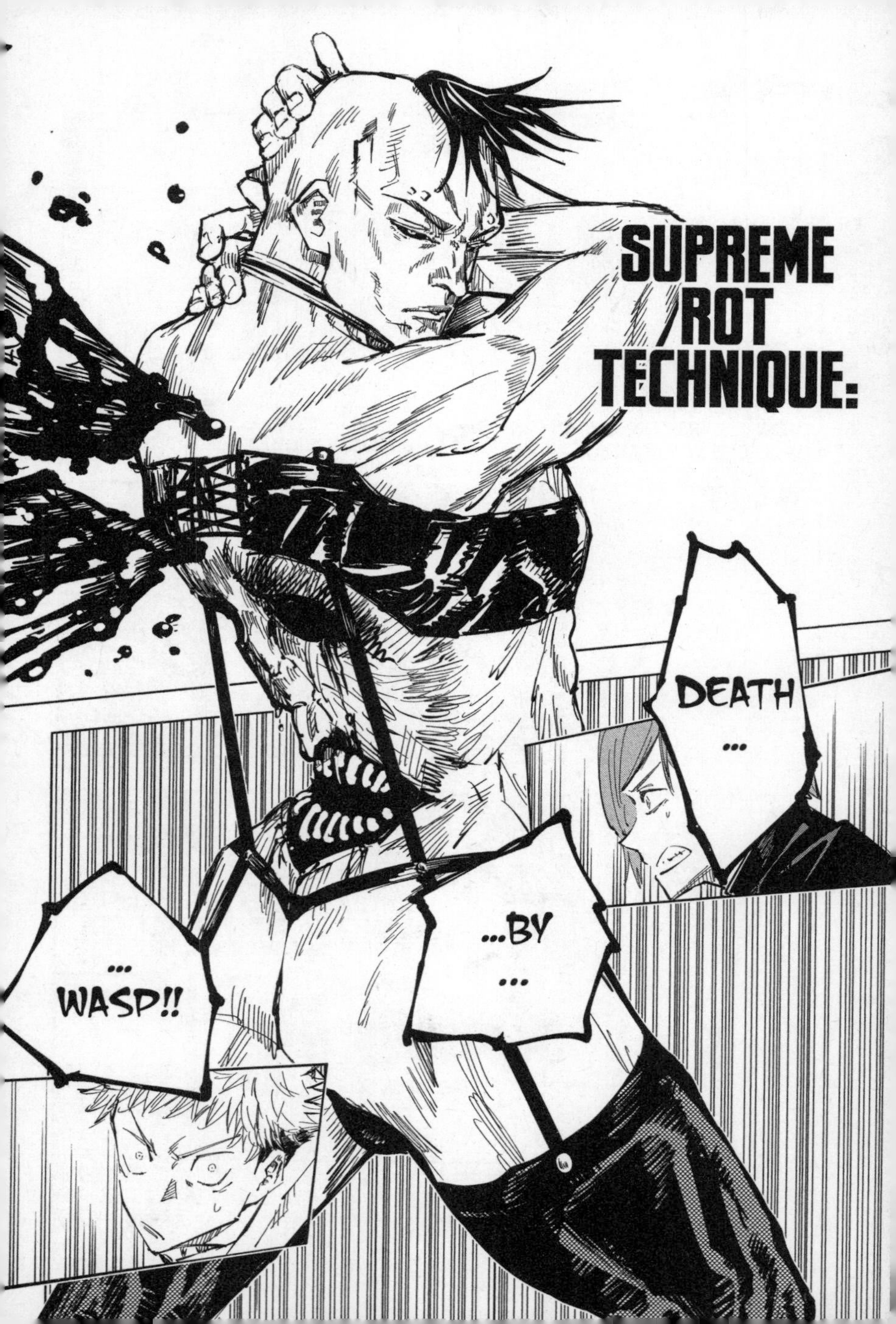
SUPREME ROT TECHNIQUE:
DEATH ...
...BY ...
... WASP!!

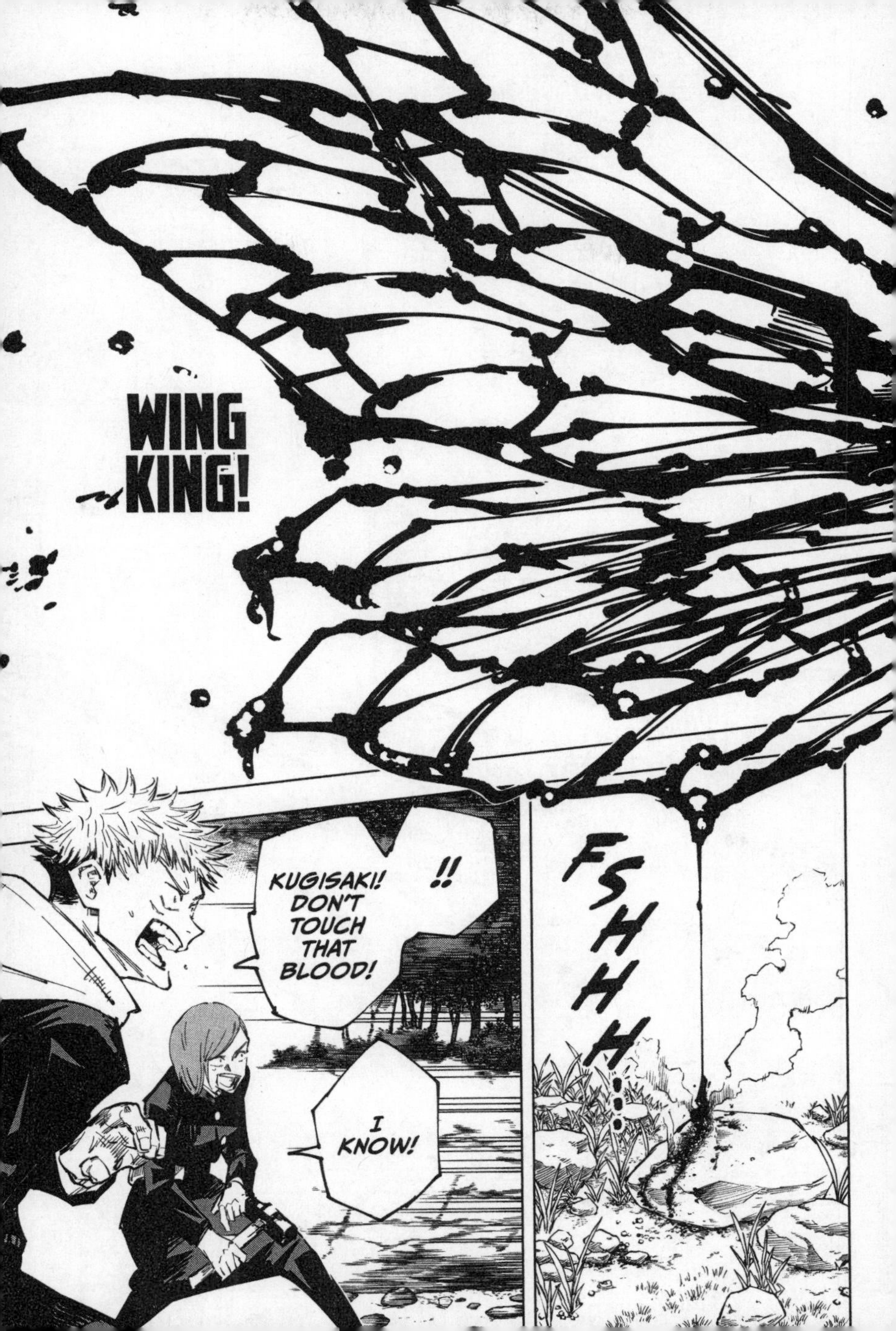
WING KING!
FSHHH...
KUGISAKI! DON'T TOUCH THAT BLOOD!
!!
I KNOW!

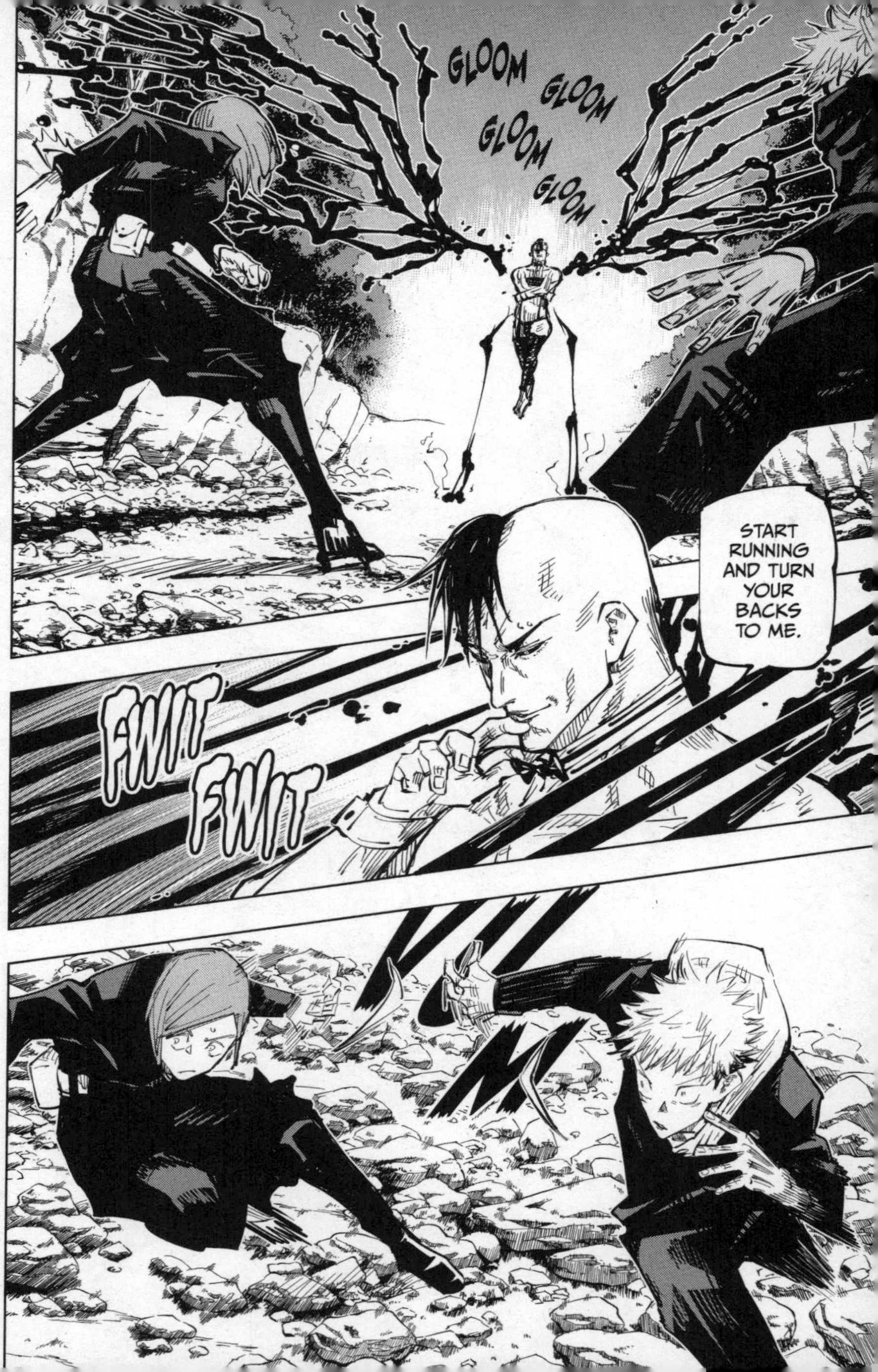
GLOOM
GLOOM
GLOOM
GLOOM
START RUNNING AND TURN YOUR BACKS TO ME.
FWIT
FWIT

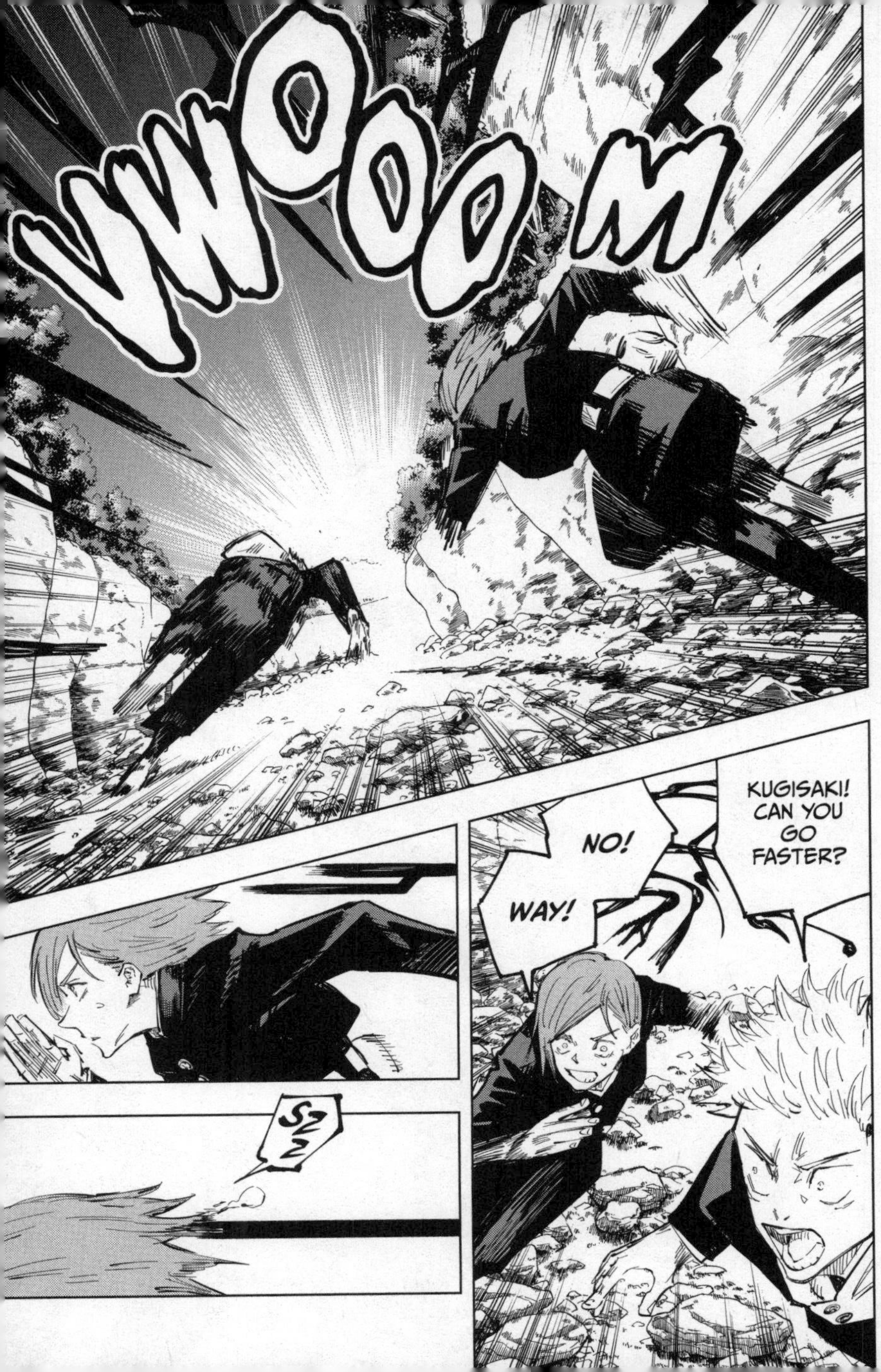
VWOOOM
KUGISAKI! CAN YOU GO FASTER?
NO!
WAY!
SZZ

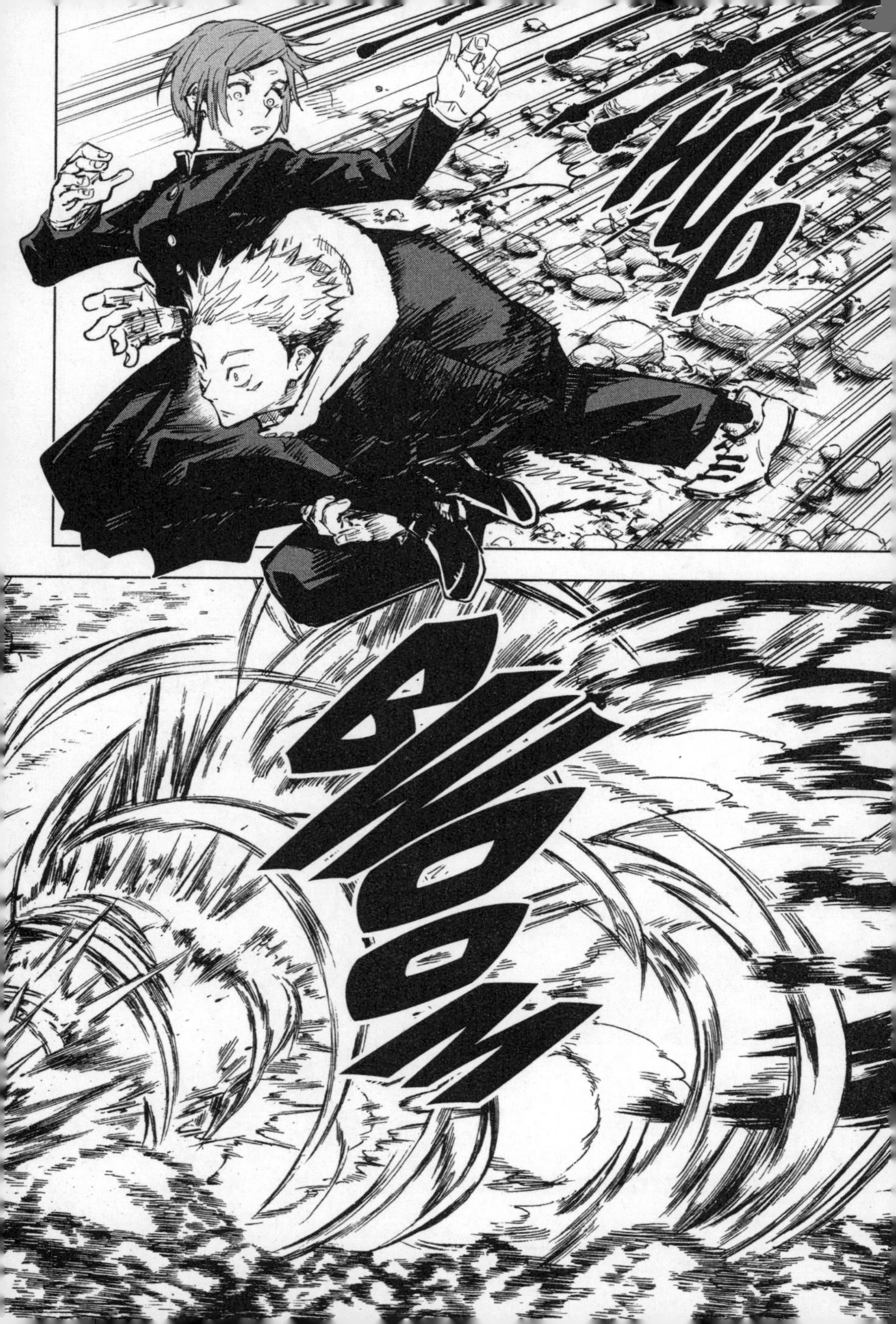
THUD
BWOOM

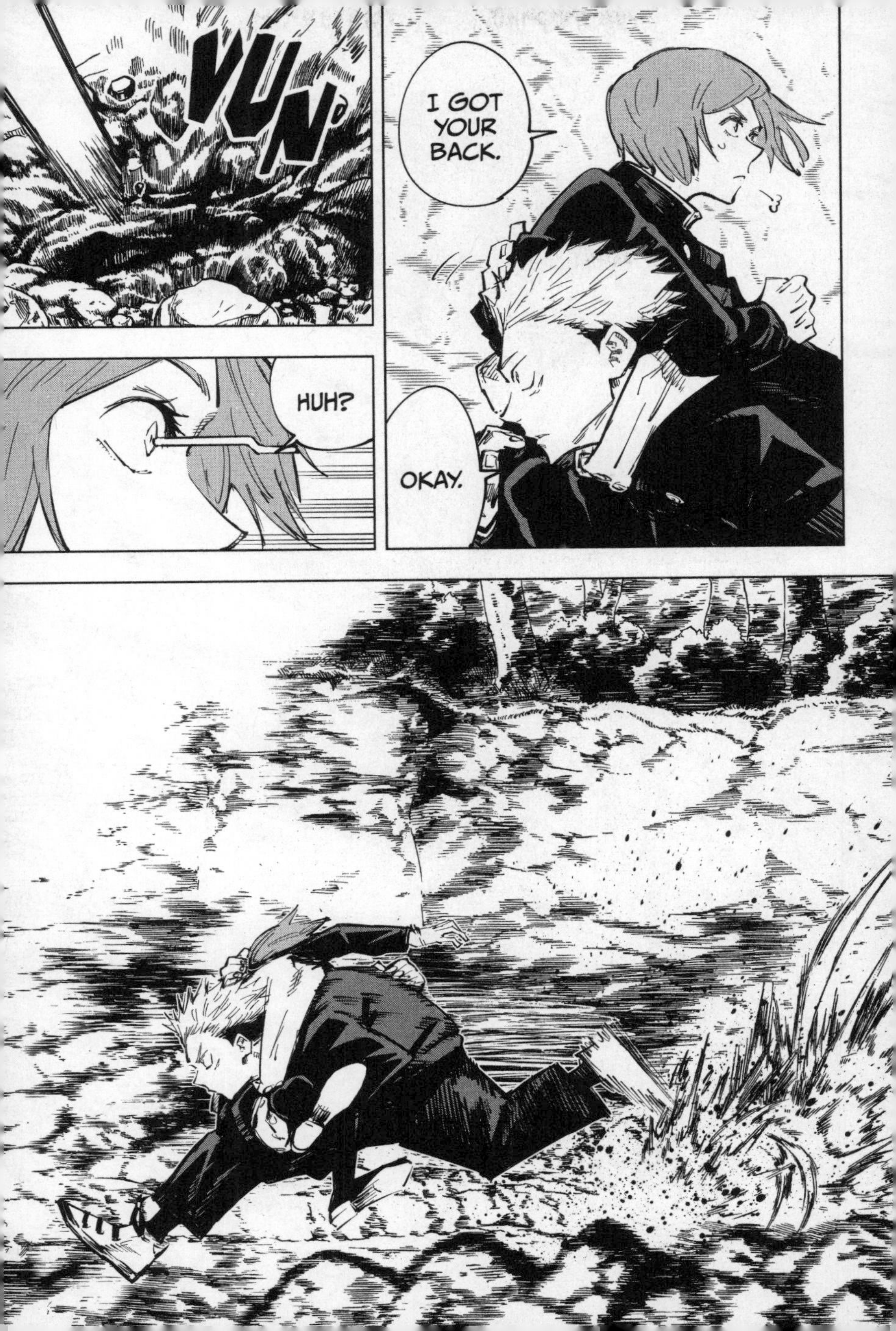
I GOT YOUR BACK.
OKAY.
VUN
HUH?

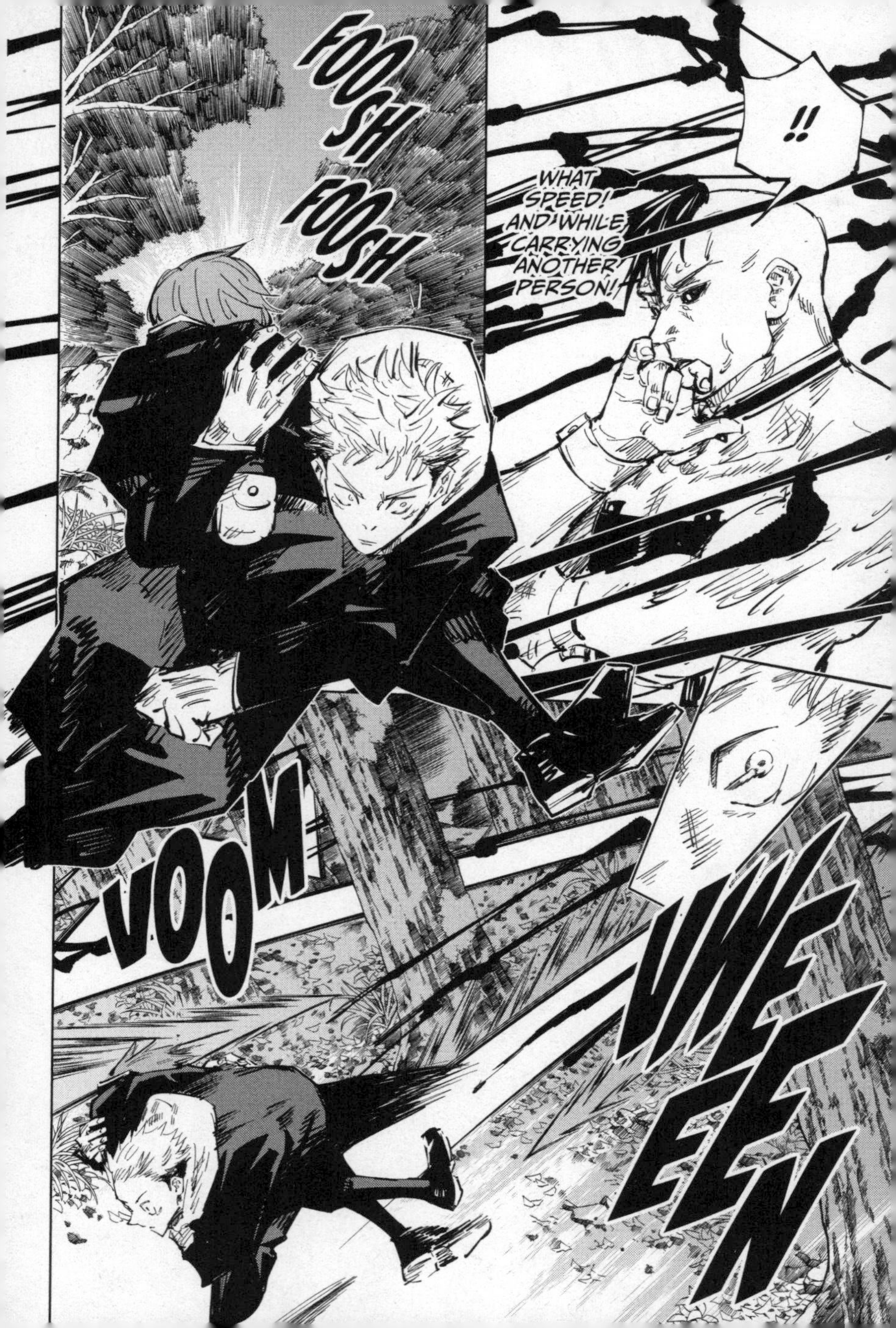
!!
WHAT SPEED! AND WHILE CARRYING ANOTHER PERSON!
FOOSH FOOSH
VOOM
VWEEEN

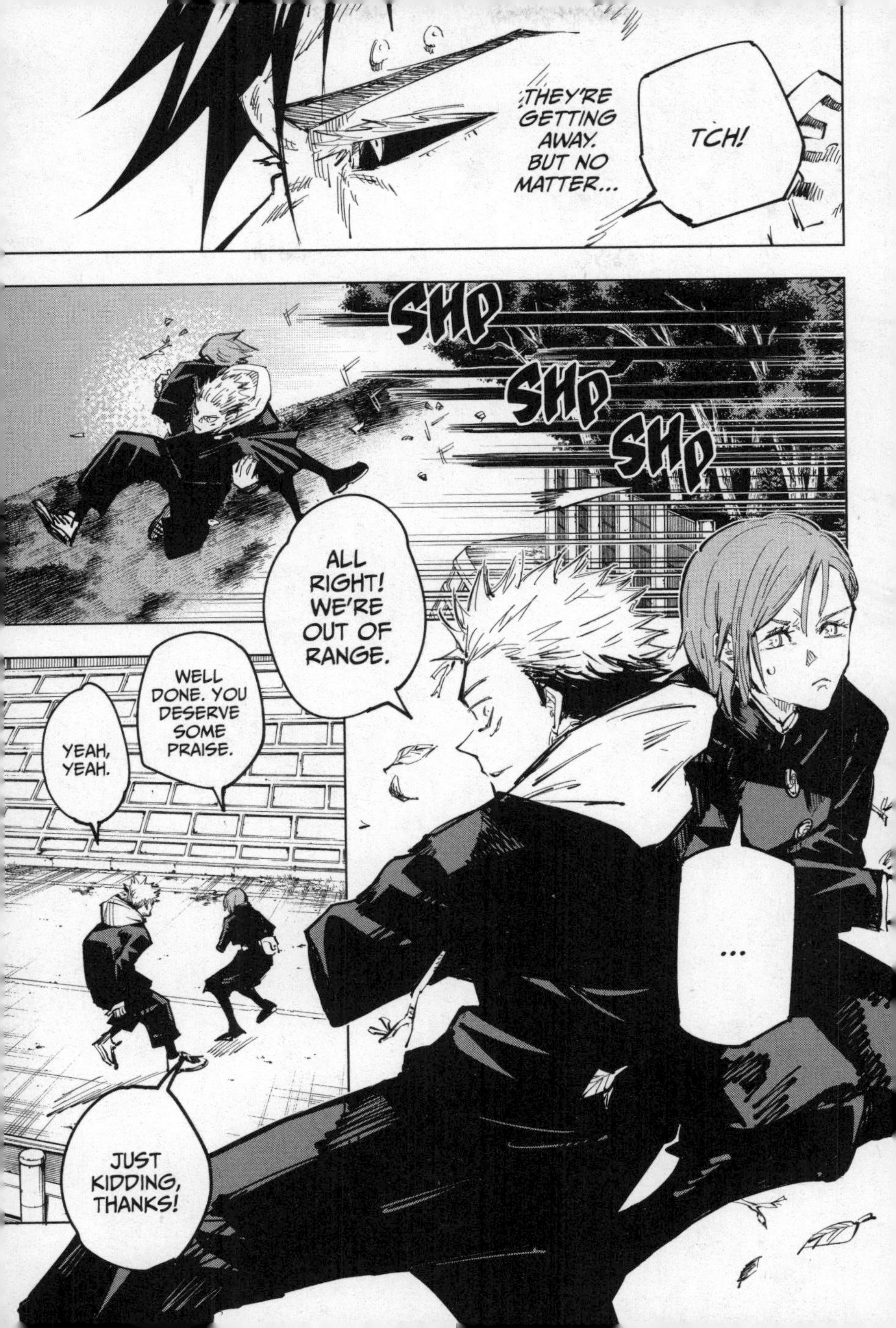
TCH!
THEY'RE GETTING AWAY. BUT NO MATTER...
SHP SHP SHP
ALL RIGHT! WE'RE OUT OF RANGE.
WELL DONE. YOU DESERVE SOME PRAISE.
YEAH, YEAH.
...
JUST KIDDING, THANKS!

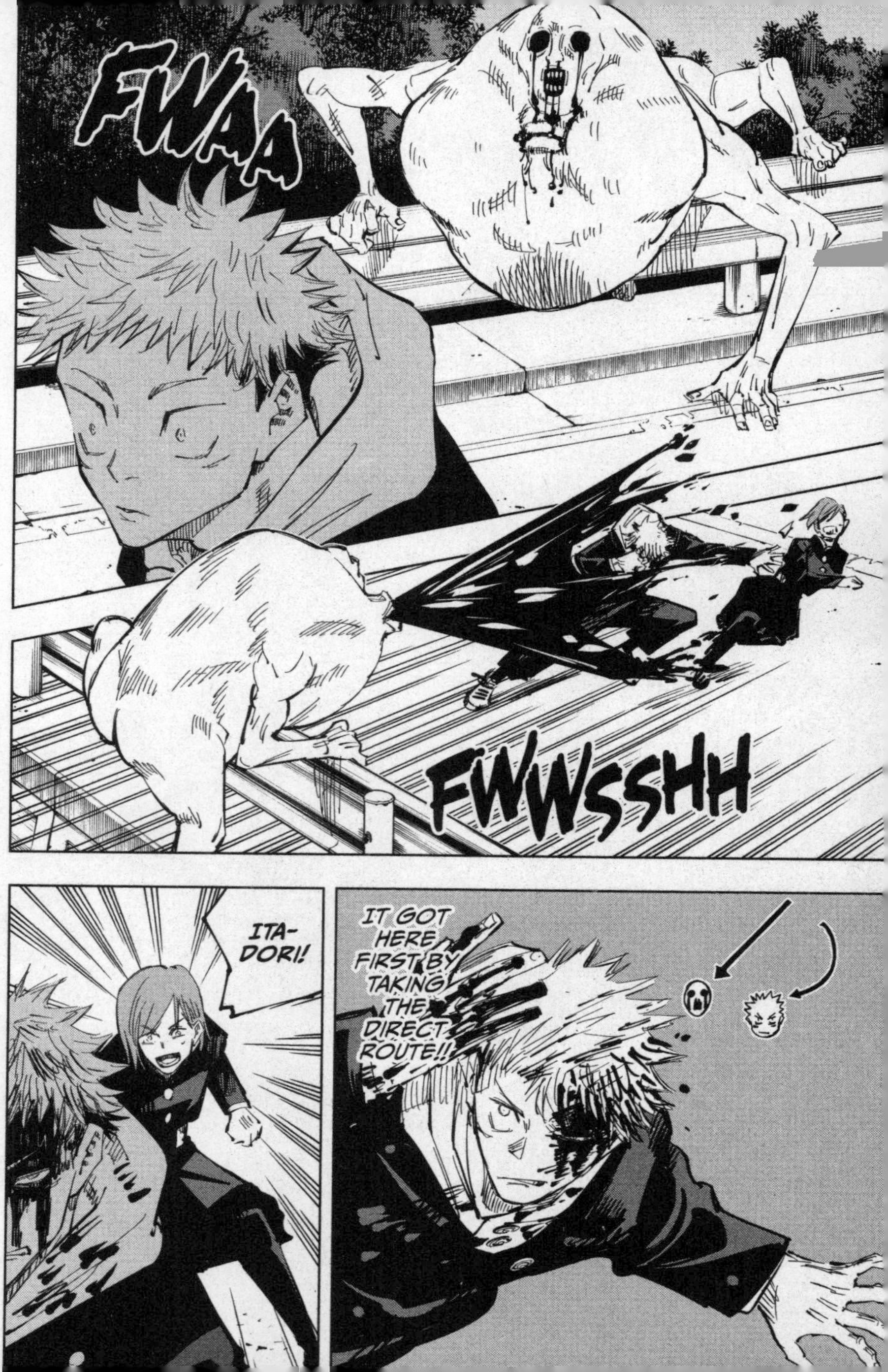
FWAA
FWWSSHH
IT GOT HERE FIRST BY TAKING THE DIRECT ROUTE!!
ITA-DORI!

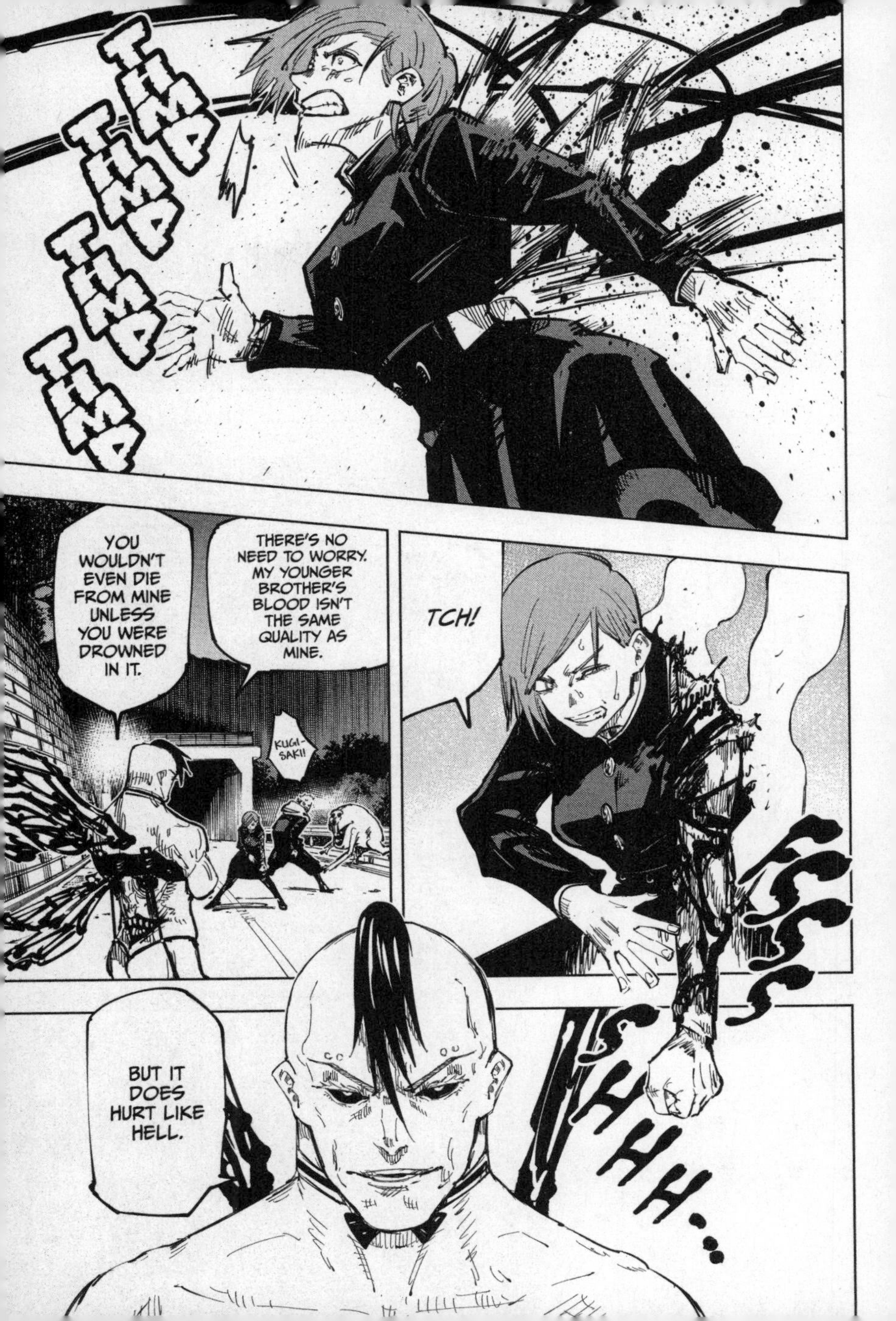
THMP THMP THMP THMP THMP
TCH!
THERE'S NO NEED TO WORRY. MY YOUNGER BROTHER'S BLOOD ISN'T THE SAME QUALITY AS MINE.
YOU WOULDN'T EVEN DIE FROM MINE UNLESS YOU WERE DROWNED IN IT.
KUGISAKI!
FSSSSHHHH...
BUT IT DOES HURT LIKE HELL.

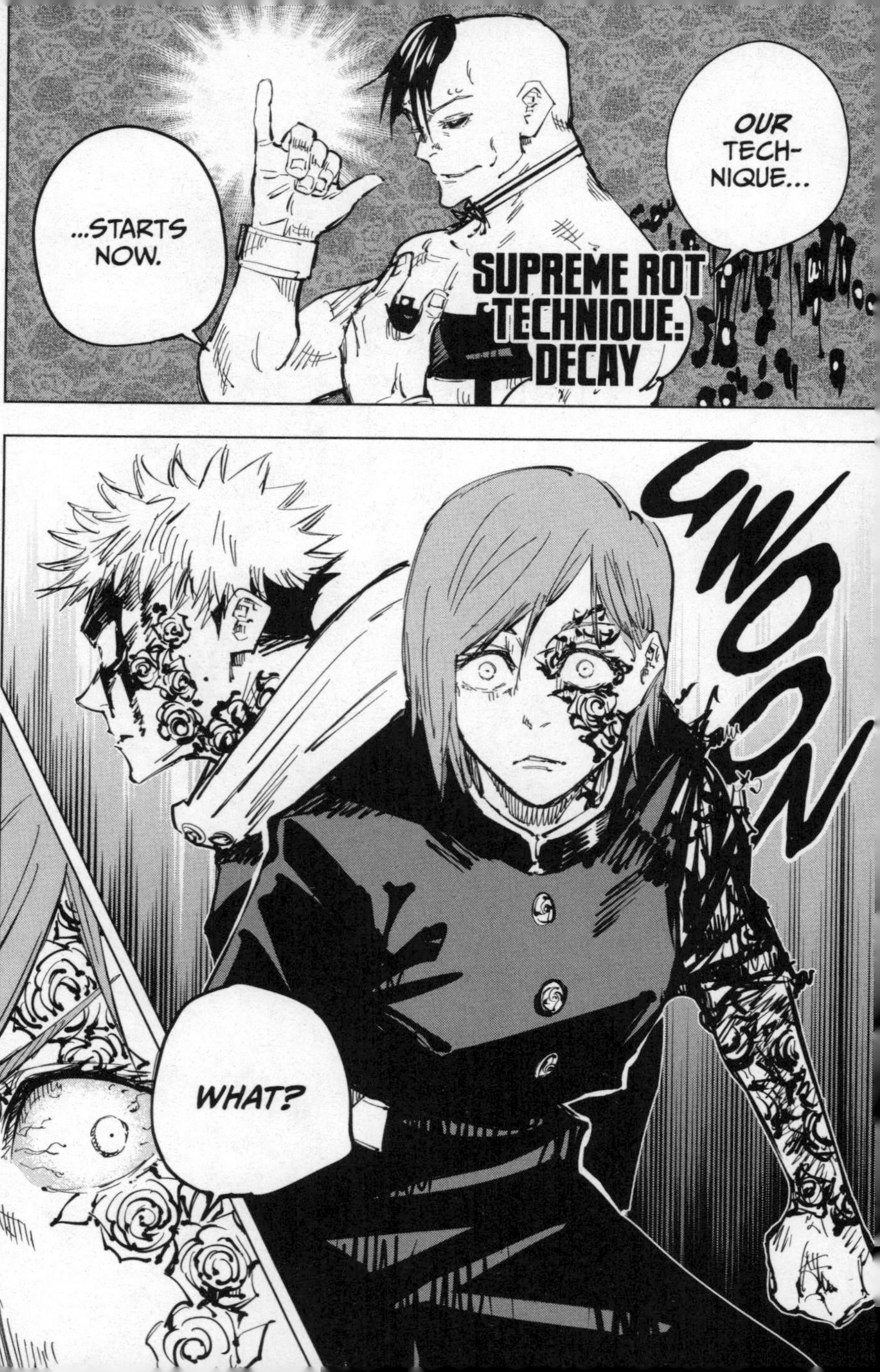
OUR TECHNIQUE...
...STARTS NOW.
SUPREME ROT TECHNIQUE: DECAY
WHAT?

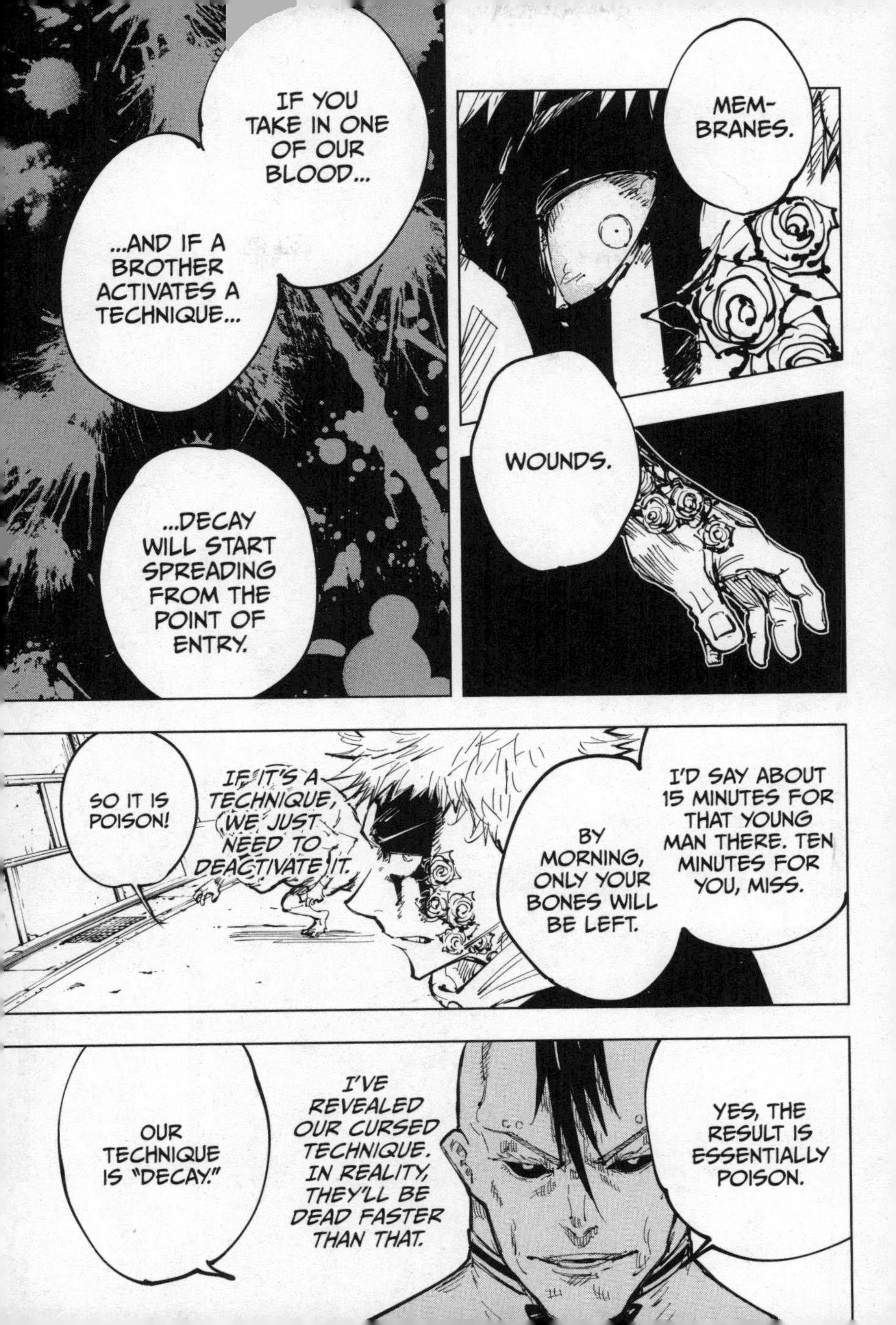
MEM-BRANES.
WOUNDS.
IF YOU TAKE IN ONE OF OUR BLOOD...
...AND IF A BROTHER ACTIVATES A TECHNIQUE...
...DECAY WILL START SPREADING FROM THE POINT OF ENTRY.
I'D SAY ABOUT 15 MINUTES FOR THAT YOUNG MAN THERE. TEN MINUTES FOR YOU, MISS.
BY MORNING, ONLY YOUR BONES WILL BE LEFT.
IF IT'S A TECHNIQUE, WE JUST NEED TO DEACTIVATE IT.
SO IT IS POISON!
YES, THE RESULT IS ESSENTIALLY POISON.
I'VE REVEALED OUR CURSED TECHNIQUE. IN REALITY, THEY'LL BE DEAD FASTER THAN THAT.
OUR TECHNIQUE IS "DECAY."

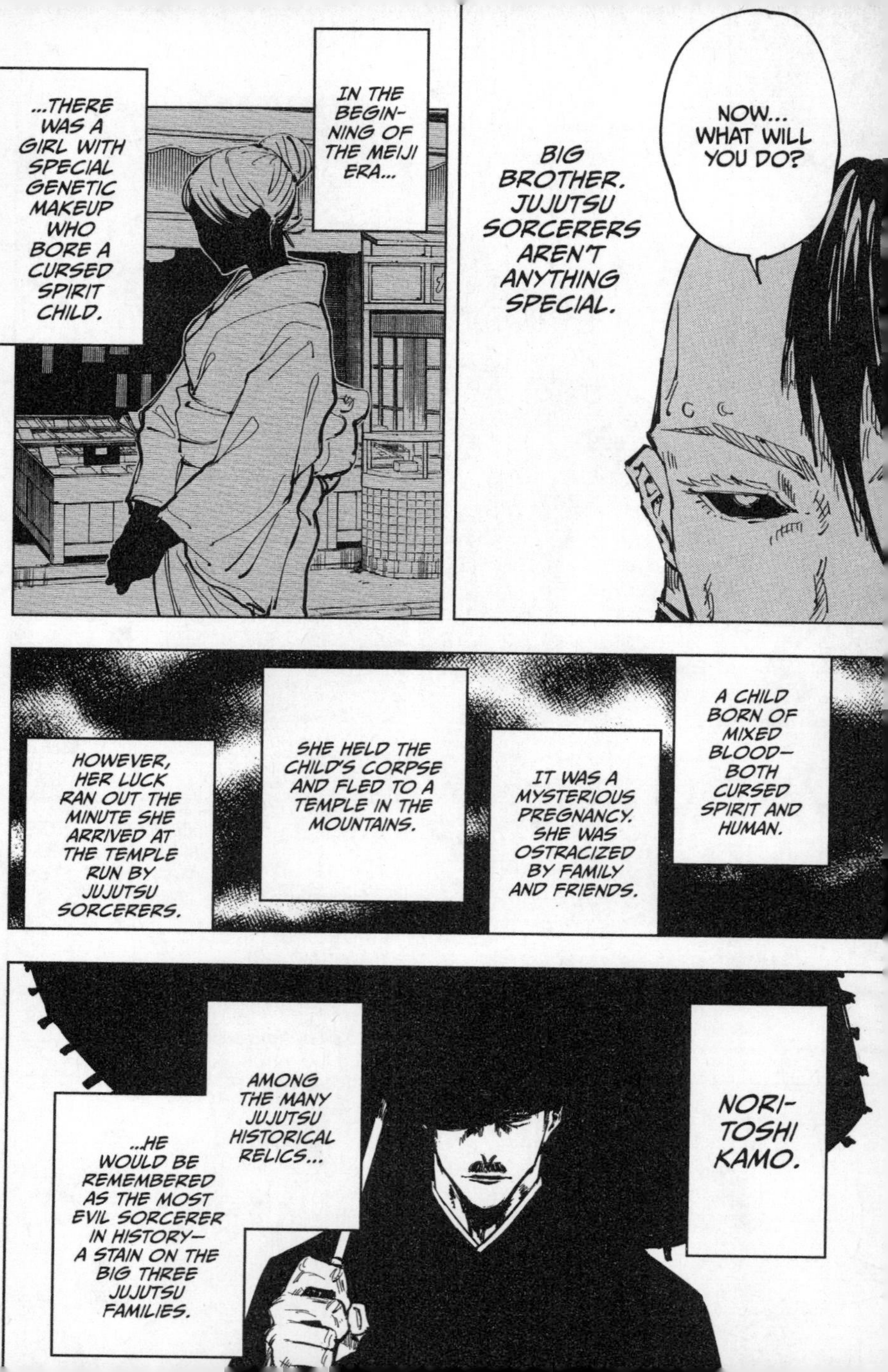
NOW... WHAT WILL YOU DO?
BIG BROTHER. JUJUTSU SORCERERS AREN'T ANYTHING SPECIAL.
IN THE BEGINNING OF THE MEIJI ERA...
...THERE WAS A GIRL WITH SPECIAL GENETIC MAKEUP WHO BORE A CURSED SPIRIT CHILD.
A CHILD BORN OF MIXED BLOOD—BOTH CURSED SPIRIT AND HUMAN.
IT WAS A MYSTERIOUS PREGNANCY. SHE WAS OSTRACIZED BY FAMILY AND FRIENDS.
SHE HELD THE CHILD'S CORPSE AND FLED TO A TEMPLE IN THE MOUNTAINS.
HOWEVER, HER LUCK RAN OUT THE MINUTE SHE ARRIVED AT THE TEMPLE RUN BY JUJUTSU SORCERERS.
NORITOSHI KAMO.
AMONG THE MANY JUJUTSU HISTORICAL RELICS...
...HE WOULD BE REMEMBERED AS THE MOST EVIL SORCERER IN HISTORY—A STAIN ON THE BIG THREE JUJUTSU FAMILIES.

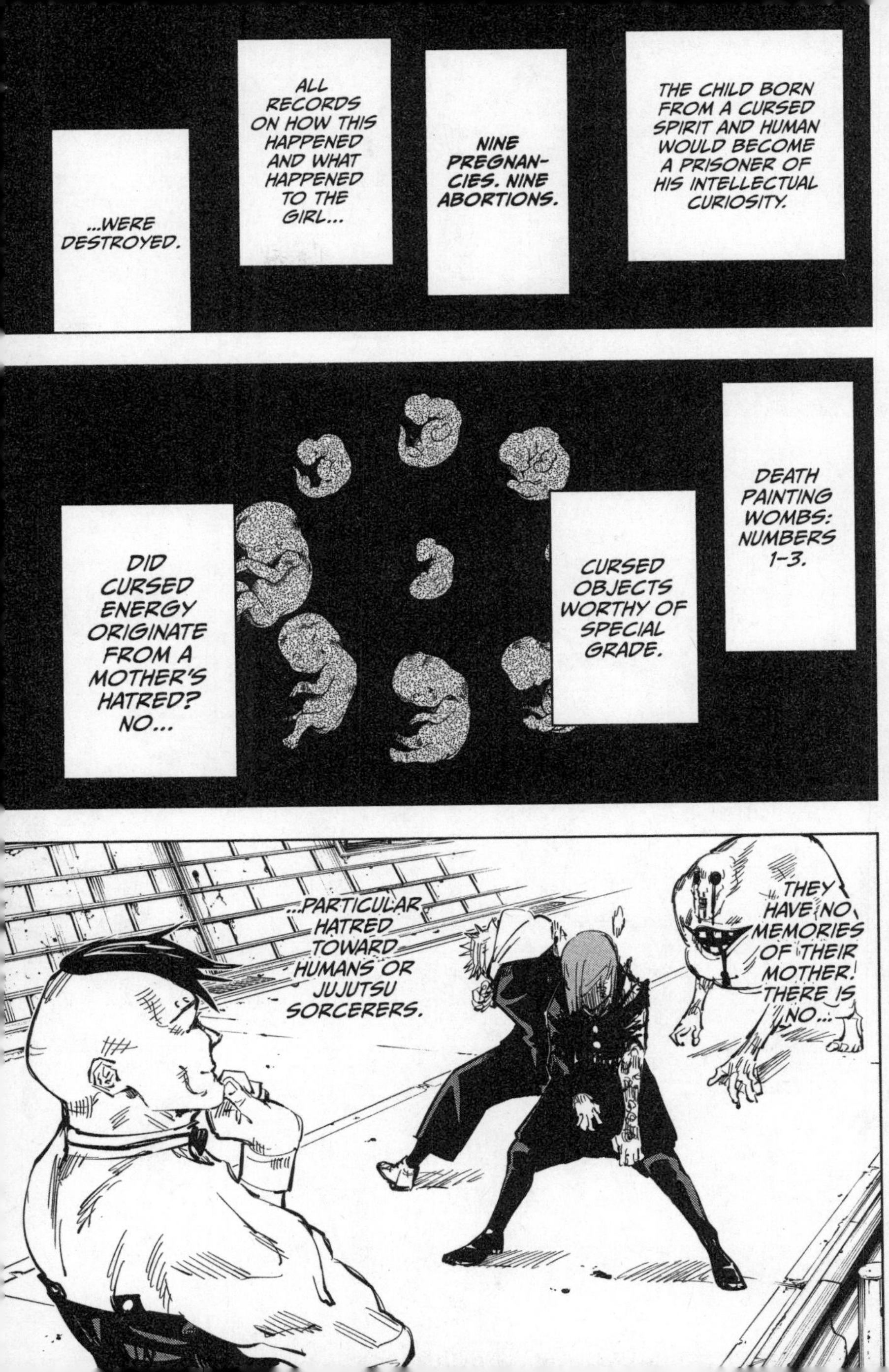
THE CHILD BORN FROM A CURSED SPIRIT AND HUMAN WOULD BECOME A PRISONER OF HIS INTELLECTUAL CURIOSITY.
NINE PREGNAN-CIES. NINE ABORTIONS.
ALL RECORDS ON HOW THIS HAPPENED AND WHAT HAPPENED TO THE GIRL...
...WERE DESTROYED.
DEATH PAINTING WOMBS: NUMBERS 1-3.
CURSED OBJECTS WORTHY OF SPECIAL GRADE.
DID CURSED ENERGY ORIGINATE FROM A MOTHER'S HATRED? NO...
THEY HAVE NO MEMORIES OF THEIR MOTHER! THERE IS NO...
...PARTICULAR HATRED TOWARD HUMANS OR JUJUTSU SORCERERS.

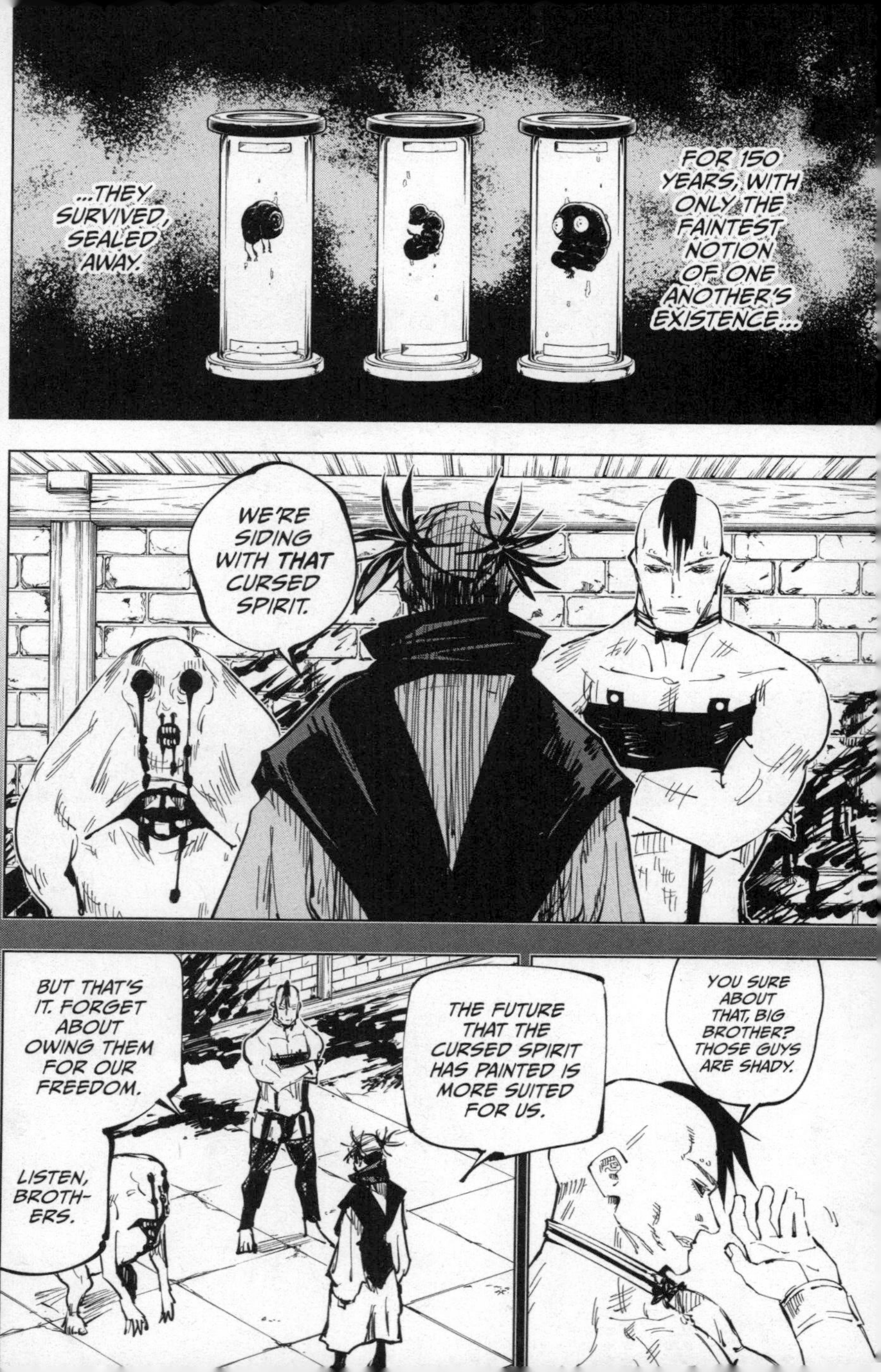
FOR 150 YEARS, WITH ONLY THE FAINTEST NOTION OF ONE ANOTHER'S EXISTENCE...
...THEY SURVIVED, SEALED AWAY.
WE'RE SIDING WITH THAT CURSED SPIRIT.
YOU SURE ABOUT THAT, BIG BROTHER? THOSE GUYS ARE SHADY.
THE FUTURE THAT THE CURSED SPIRIT HAS PAINTED IS MORE SUITED FOR US.
BUT THAT'S IT. FORGET ABOUT OWING THEM FOR OUR FREEDOM.
LISTEN, BROTHERS.

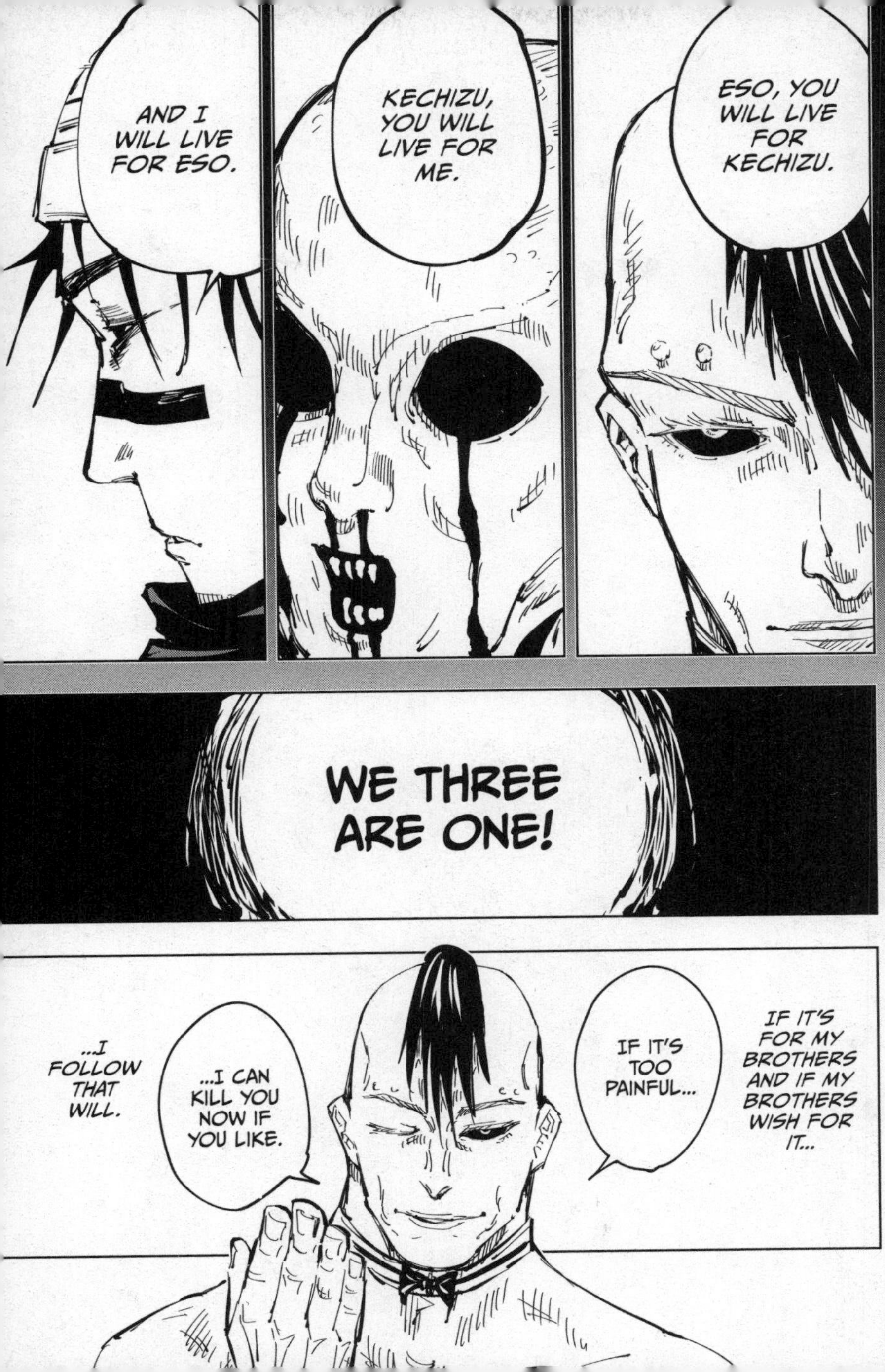
ESO, YOU WILL LIVE FOR KECHIZU.
KECHIZU, YOU WILL LIVE FOR ME.
AND I WILL LIVE FOR ESO.
WE THREE ARE ONE!
IF IT'S FOR MY BROTHERS AND IF MY BROTHERS WISH FOR IT...
IF IT'S TOO PAINFUL...
...I CAN KILL YOU NOW IF YOU LIKE.
...I FOLLOW THAT WILL.

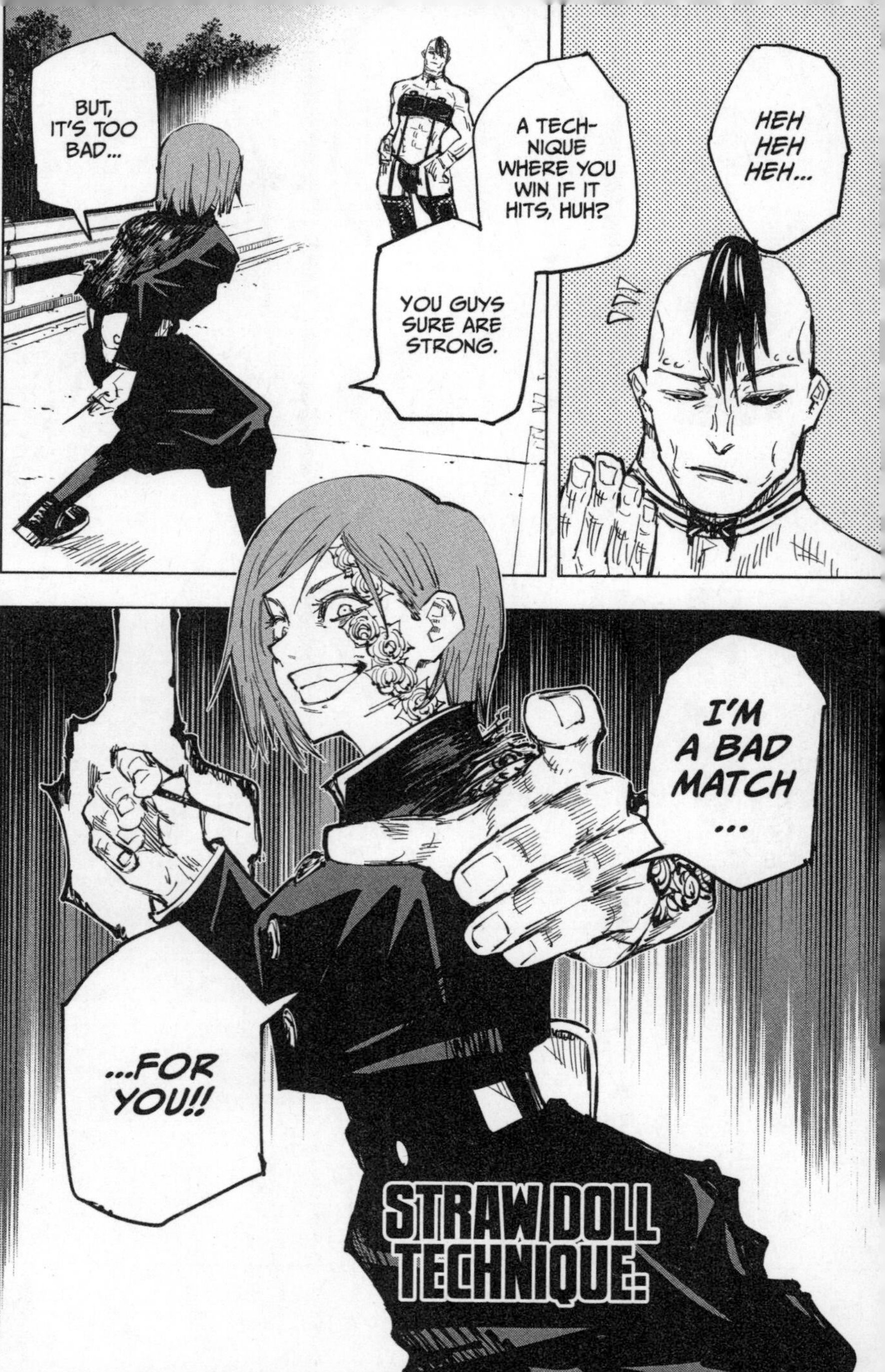
HEH HEH HEH...
A TECH-NIQUE WHERE YOU WIN IF IT HITS, HUH?
YOU GUYS SURE ARE STRONG.
BUT, IT'S TOO BAD...
I'M A BAD MATCH ...
...FOR YOU!!
STRAW DOLL TECHNIQUE.

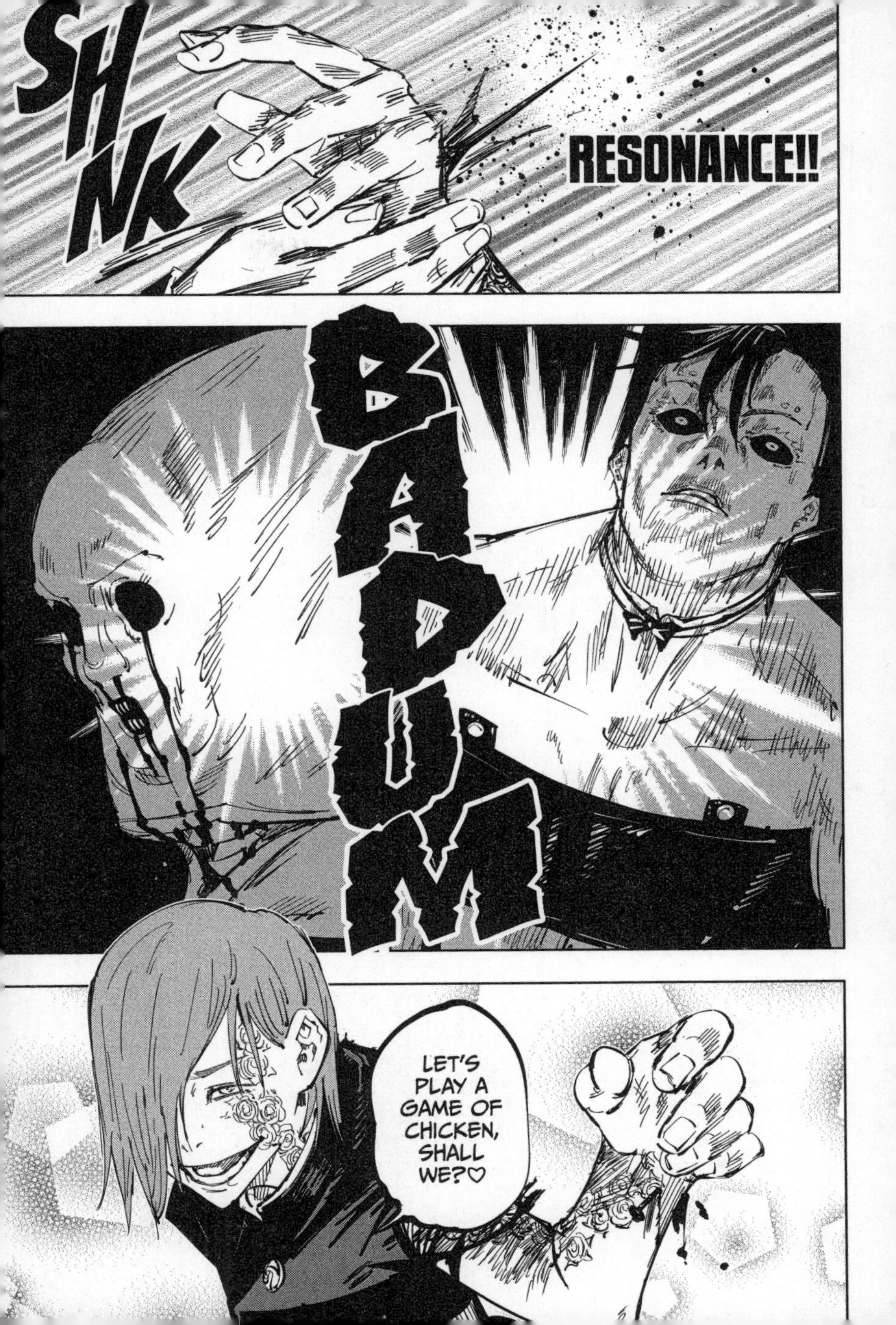
RESONANCE!!
SHNK
BADUM
LET'S PLAY A GAME OF CHICKEN, SHALL WE?♡

MASAMICHI YAGA
(47 YEARS OLD)

• I decided on his easily recognizable design while I was working on volume 0.

• His catchphrase, "God-damn!" seems appropriate for Jujutsu as well.

• He owns a lot of sunglasses.

• Although he likes cute things, it's not his intention to make his cursed corpses cute.

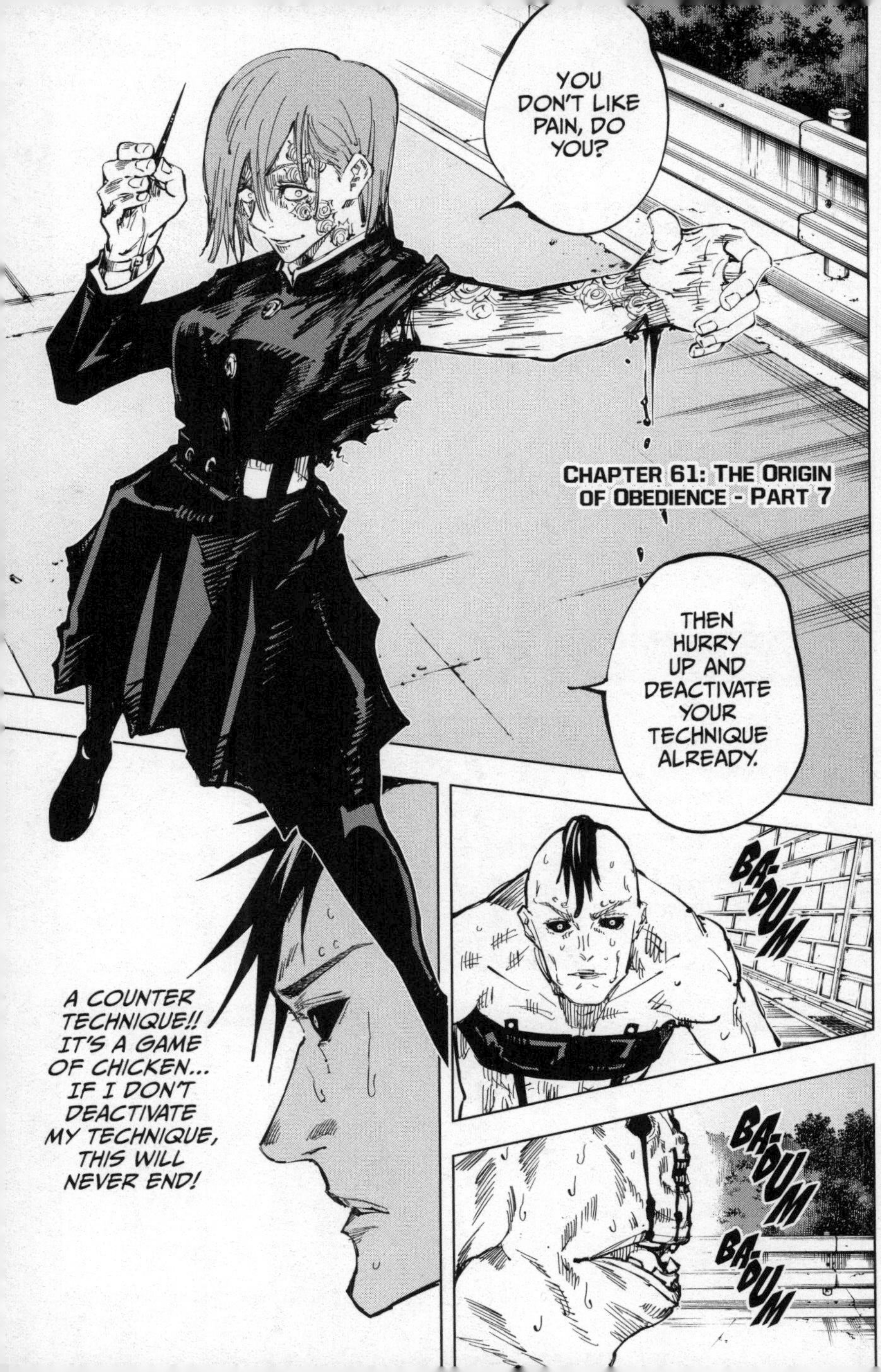
YOU DON'T LIKE PAIN, DO YOU?
CHAPTER 61: THE ORIGIN OF OBEDIENCE - PART 7
THEN HURRY UP AND DEACTIVATE YOUR TECHNIQUE ALREADY.
BA-DUM
BA-DUM
BA-DUM
BA-DUM
A COUNTER TECHNIQUE!! IT'S A GAME OF CHICKEN... IF I DON'T DEACTIVATE MY TECHNIQUE, THIS WILL NEVER END!

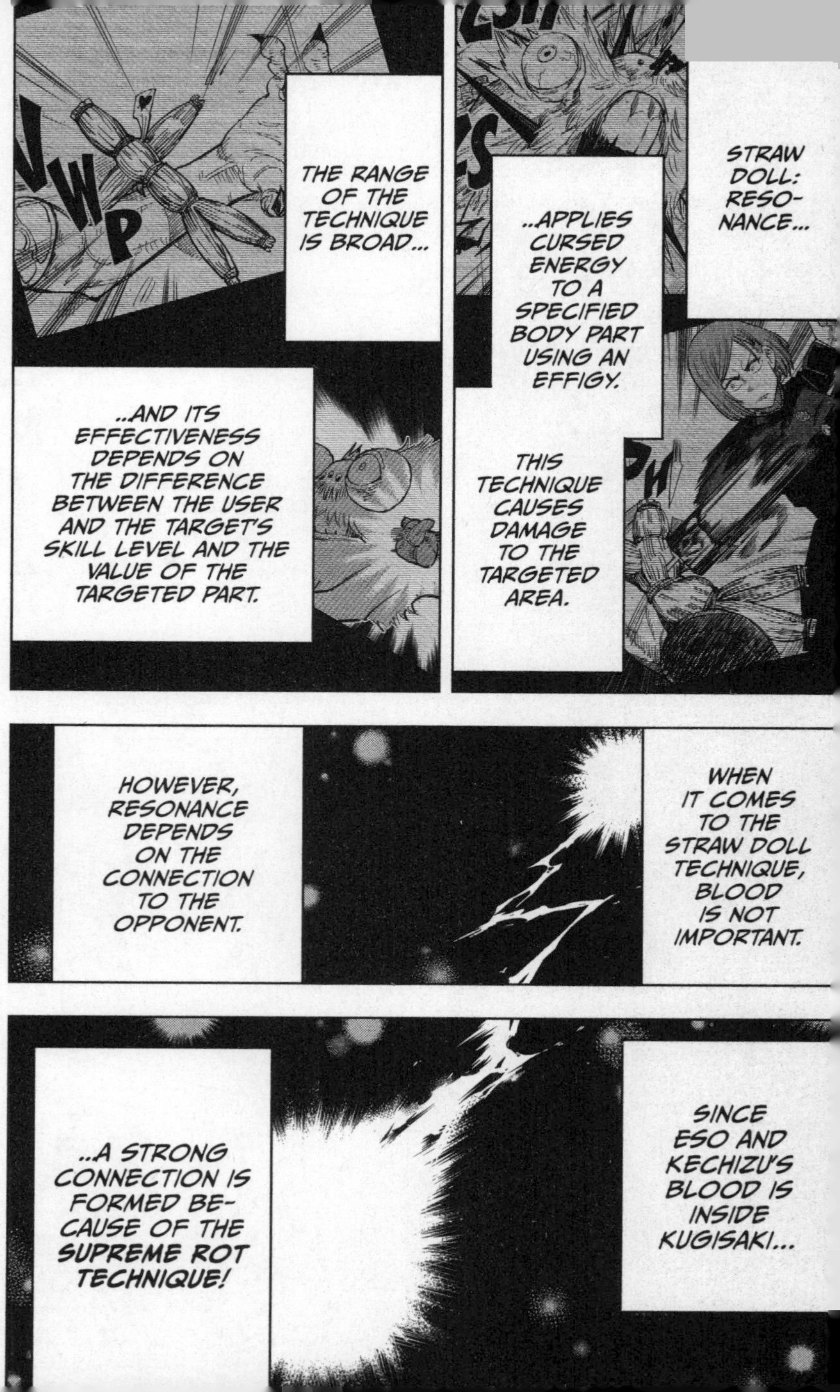
STRAW DOLL: RESO- NANCE...
...APPLIES CURSED ENERGY TO A SPECIFIED BODY PART USING AN EFFIGY.
THIS TECHNIQUE CAUSES DAMAGE TO THE TARGETED AREA.
THE RANGE OF THE TECHNIQUE IS BROAD...
...AND ITS EFFECTIVENESS DEPENDS ON THE DIFFERENCE BETWEEN THE USER AND THE TARGET'S SKILL LEVEL AND THE VALUE OF THE TARGETED PART.
WHEN IT COMES TO THE STRAW DOLL TECHNIQUE, BLOOD IS NOT IMPORTANT.
HOWEVER, RESONANCE DEPENDS ON THE CONNECTION TO THE OPPONENT.
SINCE ESO AND KECHIZU'S BLOOD IS INSIDE KUGISAKI...
...A STRONG CONNECTION IS FORMED BE- CAUSE OF THE SUPREME ROT TECHNIQUE!

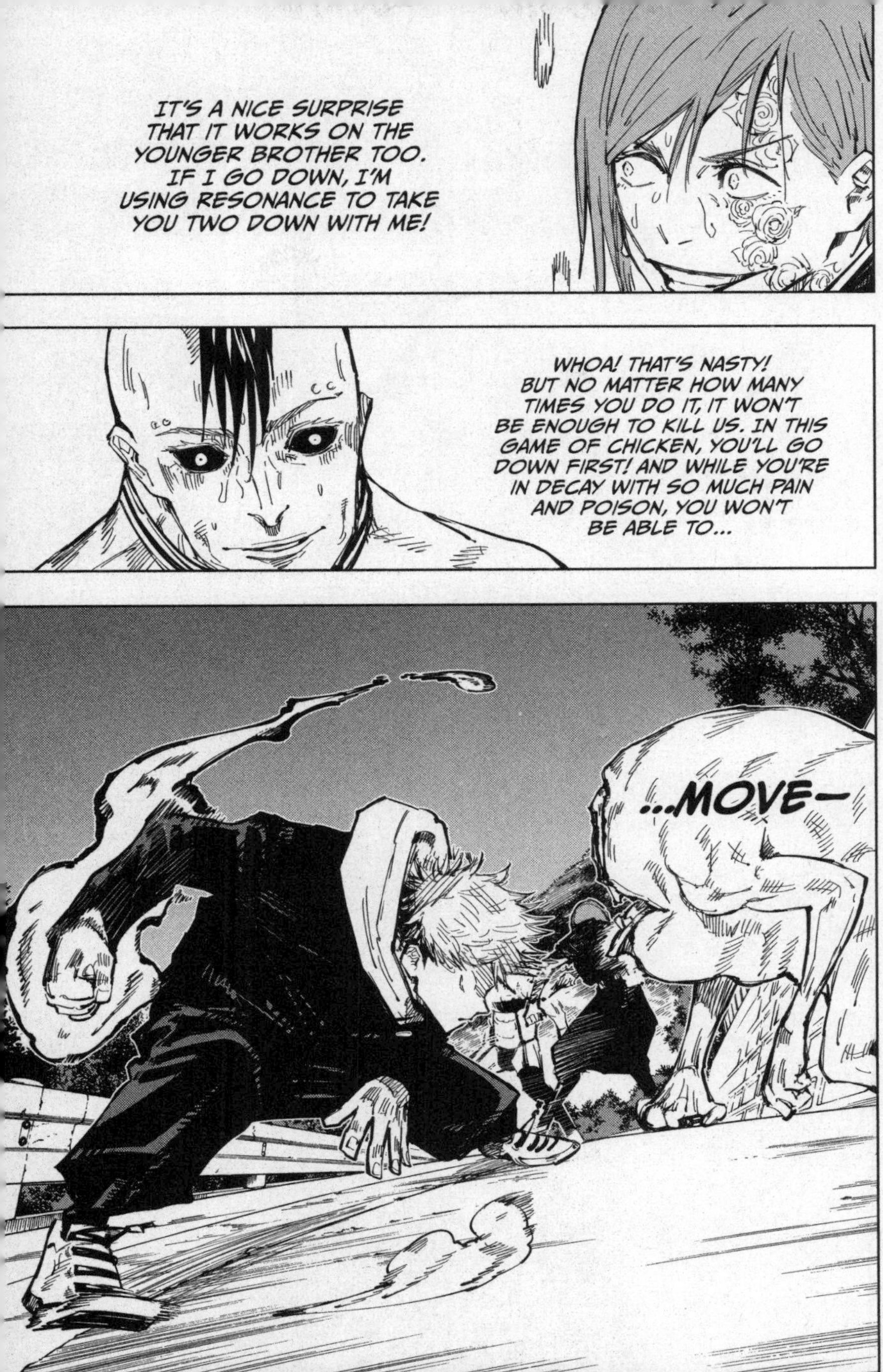
IT'S A NICE SURPRISE THAT IT WORKS ON THE YOUNGER BROTHER TOO. IF I GO DOWN, I'M USING RESONANCE TO TAKE YOU TWO DOWN WITH ME!
WHOA! THAT'S NASTY! BUT NO MATTER HOW MANY TIMES YOU DO IT, IT WON'T BE ENOUGH TO KILL US. IN THIS GAME OF CHICKEN, YOU'LL GO DOWN FIRST! AND WHILE YOU'RE IN DECAY WITH SO MUCH PAIN AND POISON, YOU WON'T BE ABLE TO...
...MOVE–

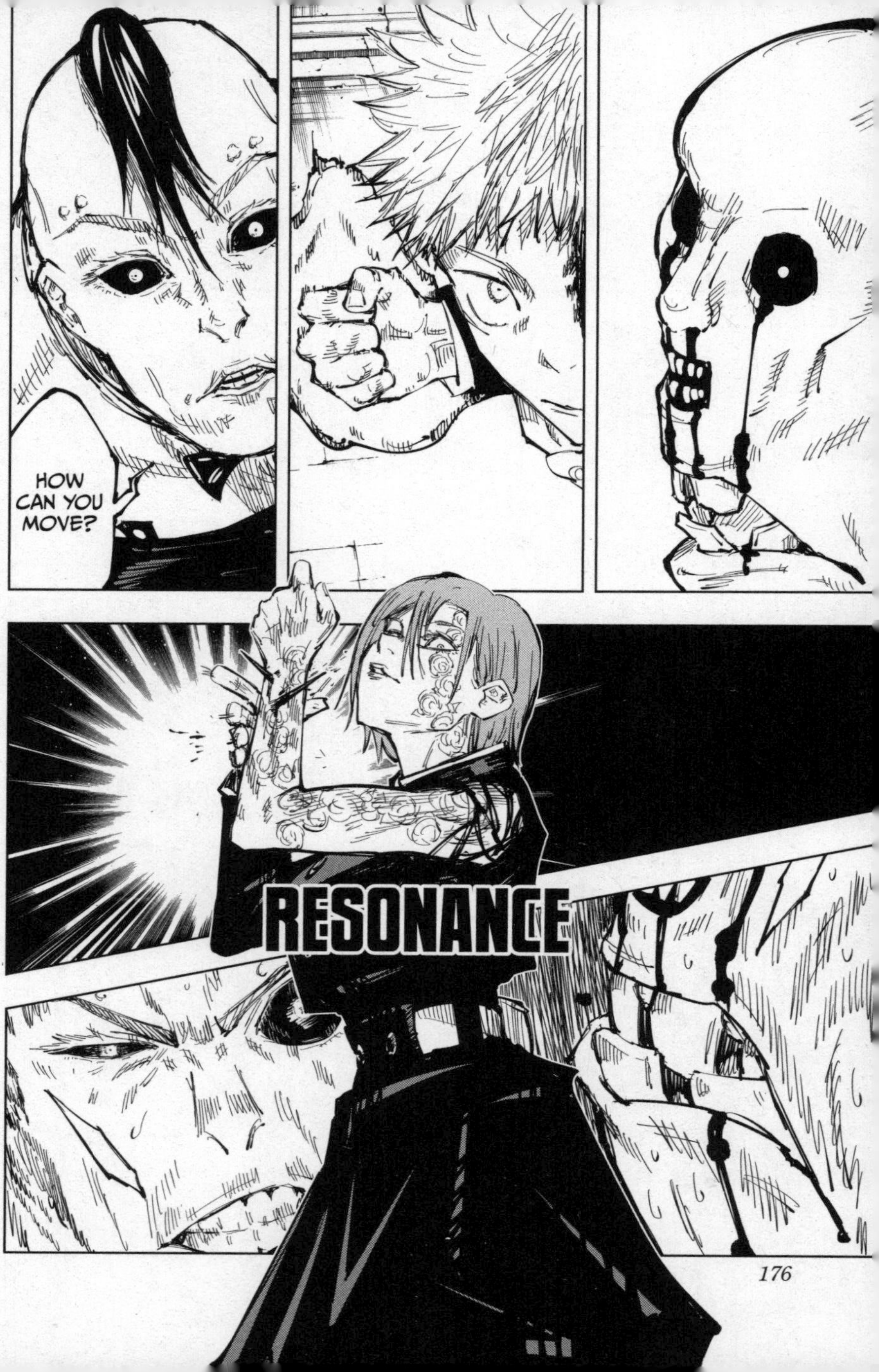
HOW CAN YOU MOVE?
RESONANCE

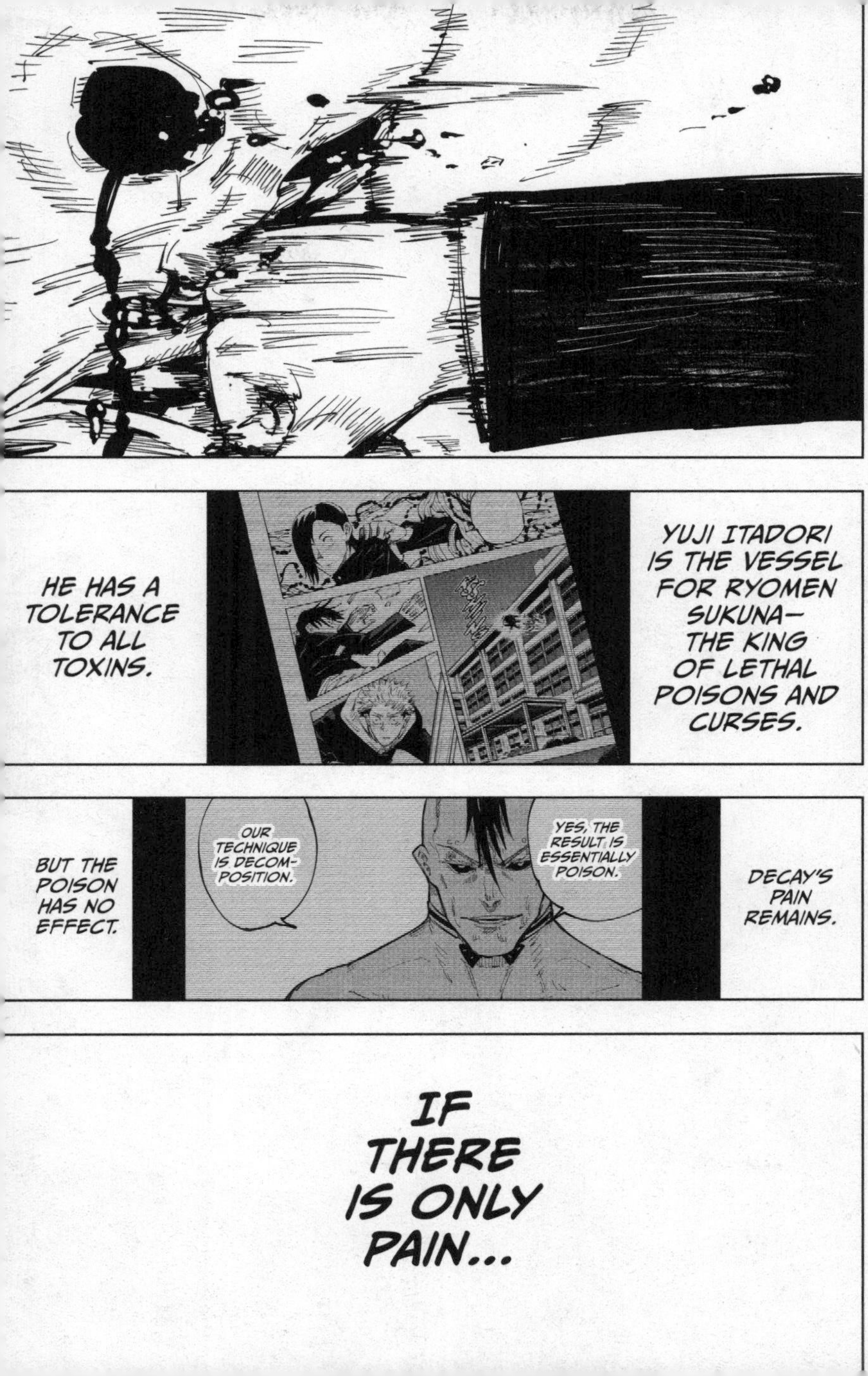
YUJI ITADORI IS THE VESSEL FOR RYOMEN SUKUNA— THE KING OF LETHAL POISONS AND CURSES.
HE HAS A TOLERANCE TO ALL TOXINS.
DECAY'S PAIN REMAINS.
YES, THE RESULT IS ESSENTIALLY POISON.
OUR TECHNIQUE IS DECOMPOSITION.
BUT THE POISON HAS NO EFFECT.
IF THERE IS ONLY PAIN...

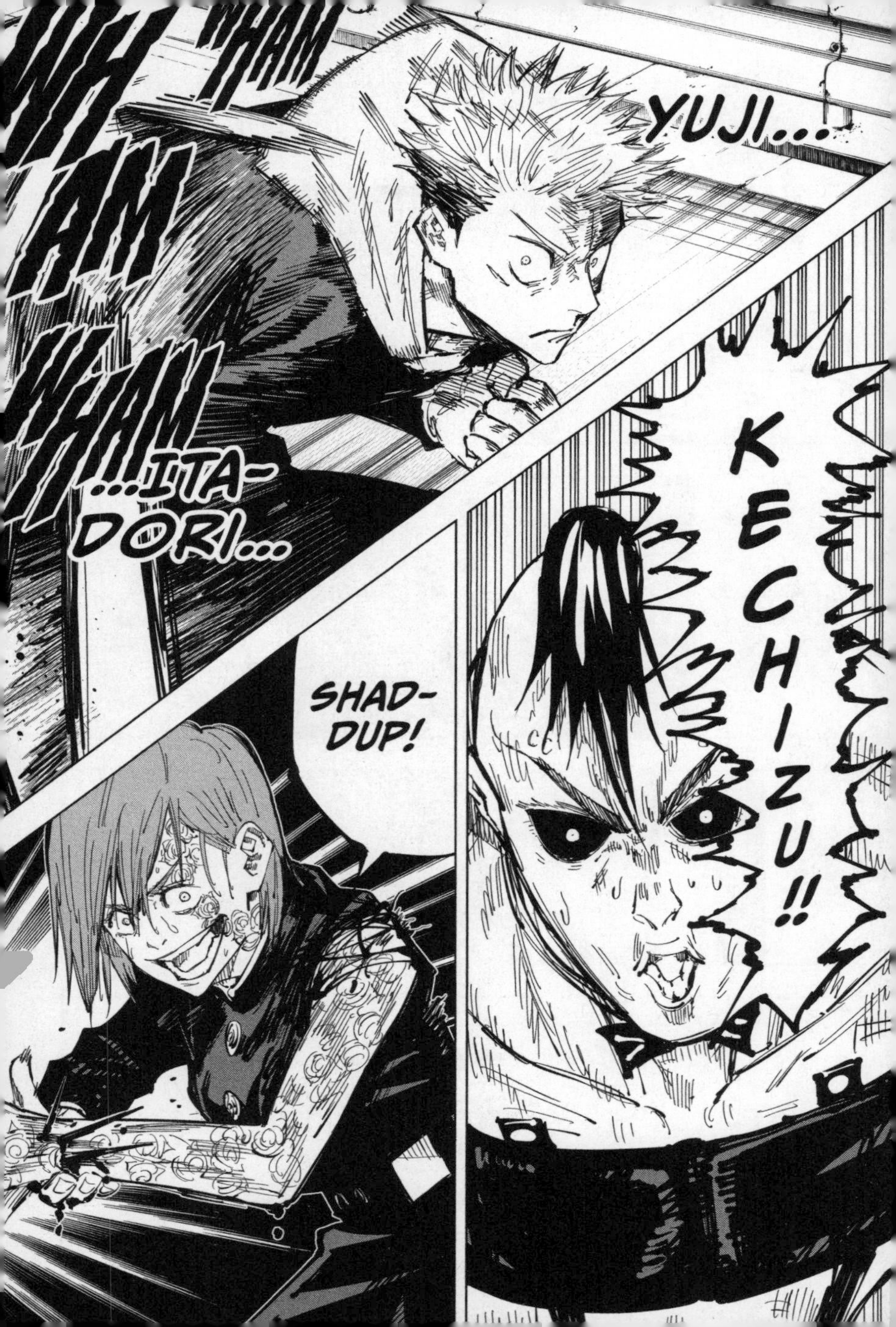
YUJI...!
WHAM
WHAM WHAM WHAM
...ITA-DORI...
KECHIZU!!
SHAD-DUP!

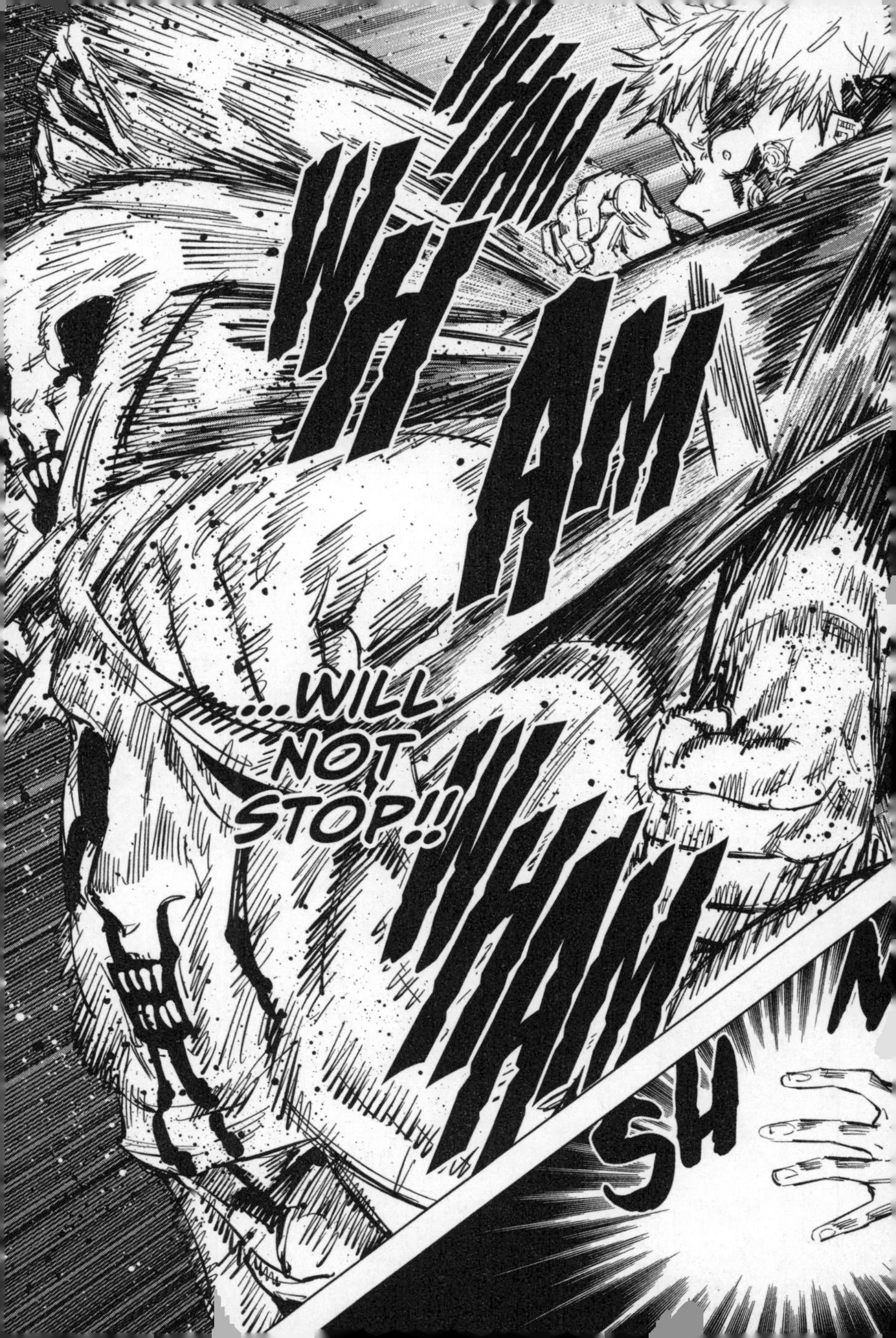
WHAM
WHAM
...WILL NOT STOP!!
WHAM
SH

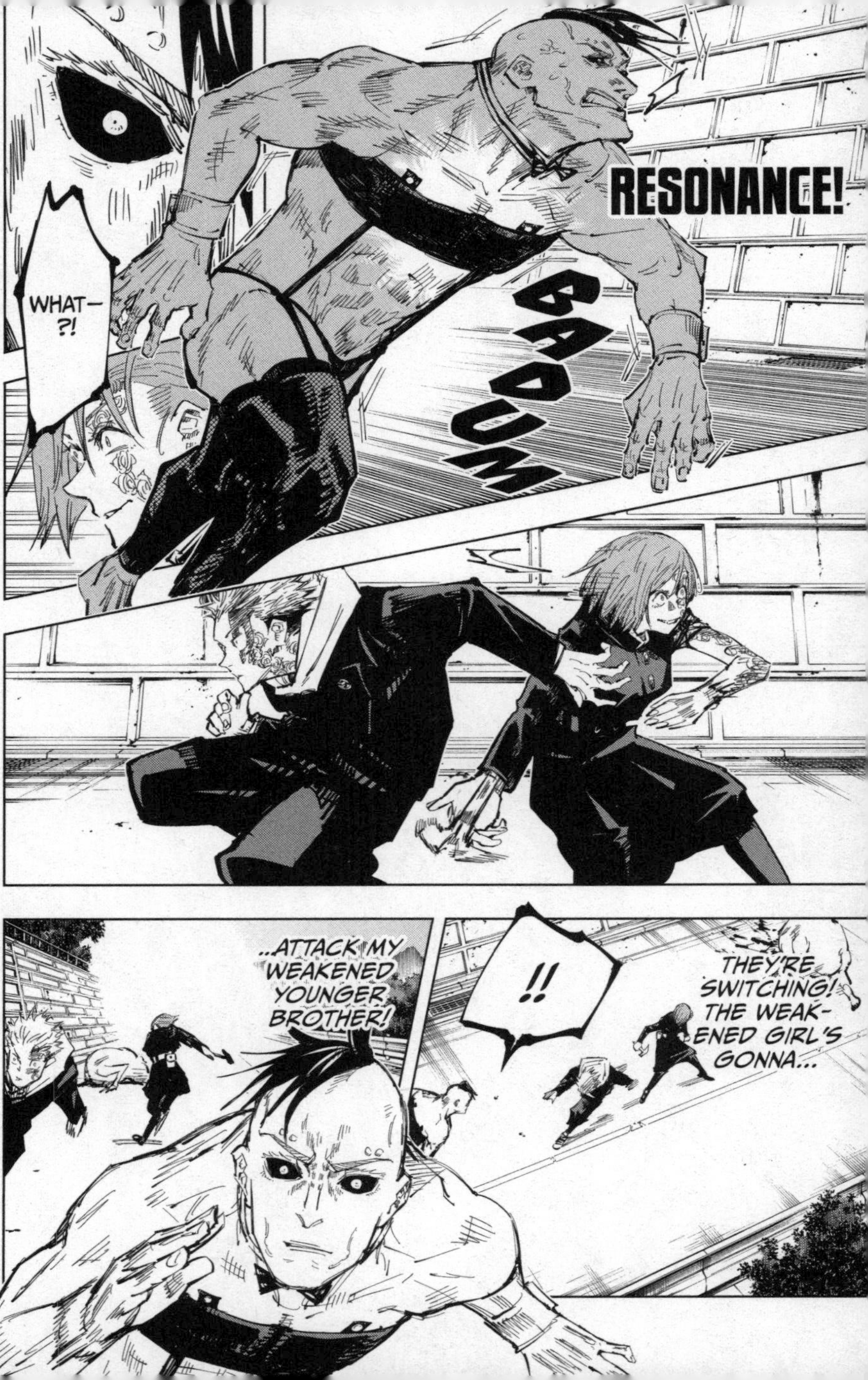
RESONANCE!
BADUM
WHAT—?!
THEY'RE SWITCHING! THE WEAK-ENED GIRL'S GONNA...
!!
...ATTACK MY WEAKENED YOUNGER BROTHER!

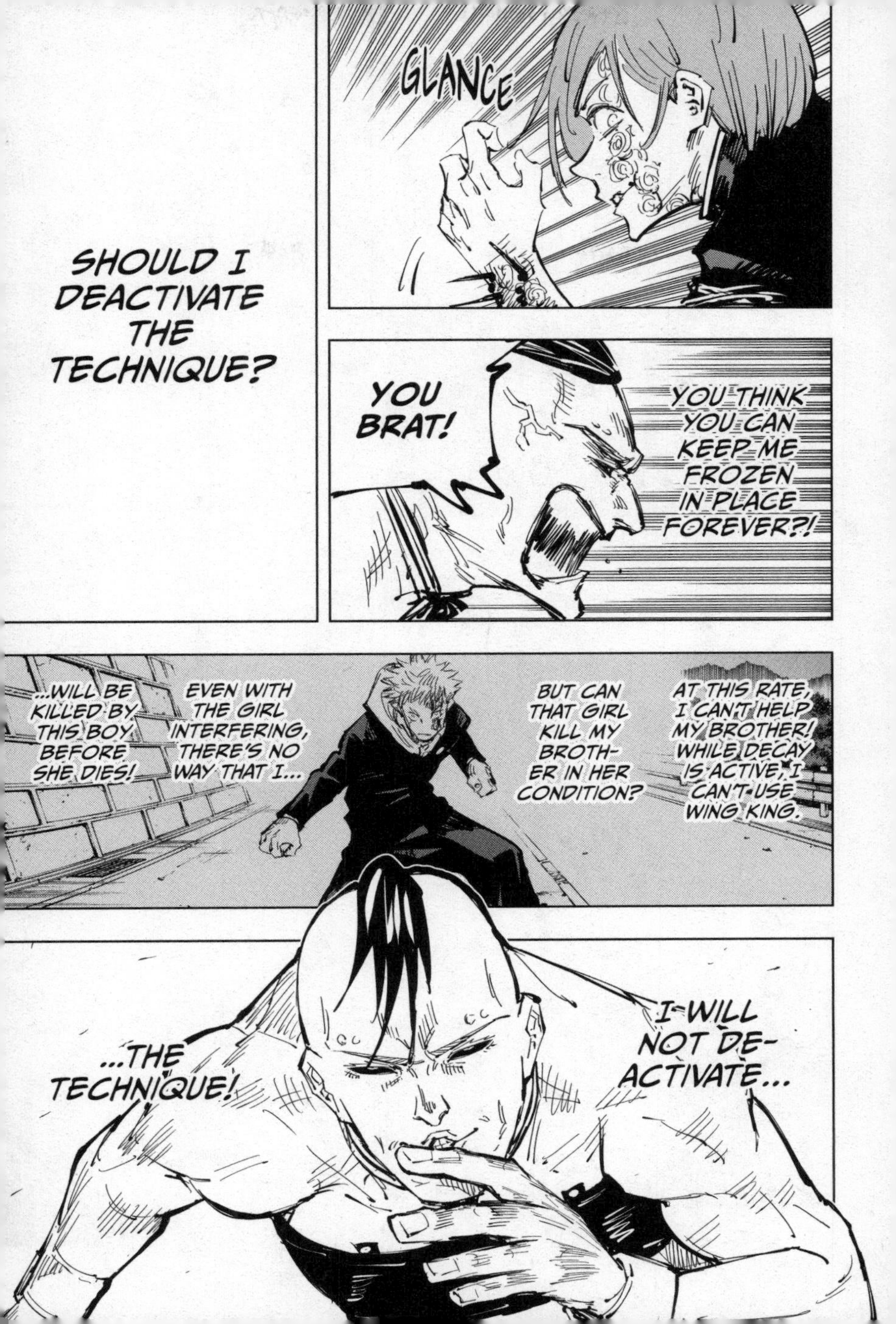
GLANCE
YOU THINK YOU CAN KEEP ME FROZEN IN PLACE FOREVER?!
YOU BRAT!
SHOULD I DEACTIVATE THE TECHNIQUE?
AT THIS RATE, I CAN'T HELP MY BROTHER! WHILE DECAY IS ACTIVE, I CAN'T USE WING KING.
BUT CAN THAT GIRL KILL MY BROTH-ER IN HER CONDITION?
EVEN WITH THE GIRL INTERFERING, THERE'S NO WAY THAT I...
...WILL BE KILLED BY THIS BOY BEFORE SHE DIES!
I WILL NOT DE-ACTIVATE...
...THE TECHNIQUE!

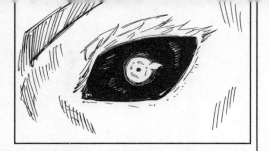

BIG BRO...

WE THREE
ARE ONE.

FOOSH

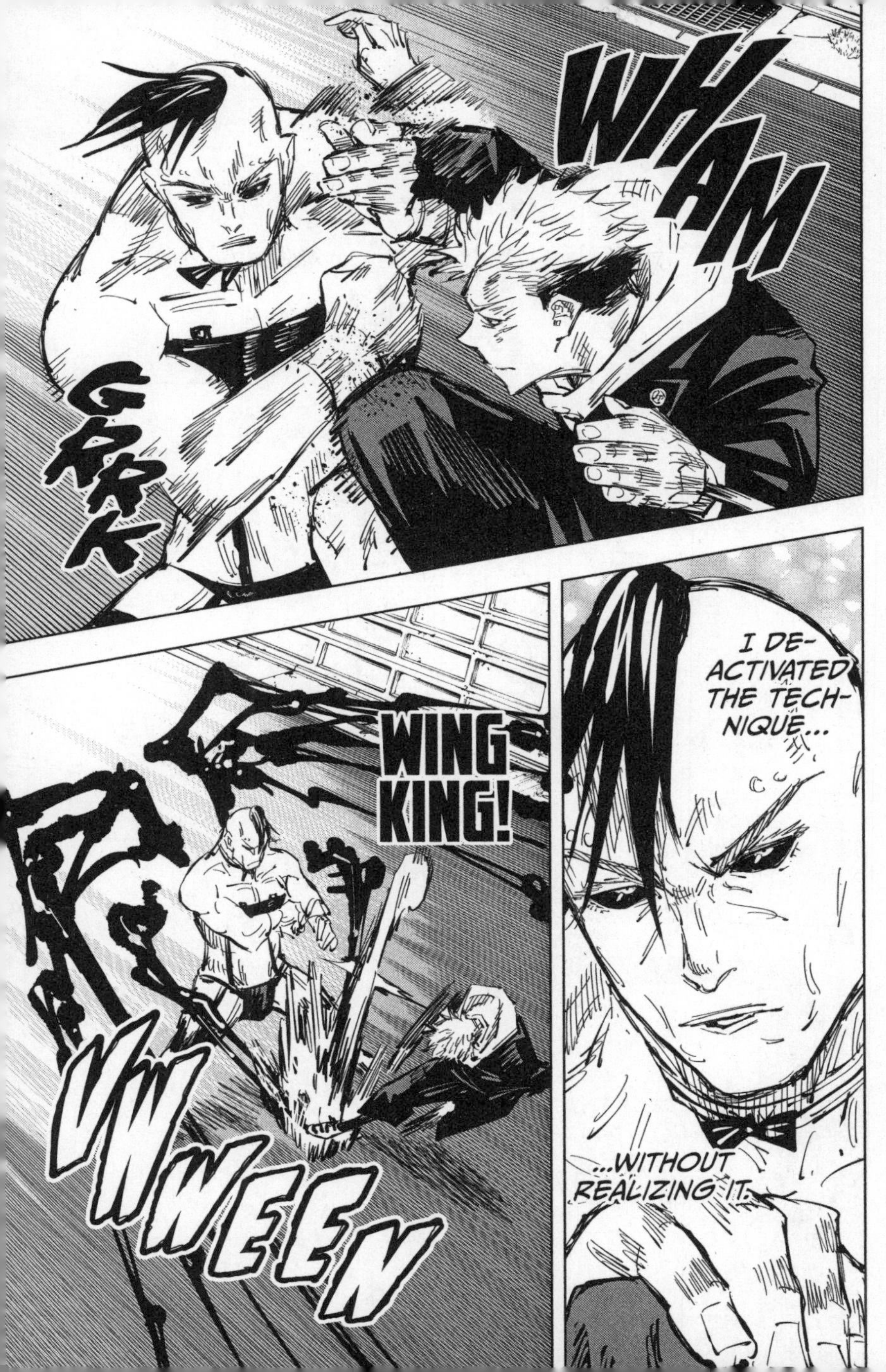
WHAM
GRRK
I DE-ACTIVATED THE TECH-NIQUE...
...WITHOUT REALIZING IT.
WING KING!
VWEEN

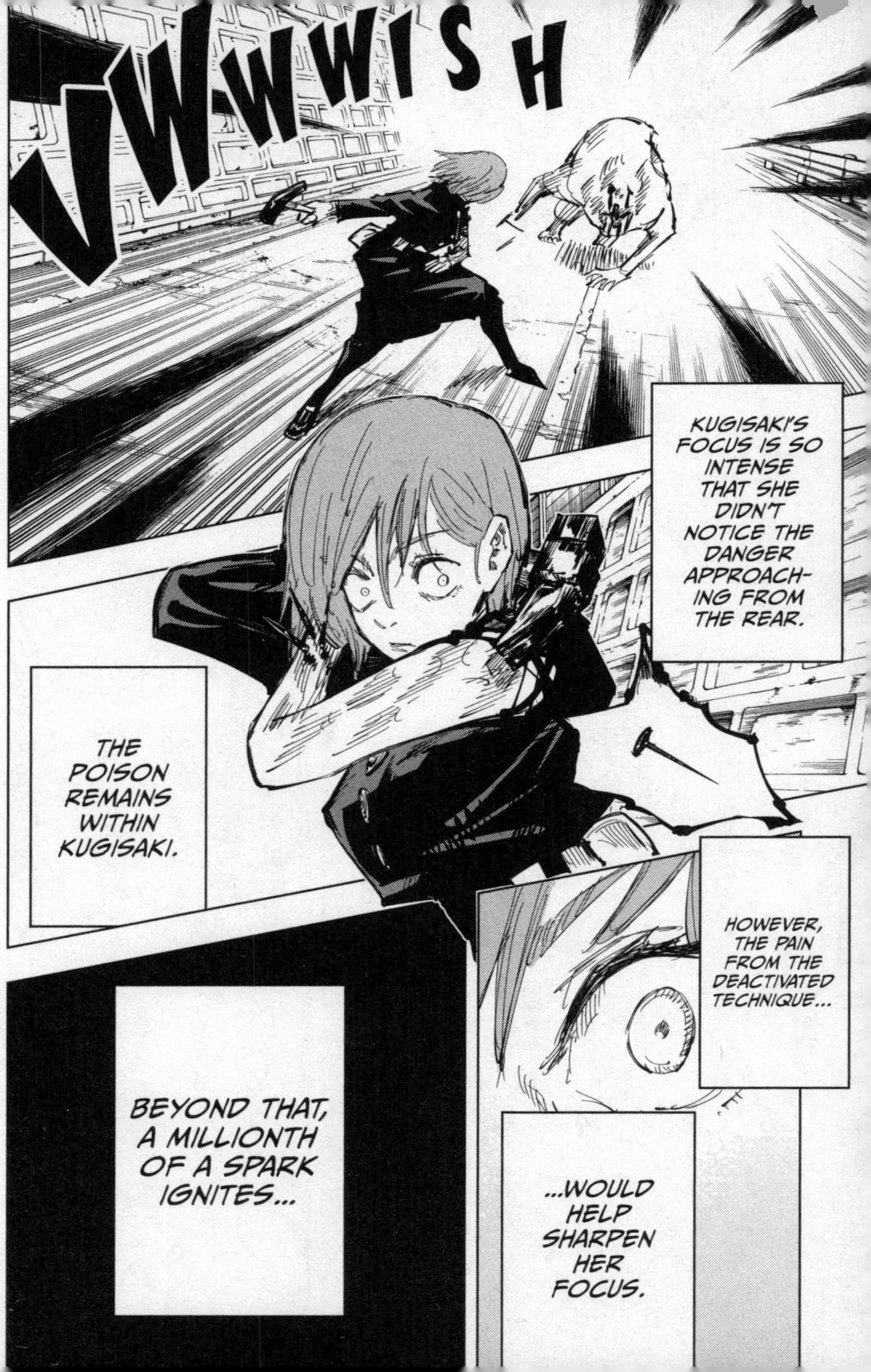
VWWWISH
KUGISAKI'S FOCUS IS SO INTENSE THAT SHE DIDN'T NOTICE THE DANGER APPROACHING FROM THE REAR.
THE POISON REMAINS WITHIN KUGISAKI.
HOWEVER, THE PAIN FROM THE DEACTIVATED TECHNIQUE...
...WOULD HELP SHARPEN HER FOCUS.
BEYOND THAT, A MILLIONTH OF A SPARK IGNITES...

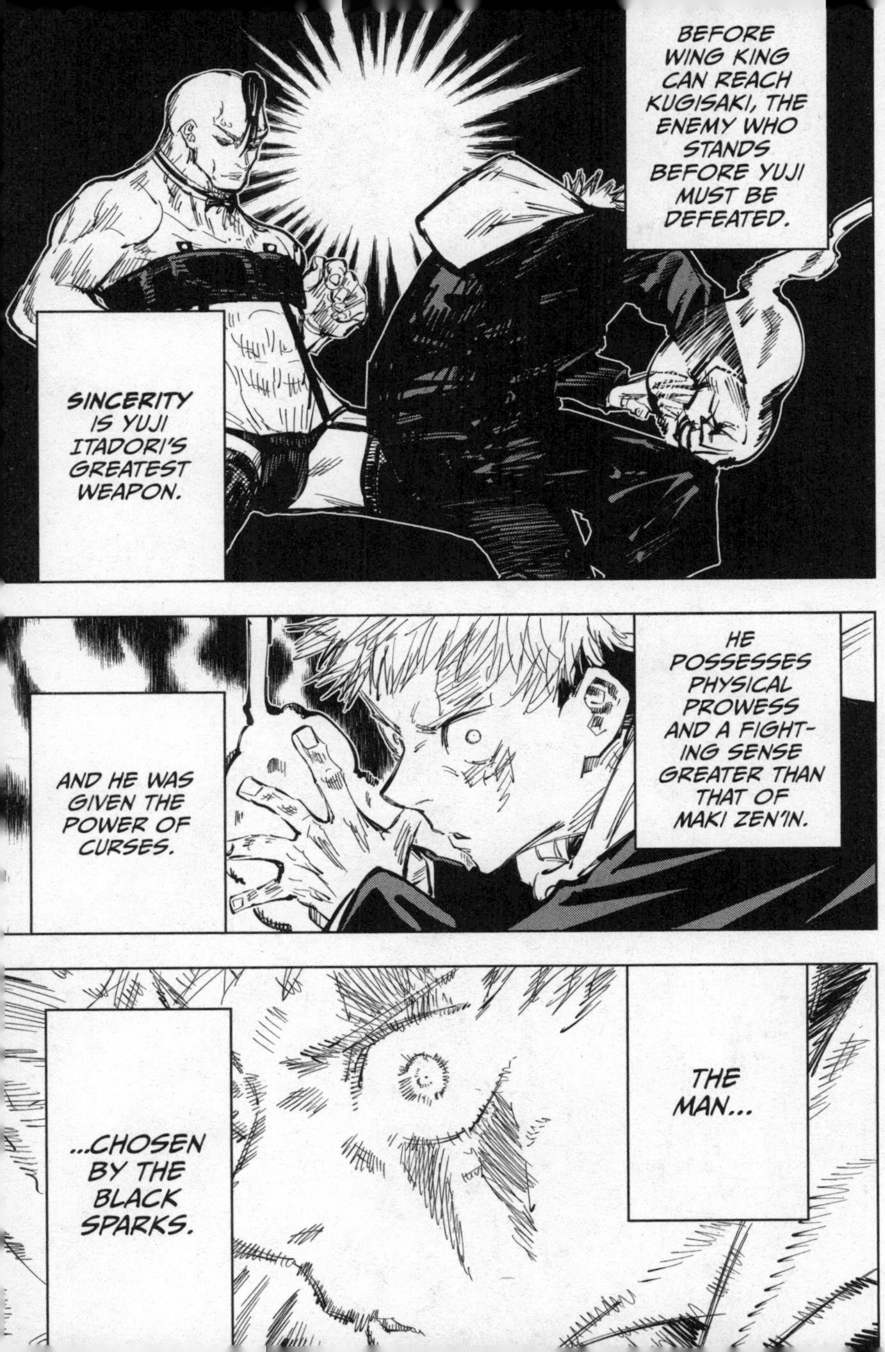
BEFORE WING KING CAN REACH KUGISAKI, THE ENEMY WHO STANDS BEFORE YUJI MUST BE DEFEATED.
SINCERITY IS YUJI ITADORI'S GREATEST WEAPON.
HE POSSESSES PHYSICAL PROWESS AND A FIGHTING SENSE GREATER THAN THAT OF MAKI ZEN'IN.
AND HE WAS GIVEN THE POWER OF CURSES.
THE MAN...
...CHOSEN BY THE BLACK SPARKS.

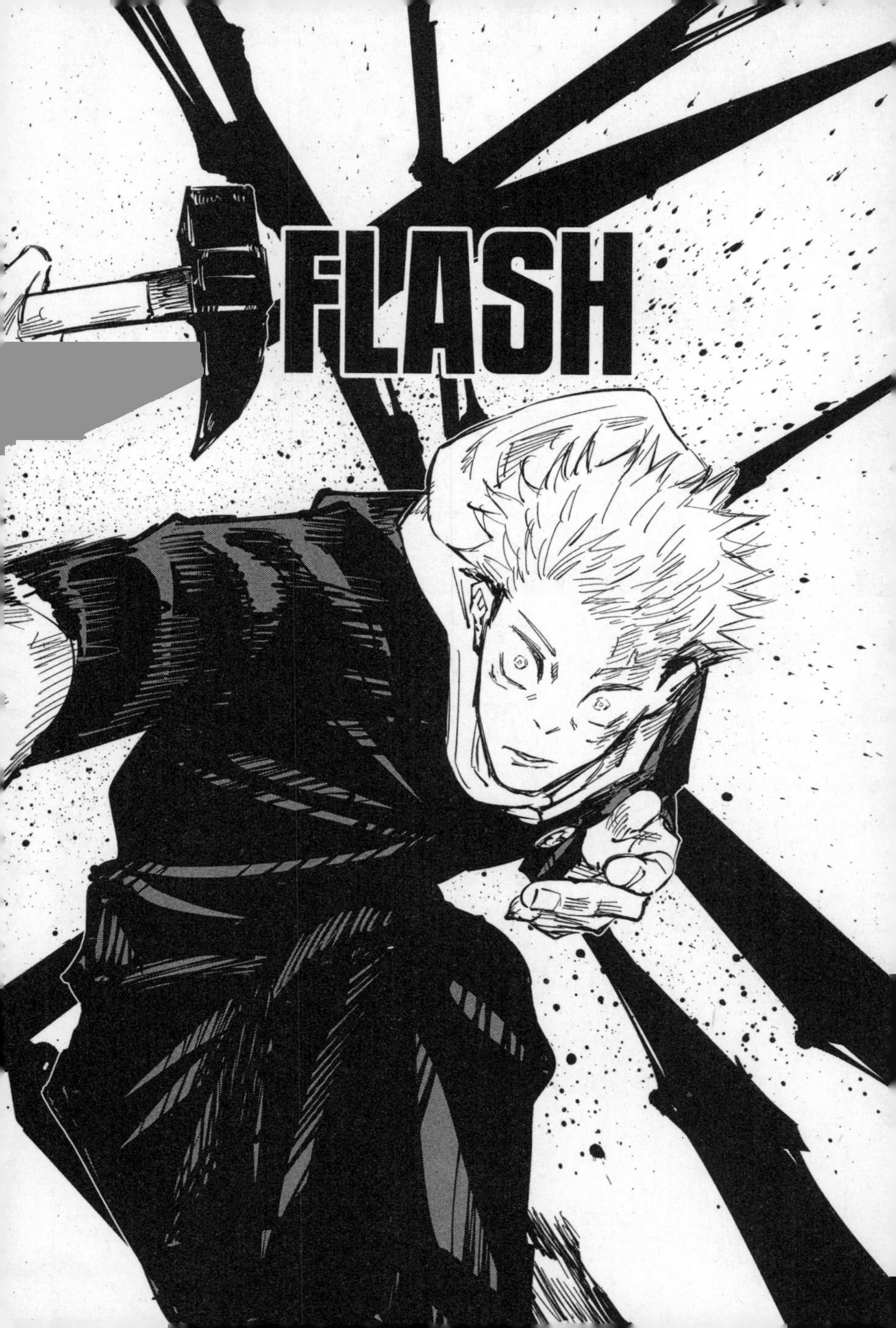
FLASH

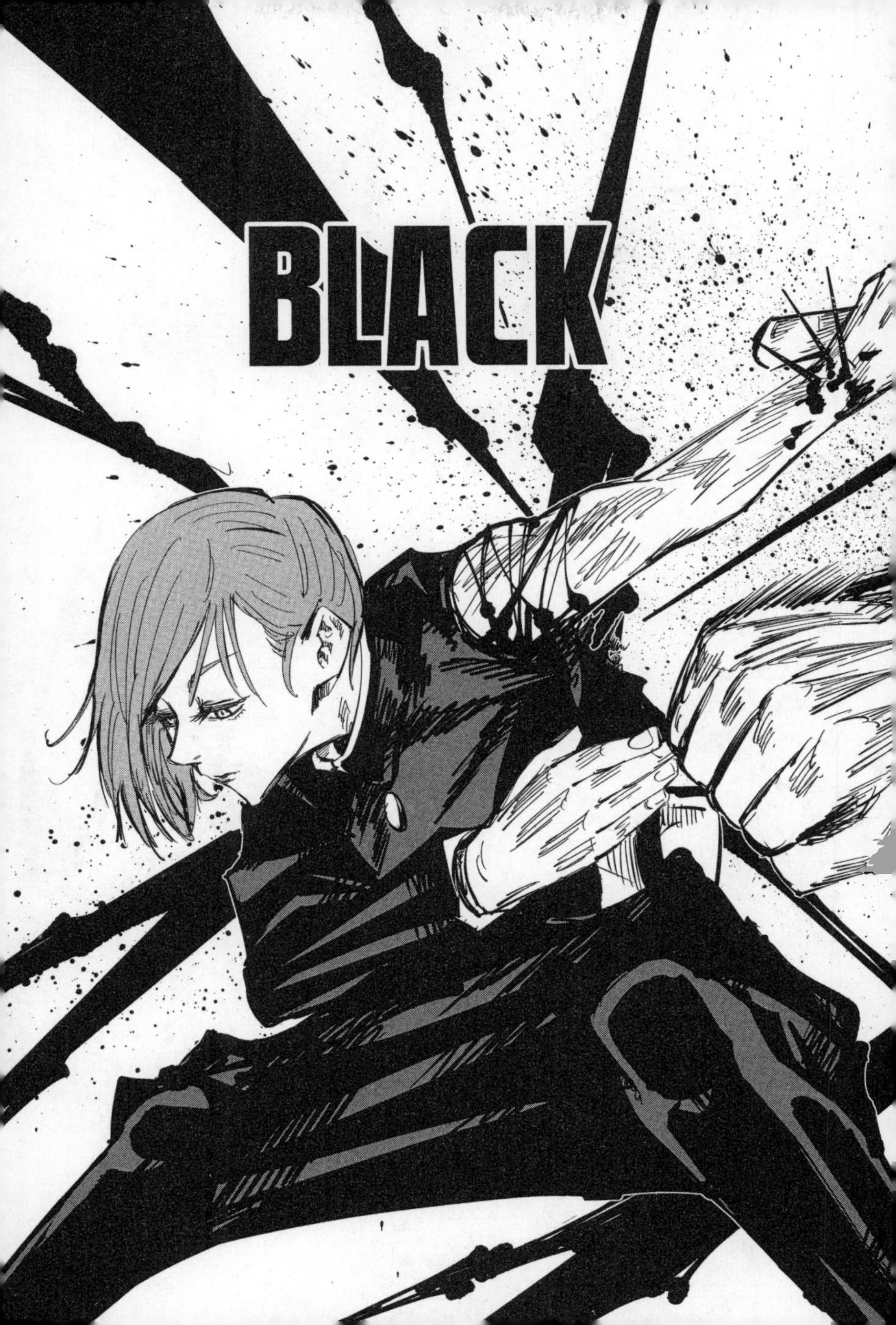
BLACK

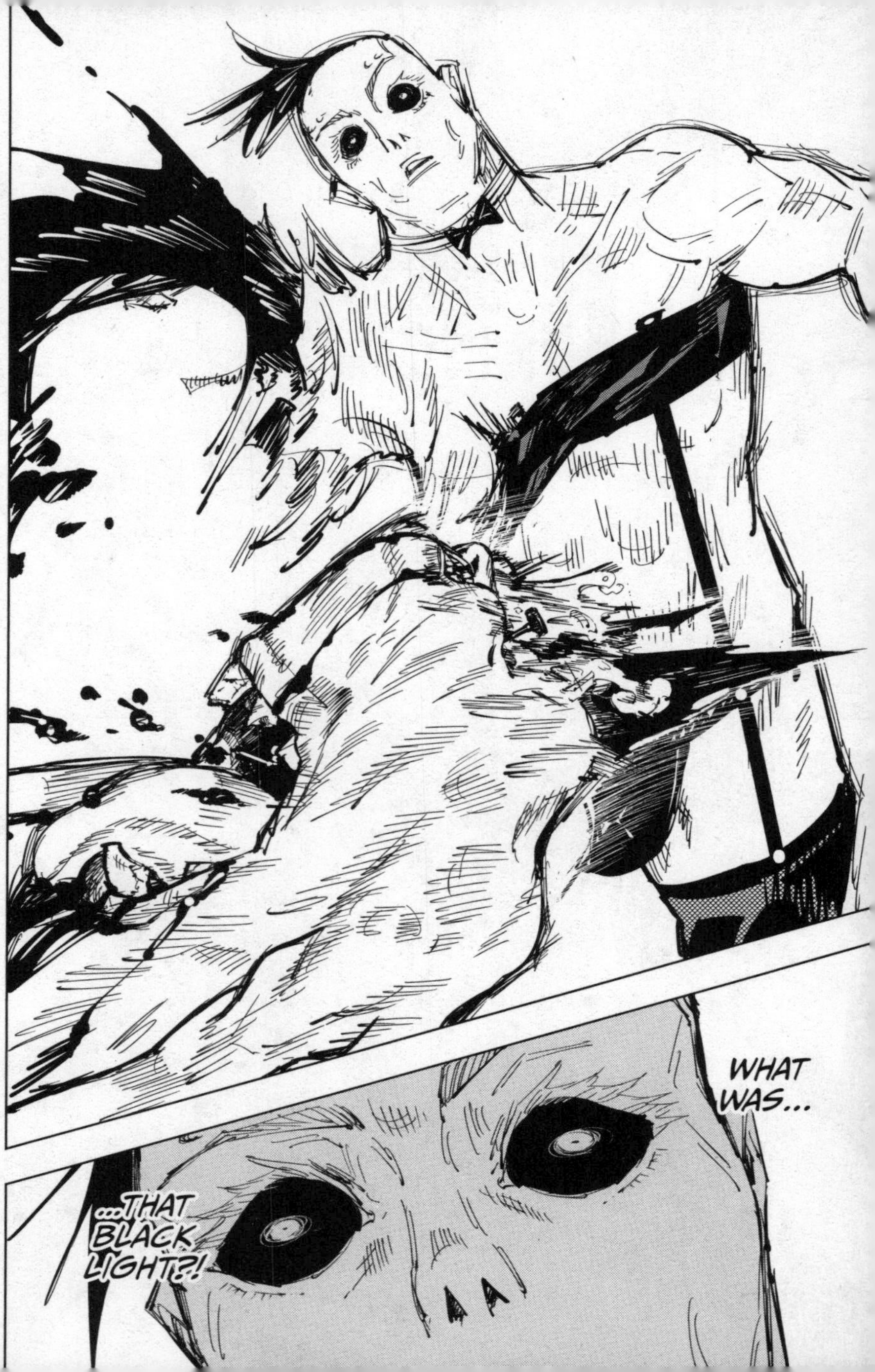
WHAT WAS...
...THAT BLACK LIGHT?!

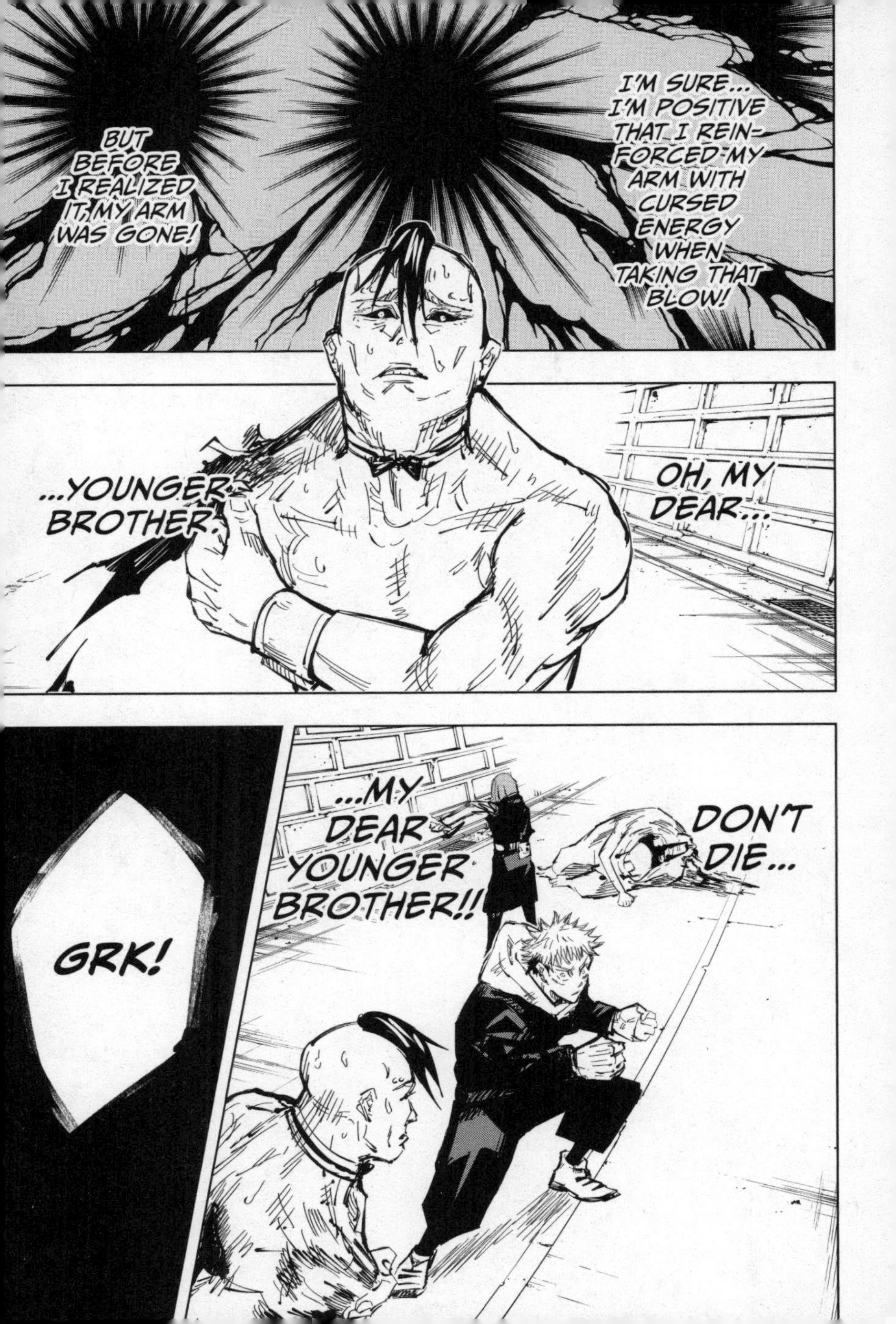
I'M SURE... I'M POSITIVE THAT I REIN-FORCED MY ARM WITH CURSED ENERGY WHEN TAKING THAT BLOW!
BUT BEFORE I REALIZED IT, MY ARM WAS GONE!
OH, MY DEAR...
...YOUNGER BROTHER.
DON'T DIE...
...MY DEAR YOUNGER BROTHER!!
GRK!

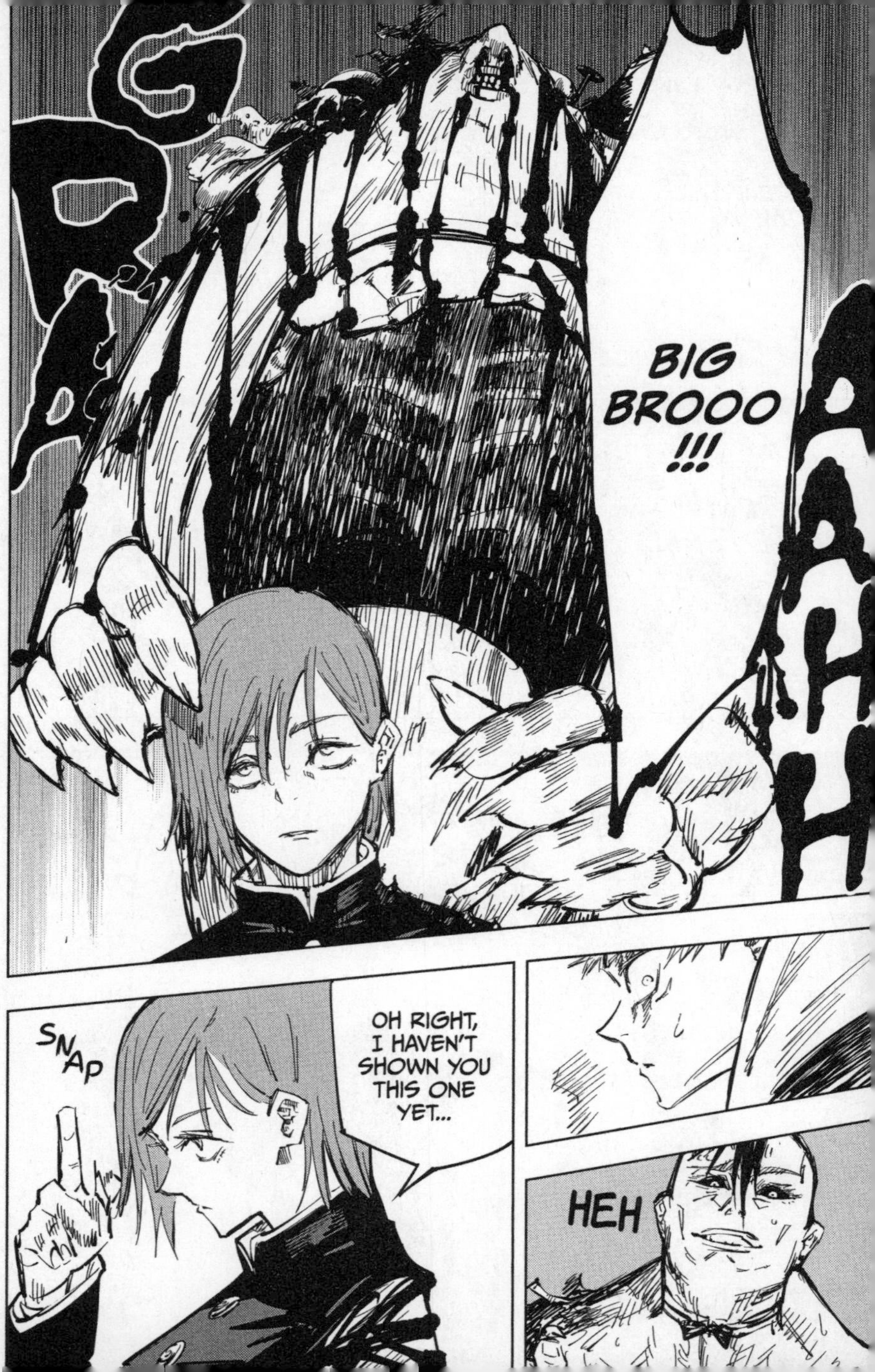
BIG BROOO !!!
HEH
OH RIGHT, I HAVEN'T SHOWN YOU THIS ONE YET...
SNAP

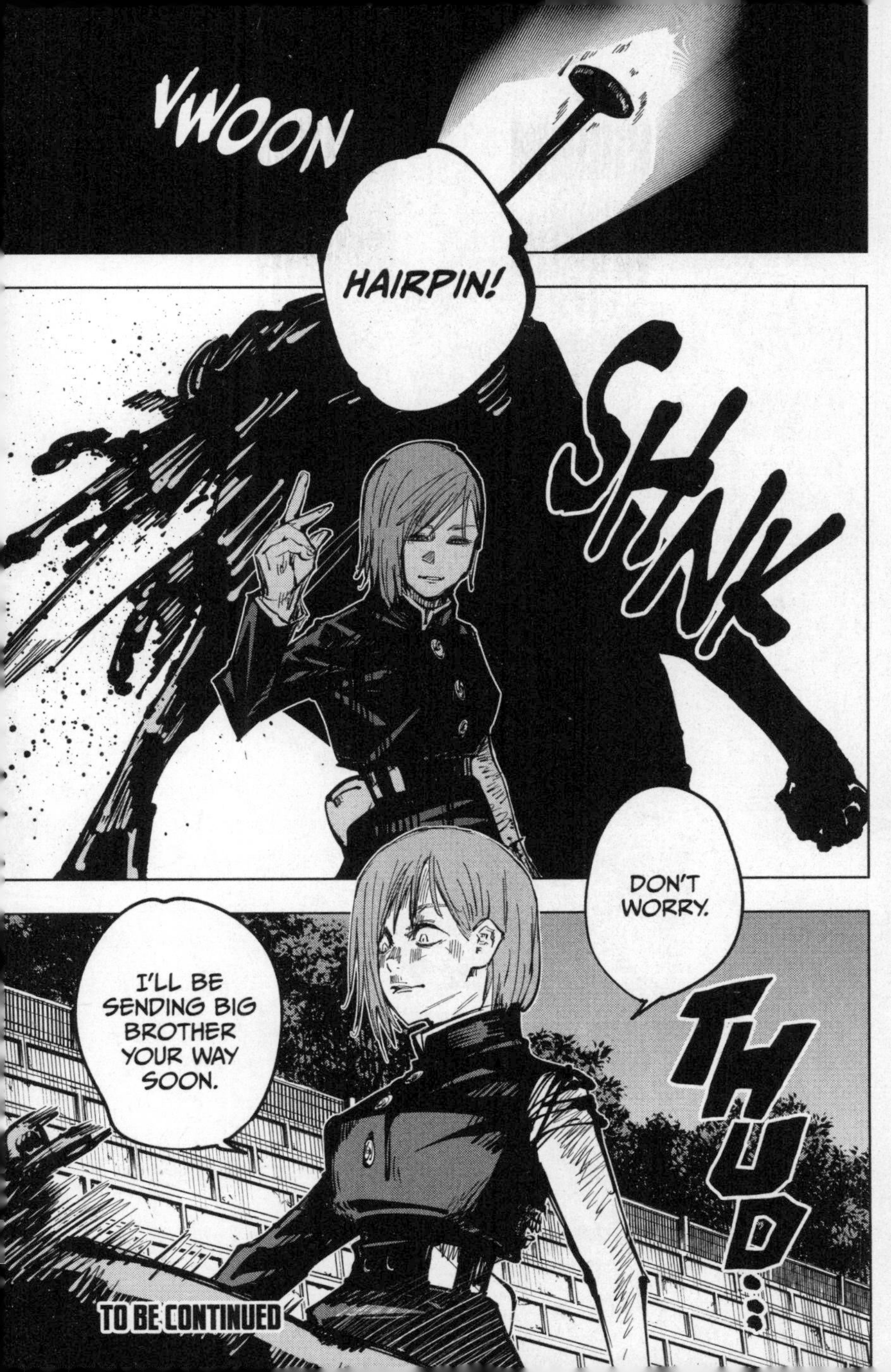
VWOON
HAIRPIN!
SHUNK
DON'T WORRY.
I'LL BE SENDING BIG BROTHER YOUR WAY SOON.
THUD...
TO BE CONTINUED

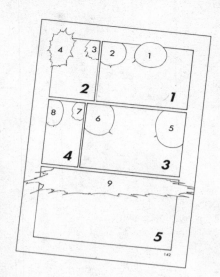

JUJUTSU KAISEN

reads from right to left, starting in the upper-right corner. Japanese is read from right to left, meaning that action, sound effects and word-balloon order are completely reversed from English order.